Unspeakable Acts

Unspeakable Acts

Why Men Sexually Abuse Children

DOUGLAS W. PRYOR

NEW YORK UNIVERSITY PRESS
New York and London

NEW YORK UNIVERSITY PRESS
New York and London

© 1996 by Douglas W. Pryor

Library of Congress Cataloging-in-Publication Data
Pryor, Douglas W.
    Unspeakable acts: why men sexually abuse children / Douglas W. Pryor
      p.   cm.
    Includes bibliographical references and index.
    ISBN 0-8147-6637-4 (alk. paper)
     1. Child molesters—United States—Interviews.   2. Child sexual abuse—United
States—Case studies.   I. Title.
HV6570.2P77   1996
364.1'536—dc20   96-9938
                         CIP

New York University Press books are printed on acid-free paper,
and their binding materials are chosen for strength and durability.

Manufactured in the United States of America

10 9 8 7 6 5 4 3 2 1

To Amy, Hannah, and Naomi

Contents

Preface

The act of molesting a child challenges the most deeply held morals of contemporary society. This is not a topic most people want to think about, short of locking offenders up and throwing away the key, or worse. I have surveyed hundreds of college students over the past five years, seeking their opinion on the following question: What should the state do to a thirty-five-year-old man who has sexual intercourse with an eleven-year-old girl? Fewer than ten people have replied that maybe we should talk to the man to figure out why he acted as he did. I have had professional colleagues yell at me or advise me not to study offenders. I have met with numerous students who were distraught, even in tears, after hearing a lecture on my research. And even now, with the publication of this manuscript, I have seldom talked about my work in any detail with relatives or friends. Indeed, only my wife and a handful of other people have been willing to discuss the findings of this project openly.

Research shows that millions of people in the United States have been involved in child sexual abuse as either victims, nonoffending parents or relatives, and/or perpetrators. Reducing the sexual risk our children face cannot begin in earnest until we learn to talk about this issue on a public level, in a constructive and rational manner. We cannot possibly hope to address solutions to the problem until we are willing to look past our anger and outrage and meet with those who have violated children sexually. It is critical that we examine the lives of such people in order to figure out how and why sexual abuse occurs. This research is dedicated to doing just that, to trying to formulate new understandings about offenders, by reporting their stories in the most objective and forthright manner possible. I urge those who have the interest to begin this book, for whatever reason, to confront their fears and views about the subject matter and to read until they finish it.

I wish to thank the thirty men who participated in this study for their willingness to trust me by meeting with me face-to-face and answering my questions. It took a great deal of courage on their part to relive what for most was an extremely shameful and embarrassing chapter in their lives. As I spoke with different offenders, I found that each had his own story about how he became involved in child molesting and how he eventually ended up in treatment or prison. Some men cried while they described what they had done; others became extremely angry with themselves; still others shook their heads in disbelief at what they were saying. What I discovered was the human side of the men; I found that their lives had often been filled with what to them was pain and turmoil, and that many, though not all, I believe, were genuinely sorry for the acts they had committed.

Most important to the success of this research was the assistance and trust of four clinicians who provided me with open access to their records and the offenders with whom they worked. As with most research on sensitive topics, there were a few bureaucrats in the different field settings I frequented who made doing the study problematic at times, but these four clinicians went to great lengths to sponsor the research. Unrecognized for their contribution to society, these four individuals day in and day out found the willpower and fortitude to work with people that most others would prefer to avoid. I wish I could thank them by name, but for reasons of confidentiality, which I promised to the men who participated in the study, I cannot.

This book would not be possible without the help of a number of people. I would like to acknowledge three faculty in the department of sociology and one colleague in the department of criminal justice at Indiana University for reading my manuscript and making many insightful comments—Martin S. Weinberg, Colin J. Williams, William B. Corsaro, and especially Harold E. Pepinsky for his eternal optimism and positive response to my inquiries. I would also like to express my appreciation to Philip Perricone and Ian Taplin in the department of sociology at Wake Forest University for the supportive and encouraging academic atmosphere they always provided. Likewise, my gratitude and respect to my editor, Timothy Bartlett, at New York University Press, whose enthusiasm about this book and courage to publish it will always be remembered. But most important, I would like to thank my wife, Amy Kopel, who has shared her reactions to this study many times, acting as a type of public barometer on an extremely sensitive topic. Long experienced in working with the victims of childhood sexual abuse, she frequently provided an important perspective on the data. Her belief in the significance of this project has helped me to see it finished.

ONE

Studying Offenders and Their Behavior

R: I was about twenty-eight or twenty-nine . . . . And it was weird. I was playing around with [my daughter]. I was tickling her . . . . And I just started
tickling her in the wrong places. I thought she liked it. At first . . . I enjoyed
it, but at the same time, I felt real bad about it too. Like, "I can't believe I'm
doing this to my own daughter. What kind of father am I?" But . . . it was
probably a month later or so, I did it again. And I'm not going to lie. I did
enjoy it. I felt bad about it [again] . . . . And then I got scared. I was fearful.
I had convinced myself that she likes this . . . . I said, "Well, if I don't do it
she's going to tell on me . . . ." I felt kind of trapped. I didn't know how to
stop. I'd keep telling myself, "I'll never do that again . . . ." But I did.

The above example is unsettling. It is meant to introduce the topic of
this book: men who have molested children, either their own children or
those of relatives, neighbors, or friends. The mere mention of offenders
and their acts can stir intense emotions, including anger, contempt,
shock, and disgust.[1] I know. I have experienced these and other feelings
across the course of the investigation that led to the book you are about
to read, and have experienced them particularly strongly because I myself
am the father of two young daughters. But however repulsed one might
feel about the issue to be addressed here, such feelings do not diminish
the importance of trying to understand how and why sexual situations
between adults and children occur. My research explores the reality and

lives of men who became offenders. I have attempted to listen to and document their stories, to capture in their experiences and their words how involvement in sexual offending unfolded.

One of the most significant problems children as a group face today is the threat of sexual abuse. Data about the number of children who become victims of sex crimes are startling. In eight recent studies, 8 percent to 62 percent of females and 3 percent to 16 percent of males who were surveyed reported having experienced unwanted sex of some type before they reached adulthood.[2] In two studies of homosexual and bisexual men, the incidence of incest during childhood was 37 percent and 46 percent, and in one of these studies among homosexual women it was 38 percent.[3] (For a detailed listing of all ten studies see table 1.) Extrapolating from these findings, researchers have estimated that roughly one in every four girls and one in ten boys are sexually victimized as children.[4] While the accuracy of any given incidence figure is far from certain, we can still draw the conclusion that the experience of unwanted sex, however broadly or narrowly defined, is a common occurrence.

The sheer number of child victims is only one reason the study of offenders is imperative. Sexual abuse in childhood has been shown to be very traumatic, upsetting, and life altering in its impact. Therapists and researchers have documented major emotional, social, economic, behavioral, and sexual effects. Evidence suggests that the closer the relationship between victim and offender, and the longer and more involved the sexual encounter, the greater the devastation overall.[5] We know also that in the case of women who are victims, even years after their abuse experiences, many still think about what happened to them and frequently spend time searching for answers or reasons about why they were molested.[6] In short, the cost in human suffering is too great for us to do anything other than try to figure out why it is that people violate sexual boundaries.

Societal Concern about Sexual Abuse

If nominations were taken for a poll that measured crimes of the decade, child sexual abuse would probably rank at the top of the list. Since the early to mid-1980s and into the 1990s, the mass media have focused nearly unprecedented attention on the topic. Numerous celebrated legal cases involving allegations of child molestation have been reported in the national news—stories involving entertainment figures, day care workers, as well as everyday people.[7] In many places, announcements about men arrested for child molesting and public warnings about offenders due for release from prison have been broadcast on television and printed in the newspaper.[8] Popular television and film have been quick to recognize a hot subject, as scores of television talk shows, movie dramas, and television documentaries that depict the horrors of sexual victimization have been produced for public viewing.[9] A few popular entertainment figures such as Oprah Winfrey and Roseanne have openly confessed in the national spotlight that they were the victims of sexual abuse as children. In addition, grassroots victim support organizations like Society's League Against Molestation (SLAM), Alliance for the Rights of Children (ARCH), and the Underground Railroad have received widespread media exposure.[10]

Perhaps as much or more than any contemporary crime or public health issue, the sexual abuse of children has attracted the interest of researchers from a range of fields: social workers, psychiatrists, psychologists, pediatric physicians, and, to a more limited degree, sociologists. Prior to the mid-1970s, there was little scientific literature that focused on child sexual abuse or child molestation. The turning point was the publication of an article in 1975 by Suzanne Sgroi, "The Sexual Molestation of Children: The Last Frontier in Child Abuse." The author, a medical doctor, issued a declaration of war to stop the secrecy and silence surrounding the behavior.[11] Since that time, scientific studies on the topic have proliferated. At least four academic journals have sprung up devoted substantially, if not entirely, to research in the area: *Child Abuse and Neglect, Journal of Interpersonal Violence, Violence and Victims*, and most recently, *Child Sexual Abuse*.

This increased concern with sexual abuse as a major problem has not gone unnoticed by the criminal justice system. Between 1983 and 1992, the number of Uniform Crime Report arrests for "rape" increased 15.5 percent, and for "other sex offenses" (prostitution excluded) the increase was 24.7 percent. In 1992, approximately 125,000 people were arrested on charges involving these crimes. By the end of 1993, slightly over ninety-seven thousand inmates who were serving sentences in state prisons were convicted sex offenders, constituting about 12.6 percent of the overall prison population. Corollary data suggest that these crimes frequently are perpetrated against children. In 1991, roughly 44 percent of the victims of violent crimes committed by inmates in state prisons whose most serious offense was rape, and 81 percent of victims of inmates whose most serious offense was some other sexual assault were minors.[12]

Coupled with this trend in the criminal justice system, the discovery of childhood sexual victimization has fueled a substantial market in victim and perpetrator mental health care, a market that the mental health industry has been quick to meet. In a voluntary survey conducted during the late 1980s, 553 public and private agencies and independent treatment programs across the United States responded that they currently provided mental health services specifically in the area of sexual abuse.[13] About three-fifths of these programs concentrated on victims and their families, the other two-fifths reported a combined or exclusive focus on perpetrators. As of 1993, forty-eight states provided some type of treatment programming for incarcerated sex offenders.[14] In recent years, professional organizations such as the American Professional Society on the Abuse of Children[15] and various professional conferences at the state and national level on sexual abuse treatment have expanded their reach. What is more, in many bookstores today, numerous self-help books for people who are sexual abuse "survivors" are readily available.[16]

Unlike some behaviors that currently are the focus of serious differences in moral opinion, for instance, homosexuality or abortion, child sexual abuse has been unanimously condemned by public figures and scholars alike with resounding moral conviction. The language used to describe sexual abuse and the people who commit it conveys an especially vehement sense of repugnance and outrage. As one local television news anchor from the area where I lived expressed it in an information pamphlet, "The sexual abuse of children is an ugly and terrible crime." He added that as a society, "we must confront this terrible act."[17] And at the time this study began, a state senator, from the same state as myself, proposed a legislative bill calling for the voluntary castration of sex offenders. He underscored his reasons: "We've got some criminals out there who are real animals . . . . All rapes and molestations are real bad. This is the worst thing that could happen to a woman or a child."[18] In the scientific community, it has been emphasized that, because of the age and limited knowledge of children, any instance of sexual contact between an adult and a minor is, by nature, exploitive, nonconsensual, violent, and thus, reprehensible and deplorable.[19] Take as evidence the words of the authors of a book on incest: "Adult-child incest strikes at the very core of civilization." They refer to "the horror of incest"; they also define such behavior as "one of the most heinous forms of rape."[20]

These social currents and reactions, I contend, make the question of why sexual violations against children occur both perplexing and intriguing. On the one hand, they would seem to suggest a cultural shift toward clarification of the moral boundary surrounding such behavior. That is, it should be more apparent than ever that sexual contact with a child is socially unacceptable. The moral line in the sand would appear to be clear. On the other hand, the sheer number of identified victims, incarcerated offenders, and treatment programs leads to the obvious conclusion that many adults violate sexual boundaries with children anyway. What, then, is the meaning of this apparent boundary, and how do people get to the other side of it not once, but repeatedly? How is it that some (apparently) otherwise everyday people become capable of doing the unspeakable? I delve into what many might regard as the dark side of human desire, the most secretive aspects of social being. My findings indicate that the moral wall that separates us from what is routinely defined as extreme behavior may not be as opaque as we would like to think.

Sexual Abuse Research in Context

The data I have collected and report herein represent a small contribution to a significant but mostly ignored aspect of the general field of child sexual abuse research. Over the last twenty years, considerable emphasis has been placed on studying child sexual abuse victims. Three core themes in particular have received major attention: the percentage of people in the general population who have been molested, the social characteristics of victims, and the short- and long-term consequences of unwanted sex.[21] Questions about offenders and the empirical analysis of why child molesting occurs have received comparatively less scrutiny. The many reasons for this probably include a primary concern among the public in general for people who are the victims of crime; the unwillingness of researchers to study what are regarded as unspeakable acts against children; a lack of easy or immediate access to samples of sexual offenders; and the perception that people who commit sex crimes of any nature would be unwilling to talk openly and honestly about their behavior.

Perhaps more striking than the overall lack of research on molestation offenders is the kind of research that *has* been conducted on this group. Some studies, for example, consist of surface descriptions of offense situations: who is most likely to engage in such behavior, the types of acts most likely to be committed, the frequency of offending and the number of victims molested, the range of offense tactics most commonly used, and the kinds of fixed motives that most often operate. The conclusion drawn from this kind of research about offenders is that they are nearly always men, generally men from every social grouping, or walk of life. No category of men as such is exempt from suspicion. In addition, offenders are usually portrayed as predatory: they preselect and groom children as targets, coerce and threaten their victims into submission and silence, enjoy exerting power and releasing anger, and progress to more serious behavior over time. Questions about what offenders think and feel in relation to their victims and their behavior are not rigorously addressed. But more, many of these studies are based on descriptive data gathered from sexual abuse survivors, from surveys administered to treatment providers, and from searches of official records.[22] Thus, much of what we know about sexual offending is framed from the standpoint of the victim or the audience, not from the perpetrator directly.

Still, there is a growing body of research that looks specifically at offenders and is based on firsthand data. Three groups of studies are most common. "Erection" studies examine the degree of sexual arousal offenders experience, based on measures of penis size, after being exposed to sexual descriptions or nude pictures of children.[23] "Personality attribute" studies involve the use of personality inventories like the MMPI, which are administered to offenders to assess levels of emotional, mental, sexual, or social disturbance; or they include general descriptions of personality problems based on case analyses.[24] "Program evaluation" studies concentrate on identifying the various factors that affect whether or not offenders complete treatment, who should be incarcerated, the impact of treatment on the likelihood of reoffending, and the relative success of treatment for instilling feelings such as empathy toward victims or acceptance of personal responsibility.[25] Research of this nature, clearly more psychological than sociological in direction, tells us little about how the lives of offenders unfold prior to their crimes, little about what offenders do to their victims when they molest them, and little about how situations of sexual abuse stop. Indeed, it would appear that the context in which sexual violations occur is largely ignored.

This is not to say that offenders and their behavior have not been the focus of serious attempted explanation. Indeed, there are many theories that specifically address why men molest children. These can be grouped into two broad categories. First are personality theories that emphasize the internal makeup of offenders. Offenders have been classified, or generally described, as fixated, regressed, alcoholic, psychopathic, sexually addicted, senile or senescent, narcissistic, sadistic, perverse, psychotic, and passive-dependent.[26] Second are social theories about problems and circumstances people encounter in life. It has been suggested that men may molest children because of, among other things, sexual failure with women, cultural objectification and patriarchy, role confusion within families, sexual abuse trauma in childhood, and moral erosion linked to pornography and divorce.[27] Reflecting the thinking about offending in general, A. Nicholas Groth has stated that "symptom formation . . . may involve genetic defects, constitutional vulnerabilities, parental deprivations, pathogenic family patterns, social pathology, and developmental traumas."[28] Central to most theories is the presumption that men who commit sexual abuse have been exposed to some type of pathology in their lives that can be identified and, if not too extreme, may even possibly be treatable. There has been little interest, however, in exploring the more routine interactional processes between men and children through which sexual offending unfolds.

On the whole, mainstream theories about child molesting raise as many questions as they seem to resolve. Most important, there is no consistent understanding as to what the theories are supposed to be explaining or what kind of act is being perpetrated. We still do not know whether sex crimes against children are crimes of physical violence, crimes of sex, or both.[29] Are we trying to explain why some people decide to harm or hurt children and use sex as a means to do that, or why some people find children sexually interesting and desirable? In part, this may be because much of the debate about sex crimes has been framed from the point of view of victims, or by people who work with victims and who themselves conduct research. The perspective of the offender is considered less relevant, or not relevant at all.

Equally confusing is the question of what triggers offenders to zero in specifically on children as sexual targets. If a guy is having sexual problems, or if he is narcissistic or psychopathic, why does he turn to this specific form of deviant behavior? Or conversely, if some type of pathology predisposes people to molest children, why then does such a condition suddenly become active?[30] To illustrate, while nearly everyone assumes that having been molested as a child is related to becoming an offender as an adult, no one has clearly explained the mechanism by which this occurs.[31] Men who molest children frequently do not begin offending until well into adulthood.[32] Yet the existence of this type of background experience, presumed present in many cases, would seem to predict an earlier and more constant pattern of behavior. And yet it does not. Why not? Still more, why do some offenders commit only a few episodes, while others commit dozens? Or why do some limit their behavior to fondling, while others subject their victims to intercourse?

The premise of the present study therefore is simple—that we will never fully understand why men have sex with children without firsthand research on offenders, especially research that analyzes how offenders view their own lives, their crimes, and their victims. Talking with offenders directly, then drawing on what they say to build theory, is a logical starting point, not ending point, for the study of child sexual abuse. I contend that in order to understand why this kind of behavior happens, we need to step inside the world of the offender, to visit the person on the other side of the boundary, to learn from the individual who has engaged in what needs to be explained. It is this approach, looking at offenders from their position, and trying to get beyond the fear, hatred, and stereotypes such a task entails, that I have chosen to undertake. I suspect that research of this type may begin to break down the image of molesters as despicable animals, and in the process shift the focus of explanation away from "odd person" theories and toward more common social dynamics and cultural realities.

Studying the Offending Career

Rather than simply analyzing a list of variables, I decided to use a "social process" approach to explore the question of why men molest children: I focus on the stages of experience that characterize movement into and out of the active offending role.[33] I look at how men reached the point where they began sexual contact with children, the patterns of adjustment they experienced between episodes, the ways their involvement varied over time, the changing views of sexual boundaries that unfolded, and how all the men were eventually caught and exposed. That is, I examine the dynamics of the sexual offender "career."[34] At first, I tried to determine whether there were distinct pathways that specific sub-groups of men followed. For example, I examined whether men who had been molested as children began and stopped offending through a different route or unique chain of events compared to those who had not been molested. However, no differences of this kind emerged. Instead, there were broader stages or general phases of involvement men described passing through, but overall a wide variation of experiences within each. Every offender, in other words, entered, sustained, and exited from sexual offending in a complex mix of ways.

Consistent with recent advances by other researchers in the study of deviant behavior, I separate involvement in sexual offending into two realms, the "objective" and the "subjective" careers.[35] The objective career consists of the external organization of behavior, *to what offenders say and do and how they interact with their victims.* This includes, for example, the tactics used to instigate sex with victims, the barriers and opportunities that shape the level or frequency of sexual violations, or the statements made to victims to prevent being discovered. In contrast, the subjective career refers to the interpretive stream of definition and reflection, to *what offenders think and feel about their experiences.* For the men in the present research, this consists of the emotions and ratio-nalizations that unfold prior to, during, and after sexual episodes involving children, and any changes in sense of self or sexual desires that impact on the willingness to continue offending. Usually studies focus on only one aspect of offending, either the internal aspect alone—what offenders think about their actions—or the external aspect alone—what offenders actually do. But I contend that to reach a fuller understanding of sexual boundary violations, we must focus on both aspects of offending simultaneously.

Locating Respondents

One of the most frequent questions I have been asked about this research is how I went about finding the men I studied. Locating offenders was much easier than one might think. The first issue I had to address, in starting my investigation, was whether to limit the sample to offenders who had been detected, or to include men who had not, thus running the risk that they might still be molesting children. Which was more important—the generalizability of the data or my own legal liability and social responsibility? In the state where I conducted my research, the law did not provide immunity to any professional person who had knowledge about a minor who was being sexually abused.[36] Thus in the course of my work, if I studied someone who was actively offending, I would have been in a serious legal bind, and would have risked criminal charges, if I did not report what I knew. Legal concerns aside, I was unable to detach my "scientific" self from my "moral" self. Personally, especially being a parent, I could not protect the identity of someone who was actively involved in child molesting. In the end, I drew a moral line, and I decided to reduce my legal risk, by narrowing my search for offenders to the correction/legal system only.[37]

While I knew that there were prison, jail, probation, welfare, and mental health settings where I could find child molesters, I did not know exactly where to begin looking. I started from scratch, with no prior experience in relation to the group I wanted to study, no inside contacts anywhere from which to build. The problem I faced was one of securing blind access to various settings where I had never previously been, and making contact with and gaining the trust of a relatively hidden official population, one that no doubt highly feared the potential reaction of society. I started by consulting the yellow pages in the city where I lived under various social service headings. The entries were extensive, but there were no specific listings for programs dealing with sex offenders. Striking out, I decided to employ a "networking" or snowball sampling method to locate respondents.[38] To begin building a list of possible leads, I spread word of my research by talking to the professional people I associated with in my everyday life—academic colleagues, social work-er friends, police officers, lawyers, and the director of a Guardian Ad Litem (i.e., juvenile court child victim advocate) program. I asked these people for the names of any possible field contacts and whether I could mention them as the source of my referral.

Over a period of two years, I developed fruitful leads in four settings from which I ultimately drew my respondents. Through extensive word of mouth, I was introduced to a clinician who provided treatment to child sexual abuse offenders at a private counseling practice. Then, while attending a criminal justice conference, I met a professor who, as it turned out, was a key member of a special state task force on mental health. Through this contact I was referred to an administrator in the state correction system where I lived. This official later introduced me to a group of clinicians at a medium-security prison who worked exten-sively with sex offenders. Both of these initial contacts then told me about a third referral source, a therapist who ran a nonsecure community group treatment program for familial child molesters. The final breakthrough in this networking process occurred after I learned about a statewide conference on child sexual abuse from my wife (a social worker). At the conference I was introduced to yet another counselor who staffed offender treatment groups similar to the other group program in a third nonsecure setting.

I scheduled appointments with every contact to whom I had been referred, traveled to their offices, and presented my research plans to them. Everyone responded favorably and was willing to help. This was surprising. In particular, I was concerned that I might encounter resistance to the research because of the problem of patient-client privilege. Instead, I discovered that building trust and rapport was relatively easy. One thing I quickly learned about the field contacts I came to know was that they were somewhat isolated professionally. As clinicians, they all had more cases than they knew what to do with, yet very few resources to guide them with treatment. Even more, as a group, they were embedded in a mental health system organized more toward the needs of victims, where offenders were basically "rabble" or "social junk."[39] Realizing this, I set myself up as a supportive resource and sounding board, sharing my knowledge of the sexual abuse literature, copying articles I was asked if I had seen, and listening to ideas and complaints about the legal system. All of this helped to build an atmosphere of trust and reciprocity.

In each setting I entered, I spoke with my contacts many times before I spoke with any offenders. I tried to find out as much as I could concerning my contacts, the kinds of cases they handled, the feelings they had regarding their clients, and any working theories they formulated about child molesting. My purpose in doing this was to gather information that might facilitate subsequent access to the people I intended to study.[40] Also, I wanted to identify any scripted or borrowed accounts about child molesting passed on through treatment that might have tainted how offenders described their behavior.[41] I requested the advice of my field contacts about what to expect from the men I hoped to meet: what they were generally like, their typical dress and appearance, and what they might want to know about me and my research. The most frequent suggestion was to be honest, because the men were extremely sensitive to and quick to spot dishonesty. I was also told that the men would want specific information about the purpose of the research and would need to hear convincing reassurances from me that their confidentiality would be carefully protected.

The fact that I was able to cultivate trusting relationships with my field contacts ultimately proved invaluable. The information they supplied helped me anticipate some of the questions offenders asked when I approached them about participating in the research. Even more important, these contacts acted as my intermediary and sponsor, personally introducing me to the respondents I studied. They facilitated the research by telling offenders about what I was doing and arranging times and places for initial face-to-face meetings. As the research progressed, I found that men who participated in the study often disclosed to me that they agreed to these initial meetings because their clinicians, my field contacts, had vouched for my trustworthiness and credentials as a researcher.[42]

The four study sites where I conducted my research were all located in the same Midwestern state. The private therapy practice and the two nonsecure treatment programs were situated in the same city, with a population of over 500,000 residents. The prison was in a rural area within two hours' drive from this city. The offenders lived (or had lived prior to being incarcerated) all across the state, in every type of region, including rural, suburban, and urban areas. In addition, the four sites served somewhat different populations; thus I was provided access to a mix of offenders in terms of class and case characteristics. One group program catered primarily to poor clients and/or offenders who had been arrested for the first time for a sex offense involving a minor. The other group program handled men rejected from the first program and/or men who sought treatment following their release from prison. The prison pool was skewed toward those who committed more serious sexual acts and/or offenders who had been convicted for child molesting at least two times. The private clinician provided services to clients who were more economically well off or who sought follow-up counseling after completion of group therapy.

Deciding Which Offenders to Study

The core group of respondents in this research consisted of twenty-seven adult men who engaged in sexual contact with at least one child or adolescent under the age of sixteen at the onset of offending. Rather than selecting a random or probability sample of offenders, I selected a "theoretical sample." This latter type of sample is one that is chosen ongoingly, as the research proceeds, as opposed to being decided in advance, with cases drawn blindly from a list based on some numerical priority. The main criteria for inclusion of a given case are "theoretical purpose and relevance."[43] In other words, the aim is to enhance the emerging theoretical focus of the study, to continually fill out and confirm concepts and ideas as they are discovered, based on the analysis of data from each preceding case.

While a number of criteria were used to select cases, two factors stood out as most important. First, I decided to focus specifically on *family-based* offenses, situations in which the offender knows the victim and is part of the victim's family circle or lifeworld. Thus, I included cases involving incest, where the offender was a blood relative or related by marriage.[44] I also included cases where the offender was a close acquaintance of the victim and his or her family—a family friend, a baby-sitter, a neighbor. Other researchers have raised the question about whether incest and acquaintance offenders should be studied together.[45] I found that it was difficult to separate the two. There were some men who had sex with their own children, but also with other children who knew their children. There were other men who had molested their friends' children, but had no children of their own. It seemed arbitrary to exclude these cases on the grounds that they were not strictly incest cases. In particular, I was interested in violations of family and parental trust, and how this might have impacted on offenders emotionally, as well as the ways this might have shaped how they carried out their offenses and maintained secrecy.

As my research proceeded, I narrowed my sample in a second critical direction. I limited my respondents to men who had *a history of sex with other adults* after they had become adults themselves (i.e., reached age eighteen), prior to any transition into offending, and/or who stated that they preferred adults as sexual partners. Men with sexual histories or interests that involved only underage youth or a stated sexual preference for children were excluded from the research. Family and/or incest offenders are more likely to fit this first profile, compared to distant acquaintance or stranger offenders, who are more likely to display fixated desires for children. In addition, the former are probably more likely to molest the same victim repeatedly over a longer span of time, the latter in contrast to report a greater overall number of victims and to molest boys instead of girls.[46] Most important, this type of case exclusion presented, I felt, a more interesting sociological question: *Why and how did men with apparently "normal" sexual lives cross the sexual boundary with children?* Why did such a major shift in sexual direction occur?

Still other contingencies shaped the cases I selected, for both theoretical and practical reasons. In particular, I focused my study specifically on offenders who had engaged in *sexual contact* with children—as opposed to peepers, exhibitionists, or child pornographers[47]—and who admitted and were willing to talk about their involvement. I wanted to look at men who had crossed the touch boundary, and to pass on those who exploited children sexually for profit. Also, I was not interested in offenders who denied guilt or who refused to describe what they had done. Respondents were also restricted by age and gender, to adult men twenty years old or older at the time they first offended. While growing numbers of adolescent and female offenders have been documented by others, access to these groups was much more difficult and limited, and such cases could potentially vary widely from the dynamics of the kinds of cases I studied. Female offenders, for instance, are probably equally or more likely to offend with a male accomplice rather than alone, or may molest less repetitively compared to men, though this latter hypothesis is largely my speculation.[48]

Two added criteria about who was included as a respondent were likewise relevant. Offenders who had molested children under sixteen at onset, whatever the age, qualified for the sample. Certainly there are grounds for the argument that sexual contact with a fifteen-year-old child is different from that with a three-year-old. However, I found that in the few cases I sampled of this nature, offenders who began molesting very young children often continued for years until the victim was substantially older. The young age made it easier to begin acting without repercussions, and represented an important route into the offending career. Finally, I decided to include both heterosexual and homosexual offenders. Rather than presuming a fundamental difference between the two, I was interested in whether men in each group became offenders in similar or different ways. In addition, the fact that some men molest children of both sexes[49] makes such exclusions even more problematic.

Among the twenty-seven principal cases I analyzed, the breakdown from the four study sites is as follows: nine men from the first group treatment program, three men from the medium-security prison, eight men from the agency of the private clinician, and seven men from the second group treatment program. Overall, there are considerably more offenders in the sample who had been selected from the nonsecure treatment settings instead of from prison. However, three other respondents from two of the three nonsecure research sites had served time in the state prison system prior to being interviewed, and three more were sentenced to prison terms after I finished my research.

In addition to the main sample, three other respondents were included in the research, bringing the total number of cases to thirty. Their situations differed theoretically from the rest of the sample, and the data collected on them are not as extensive, nor as rich. One man, Eric, expressed a clear lifelong preference for boys as sexual partners, though he admitted he had been sexual with adult men too. A second man, Keith, denied having had sexual contact with his twelve-year-old niece, but pled guilty to charges anyway. This offender did admit to touching the breasts of the alleged victim, but insisted that it was an accident. He said his hand happened to get caught under her halter-top while he was wrestling with her. A third man, Stuart, had just been arrested because he had his biological daughter perform oral sex on him; he was in a state of shock and turmoil. He had not been exposed to any sex offender treatment, and unlike the other respondents, had never talked about his behavior before. I was allowed to sit in and take fieldnotes during a day-long court-ordered psychological assessment.

Interviewing the Offenders

I conducted "depth" or "long" interviews with the men I studied.[50] I met each offender alone, in a private room, and talked face-to-face with him. I conducted the interviews at each of the research sites or in a faculty office at a local university. Initially, I was nervous and fearful about being alone with these men, especially when interviews ran late into the night, or when I was in the prison. After my first interview, which was at one of the nonsecure sites, I drove home a different way from usual because I was paranoid about being followed, and checked with my wife to make sure our phone was in her name, which was different from mine, to avoid follow-up calls. I also instructed the secretarial staff where I worked not to give out my home phone to anyone. When I exited the building where I had done the interview, about fifteen minutes after we had finished, the offender was sitting in his car with the engine idling and racing up and down. I suspected that he was masturbating with his foot on the gas pedal, that his descriptions of his sexual behaviors in the interview had excited him. As I walked toward my car, he turned on his headlights and drove off slowly behind me. I felt spooked. Fortunately he did not follow me home, though a few months later he jumped probation and disappeared.

There were other incidents that also left me uneasy. In the first prison interview I conducted, the offender pulled his chair in front of the door so no one could get in or out, and then asked how I felt being alone with him. Two other respondents I interviewed repeatedly slammed their fists on the table at which we sat, raising their voices, as they described aspects of their lives and offenses, often telling me the same answer twice in an insistent tone, so that I would be sure to understand them. And, after each interview, nearly every offender wanted to shake my hand. A few would shake my hand for a couple of minutes, not letting go, talking about how they felt we really got to know one another, and thanking me for listening to them and not getting angry. These were events that I learned to get used to over time, and to accept as part of the research process. They were necessary to collect the data. None of the men ever threatened me personally in any direct way; in fact, all were friendly and cordial. Only one offender ever called me, about four years after I interviewed him, because he wanted to read the results of the research.

I used a standardized topical interview guide, a detailed outline of specific areas to question, to conduct the interviews. The interview guide was arranged in a natural time sequence to help capture a sense of movement across the life of the offender (see appendix A). In twenty-five of the interviews the data were tape-recorded; in the five remaining cases the data were recorded by hand. Prison administrators would not allow a tape recorder inside the prison grounds and thus interviews with the three incarcerated respondents could not be tape-recorded. The stated reason, which struck me as odd, was that the inmates might steal the tape deck and make a tatoo gun. I suspect the real reason was fear about what inmates might have said regarding the conditions of the prison. Data from two of the supplemental cases were also recorded by hand. Every respondent in this study who was asked about being tape-recorded agreed to the procedure. A couple of men, however, did request that the tape recorder be turned off when they described their occupations. They felt this information might identify them and asked that the exact nature of their occupations, which they disclosed off-tape, not be specifically reported in the study.

Most of the interviews took between three and five hours to complete, though a few lasted longer. The interviews at the prison, in particular, lasted from ten to fifteen hours each and involved from three to nine sessions. When I had to record the data by hand, the interviews took much longer. This was why I completed only three interviews at the prison setting. In contrast, nearly all the taped interviews were conducted in one or two interview sessions. In general, some men had molested their victims so many times, or had been molested so extensively themselves as children, that it took a long time for them to describe their histories. Hundreds of such episodes were common. Many men also provided extensive details about offenses, at my prompting, focusing on what they did, how the victim reacted, and the like. In fact, sometimes the data became so detailed and graphic I felt reluctant to report it, though I have done so. The handwritten data were recorded in near verbatim format. A great deal of care was taken to record the exact words of the respondents, minus pauses and linguistic fillers. Also, the tape-recorded interviews were transcribed verbatim, again minus breaks, false starts, and dialects.

In addition to conducting interviews with offenders, I collected two other types of supplemental data. First, I conducted informal interviews with two of the clinicians who referred many of the men in the research. The focus was on following up with what happened to offenders over time, from six months to three years after each interview, and with *corroborating* the stories they shared about their cases. I wanted to know whether the men had told me more or less than they had disclosed to the authorities. I found the former to be mainly true. I also wanted to find out who finished treatment, who did not, and who ended up in prison later. While I do not specifically report these data in my analysis, some of what I learned is interesting. One offender, for instance, became a male strip dancer. Another worked out a peeping arrangement with his wife, who stayed married to him. He would sneak outside, peer through his bedroom window, and masturbate while his wife undressed. Still other men ended up getting divorced, marrying new wives, putting their marriages back together, relocating in new communities where no one knew their past, though none of the men I know of ever reoffended. Second, I sifted through and selectively recorded information from the official files on twenty-two of thirty respondents at three of the four places I sampled. This information was used as well to check the validity of responses. Further, it was used to fill out demographic or legal information glossed over in the interviews, especially to clarify legal charges.

Convincing Respondents to Participate

After I located the settings where I conducted my study and had secured initial introductions to offenders, I still had to meet with the men, tell them about my research, and then convince them to participate in an interview. I have often been asked how I persuaded men who molested children to tell me about all the sordid details of their lives. The hard part was getting them to agree to an interview, which more often than not they did decide to do. Once in the interview situation, they would tell me basically anything I asked. My experience is that people like to talk about sex, even illicit sex, because for the most part they need to talk with someone. Before I conducted any formal interviews, I held pre-interview meetings with potential respondents to explain the focus and aims of my research. I conducted two types of pre-interviews. In the first, I visited a number of treatment groups run by two of my contacts and talked with the men in a group context. Afterwards, I scheduled appointments with those who were interested and who fit the sample criteria. In the second type, I held one-on-one discussions with offenders either the day before or just prior to the interviews. This type of meeting occurred in the prison and in the private therapist's office.

Since the pre-interview meetings were the only chance I had to convince the offenders to participate in an interview, they were critical to the success of the study. Routinely, I paced back and forth in private, rehearsing the areas I planned to cover with the men, and trying to shift myself into a detached, value-neutral role. This always required effort. What I was studying was unsettling to me. Every meeting began the same way. I told the men who I was and where I was from, what the research was about, why I was doing the research, the amount of time needed for an interview (three to five hours), the steps that would be followed to protect their confidentiality, and what I planned to do with the data after I collected it. Then I asked the men whether they had any questions. Usually I received a barrage of them. The questions were occasionally technical, but often personal. They asked about my last name, where I lived, whether or not I had been molested as a child, why I had decided to study what I was studying, whether I was married, whether I had any children, what theory I was testing about sexual abuse, and what I thought of people who had done what they did.

In response to what the men asked, the primary strategy I used to build trust was to demonstrate trust through self-disclosure.[51] If I expected honesty and openness, and if I were going to probe people about the intimate details of their lives, especially about what they had done sexually with children, I realized I had to answer their questions about me, honestly. I did so as sincerely as I could, though personally I was never comfortable with this task. I told them generally where I lived, my last name, that I was married, that I did not have children, that I did have a child later in the study, and that child molesting was not something I approved of personally, but that as a researcher I was trying to understand how and why men got involved in these situations. I stressed that as a researcher, unlike the public or the press, I intended to take an objective and value-neutral look at the topic.

I used other strategies to build trust with the men as well. In particular, I attempted to present my research using a naive front in order to minimize any perceived power differences and to shift a sense of authority to the respondents.[52] I did this by portraying a sense of methodological expertise, for example, by elaborating briefly on my experience as a researcher, while at the same time admitting to knowing relatively little about the subject matter I wanted to study. I routinely mentioned to the men that they should think of me as a "student," and that they needed to teach me about themselves. I stated to every respondent that my role as a researcher involved listening to and reporting on their lives, and that the more they told me, the more accurate the portrait I would be able to draw. I emphasized that I wanted to learn from them about their experiences. I likewise pointed out that they controlled the information disclosed in their interviews—that I was not going to make them tell me anything they did not want to tell me, and that it was their decision to decide what to reveal.

Also, for more than a few of the interviewees, building trust seemed to depend on my passing moral tests.[53] Routinely, there were attempts to test my politics about the issue of sexual abuse. Some men asked whether or not I believed that people convicted of child molesting should be incarcerated. My standard reply was that I did not know, that it depended on what the person was willing to do to keep from reoffending. I also observed that during their interviews, many men monitored my reactions as they described their molestation offenses. In these instances, I maintained a serious demeanor and often leaned forward to encourage

acceptable framework. "The reason that I'm participating is to let people know that it could happen to anybody. Those of us . . . in my group aren't people that hung out on the street corners with long overcoats."

The reasons men gave for deciding to tell their stories often too were more personal, more idiosyncratic. One offender simply wanted to talk to someone who might be willing to listen so he could work through his problems. He saw the world as "woefully deficient of people who are seeking to understand this problem," and added that he was glad "to find somebody that I can talk to about it." A second offender mentioned being "curious" about the process of social research. He found it "exciting" to be part of a study, even if the topic was, as he put it, "not something to be proud of." A third respondent seemed to like the angle that the research was taking, that someone was finally paying attention to offenders. "You're attacking it from a whole different point of view. There's thousands of researchers out there just dying to talk to the victims, but go and talk to some of the child molesters and try to get their views." As with other men, with this same offender, my presentation of self as a researcher was also critical: "You were pretty well up front. You didn't give the impression that you were saying one thing while thinking another . . . . You more or less made yourself convenient for us . . . . You didn't give off that 'I'm superior' attitude."

I also asked a few offenders I interviewed to explain why they thought some men might have declined to participate in the research. Three primary reasons, among others, were cited. The first centered around the fear of a breach in confidentiality. Some apparently felt that their stories were unique and that any type of description of what they did would identify them to the victim, their spouse, or others. The second was that some men, it was said, had not reached a point where they were able to talk about what they had done with anyone. They still felt too much embarrassment and shame. Finally, some were simply trying to put things behind them, did not want to keep dredging up the past, and wanted to get on with their lives. In the end, the men who did participate in the research reported that the decision to do so was not always immediately clear-cut and that they sometimes wavered—initially saying yes to the research, but then hedging back and forth up until the time of the actual interview.

Description of the Men and Their Cases

The descriptive profile of the respondents in the sample (see appendix C) is as follows: The average age of the men at the onset of first sexual contact with someone under sixteen was 32.9 years. The age range was twenty to fifty-two years. The average age when they stopped offending was 35.7 years. At the time of the interview, the average age of the men was 38.5 years. When they began offending, 70 percent of the sample were married, 80 percent either had completed high school or had some college education, 57 percent had prior military experience, and 93 percent were employed. Fifty-two percent said that their highest yearly income any year from the onset of offending to when they were interviewed was between $15,000 and $34,999 per year, the rest reported incomes roughly equally above or below that amount. One offender earned $100,000 per year. The occupations of the men were wide ranging, but more were employed in semiskilled or trade jobs. The religious composition of the sample was 52 percent Protestant and 34 percent no affiliation. All but one of the men in the study were white; the other was African American.

The men gave the following description of their victims and the nature of their everyday relationship to them: The average age of all the victims reported by the men at the onset of sexual contact was 9.4 years. The range was two to fourteen years. The average age of the victims when sexual contact ended was 11.0 years. The age range was six to twenty years. Eighty-three percent of all reported victims were female; 17 percent were male. There were fifty-two total victims reported by all the offenders in the sample. One victim was African American; all the others were white. The offender's relationship to the victim was 23 percent biological father, 38 percent stepfather, adopted father, or mother's boyfriend, 27 percent acquaintance, and 12 percent other relative. (The types of offenses the men committed and the frequency and duration of their involvement are reported later in chapter 7.)

The legal outcomes for the respondents consisted of the following: At the time they were interviewed, 63 percent of the men had pled guilty to at least one charge of felony child molesting; 20 percent had pled guilty to a lesser charge—usually misdemeanor battery—after being charged initially with child molesting; and 10 percent reported being charged with felony child molesting but their cases were still pending. The other 7 percent of the sample (two men) were never charged with any crime because in one case the statute of limitations (five years) had expired and in the second the offenses had been committed in another state. The length of sentence (time served or to be served) the men received was relatively short: 33 percent less than one week, 37 percent from one week to six months, and 30 percent one year or longer. The longest sentence was ten years, five years served. Nearly half, 48 percent of the sample, received a sentence that included three or more years probation. The longest assigned probation was ten years. At the time of the interview, 80 percent of the men had participated in at least one year of individual and/or group counseling.

The Question of Honesty

Certainly a range of methodological criticisms can be leveled at this research. Because of the small size of my sample, and because I restricted my respondents to official cases, *the data I present should be regarded as exploratory, the conclusions I draw as suggestive.* There is simply no way to know for sure how this sample of offenders differs from others who never get detected. Also, because of the nature of the research design, one involving the use of depth interviews, some concern about the problem of retrospective interpretation is warranted. That is, the stories men told about their lives and offenses were certainly affected by the history of their apprehension and exposure to treatment. (See appendix D for a more detailed discussion of this problem.)

Despite these drawbacks, the greatest concern I had was whether or not the offenders I interviewed were telling me the truth as they knew it. The stereotyped image of criminal offenders is that they are dishonest. This image is especially relevant in the situation of sex offenders.[55] The stigma attached to sex crimes suggests extensive efforts to avoid detection and to save face. During my early fieldwork in this research, a few clinicians repeatedly advised me not to expect a complete or reliable accounting from any respondent. One therapist in particular, who referred cases in the research, commented that the offenders he knew were "like electricity": "they follow the path of least resistance. They'll reveal only as much as they have to." The question, then, is whether any researcher can ever honestly capture the reality of this particular group of people.

Contrary to popular expectations, the respondents in this study seemed open, interested in and committed to the research, frank and explicit, and consistent in their accounts in the face of a litany of questions. In order to assess their honesty, I asked a number of the men a few questions twice, occasionally on different days. Their answers rarely varied. I emphasized a second internal check involving cross-referencing answers against data from official records. The most common discrepancies were underreports by offenders about the level of force used, comments to victims about keeping quiet, or the level of sexual contact. Also common, but less frequent, were overreports by men in each of these realms and others, particularly confessions about additional behaviors previously undocumented by authorities.

In the end, it was difficult to assess the honesty of respondents based on comparisons with the official records in their cases. The official records routinely contained enormous gaps and omissions about the lives of the men and their offenses. The men were more likely to match the official record, but the official record seldom seemed to tell the complete story about the men. Other researchers have tried to gauge the honesty of criminal offenders by comparing their accounts against official records.[56] This assumes, though, that official records themselves are valid indicators of events, which they very often may not be,[57] especially when the type of offense being documented is as highly charged as child molesting. The point is that official records are weak indicators of honesty, despite the continued persistence of researchers trying to defend the integrity of their data by using them.

To try to address the issue of honesty more thoroughly, I decided to explore the nature of the research experience for the men in this study. Respondents were asked how they felt about participating in the research at the start of the interview. At the close of the interview, they were then asked how they felt about having participated. A third question at the end as well involved confronting the men as to whether or not they had been honest. The idea was to take a type of barometer reading, to see whether anything the men said relating to the research might indicate a propensity to lie, and to let readers judge for themselves whether the men were honest.

At the start of the interviews, the vast majority of the men reported feeling comfortable, having no overriding concern regarding their confidentiality, feeling safe with the idea of being tape-recorded, and feeling ready to go ahead with things. Often they stated that they had nothing left to hide and that they were eager to talk.

I: How [do] you feel . . . being here, talking with me?

R: Well, it doesn't bother me a bit.

I: Do you have any reservations about this study at all?

R: I have nothing to hide. I don't care if the information does get released. It doesn't bother me.

I: Do you have any reservations about describing very detailed things about your situation?

R: No.

I: How do you feel telling me about all this?

R: Well, I've been telling other people, and I really am at the point where I don't want to hide it anymore . . . . There was another scripture that says, "Whatever is brought to the light becomes light." So it gets out and it's dealt with, it'll stop. I mean that's the way I look at it. It will stop. It has stopped. And therein lies my hope.

A few men admitted that they felt ashamed and embarrassed, casting a very serious and somber mood over the interview, but this feeling did not seem to preclude them from participating. They noted that they had told their story before, which seemed to make it easier for them to talk.

R: I just feel nervous . . . . I'm still ashamed of why I'm here. It's embarrassing, but I know you've met a lot of people that's been in my shoes . . . . So [it] might make it a little easier for me . . . . I don't particularly like to talk about it but I've been having to now for a year and a half.

I: . . . Is there anything that you would be unwilling to tell me about the molest situation or your treatment program?

R: I don't think so.

One man sounded a somewhat different note; he said that he was willing to participate in an interview, but was tired of describing to everyone what he had done. He too hinted that the subject was difficult to talk about.

R: I feel fine. It just gets old telling so many people all the time. It seems like over and over . . . . But I have to tell you it's a little uncomfortable to tell someone.

Other men mentioned being uncomfortable with the prospect of being interviewed, more, it seemed, because they did not know the interviewer and the research process seemed unfamiliar to them than because of any deep underlying embarrassment.

R: I'm kind of leery about it [being interviewed] because I've never done this before. Kind of semi-uncomfortable. But I'm willing to go through with it to help you, . . . to make more people out there in the public really understand . . . .

I: Will talking on tape affect the . . . things you might say?

R: Oh no! . . . The reason why I'm a little uncomfortable is because like you're somebody new . . . . We never got together to discuss my problem before.

R: There's the nervousness associated with unfamiliar circumstances. But I have become accustomed to this situation . . . and I've learned to relax and handle the situation easier.

I: . . . You've talked about it to more than one other person?

R: Not in a research setting.

When I asked them what they would say to convince readers that they were being honest, the men emphasized that there was really no way to convince people they were telling the truth. They admitted that some offenders do lie, and that the image of dishonesty was not unfounded. They sometimes acknowledged having lied to their counselors themselves because of the fear of legal repercussions. Often they spoke about having nothing to gain by lying since they had already confessed to being guilty.

I: There is a strong belief among social scientists and . . . the public that child molesters don't tell the truth. What would you say in that regard to help me answer my critics?

R: Well, you know, there's nothing I can say. I think you're right. I think that one of the biggest traits among child molesters is the fact that they lie . . . . I think a lot of the times people in therapy, people like myself, we realize how damaging lies can be. I don't lie anymore . . . about the smallest of things. But I can't say that for everybody. And I mean how am I supposed to make you believe that?

I: Why should readers believe what you say?

R: . . . There's no reason for anybody to believe me . . . . I think I can look you in the eye and say, "Hey, I am telling you the truth . . . ." If you believe that I've fed you a line of shit, there's just nothing I can do to make you believe me . . . . I have a daughter that I really want to see protected from the type of person that I am. I know what I am. I don't want to see anybody else ever have to go through this. Man, woman, child, nobody! I made a commitment that I'm going to do everything I can to prevent this from happening again . . . . If people can't accept that, they'll just have to believe what they want.

I: What can you say to . . . readers that your accounts were honest?

R: . . . They asked me if I did it and I said yes. If I'm not going to lie about that, why would I lie about anything else? That probably wouldn't convince very many people . . . .

I: There's also a presumption . . . men in your situation . . . wouldn't tell everything. What would you like to say about that?

R: I'd say in a lot of situations that may be true because they have not been charged with more than a certain amount.

I: How about in your case?

R: . . . I wasn't charged with some of what I told you!

I: Why should [people] believe what you're telling me?

R: The biggest thing is that we agreed to the interview without any sort of promise or consideration . . . . Nobody forced me in here to do this interview . . . . Technically speaking there's very little of it that can't be checked. I mean hospital records, arrest records, that sort of thing are easy to look up. So it'd be kind of silly for me to sit there and make up a story trying to get pity or making excuses for what I did. I'm not making excuses for the molest; I did it, absolutely. I regret it and there's nothing to be gained by lying now.

I: . . . Is there anything you want to say to convince the readers that what you told me is the truth?

R: . . . I trust you to the extent I feel you have nothing to gain. You're not prosecuting me. You're not working for them . . . . So you trust somebody like that . . . . And maybe I would modify my views five minutes from now, but at the time the words came out, that's how I felt at the time . . . . From other people's point of view, they say, "Well, that guy's sick anyway . . . so you can't believe anything he'd say anyhow . . . ." But I guess the bottom line is I have nothing to gain, so why shouldn't I be credible? But whether somebody would buy that?

When I asked my respondents what it had been like doing the interview, everyone reacted positively. They described it as therapeutic and said that it provided an emotional release and made them think about things they had not considered before. There was a sense that the men put a lot of effort and self into the interview. Almost everyone felt they had grown from the experience. The feeling was one of honesty.

R: I feel like I have told my story.

I: Are you okay? . . . You feel all right after it all?

R: I feel okay. I feel good. I feel good. Especially a little emotional release. I feel good. Yeah. I really do. I'm glad we did this . . . . I think you're into fascinating stuff. I've thought about doing something like this myself.

R: I'd like to say it was a very intriguing three hours . . . .

I: How do you feel having talked with me?

R: . . . I feel kind of better now. I feel comfortable now, coming to the close of it. I didn't know I was going to take so much time . . . . I thought I was going to come in here and wrap it up in about an hour . . . . You took me back into time. And that was great . . . . I feel a little bit more relieved that I've talked about it. But I kind of [feel] hurt again thinking, I kind of relived what . . . went on in my life . . . . I'm very, very, very, very sorry I committed this offense.

R: You asked questions that were not asked before by others that got me thinking about various things. And it was good . . . . I got a lot out of it that way . . . . It was kind of like a catalyst for a lot of thoughts to flow that hadn't been flowing prior. And it opened up a lot of avenues to me in thinking and observing and kind of analyzing things from years ago . . . . You're opening up doors that maybe somebody else missed and didn't push the right button to stimulate a thought.

Overview of the Study

In the pages to follow, I present the stories of thirty men who engaged in very serious sexual crimes. Using detailed depth interviews, I show how men with no prior history of child molesting as adults transitioned into and out of sexual relations with children. Together we will explore the early lives of offenders, including the sexual violations many reported experiencing as children, that set the stage for the boundary violations they later committed. We will also look at how the lives of men who became offenders began to erode in various realms during their adult years. Having described some of the factors that lead up to offending, we will turn next to the question of how the idea of having sex with a child or children actually surfaced. In addition, the offenders will tell you in their own words the methods and tactics they used to initiate sexual contact with their victims. Since most men molested their victims repeatedly, we will then examine how offenders viewed what they did and coped with their feelings afterwards, and how their involvement in offending usually continued over time. To close their stories, I will describe the unsuccessful attempts many offenders made to stop their behavior and the different ways all the men eventually got caught. At the end, bringing what the men said together, I will propose a working theory about why situational involvement in child molesting occurs.

The accounts of offenders about their behavior probably will be shocking and upsetting for many who decide to continue reading this book. It is my hope that, by allowing offenders who have sexually abused children to speak about the unspeakable, we can begin the process of explaining the basis for such behavior. I believe that this is a crucial step that will possibly prevent others in the future from crossing these same boundaries. The more we as a culture hear about these acts and talk about them, the clearer the moral boundary will become. At the very least, research on offenders might help some victims answer questions about what happened to them. It might help those who are currently offending or who have offended to recognize what they are doing or what they have done. It might help the nonoffending spouses, parents, and relatives of offenders make sense of someone close to them. And for therapists, police, and prosecutors dealing with cases of sexual abuse, it might help to assess the scope and magnitude of what routinely happens in these situations. I strongly encourage you, the reader, whatever your reason for reading this research, to set aside what you currently think and know about this issue, and to open your mind to understanding these men and their acts, so that we can all become part of the solution to this unsettling problem.

TWO

Blurring of Boundaries in Childhood

Why would an adult turn to a child for sex? Where does the interest start? How do people become so unglued morally that they engage in such behavior? Maybe some individuals are genetically disposed to become molesters. Maybe certain men have core personalities that make sexual abuse inevitable. Or is this conduct more possibly the result of social experience and learning? The answer begins, I think, with the last of these. Child molestation involves the violation of sexual, physical, age, emotional, and even parental boundaries, an act widely thought to inflict enormous harm. What I wondered as I set out with this study was whether certain kinds of life events might possibly blur or erode the way offenders view these boundaries or increase the likelihood of focusing in on a child sexually. Since much of what people learn about sexual desire and morality is acquired early in life, I decided to explore the childhood histories of offenders. Were their backgrounds unique in some way? To get at this question, I asked my respondents to trace their sexual development from as far back as they could recall and to describe what their family life was like while they were growing up.

Three types of early life experiences that were commonly reported by offenders seemed to contribute to the sexual crimes they committed later. Included were genital sexual contact before age sixteen with someone substantially older, genital sexual contact by age thirteen with age peers involving incest or sex with force, and nonsexual physical violence perpetrated primarily by parents. Overall, 83 percent mentioned at least one of these, a majority all three. Other researchers have discussed and investigated the possible link between exposure to childhood sexual trauma,[1] physical violence,[2] or early sexual activation[3] and subsequent adult participation in sexual or violent crime. The focus is often on the comparison of incidence rates between offenders and nonoffenders. In contrast, I explore what offenders said they remembered about the abuse in their past, what their experience and reality had been, and what the long-term impact was for them, as they saw it, both emotionally and erotically, and also in terms of how they viewed the sexual boundaries they violated. While the histories I present could be regarded as sympathy ploys, they also reveal that, rather than being predatory beasts, offenders were often victims themselves. If so, do they deserve more compassion?

Childhood Sex with Someone Older

Over half the offenders who were interviewed (57 percent) reported having experienced sexual contact before they were sixteen with someone at least five years older. As a comparison, the incidence rate of adult-child sexual contact found in various population surveys of adult males has been found to range between 3 percent and 16 percent (see table 1). Among those who reported such an involvement, 47 percent said it had occurred with one person only, 53 percent with two or more people. Two-fifths (41 percent) said the older person or persons involved had been male; 35 percent reported separate episodes with both sexes; the remaining 24 percent said their experience was limited to an older female or females. The average age when the experience first occurred was 9.9 years. The older person was most often an acquaintance (37 percent—e.g., baby-sitter, neighbor, associate of father), then a relative (29 percent—e.g., uncle, aunt, cousin, grandfather), a stranger (23 percent—e.g., someone at a park or rest room), and finally a parent (11 percent).

Simply being a victim of sexual abuse as a child, it must be noted, does not cause people to become offenders. This can most readily be seen by the obvious fact that girls are much more likely than boys to be victims of sexual abuse (see table 1). Yet statistically, we know that men are much more likely than women to be offenders.[4] If there were a direct correlation between the two, the number of female offenders would far outweigh the number of male offenders.[5] There are two possible reasons for this discrepancy. It might be that women are involved in sexual offending more than is known and that our culture and justice system are less likely to identify them as offenders. Or it could be that among men who become offenders who do report sexual contact with someone older as children, the experience and interpretation of these events are different than for others with similar biographies who do not become offenders. It is the second of these possibilities that I believe is key and that I explore here.

In this study, there were two realities offenders constructed that could explain the gender-based discrepancy between childhood sex with someone older and sexual offending in later life. First, some men with such biographies did not see what happened to them as "traumatic" and they had no noteworthy, lasting, or long-term negative memories of having been victimized or molested. Instead, they defined their experiences as either affectionate and caring or physically pleasureful. Comments about feeling turned on to sex or feeling special and loved were common. This is quite the opposite from reports of both the immediate and long-term negative effects of childhood sexual abuse almost always mentioned by female victims.[6] The meanings these men attributed to their experiences, I argue, facilitated a greater openness to seeing children in sexual terms as adults, and provided a framework for minimizing any feelings of harm that surfaced in relation to their own victims years later.

William, for example, reported having had sexual contact with two adults during his early adolescence. One of the offenders, his father, who was drunk at the time, asked William at age twelve to fondle his penis for him, which he did. To William, the incident felt abnormal because of the homosexual dimension to it. He did not see himself as having been victimized by an older, more powerful adult. The second sexual contact, during his early youth, was with an adult female.

R: At about thirteen, my mother was renting a room out to a lady she worked with who was maybe twenty-four. And I remember her calling me into her bedroom when no one else was at home and taking off her clothes, asking me to take off my clothes, and we had intercourse. She taught me my first lessons about sex with a woman. And we had sex probably weekly, I guess, for the next seven or eight months.

As he saw it, this relationship taught him that sex and affection were linked. He stated that the experience was physically pleasurable and made him feel important on an emotional level, not bad or traumatized.

R: My parents were never what you would call very affectionate or intimate as far as hugging, stroking, kissing, or verbally praising my brother and I . . . . Therefore, when this woman showed me sex it was very enjoyable, exciting, fun, and a way of feeling needed and important to someone . . . . The sex gave me physical pleasure, an orgasm. But the idea that she wanted sex with me gave me an emotional satisfaction I was not getting from my parents . . . . It was like having a first girlfriend but she was twenty-four instead of age thirteen.

William believed that his experience with the older female contributed to an overly permissive attitude toward sex and that he lost track of the boundaries between acceptable versus unacceptable conduct. He figured he was the product of what he had learned, that sex with his girls was his way of showing affection, just as he had been shown.

R: In hindsight, I believe it helped de-emphasize any sexual taboos that maybe should've existed for a thirteen-year-old boy . . . . All this presented me with the idea that sex was okay. Especially between someone my age and someone their age, sex was okay.

R: I thought I was showing affection in the same way . . . . The molest [was not out of] anger, hostility, revenge. I always saw it as something intimate, affectionate, and as trying to please another person.

Kevin, a second case, did not recall his own childhood sexual experience with an adult male until after he had molested his daughter, had been caught, and was in offender treatment. It was not that his memory was blocked as a consequence of being traumatized; rather, he never thought much about what happened to him. He remembered the experience as being strange, though he also described feeling that the offender cared about him. Thus Kevin too organized his own apparent "victimization" as an odd event that had affectionate meaning to him, not something that was necessarily distressing. Kevin stated that he was six years old when the contact occurred and that the offender was his uncle, whom he estimated as being seventeen or eighteen at the time. There were at least ten episodes during which he rubbed the penis of his uncle or watched his uncle masturbate himself to orgasm.

R: I had buried it so far down I didn't even remember . . . . I was about six years old. And it was an uncle.... We slept together and he would get me to rub his penis for him and stuff like that. And it was weird. I thought . . . he must really care a lot about me because none of the other uncles do that. And I just never did put it together.

I: . . . That's what you felt at the time?

R: [Yes], closeness.

Later in the interview, Kevin explained the connection between his own childhood experience and what he later did to his biological daughter. As he saw it, he was doing to her exactly what he experienced as a child.

R: I molested [my daughter] about the same age I was molested . . . . The feelings that I had for my uncle at that time, I had the same feelings for [my daughter] . . . . As far as what I was feel[ing] when ...my uncle was molesting me like that, I was thinking he must really love me. He's the only one that does that. None of the others do it. And at that time that's what I thought.

I: And then with [your daughter] . . . you thought?

R: I was showing her . . . love and affection.

Scott stated that he had been "molested" two or three times by a male baby-sitter around age four or five. When asked the age of the offender, he said that he learned from his mother after being arrested that the baby-sitter was about eighteen. Scott said he remembered the man as being much older.

R: Basically he would come in the room when I was sleeping, or when I was in bed, and suck on my penis and fondle my genitals and that would be about it. Then one night he went into the other bedroom and he wanted me to handle him . . . . He had come in and he had fondled me and then he asked me to come into the other room with him . . . . But anyway . . . he pulled his pants down and had an erect penis and wanted me to handle it and wanted me to put it in my mouth, which I wouldn't do.

Contrary to the sexual trauma thesis, Scott did not define the experience as harmful or frightening, but as physically stimulating and pleasureful. Asked how the experience felt at the time, his reply was "It felt great!" He recalled having had an erection and having reached some type of orgasm, though he admitted that because of his age he did not ejaculate.

R: I did experience very pleasurable feelings and if I look back at the experience, other than the time when he wanted me to put my mouth on him, I can really only think of pleasurable feelings from the experience. It didn't frighten me that I'm aware of. And I just don't really remember anything bad about it.

Again, unlike female victims of child sexual abuse, Scott never remembered being threatened or forced against his will to engage in sex. In fact, he described just the opposite, that he asked the male involved to do more. To him, as he remembered at the time, the experience was a physical turn-on.

R: As a matter of fact one time I had asked him—I'm a little embarrassed to discuss this—but I had asked him if there was something for the other side, speaking of the rectal area or my fanny. Because it, I just really found it a pleasurable experience. And he turned me over and played with my fanny a little bit, but he never inserted anything in my rectum or anything like that. And it was only like two or three times that I can recall.

Scott knew that his younger brother, at age two or three, had also been fondled by this man. His brother told his mother, and Scott had no memory of her doing anything about it. There was no external reaction, no definition from anyone else, to change the meaning of the situation as he saw it. This lack of definition carried over later, when he offended, at which time he remembered thinking, "I felt like, hey it happened to me and I didn't get destroyed, so it's not *that* bad." Feelings of physical pleasure coupled with no negative reaction led him to normalize the experience.

Randy likewise defined the sexual contact he had with a thirty-five-year-old woman at age thirteen as positive. As he explained it, the woman used to invite him and his friends into her house to keep warm in the winter while they waited for their school bus. He believed that society does not see sexual approaches by adult females in the same negative light as approaches by adult males; there is more tolerance and less anger, especially among men. The message as he saw it was that sex between young people and adults was okay on some level. Randy was keenly aware that his status with his friends escalated when they learned that he had had sex with an older woman. There was a sense of pride in his description.

R: She was talking to me and just kind of walked up and kissed me. I mean and then she started rubbing me, and she unbuttoned my pants and gave me head. That's like the first [sexual] experience I ever remember.

I: ...Was it pleasureful for you?

R: Well sure, definitely.

I: Do you think of that as a positive or negative experience?

R: ...I would say probably positive because . . . this was an older woman that liked a younger guy and I come to find out that she's doing it with the other guys . . . . It's kind of a different situation with a woman and a man when you're thirteen and you get a thirty-five-year-old woman. You're considered a stud! You become part of the stud factory. That's what we used to call it.

While Randy stated that what happened with this older woman was his first sexual experience, there was also an earlier period from ages seven to eleven where his grandfather engaged him in genital sex twenty to thirty times. Raised by his grandparents, his grandfather would approach him at night when his grandmother was out of town. As he grew older and more aware of his sexuality, the sexual advances became something he disliked, especially in light of the homosexual sex involved. Still, like other men in the study, he never remembered thinking he had been victimized or abused by the older person until he entered treatment as an offender. Instead, he described the sexual contact as mechanical and business-like, yet strangely affectional. Between both situations, the older woman and his grandfather, it is not hard to imagine that Randy probably developed a blurred understanding of sexual boundaries. He shared his story about what his grandfather did and the feelings that resulted for him.

R: He put . . . my hand over on his penis and then wanted me to suck it . . . . I didn't know what the hell it was all about....

I: How did it make you feel when it was happening?

R: ...I don't remember any feelings one way or the other as far as being excited . . . . To me it was just something he wanted done . . . . It was more like an affection thing than a sexual thing for me. It was like he was my protector.

Not everyone, however, had such positive or at least neutral memories of childhood sexual contact at the hands of older teenagers and adults. A second group of men defined their experiences as violent, unwanted, and/or deeply upsetting and confusing. In these cases, although others apparently knew that something had happened, there was no negative audience reaction built around the experience, and consequently no sense that sex between adults and children was considered culturally unacceptable and wrong. Even though the experience was unsettling for them, these men routinely said they came to define what happened as normal, the type of thing that all kids went through. Again, in the cases of adult male offenders, it might be that the reaction to the situation involved greater tolerance and less condemnation compared to the situations of female victims more generally.

Harry, one case in point, was the victim of ritualistic and sadistic sexual abuse committed by his father from as early as he could remember until about age twelve. His first memory of sex involved his father taping a crayon to his penis and making him insert it in the vagina of his younger sister. Harry figured he was probably three at the time, and his sister was wearing diapers. Many times over the years Harry was asked to perform sexual acts on his sister. He recalled an episode in which his father tied his sister naked to a chair, poured cold water over her, took her outside and tied her to a tree, and instructed Harry and his brothers to thrash the girl with sticks.

By his own admission, Harry had few sexual boundaries when he was growing up. He stated that his father sodomized him on several occasions, starting when Harry was five and lasting until he was seven or eight. He recalled bleeding heavily after the first offense, vomiting afterwards, and thinking he was going to die. He also remembered a great deal of physical pain and yelling whenever he was penetrated anally, and learning to bite on the corner of a pillow to keep quiet. Often when he yelled, he said, his mother yelled back from another room to stop making so much noise, or he got in trouble the next morning. For Harry, sexual contact with his father was a way of life, something that happened virtually every day.

R: If you were in the bathroom using the bathroom, he'd come in there and grab you then. There wasn't any privacy anywhere....
I: And what would he do when he grabbed you?
R: Just squeeze . . . just to hurt us, that's what he did....
I: He'd squeeze your genitals to hurt you?
R: Yes, then he'd laugh and say something like it was a joke and then he'd leave . . . . That was a common thing.

Harry drew a series of connections between the past and his molestation offenses with his father. He admitted, for example, that he "focused on sex a lot" throughout his adolescence and early adulthood. He also claimed that he was left with the impression that sex between adults and children was, as he put it, not really morally wrong and certainly not legally wrong. There were never any negative reactions from other adults who, he claimed, knew what his father was doing.

R: I didn't think it was morally wrong because my grandmother was real religious. She worked for [a] church and I grew up and went to a Catholic grade school . . . and she knew what my father was doing and it was okay . . . . And I considered her a moral person, so I guess I didn't consider that morally wrong because she didn't apparently. I didn't think it was wrong.

Since he perceived no negative reactions, Harry appeared to accept the events as normal, believing he had not been hurt by what happened, and that it was something every child experienced. When asked whether he ever thought that the sexual contact with the seven children he offended might be harmful for them, he recalled his own sadistic background, which led him to conclude that physical pain was possible, but emotional injury was not in his vocabulary. He never thought that he might have been harmed on this level.

R: I didn't think it would be emotionally harmful because I didn't think I had been emotionally harmed. I thought everyone was the same way I was. I thought I was just a normal person, or an average person, and I wasn't.
I: . . . You didn't feel that you had been emotionally harmed?
R: I actually believed that everyone did that. That all children's parents did that to them.

Larry was molested at age nine by a male and at age ten by a female; both experiences were described as unwanted. At age nine he was pulled into a rest room at a gas station by a stranger and anally sodomized. The experience profoundly affected his feelings of sexual competence throughout his life, and the reaction of his parents left him feeling responsible. They basically told him he got what he deserved for not listening to them.

R: He pulled me in, he jerked my pants down, and he raped me . . . . And that was where part of my problem was as far as . . . being sexual with my wife . . . . I had a lot of confused thoughts . . . . I mean I . . . didn't think I was all a man because I let somebody rape me. I let somebody rape me.
I: Why do you say that you let them?

R: . . . I tried to tell my dad and my dad told me that if I had been in the yard where I was told to be that it wouldn't have happened. So in a sense, I let it happen . . . . That's what I carried with me all these years was I was responsible for the rape.

The older female who had sex with him was a baby-sitter estimated to be around age twenty. He remembered a combination of feelings—fear, curiosity, and confusion.

R: She started playing with me and stuff and I was really scared. I didn't know what was going on. And she really got pissed off because I couldn't get a hard-on. And she made fun of me and so that really made me feel even worse . . . . She would shave herself [her pubic hair] (*chuckles*).
I: What, while you were watching?
R: Yeah. I still have problems with that sometimes. Even today I think, why would she shave herself? She sat me down and she shaved herself. I mean she was just doing all kinds of crazy stuff. She had me real scared.

Larry said he did not feel there was anyone he could talk to about what happened to him. He figured if he told his mother she would hit him. In the end, he tried to emulate the behavior with someone else his own age, indicating a disintegration in his sense of sexual boundaries as a child.

R: The guy that we were living with had two daughters and his oldest was about two years younger than me. So I tried to do it to her (*chuckles*). I didn't know what I was doing . . . . I thought it was natural. She was hitting on me and maybe I can hit on her. She was more my size . . . . I guess what it was was it got my curiosity up. And I was afraid to go to mom because mom . . . , she would beat us pretty bad. She would do shit to us that I didn't like.

Reactions of toleration from his parents and feelings of powerlessness extended to a sexual attack against his sister. Larry remembered that when he was around nine, he saw a man about age twenty who lived in the neighborhood force his five-year-old sister to perform oral sex on him. Two brothers also observed the event. When he and his brothers told his parents what happened, their reaction sent the implicit message that adults can do what they want and children are responsible for what happens to them.

R: I witnessed it, yeah. [My brother] witnessed it; [my other brother] witnessed it. And it wasn't that she did it freely. I mean he had a hold of her. He was forcing her. And dad got home and it ended up that they blamed her. They sat her at a table like this and kept telling her it was her fault .... Just out and out told her it was her fault. And just kept badgering her and badgering her.

John stated that his first sexual experience occurred at age ten with a man who worked for his father and who spent a great deal of time with the family. One day, while in a car alone with the man, he was propositioned for sex. John described feeling trapped, and his account suggested that the sex was unwanted.

R: He asked me if I'd do something for him and I said, "What?" And he says, "Well, I want you to stick your hand inside of my pants...." I said, "You're nuts, ain't no way." And he said, "Well, . . . do you mind if I put my hand inside your pants?" And all of a sudden, oh it's hard to describe the feeling . . . , I felt like I was trapped in a situation . . . . And he put his hands inside of my pants and started fondling me. And I remember sitting there in the car and the greatest fear I had was somebody would walk by, see us, and think that I was doing this because I wanted to. I mean that scared me to death. So he asked me how it felt and I said, "Well, okay...." I was confused more than anything else about what was going on . . . . He asked me if he could show me something that felt even better. And I think what I said was "I don't know." And what he did was push my pants down and perform oral sex on me . . . . After it was over I remember I went . . . to the bathroom and I was sick.

For John, much of the meaning of his own victimization came a few years later, when he heard a comment from his father. He realized his father knew what was going on but did nothing to protect his sons and daughters, who were all eventually molested, by a man who had a reputation for messing with children. He claimed feeling and having reached the conclusion that nothing happened to people who had sex with children; that while it might be morally wrong, there were no consequences. He felt this view extended to his own offending.

R: Everybody's attitude . . . was . . . maybe it's wrong but we won't say nothing about it . . . . After we was molested, both me and my brothers and eventually my sisters a few years later, I'd always assumed that my father never knew about it, but one day we were out working on the job and . . . someone made a comment about [the guy] being too friendly and he says, "Yeah, but only with young kids." And I thought, "You knew! You *knew* what he was like and what he might do and you *still* let us go with him." . . . And in my own mind was, "You approved of it; . . . it was okay with you."

I: Do you think that affected you when you molested?

R: Yeah, I think it did . . . . I thought of it as being wrong . . . the same way of going in and breaking something that belongs to somebody else as being wrong . . . . But I didn't think of it as being illegal, that I might be arrested for it.

As John described, people in his family tolerated adult-child sex. He reported that he grew up in a family in which incest was known to occur and that people joked about it and never drew strong boundaries against it.

R: I had a cousin . . . , everyone knew she was being molested by her grandfather. We all knew it. He was constantly giving her money …and he'd arrange for her to be alone with him whenever he could. We all knew that something was going on but it was ignored . . . . Or jokes were made about it. And it was more or less like the family knew about it; . . . they didn't approve of it, but they protected it . . . . I can also remember just wanting to talk to the girl, my cousin, about it. Just, . . . you get curious.

Sometimes sex that was experienced as unwanted and distressing as a child resulted in long-term anger, hardened the offender emotionally, and then seemed to get played out later symbolically in adulthood. Earl said that from age three to ten he was the victim of unwanted sex by his aunt, who was thirteen at the time things began. He remembered what happened to him as extremely unpleasant. In the beginning, he said, the frequency was once or twice a month, and later on it occurred whenever he was alone with her, as often as twice a week.

R: I was made to perform oral sex on her. And I wasn't the only nephew . . . . If I didn't I wasn't allowed out to play . . . . She'd just motion for me to come to the house . . . . The first couple of times I got sick . . . , vomit . . . . I was always told if you [don't do this], this's what's going to happen. Under threat . . . . It really quit when I tried to kill her with a butcher knife.

When asked how the experience affected him over the years, he conveyed strong feelings of anger and hate. This eventually seemed to translate into sexual domination over his girlfriend's daughter.

R: I think it's really made me tough. Yeah. I thought years ago I could show love and affection. I can show you anger in a second. To show you love and affection, it might take me a year. It's just a . . . , a lot of anger toward women.

He added that he had a distinct dislike for women with a certain hair color (his aunt's), which unfortunately was the same as that of his stepdaughter, whom he victimized using force. His offense seemed to involve a similar reenactment of what had happened to him years earlier.

R: She was a little bit heavier than my aunt. Hair almost the same color....
I: Were you thinking about your aunt when you looked at her?
R: Oh yeah! . . . Her hair, like I said before, blondes and redheads and she's reddish blonde, yeah. I don't hate or dislike . . . my stepdaughter. I didn't at the time; I don't now. But other girls with her hair . . . , most of the women that's got red hair, blondes, . . . I just don't like them.

There were also a few men who remembered negative feelings about sex with an older person of one gender, but positive feelings about sex that occurred with the other gender. This seemed to close off sexual interest in the first direction and enhance it in the opposite. Bob was repulsed by sex as a child with an older aunt, which occurred at age six or seven and spanned eight to nine years at a rate of three to four times a week each summer.

R: I had an older aunt who used to fondle me....
I: How old was she when it started with you?
R: She must have been in her mid-twenties . . . . In my younger years, she'd give me my bath and that would usually end up with her trying to get me to have some kind of sex with her.
I: What kind?
R: It was just usually my finger . . . in her vagina. And I would suck on her breasts.
I: What did you think of all this?
R: I did it, but I didn't want to . . . . I thought it was repulsive. When she would kiss me, I tried to pull away from her, or make excuses.

At the same time, he felt a special attachment during sex with older male cousins, which occurred at about the same ages and was just as extensive. Bob had sex with two boys, a neighbor and a nephew, as an adult. He was married, but often felt homosexual desires, which led to feelings of sexual confusion. Sexual relations with adult men did not seem like a practical option to him, partly because he had trouble accept-ing his same-sex feelings, and partly because finding such an outlet was too difficult to secretly engineer while living with his wife.

R: I had older male cousins, and some of their friends too, that I had homosex-ual sex with . . . .

I: Tell me a little more about the homosexual acts.

R: They were always with older males . . . . It was mostly oral . . . , I sucked their dicks. I often thought about it as getting the attention from older males that I didn't get from dad.

I: How old were the males, generally?

R: Most of them would have been in their late teens, high school seniors, that age . . . .

I: Why did you choose boys instead of girls?

R: Probably because of my aunt. I said before I felt her advances were repul-sive, like I wanted to . . . get away from her. And I felt that way about my wife too in later years.

Early First Sex with Age Mates

Many of the men, in addition to having been exposed to sex with adults during childhood, indicated that they had engaged in sexual activities with other children very early in their lives. Forty-seven percent said that their first sexual experience with age peers, involving at least breast or genital contact, occurred by age twelve or younger. Sixty percent said it occurred by age fourteen or younger; 70 percent by age fifteen or younger. The average age of first sexual experience with age peers was 13.4 years; the range was five to twenty-four. When the oldest case was excluded from the distribution, the average age of first genital sex with age mates was thirteen. This age is substantially earlier than that report-ed in a recent study of heterosexual, bisexual, and homosexual men,[7] and very similar to what was reported in two studies of female prosti-tutes.[8] The latter two studies in particular showed that early sex set a trajectory for involvement in certain sexual behaviors that came later, and in the cases of the men here, such experiences occurred even earlier.

More than the actual experience itself, it was the men's interpretation of these early activities, both at the time they occurred and later as their life progressed, that seemed most revealing. They remembered being excit-ed and highly eroticized by what happened, carried the memory with them for years, often became heavily involved in getting themselves off sexually, felt that as a result they had always been interested in sex, saw sex as having made them feel better emotionally, typically believed that other children—especially in situations with girls—had been sexual teases and instigators, sometimes recalled their childhood activities when they offended, built up positive rather than negative meanings around sex with children, and generally had little sense that childhood sex might not be as exciting for their victims as it was for them.

Sometimes the first peer sex the men reported involved sexual offending against another child. This was sex that involved the use of force or coercion, the seriousness of which the men minimized in their interpretations. The victim was typically a sister, though not always, and the behavior was never discovered by others or was lightly sanctioned and dismissed by parents. Conrad, for example, reported trying to force his ten-year-old sister to have sex on roughly six different occasions spanning five years, starting when he was thirteen.

R: I took my clothes off one day and come into her room with an erection and tried to get her clothes off and tried to have sex with her. And she said no. She put up enough of a resistance that I didn't try to force her . . . . She left and went and told mom and dad . . . . And we just talked about it, . . . saying, "Well, that's something you shouldn't do. Why'd you do that?" So I said, "I don't know why."
I: Did you take her clothes off or not?
R: . . . Well yeah, yeah, I had her clothes off. And I tried to get between her legs but she resisted enough that I couldn't. And I didn't. I didn't violently force it.
I: . . . Were you physical with her in some way... ?
R: I succeeded in forcing her to, getting her to take her clothes off. I took them off myself . . . . It wasn't violence in the sense that I caused her physical harm or bruising or anything like that. It was more psychological and emotional type of damage.

The attacks Conrad instigated on his sister involved a progression of sexual behavior that began about six months earlier. First there was masturbation to orgasm, which he said he remembered gave him "solace" and "comfort," followed by extensive fantasies about nude girls, the latter of which were so strong in the case of one girl that he named his daughter (whom he offended) after her. At the same time, Conrad grew up in a fundamentalist religious upbringing, with parents who he felt had a very narrow view of sex, believing that it was something that only married people did, and that the topic was out of bounds for discussion with them. He commented, "I grew up in a vacuum, an information vacuum about sex." As he saw it, his curiosity and ultimately the advances he made toward his sister were fueled by the rigid sexual ethos of his family. These same feelings, he speculated, carried over years later and could account in part for the sexual contact he had with his biological daughter.

R: I guess the reason why I did it [to my sister] was because I was curious about it. I wanted to know about it. I wanted to see what it was like . . . . [And] the connection between my childhood experience . . . and . . . with my daughter . . . was the fact that sex was enshrouded in mystery and it was something that was, it was something only for married people. The mystique around sex was [what] led up to my behavior.

Phil likewise admitted to having had sex with his sister, six different times, when she was ten or eleven and he was thirteen. The contact escalated to vaginal intercourse, and as he saw it, she initially was a willing partner. At first his sister returned his kisses and apparently told him, "You can do what you want," but later she had to be persuaded to participate. He continued to initiate even though he knew she had become uncomfortable with the interaction. He indicated that he felt remorse a few years later, but had buried the feelings and never really gave them much thought again.

R: This would occur in her bedroom, . . . and we would be kissing, and then I would ask if I could touch her . . . and she would say yes, and then from there it went to the intercourse.
I: . . . She said you could do what you wanted and then you proceeded to do that?
R: Right . . . , and then after this, she became more resistant . . . , after the first intercourse, she did not want to continue....
I: But yet there were five or six episodes?
R: After that, right . . . . I would talk her into it basically.
I: What was your sense of the interaction for her?
R: I don't think she enjoyed the interaction . . . . She may have thought she might enjoy it, but she did not . . . . Probably because I ejaculated in her. And she didn't like the sensation. She thought I was peeing in her.
I: . . . What was the situation like for you?
R: It was a pleasurable situation, though it was something we did in secret.

I: ... In what way was it pleasureful?

R: It's hard to describe. An orgasm, I mean, is a pleasurable situation.

The incest reported by Phil was not an isolated aspect of his childhood sexuality. His first sexual contact occurred at age eight, when he had intercourse with an eleven-year-old girl, the sister of a male friend, following a game of show and tell. He claimed he went along with it when the girl instigated the sex—"she showed hers," "she gave me a french kiss," "she had me expose myself." This first experience seemed to set an early sexual trajectory to his life.

R: It was very, it was a pleasurable feeling. And then a desire for that feeling over and over again, that's what I had afterwards. I just wanted to repeat, I wanted to have sex with her again. That was the only time I had sex with her . . . . I remember the feeling, ...the pleasurable sensations. And then that led to masturbation, so prior to that night I had never masturbated. And then after that it was masturbation on a regular basis.

By age ten, he said, he tried to have intercourse with a five-year-old cousin, but she was too young. He claimed to be cued to act in part by the victim—"She was curious as to wanting to know more about it." He also admitted to watching friends who were brother and sister have vaginal intercourse together. Shortly afterwards, he had sex with his own sister. Finally, at age fifteen, he began a sexual relationship with a twenty-five-year-old married woman who was a friend of his parents and who lived in the same neighborhood.

I: How did you feel having sex with an older woman at fifteen?

R: . . . I didn't really have any moral convictions about it at that time. Now looking back, I see it . . . as wrong. Though I, because of my sexual desires, I would probably . . . repeat the same thing.

Other men reported becoming involved in incestuous relations early on with cousins or siblings that had a less coercive, more mutual quality to them. In these cases, the overall volume of contact was greater. Steve began having sexual relations with girls his age, as best he could recall, when he was five. Usually it occurred with a cousin when he visited his grandparents; occasionally it took place with girls who lived near him.

R: It started out as "Gee, I wonder what they look like," the usual things I've read anyway that kids play to see if, to notice the other person is different.

Somehow, somewhere in there, it developed into more than just that.

The behaviors included having girls pull their pants down to see their genitals, touching their genitals with his hands, rubbing his penis in their vaginal region, and even intercourse. Steve reported fond and pleasurable memories of these early sexual experiences.

R: It was something that was fun. I guess it was pleasurable. It felt good to touch. It was a touching thing I suppose. Close, warm. As I look back and think about it, it was probably where I first learned that women are a source of pleasure, girls of course, but it was pleasurable.

Steve admitted that from his earliest days he had always been interested in girls, and that looking back at his sexual experiences, he realized he had long wondered how girls developed. He described his parents as sexually repressed—they did not sleep together at night and sex was never discussed—and he believed that this contributed to his curiosity. During his adulthood, and through the years prior to offending, his childhood experiences began to feel incomplete and unresolved to him.

R: I had an interest in girls, sure. You don't start off that young and not be interested in girls. I had no sisters so I didn't know much about the development of, how do girls develop? Who knows? It was all cut off before they reached the age of being able to tell. So, "When do girls start growing breasts?" Geez.

When he was ten, Steve said, his uncle caught him and his cousin having intercourse together and gave them a warning about not doing it again, which they did not. Later his mother had his father talk to him about what happened, and in light of what occurred, made no attempt to establish a moral boundary around sexual relations.

R: She had my dad come in and talk to me, and he talked very little, . . . he may have said more, but all I remember is that that's how, basically keep it in your pants because that's how girls get pregnant.

Again, Steve believed that his early sexual experiences with girls set in motion his tendency to view girls and women in sexual terms and as sexual objects. To him, the source of his offending began long ago at an age when he was more innocent.

R: The point I'm trying to get at is sex has always been a motivation. As I look back, . . . even back to when I was a kid, [sex was] always a motivating factor in there. It was a good feeling. I liked the feeling of the touching.

Like other men, Steve said that the child he molested was similar in appearance and about the same age at first as a relative he had early sex with when he was young. This was not something he or others typically recognized prior to offending, but came to understand later, after the fact. Still, as Steve saw it, he was reenacting what he had learned as a child and was seeking out answers to questions he reflectively had constructed about his childhood experiences with sex.

R: I think she might have reminded me a bit too of one of my cousins. A dark-haired cousin I had.

I: [The] one that you were sexual with?

R: Yeah, . . . when we were little kids . . . . I've since noticed, she was tall, my stepdaughter's tall . . . . Kind of built the same. There was a lot of similarities . . . . And the curiosity, back to the old case, never had sisters. Never had, "What do little girls look like?" Like some unfulfilled curiosity that never got satisfied when I was younger. From that standpoint I mean, [it] seemed to come up again, I guess.

Other men revealed that engaging in incest with someone about their own age left them with different feelings about sex other than curiosity. In one case in particular, early sex was linked to emotional expressiveness and became defined as a way of communicating. Harry admitted to an extensive history of incest with his sister, who was about two years younger, that spanned his childhood until around age thirteen. As reported earlier, Harry was ritualistically sexually abused by his father, and was often forced to have sex with his sister while his father watched. There was also extensive physical violence against the two—being whacked with steel tools, being tied up and whipped, having cans shot off his stomach. According to his account, he and his sister adapted by turning to each other for support. He claimed they developed their own language that no one else understood so they could talk together. And sex between them represented a type of communication as well.

R: Me and my sister both hated it when my dad made us do things together but on our own we would do things anyway . . . . It was kind of a way to keep each other feeling secure. It's like saying we have each other. It was more of a way of telling each other something rather than just intercourse. When it started . . . , well for years, I don't remember even having an orgasm. That wasn't part of it. That wasn't involved in the intent anywhere. It was just the way we communicated.

Harry learned early on in life that sex was a safe way to express his feelings, and he linked sex to feeling secure. He did not view the incest he was involved in as bad; on the contrary, it was such a normal aspect of his life that he and his sister made no attempt to hide it.

R: I think that made us closer because it was never a forced thing. It was mutual. At first it was a mutual way to talk to each other and then, by the time the
both of us started having orgasms, . . . that changed everything so it was kind
of an adventure or something. A learning experience, I'd say . . . . We really
didn't seem that concerned about hiding it from anyone else because it was just
like talking. We didn't see it as something bad. It wasn't bad to talk so why was
it bad to do that? That was talking too. That's the way we looked at it.

There were yet other men who became involved in sex with boys or girls at an early age who were friends, schoolmates, or neighbors. Usually the men described fond sexual memories that stayed with them and resurfaced when they offended. Sam was fourteen when a sixteen-year-old male friend initiated sex with him. This was the first sexual experience he ever had, and it was followed by a period of sexual abstinence until his early thirties, when he married.

R: He was about sixteen and I was about fourteen . . . . I don't remember
what . . . brought it about or how we got into that situation. But as I recall
he told me about the birds and the bees, if you will. About sex. Introduced me
into masturbation . . . . At fourteen, I wasn't able to masturbate to climax and
so that was a unique experience that he brought me into . . . . We masturbated each other but it never was to the point of climax. As we got close each
of us would masturbate to climax ourselves . . . . He was my good friend.

Sam remembered that the sex was physically enjoyable and that his partner made him feel cared about and important. He also indicated that this person filled a void in his life. From his earliest experiences, Sam formulated the script that sex was something that made him feel good about himself and helped him feel more connected to people.

R: He filled a void, by telling me things . . . , making me feel good about myself,
in a sense . . . that I was . . . , what would I say, adequate . . . . I always felt

that I was underdeveloped....

I: So that first same-sex experience then was . . . quite important in your life?

R: Yeah, and it was a good experience . . . . It was a[n] . . . uplifting experience and I didn't find any ill effects from it.

I: Was it physically pleasurable?

R: Yeah . . . . I guess it's just closeness, closeness to somebody, to be touching. And of course there was the . . . physical release itself when I was able to masturbate to climax. But I think it was . . . being cared about that was important.

As a result of this initial history too, Sam saw homosexual sex as something "natural." This view carried over to what he later told his stepson.

R: I convinced myself that it was, . . . just a natural thing that boys did . . . . And . . . that's exactly the same thing that I did, telling my victim . . . . I convinced myself that . . . it was just a normal thing. And I guess I would say that, that at some age, I probably would still tend to think that some sort of sexual contact, . . . between two boys at some young age is not all that unusual or immoral or homosexual either. But just a matter of curiosity and development.

Sam approached his stepson when the latter was eleven, a couple of years earlier than the age at which he was introduced to sex, but still around puberty. He felt he was doing for his stepson what had been done to him, all viewed within a positive light. He never constructed his own experience as having been harmful; consequently it never occurred to him that he was doing anything wrong.

R: I recall how I started saying to him the same sort of things that I . . . remember [my friend] telling me . . . . I told him that he had a big penis and that he was . . . really growing up. And he was going to be a real stud . . . . Some sort of flattery . . . . I look back at my relationship with [my friend] and that was a good relationship.

I: Did that help you think you weren't doing any harm then? ...Because you weren't harmed... ?

R: I didn't think I was harmed and neither was he. And we're still friends. He's married and had a family and doing just fine . . . . Well of course now I look and say, "Well, there was harm done because I did the very same thing that was done to me."

Ian reported a series of three voyeuristic sexual encounters with young girls that progressed to the level of sexual contact when he was between the ages of six and ten. Years later he defined the girls as aggressive, loose, initiators, and as really having wanted sex even though they said no. A *rape ideology* of sorts was formulated. One incident he described had him and a friend barging in on his friend's sister taking a bath.

R: The girl next door was real loose with her morals. And her brother, . . . the three of us were about roughly the same age and would run around togeth-er . . . . So she was taking a bath and her brother was constantly interrupt-ing . . . and she was pretending to be annoyed by it. "You boys get out of here," and on and on and, one of these kinds of things. And so we went in just playfully and he'd tickle her and expose her parts . . . . And she was enjoy-ing the whole thing. She was having a ball with this. Pretending to be annoyed. If she was really annoyed why didn't she lock the bathroom door? (*laughs*) . . . Or really get angry? But she didn't and she enjoyed it. And I got my first real glimpse of a fully developed female body at that point. And I wasn't exactly what you'd call aroused. I didn't have an erection or anything like that. But . . . there was curiosity. She had well-developed breasts and she was a very attractive girl. And that was probably a key thing in my sexual development, . . . being aware of her.

Ian provided excruciatingly detailed descriptions of the anatomies of the girls he had seen naked. Even years later, the memories seemed to stick with him.

R: There was one in fourth grade where a girl was very aggressive and . . . this particular girl had been well developed . . . . It was after school on the bus. She wants to get off early . . . and we went into the woods along a parkway area and she exposes herself and wants me to do it . . . . And I'm reluctant to do that, . . . I'm this naive kid . . . raised up in this real religious environment.
I: . . . What did she expose?
R: Vagina and her breasts . . . . I don't think I even touched anything. I think I was kind of repulsed by it. Because by this time she was well developed with a lot of hair and . . . the vagina . . . was pretty much open there. And wow!

He admitted that maybe the curiosity and fascination he felt for girls growing up carried over to his own daughters as they matured physi-cally. Indeed, Ian, like other men, recognized that they initiated sex with their daughters or victims only after they reached the same stage of devel-opment as the girls they had done things with when they were young. In

Ian's case, his "curiosity" resurfaced when his daughters entered puberty and their breasts started to develop.

R: Maybe some of these events with the younger girls . . . . Maybe this is an incomplete thing . . . . It didn't go to the point where I got the end conclusion or learned what it was all about . . . . Maybe it was the kind of thing where here right now I know about what it is and how much fun it is and how exciting it is and I didn't then, I didn't understand what was going on, and now I do. And then here's a young developing body that's attractive. I mean all three of my daughters are beautiful girls . . . . And I don't know if one of them were ugly that it would have made any difference. But in developing, they were real cute girls.

Last, not all early peer sex facilitated erotic sexual scripts per se. In a few instances, offenders reported being the victims of violent sex inflicted *against them by age peers.* The reaction seemed to be one of anger and rage, coupled with the implicit message of tolerance toward offenders. Brian described being raped—orally and anally—while incarcerated in a group home between placements with foster families at age fifteen.

R: I was put in this cell with five very large black dudes. And they raped me. Four held me down and one took his turn until all of them had their turns. And the security guard out the door sat and watched the whole thing . . . . You name it, they did it. And the only way that I could get any attention was, after they had done what they were doing, I went crazy. And I just started throwing punches anywhere . . . . I got behind the iron bunk beds and I tipped them over on them . . . . And they covered the whole thing up. They never did anything about it . . . . I called my social worker and told him, if you don't get me out of here I will kill myself . . . . I always wondered ...what I had done to deserve such a life like this.

Brian, like the others who reported violent sexual victimization in their backgrounds, or who had experienced incest, did nothing to deal with his feelings about what happened, then or later. His experience being raped and the anger associated with it were buried away and in part fueled a hostile demeanor throughout his adult life.

R: I never really dealt with . . . being molested or raped or whatever you want to call it. I turned it off. I didn't know where to go. I didn't know who to talk to. I was afraid of people. I turned it off. And to this day I still have never really dealt with it.

Exposure to Nonsexual Violence

Many men related how the experience of nonsexual violence inflicted on them primarily by their parents was also related directly to the sexual crimes they committed. Violence seemed to beget violence, from one generation to the next. The more "unresponsive" the world the offender was raised in, the more "unresponsive" and emotionally detached he seemed to become with victims.[9] Among the offenders in my study, 67 percent reported a substantial amount of physical violence, often at extreme levels of seriousness, in their backgrounds, the nature of which is elaborated in a few examples. In most cases, alleged emotional hardship accompanied the violence.

Larry described a life that was tragic in a variety of ways. Besides being raped anally at age nine by a stranger in a gas station and seeing his five-year-old sister forced to perform oral sex by an older male, he was enmeshed in a world of nonsexual physical and emotional violence throughout his youth and into his young adulthood. His parents divorced when he was very young, and neither wanted custody of the children. For about seven years, he was abandoned by his mother, who took off with a boyfriend. His father drifted in and out of his life to avoid paying child support. He grew up in extreme poverty, having lived, as he put it, "like trash," and at times when overcome by hunger, ate trash.

His parents, when they were in the parental role, used severe physical force for discipline, often hitting to the point of drawing blood. Larry saw his stepmother whack one of his brothers in the mouth so hard that she knocked out a tooth. His sister had been hit so brutally that she began to bleed to the point that emergency care was necessary. There were other times when his mother, if she was angry, would make him eat coffee grinds as punishment. She was described as a heavy drinker who often left her children home alone for days. When he was thirteen, he recalled, his mother assaulted one of his girlfriends, taking her head and slamming it into a door. Even more, his father used to intimidate and control him by pointing a gun at his head in what was described as a joking manner. There were also times when his father would lock him and his siblings out of the house for hours, often in the extreme cold.

As a teenager, Larry tried to escape his family situation and he began reenacting the violent behavior he experienced throughout his life. As he described himself, "I was all mixed up." He admitted to pulling and firing a tear gas pistol at a man who challenged him to a fight and added, "what I intended to do was hurt the guy." Told to "get the hell out" by his mother, Larry left home at age thirteen and found a job, lying about his age, to survive. He was jailed at age fifteen when his mother reported him to juvenile authorities as an incorrigible runaway, having done so after he called home and said he wanted his share of her AFDC money. He joined the military at age seventeen, again lying about his age. He quickly received a bad conduct discharge after beating up a superior officer and breaking his back, leg, arm, and jaw. Larry admitted that by his late teens he had a dislike for authority and that he had more or less become a loner. By his early twenties, he married a woman who was twenty-three, was married when he met her, had been married three times, and had three children. She got pregnant while they were living together, and he decided to marry her despite being unsure he was the father.

Larry lived a life that was extremely chaotic. Many of the situations he described were boundary-disintegrating events. As such, it is difficult to imagine that he was able to develop a sense of respect for other people's physical space. There was an implicit sense of bitterness, coldness, and hardness in Larry when he talked about his life. In relation to his mother, who inflicted a great deal of pain, there was evidence of a complete emotional detachment.

R: I, to this day, cannot say I love my mother. If she was to die tomorrow, if she was to die right now, I wouldn't have no feelings. It would be like a stranger dying to me.

Still, Larry was able to describe how the violence and totality of his life experiences affected him and his relationships. His lack of emotions probably made it easier for him to offend.

R: I was afraid to get close to anybody. I was afraid to show anybody my feelings. Because throughout my life all I remember is hurt from trying to get close to somebody. So I just kind of put a block up and I was, call it male chauvinistic or whatever. Or call it being hard or call it protecting my own feelings. But I just put a block up and I was nonemotional . . . . When [my stepdaughter] turned me in and I started getting counseling is when I started showing affection.

John grew up in a world of nonsexual violence too, violence inflicted mainly by his father until John left home at age sixteen and got married. He described his father as a heavy drinker who was drunk almost every night. He recalled incidents in which he and/or his siblings were hit with a belt, car antenna, or some other object, which caused welts or bleeding, injuries that often lasted a week or longer. When asked how frequent the violence was for both himself and his siblings, he replied that it was constant.

R: Oh, one of us got it just about every night . . . . It was like roulette, your chances were one-in-six it was going to be you. On a bad day, he might get three of us.

The intensity of the violence John experienced cannot be understated. He said that his father battered his mother frequently and severely, punching, kicking, and "grabbing her by the head and slamming her against the wall," and one time throwing a fork at her that stuck in her leg. There was also "the" incident where his father asked his mother for a divorce—he had met another woman in a bar—and she refused, so he pulled out a gun, put it to her head, and told her he was going to kill her.

R: He was sitting there holding a gun to her head telling her he's had it, he was going to kill her, he's *sick* of her, he's *sick* of the kids, he's sick of all of us. And he grabbed her and shoved her down . . . and she was on her knees crying and she had her head down on the floor crying, begging him not to kill her. And he just laughed at her and he pulled the trigger [the gun was empty] . . . . And we were standing there watching this and he thought it was hilarious. I mean he just sat down at the table and just died laughing, it was the funniest thing he'd ever seen. And she was laying there crying . . . . And I remember thinking he'd been kinder if he'd actually had shot her with the gun because he'd reduced her down to nothing.

After his parents divorced, John said, his mother was left destitute, so his father gained custody of the children and quickly remarried his pregnant girlfriend, who was eighteen or nineteen at the time. The beatings by his father then continued with his stepmother, and as he put it, "he worked her over pretty good, so she'd have bruises and stuff." He related that he and his siblings hated their stepmother and so no one cared what their father was doing or even if he beat her to death. The physical violence was compounded in mid-adolescence because his father and mother began shuffling the children back and forth three to four times a year, depending on how angry each parent got with them.

The impact of the violence John experienced within his family seemed to leave an indelible impression on him. When asked whether he felt the violence by his father was related to the sexual offenses he eventually committed, around age thirty-one, behavior that involved physical force at times, the answer was yes.

R: Well, I think it more or less set the attitude . . . that women were . . . subservient and it was okay no matter what you did to them and you didn't have to explain yourself to them. Children were subservient, I mean you never talk back to an adult. If you did you got your teeth knocked out.

It was difficult to differentiate the impact of physical or emotional violence from that of the sexual violence some men had experienced. It was typical to find men, like Brian, who were subjected to experiences of harm on every level. As reported earlier, he was gang raped in a group home for delinquent children and adolescents, and this was only one incident in a life he described as filled with hardship. Brian stated that he never knew his biological parents, as he had been adopted illegally on the black market. His adoptive mother was a "common hooker" and his adoptive father was a merchant seaman. As he told it, his mother used to dress him in girl's clothing because she had hoped to adopt a girl but got a boy instead.

His adoptive parents split up when he was three, and his mother began living with another merchant seaman. The two drank heavily, and they spent most of their money on gambling and alcohol. Brian remembered often being hungry, going for days without food; he reported that one time he ate nothing but a bottle of syrup for a week. By age eight, he had learned how to drive to survive, taking over for his mother, who was frequently intoxicated. Throughout much of his childhood, because his mother drank so heavily, he said he had to fix the meals at home, clean up her vomit, undress her and put her to bed, and provide child care to an infant brother.

There was also extensive physical violence. At age ten, he "beat the hell" out of his stepfather because he got tired of him hitting his brother and mother. When his parents got drunk, they would start hitting each other. He described his mother as "wild," often causing injuries to his stepfather serious enough to warrant hospitalization. She was known to use knives and wield a rolling pin, and one time she hit his stepfather over the head with an iron skillet. The violence also extended to him and his brother.

R: I got hit every time I took a breath, seemed to me. If I didn't bring her her whiskey she would hit me, knock me across the room . . . . If I didn't stay home and take care of this, if I didn't do that. I got hit all the time. If I asked to go somewhere, I got hit.

At age thirteen, Brian ran away from home because he had "had enough" and lived off the streets as a child prostitute. He said he turned tricks with both men and women, but mostly older men, and had built up a clientele. After a year, he returned home to try again, but the violence continued, and he quickly ended up in a foster home. He described his foster mother as cruel. There was one episode in which she made her own sons eat off a plate that she put dirt and animal feces on because they kept forgetting to keep the dog's food bowl clean. His foster mother was nearly as violent as his adoptive mother.

R: She was a very explosive person temper-wise. Her temper would just go off in a split second . . . . I had seen some of the beatings she had given her own children . . . . One time I saw in this foster home the boy's mother whip him with a lamp cord and left welts . . . all over his back and legs. I had a lot of those types of welts and bruises and black eyes and things when I went to school . . . . I was very much afraid of people when I was going through all of that in those years.

Asked how the series of events in his life added up and had affected him, Brian said that he stopped trying to feel. He believed his offending was facilitated in part by his lack of emotions and his ability to turn off his emotions if he had them.

R: All my life I have felt like a discarded toy that's thrown aside and picked up once in a while . . . . I got rid of a lot of my thoughts and feelings in my lifetime. I just shut me off, flat ignored them, built a wall. They weren't there. It was easy for me to do. It was like a light switch. I could just turn them on and off.

At the time of the interview, Brian described himself as a mean and uncaring person. His predominant emotion was anger.

R: Most people describe me as a very coldhearted person. They say I have ice-water for blood . . . .
I: Do you really believe that of yourself?
R: I am a very coldhearted person. I'm not nice to anybody.

Finally, he had an expectation of obedience from children that was a carryover from his younger days. No matter what parents did, he felt that as an adult, children owed him some respect.

R: Even though my mother has done the things that she's done to me I still believe in respect. I still believe you respect your elders. Even if she asked me to come over and do something for her I might not like it but I'd probably go do it. Strangely enough, why I don't know, but I would . . . . I just wish there was some way I could take these children who think they have it so bad and take them back in time with me. See what I went through. And then take them back and point out what they have. And see how bad they really have it.

These men, subjected to years of emotional pain, intimidation, and physical violence, learned early not to trust or to share their feelings with the people around them. Their adult lives were often characterized by isolation and social marginalization. The constant betrayal, rejection, abandonment, and barrage of violence left them hurt, angry, unhappy, and without any supportive outlet to turn to for help. They routinely concluded that it was safer not to feel than to remain vulnerable and risk exposing themselves to more harm. As adults, then, they found it easier to break sexual boundaries with children once their emotions had been cut off and blunted.

Conclusion

Many offenders in this study were involved in childhood sex with someone significantly older, had engaged in early genital sex with siblings and/or age peers, and/or had been subjected to extensive physical violence, primarily at the hands of parents. What made these events critical was not so much that they had occurred (for many people with such biographies, it could be argued, do not become offenders), but how they came to be defined at the time and afterwards. Sexual contact initiated by an adult was defined by some as affectionate or erotic rather than traumatic. Or if it was experienced as unsettling and confusing, the reactions of parents and other nonoffending adults typically involved blaming the victim or ignoring what had happened. Men who said they had engaged in incest or aggressive sex as children with other children admitted having constructed erotic scripts, which they said they remembered and which resurfaced years later. And they reported that weak or nonexistent sanctions around the use of sexual force resulted in their own inability to define sexual boundaries. The effects of physical violence, according to the offenders, was either emotional detachment throughout life or a pattern of domination and aggressiveness in their interactions with others. Regardless of the individual nature and mix of the offenders' experiences, offenders seemed to develop a blurred or more confused sense of culturally acceptable boundaries about sexual respect and physical space with others. Their experiences weakened the hold that broader cultural messages about the taboo nature of adult-child sex might have otherwise had over them.

THREE

Escalating Problems in Adulthood

From abusive childhoods, we move forward with the offenders to their adult years, focusing primarily on the months, weeks, and days just prior to their initial engagement in the act of child molesting. Nearly all the men described a period of mounting troubles, personal tragedies, and unhappiness, a situation of acute life problems that seemed to facilitate an emotional slide and to isolate and disconnect them from others.[1] Sexual, marital, familial, and occupational problems and issues were widely reported. Feelings of boredom, anger, aloneness, depression, worthlessness, emptiness, lack of appreciation, inadequacy, and power-lessness routinely escalated to what were said to be extreme levels. Many remembered reaching what to them was a personal emotional low, a feeling that things had hit bottom. Some indicated reaching a distinct turning point, a stage where they wanted something different in life and where they were looking to make some type of major change.[2] Usually it was when the men felt desperate about who they were as people and about the road down which they were heading that sexual offending seemed to become a more distinct possibility.

Certainly the trials and tribulations my respondents said they experienced in the period preceding their shift into sexual offending are not unusual for men who are not offenders. The complaints I listened to—not enough sex, wife is too independent, trouble getting an erection, someone important died, job is crummy, partner is not as attractive as before, boredom with masturbation—these are situations men frequently and routinely encounter, especially men in their mid-thirties and beyond, the ages at which the offenders in this study most often began molesting their victims. Critics of this life problem model will almost certainly argue that such commonplace events are hardly enough to push men across a boundary as extreme as the one involving sex with children. To many, in an era when personal responsibility is perceived as having waned, such accounts are nothing more than excuses. In fact, one woman with a grandchild who had been molested, who read an early version of my research, specifically pointed to this aspect of the study as problematic. How could something so simple explain something so great? That is exactly the point. Childhood biography aside, in many cases, it did not take much in terms of actual objective events to set the process of offending in motion. If you think about it, this prospect is chilling.

Entrapment in an Unwanted Life

Some men stated that before they became offenders they had reached a stage of deep personal frustration, emptiness, and disappointment because they felt the life they once envisioned for themselves did not turn out the way they anticipated or wanted. They said they were living in marriages that amounted to less than they hoped for; they had lost track of their careers and the lifestyle they once led because of sacrifices for their spouses or unwanted pregnancies; their wives were unwilling to try new fun or adventurous things; they often were saddled with having to take care of their or their wives' children; and they had become burdened with economic responsibilities that seemed overwhelming. As a consequence, these men said that emotionally they felt stifled, trapped, and stuck, that their lives were going nowhere; generally they viewed their situation with anger and resentment. Routinely these men blamed their wives for their unhappiness and mentioned that when they began offending they had been looking for an escape.

Steve said that from the moment he got married he felt trapped and unhappy. Previously he had lived the fast life of women, cruising, music, and marijuana. He enjoyed the freedom of doing what he wanted and even resided in a mountain community of alternative-lifestyle "hippies." Then he met a woman and after six months he began to live with her and she got pregnant. Angry over that—he felt she had a lax attitude about birth control—he asked her to marry him but admitted he was not really ready to do so.

R: Even though I was with her I still had not let go of my footloose, fancy-free, single guy attitude. So I would go off and . . . do this and that . . . and leave her sitting behind, never thinking of the relationship side of it . . . . I really was not experienced in what it meant to be serious in a relationship . . . other than somebody to sleep with . . . . I was angry at first because she was pregnant. I thought, "Gosh, I'm trapped." And so I thought, ". . . Do I stay? Do I leave? What do I do?" I decided that I guess I'd always wanted a family because I kept ending up . . . with women that had kids.

Steve had envisioned great things for himself—a beautiful wife, successful career, moderate wealth, and a lot of adventure. As time wore on he grew dissatisfied and angry with the reality of his situation. As he saw it, there was one bad scene after the next. Soon after getting married, Steve's new wife and parents, in particular his mother, fought viciously. He felt his mother disapproved of his choice of partners, in part because his wife had been married before and had three children, and he began to wonder if he had made a terrible mistake. Then he was fired from his job and he ended up staying at home and watching his stepchildren while his wife worked. His sense of self-worth declined and he eventually needed to accept public welfare assistance to keep his family afloat. He started to feel worse and worse about himself and life in general.

R: There we were, no job, and her job was minimal . . . . We had three kids. I was stuck! One of them was four years old, so I was having to baby-sit while she worked . . . . Finally I got a part-time job at a radio station. But it was only like weekends . . . . Then our firstborn came along . . . . It was a period where we were on welfare—food stamps—the whole you go in the store and get the looks from the people . . . . So there was a lot of low self-esteem here. Here I'm wallowing down, what am I doing down here? I never expected to be here. A lot of feeling sorry for myself and miserable. And feeling trapped.

Over a period of time, in this state of personal dissatisfaction, Steve began to reassess the direction of his life and the woman he married. He reached a point at which something had to change. It was shortly after reaching this turning point of sorts that he initiated sex with his stepdaughter.

R: I began to take a look at my wife and say, "What am I doing with this person?" I began to see her as being very physically . . . homely looking. I always imagined I'd be with some foxy dame. What am I doing here in this situation? Beginning to resent where I was.

I: . . . Were you angry that you were with her?

R: Yes. Yes, I felt trapped. I felt that life wasn't supposed to be this way. I was having a good time before I met [my wife], now look where I am. So there was a lot of . . . anger, you bet ya, sure there was.

Usually men who described feeling dissatisfied and trapped when they began offending were in their late thirties and early forties. For these men, when they paused to evaluate how things had gone for themselves, they tended to identify one problem after another with their wife, family, and job, leaving the impression that there was nothing about their day-to-day existence that was fun or gave them any satisfaction. In particular, there was a pattern of placating the needs and interests of their spouses, locking themselves into a marital role and lifestyle that was personally unfulfilling, putting off the things they wanted and making what they perceived as sacrifices for everyone else. Rather than one specific event that was a defining moment for their careers as offenders, there were a number of common problems that seemed to build, numerous twists and turns they felt powerless to stop or change.

Corey is a second case in point. Asked to describe his life before he started offending, he focused on his wife being sick, her becoming overweight, problems with money, and the fact that he had to bear most of the responsibility of the children.

R: My wife at that time had been in and out of the hospital two or three times a year . . . . I took care of the kids all the time. Get the kids off to school, go to work, visit her, come home . . . . We had a lot of troubles with money. She was sick a lot . . . . She was on [a drug] . . . . It had such ungodly effects . . . . The attitude, the moods, the water buildup.

I: She gained weight?

R: Oh yes. She went from 125 pounds up to 150.

I: Did she lose her attractiveness . . . to you?

R: In essence, yeah, because . . . she become obese! And at the same time, the girls were starting to look like she did when she was a teenager.

Corey also noted that his wife's moods were basically unpredictable. From his point of view, her predominant emotions included anger, inconsolable crying, and explosiveness. He seemed to believe this was a reaction from a drug she had to take to control her illness.

R: I mean it wouldn't take nothing to set her off in a different mood . . . . You walk in the door and you say hello, and you determined the mood by the reaction you got back from her. Whether it was anger, whether it was crying; a happy mood . . . . If in a crying mood, no matter what you said, it was just total crying. And the kids and I worked around that. We worked hard . . . . We lived with it. When she would throw a temper tantrum, when the kids would do something, she would just go into a total rage. Hit, beat, whip the kids.

When his wife was happy, he felt he was ignored. The children always came first, which meant that she spent so much money on them that, when he wanted to buy something for himself, there was nothing left. He felt he could not do the things he wanted to do and might have enjoyed.

R: I felt that she was . . . doing a lot of stuff with the kids, and she was putting them before me. It always seemed like she always had to have this for the kids, that for the kids . . . . Whenever I wanted something there was nothing there to get anything, there was no money left to get it . . . . That's what I was feeling . . . . I'd spend hours upon hours upon hours working and come home and [there was] no money to do what . . . I wanted to do . . . . I was being a little on the selfish side . . . . Because I felt everything had to come first—me first, them second.

Asked to assess how he saw his life before and after he began and continued offending, Corey said that things had unraveled to the point where he felt dissatisfied with essentially everything. He reached what to him was an emotional low. He wanted some excitement in his life, and apparently molesting his biological children seemed to provide that for him.

R: I was feeling frustrated. Felt like I'm not going anywhere. Maybe it was the age, coming up on the age of forty. Dissatisfied with my job, my job performance. Dissatisfied with the things that was going on around the house. [Dissatisfied] with the attitude between my wife and myself.

Erosion of Sexual Happiness

In contrast to the cases above, for other men the transition to offending was marked by a major deterioration of sexual relations with their involved partners. In fact, many men said they had become bored, uninterested, or sexually unaroused by their partner, or that the frequency of sex together had trailed off substantially. These men took no responsibility for their feelings of sexual dissatisfaction, but instead assigned blame to their female partners. Some men, as they became more and more frustrated by their sense of sexual injustice, reached the point where they forced their wives to have sex with them.

One unpopular theory about rape and child sexual abuse proposed that when men become dissatisfied or frustrated with their sex lives, they sometimes turn to coercive or forced sex out of "sexual need" or desperation.[3] In the era of feminist scholarship on sex crimes this explanation has been rejected, and rape has come to be redefined as a crime of violence or aggression against women. The accounts of the men here, however, suggest that feelings of sexual frustration may be an important factor in their decision to engage children in sex, and as such, cannot be discounted as a catalyst.[4] Importantly, this does not mean that sexual abuse is justified in any way, or that the behavior of offenders is nonviolent. The broader nature of the situation depends on the perspective of the victim.

Ian described sexual incompatibilities with his wife that began on their honeymoon. He wanted sex, she did not, and he could not understand this, given his expectation that couples have sex when they marry. In the end, Ian had sex with his wife despite her feelings against it. He excused his action on the grounds that it was what he wanted and she never resisted.

R: On our honeymoon, she didn't want to engage in sexual intercourse at all. She just wanted to sleep. She was tired . . . . And . . . we got in a honeymoon suite with several beds and messed up one and messed up [another], . . . I was just going all night long . . . . I mean she'd have been happy not [to do it], she just wanted me, she didn't want the sex. And she put up with it. I mean she didn't argue about it. But she'd say, "Oh boy, here we go again."

I: . . . So you were sexual a number of times even though she may not have wanted to be?

R: Yeah. She . . . would cuddle up a little bit or just kind of lay there . . . . She never got angry with me about it.

There was a critical edge to Ian's view of his wife's sexuality. He felt she was uptight and repressed—"She had a lot of sexual hang-ups"—and that her sexual problems stood in the way of his sexual happiness.

His description of his sexual relationship with his wife contained many inconsistencies—efforts to present a nonproblem. Ian insisted that he had a happy sexual relationship with his wife. He mentioned being oversexed and extremely turned on with her, and that he got more than he needed in terms of frequency. But then the conversation would return to feelings of frustration and disappointment. There was much talk of his wife being unable to experience orgasm.

R: I'd say little remarks to her once in a while, that some of the friends say to their girlfriends and wives, "The cat that doesn't eat at home eats out!" . . . And I might have been putting pressure on her a little bit that way and maybe made it more difficult for her to come around and respond . . . .

I: So in other words, you were hearing things that other guys were doing with their wives and maybe you wanted a little more?

R: Well yeah. Well, I certainly wanted more response from her. Because she didn't have an orgasm, didn't even know what it was, for years. It took a long time.

Ian related that over the years he became bored with and uninterested in sex with his wife. He remembered wanting something more exciting but being unable to act on his feelings, primarily, as elaborated elsewhere in the interview, out of guilt. Still, he remembered thinking early on that one day he would have sex with someone other than his wife. He drew a parallel between sex with his wife and people who progressed to more and more potent, intoxicating substances for a high.

R: It's kind of like maybe analogous to a fella who starts on pot and after a while he doesn't get enough of a high on pot and he's got to go to what, cocaine next, or whatever's the next step. I'm not into drugs so I don't know . . . . We'd had a normal traditional heterosexual relationship; after a while you look for something more exciting. And a lot of men look for, in other beds, for something more exciting, other women. And I had fantasized about that. I flirted a little bit. But when it came down to it, I couldn't do it. I came close a few times.

Eventually there was a point in the relationship where his wife began to get more interested in sex, but he had been frustrated and unhappy for so long that his interest continued in the opposite direction.

R: She got more interested in sex. And it was really strange, it really baffled her sometimes, when I wasn't responsive. And she said, "Oh I remember the time you'd always want to have sex." "Well, I'm tired tonight," or "I've got to get up early in the morning."

In the end, Ian admitted somewhat speculatively that lack of sexual responsiveness from his wife may in part have led him to turn his attention toward his three biological daughters.

R: Maybe I tried to, especially during some difficult times there, times when she wasn't responsive to me, . . . maybe I looked upon the kids as substitutes or surrogates. And obviously inappropriately.

Scott too described reaching a stage of sexual discontentment before he began offending. His sexual and emotional relationship with his wife deteriorated to the point where he was extremely unhappy.

I: Were you . . . sexual with your wife when the molestation began?
R: (*Sighs heavily.*) If *you wanna call* (*very loudly*) what we were having as sex, yes, we were. It was very mechanical, very little feeling left in the relationship . . . . It was something that was done I think more just to release sexual tension than it was because we loved one another. I think our marriage had really burned out a long time prior . . . . And I wasn't getting the sexual fulfillment and sexual satisfaction that I wanted from my wife. I'd been masturbating for probably two years prior to the time that I molested my daughters . . . and feeling very uncared for and unloved and unrespected.

Good sex was very important to Scott, in fact so much so that he said his selection of a wife depended on it. His feelings of sexual discontentment were exacerbated by this expectation he had of a spouse.

R: I always looked for a wife that would sexually fulfill me. I mean that was something that in my way of thinking was very important, that my wife was sexually satisfying to me and that we could have good sex together. And initially when my wife and I started sex it was good.

Scott reached a stage where he was so unhappy with his sexual life that he began looking for new adventures or something new to stimulate himself sexually. At first, sex with his stepdaughters was not something he had considered. The key was that he was seeking a new outlet.

R: I just constantly walked around not feeling satisfied . . . . I was getting bored with masturbation and soft porn, and it just wasn't exciting to me anymore and I was looking for something more stimulating. Frankly . . . prior to the molest I had even started thinking about homosexuality. Just something more stimulating than just me . . . . And there wasn't that much there between my wife and I . . . , I would try to stimulate things between my wife and I, but it was a waste of time. It was like talking to a brick wall . . . . Like if she was cooking . . . and I'd come in and put my arm around her and try to . . . seduce her . . . , she'd just stonewall me, to the point of "Get out of here, I'm busy!" or "Go away!" . . . I felt like what's the use anymore? I had gotten to that point.

There were other men who simply could not accept a decline in sexual frequency with their wives. Any reduction in sexual outlet, even for a short time, set them on edge. These men saw sex in marriage as a right, not a privilege, and felt it was intolerable if their wives began denying their requests or were unavailable for sex. This was certainly the case for Earl, who initiated sex with his stepdaughter one morning, after morning sex with his wife stopped because of her new earlier work schedule. This respondent claimed that he and his longtime female partner—common law wife—had sex every day, and as much as eight to ten times a day, across their entire ten-year relationship.[5] He complained that her schedule cut into their sex life.

R: I had been used to having sex at night and . . . [in] the morning. When her job changed and she left early, . . . the sexual relationship we had every morning [after] waking up—not every morning—but she wasn't there no more.
I: So you were used to it every morning and every night and suddenly the mornings were taken away?
R: Oh yeah! . . . You can think back now and you can say, "why didn't I get up a half an hour earlier," but that's not what happened . . . . Maybe you want to call it a void, but over the years you're used to a relationship, and then all of a sudden . . . . I disliked her job . . . . It's just that everything had changed.

Kelly, likewise, initiated sex with his stepdaughter following what he felt was a period of sexual inaccessibility instigated by his wife, which in his view was unacceptable.

R: She would kind of ignore me . . . . Sex-wise. You ain't getting no love or this. And that's about where it went. Because that's really what drove me more into deeply consuming alcohol....
I: The fact that your sexual needs weren't being met?
R: Yeah. They weren't met at all! There was a blank. I'd go over there and kiss

her or something and well, "No, not right now . . . . "

I: . . . So there was no sexuality?

R: There wasn't nothing. I'd be lucky to get it . . . once a week.

I: And how long had that gone on?

R: Well . . . for a while; maybe eight months . . . .

I: How did you feel?

R: I didn't like it. I wasn't getting anything. It's kind of hard to go in the bathroom knowing that she's in the next room and you got to sit there and masturbate . . . . Tears you up. There's nothing there. I should have left. I knew I should have left. Something told me, Kelly, leave. And I didn't.

A couple of men admitted they raped their female partners who had continually refused them sex. The men maintained that feelings of sexual deprivation facilitated things. Mark, in particular, openly admitted to raping his wife on multiple occasions. She had been sleeping with other men outside the marriage because, as he said, she liked variety. Generally, Mark saw his wife as a sexual tease. She would undress in front of him, he felt, to deliberately arouse him, and then say no when he asked her for sex. He believed that his wife enjoyed the use of force, and he was oblivious, at the time, to what he was doing. As he said, "What I wanted I snatched, wrestled her for it." If he could rape his wife, what was there to stop him with his stepdaughter?

R: I asked her for [it], . . . and she knew I wanted it, but it was like the way she'd tease me: "No! No!" But then she'd get all naked, butt naked. And I didn't want to beg . . . . So naturally I had to go after her and take it.

I: . . . And then what would you do?

R: Like I'd go to her to hold her. She'd pull away. I'd go to play with her and she'd pull away. I'd say, "Come and let me eat you." She would pull away . . . . But then after [that] . . . I would hold her down and I opened [her] and I put it in.

I: You opened what?

R: Opened her legs and I'd penetrate her, and she, everything [was] just like we never had a fight . . . . It was just part of the way she wanted it.

I: Would she get into the sex then?

R: Oh yeah! She'd get right into it . . . . That was kind of freaky with me because I couldn't understand why a woman had to be dogged in that way. Rough and taking it from [her] to get into it.

When asked whether he thought what he had done was rape, he said looking back yes, but at the time no; the reason for his actions seemed to be sexual desire.

R: I look[ed] at it [as], this is my wife, and where must I go, [where] else, to get my sexual pleasure filled than her? And if she ain't going to give it to me, I'm going to take it from her.

George too described how sex with his wife reached what bordered on marital rape. He stated that he frequently went out drinking after work and when he got home, late at night, he wanted to have sex. His attitude was that he expected sex from his wife and it was her duty to comply. She would often refuse and he would not stand for it. George in general had little understanding about sexual boundaries. When his wife refused his advances, he would do what he wanted anyway. What he did with his wife was a type of stepping-stone in his offending career.

R: I'd wake her up . . . . Sometimes she'd be awake. Most times I'd wake her up.

I: And then . . . what would you do. . . ?

R: Oh I'd just roll her over and start . . . rubbing on her or something . . . . Most times she'd raise hell (*chuckles*). I couldn't understand it....

I: She'd raise hell. What would she say?

R: Just she's too tired. Or, . . . get on me for drinking so much and . . . not being at home . . . . I couldn't get my mind off of this. Because she ought to be ready. I worked everyday. Now, why shouldn't she? Because she can sleep in. Yeah, what's the hurt in waking her up. That was my thoughts then.

I: How'd you feel about the fact that she was saying no to you?

R: Well I'd get pretty disgusted; I'd always throw it up to her the next day, or say something about it.

I: . . . [So] then a lot of times she would what, agree to go ahead?

R: Yeah. And she'd, I don't know if she'd enjoyed it or [just tell me that] or something . . . . I knew she wasn't getting nothing out of it then.

Loss of Male Authority

Some men stated that their turning point before they started offending involved a loss of control and authority in their role as husband/partner and/or father.[6] In particular, they mentioned having wives, girlfriends, and/or children who did things they did not want them to do, such as spending too much money or spending money without asking, overriding or disregarding decisions they had made, and/or shucking domestic responsibilities. These men said they reached a stage in their lives where they felt taken advantage of, unappreciated, and disrespected. They usually adhered to rigid role expectations for their female partners and children. They believed that both should be subservient and loyal, and as a consequence became especially unhappy when things did not seem that way.

Sidney reported a perceived lack of power in relation to his wife and stepchildren that seemed to send him over the edge. He believed that his wife overrode decisions he made about the children and that he had no input when it came to parenting. Sidney held a very traditional view of gender roles that he said reflected how he had been raised. He was also an extremely large man (probably six feet and maybe 300 pounds or more, with tatoos on his arms), and a former biker who used to frequent strip bars.

R: Every decision seemed like it had to be cleared through her as far as raising the kids. See, the kids were stepchildren, so for a period there we had a problem where, if they weren't happy with what was going on they went to mom. If mom happened to be there when I said something, frequently she'd stopped me right in the middle and change tracks on what was being done. It was a situation where I felt the pecking order in the family was her, the kids, and me, at the time, okay? And I felt that I was at least two places out of position . . . , and in these situations with my daughter, there was only two people involved and I was the one in charge.

This case fits the "domination" theory of sexual offending. Sidney reached a point where he had to do something in the context of the family to claim some semblance of power and control. According to the therapist who referred Sidney for this research, his feelings of powerlessness were especially paramount because his spouse was "quite attractive" and "petite," while he appeared the opposite. She also allegedly was sexual with other men outside the marriage. There was a sense, in the comment by Sidney below, that the marriage was on less than solid footing.

R: Well then I reached the point where I felt like I had absolutely no authority and no responsibility in the family. And I think that was the period, just prior and during the molest where I . . . felt like . . . everything I said had to be seconded or underwritten by my wife, and that the kids had realized that if they weren't happy with the judgment I made, all they had to do was go to mom and try to get it changed. And so it was a situation where you feel like, well you're out there every day and you're working and you're supporting the people and you're doing everything you can, but you just have no input. And for me that was not tolerable . . . . I wanted the authority, but I didn't know what to do to get it.

Like Sidney, Leon stated that before he began offending he and his wife had entered a stage in their marriage where they "were fighting constantly" and he felt he was in "constant turmoil." The conflict covered all realms of their marriage, from being parents to their sexual relationship. Leon adhered to very strict and, again, traditional beliefs in his view of children and the role of men and women.

R: I expected certain things from the kids, my wife doesn't . . . . She thinks they're individuals, and in a lot of ways she's right . . . . I expect them to be not constantly in my face making a lot of noise. She says I want them out of the room all the time, but that's not true. I just want quiet peaceful existence. I don't want this constant noise and hollering and disruption. We fought about that all the time. Everything I would say to the kids she would holler at me about. "Now that's not right. You did that as a kid, blah, blah, blah, blah, blah." She was always, I thought, undermining my authority.

Leon and his wife differed philosophically on the roles of men and women. Leon was raised to believe he was responsible for earning an income and for the outside maintenance of his home, whereas he expected his wife to raise the children and manage everything inside. Apparently his wife did not concur with his view of gender roles.

R: My wife is very intelligent, very hardworking, but at her career. Now everything else is secondary. And that's what created the problems . . . . I was raised to where the male went to work and he come home and was pampered by his wife. My dad to this day is still number one in his house . . . .
I: So you had some adjustments to go through?
R: Right, and I didn't handle them all well. I mean most of the time we fought or argued about it or I resented it or sometimes I'd take it out on the kids.

Leon came to see his wife as a threat or challenge to his role as a male and his sense of masculinity. In the end, even his sexual relationship became a source of conflict as he struggled to control what he saw as his innate right or male territory.

R: She's very demanding sexually. And I had a hard time adjusting to that.

I: What do you mean by demanding?

R: Frequency—she is very sexual . . . . I don't know that I've ever allowed her to have the frequency that she wants (*laughs*).

I: How often [did] she want sex?

R: Just guessing, every other day at least . . . . I would withhold sex. Now that's a funny thing to say for a man, I guess. But if I was mad at her or whatever, I knew that that was very important to her and I would use that . . . . I found myself being the reluctant one and she . . . wanted to all the time.

I: . . . How did you feel about that?

R: I resented it. I thought I should control that. I thought that was a male prerogative and not a female [one], although a female has a right to say yes or no and a male has the right to continually pester for it, which is the way I viewed it. Man's role was to continually try, and if he didn't, he didn't.

At the time, as he watched the complete breakdown of his male role expectations, he remembered feeling "self-pity" and "being depressed." He came to feel undervalued and unappreciated, and soon began offending.

R: Her life is very glamorous compared to mine. She more or less set her own hours; . . . she had long lunches at real nice restaurants. And boy, everything about what she did just seemed great. Everything about what I did just seemed awful . . . . And I didn't get any credit from her. That's what I felt! I felt, well I'd go to work every day, I provide majority support, I provide all these benefits . . . , and . . . "I'm not getting patted on the back enough." I [wasn't] getting, somebody's not telling me, "Hey, you're doing great."

Kevin is yet another, even more dramatic, example of a man who turned to offending once he decided he lost control over his wife and blamed her for wrecking their marriage. According to Kevin, his wife, Kathy, spent money recklessly, and this led to feelings of despair, frustration, and betrayal on his part. In the end, he came to believe he had no say over how she spent what he defined as his money, and this abruptly changed how he felt about her.

R: [My wife] and I were having a lot of problems then financially . . . . The lady could go through money like water. I mean it was just terrible. And I lost all trust and confidence in her. But I didn't want to get a divorce because of the kids . . . .

I: What kind of spending was she doing?

R: Oh man! First time she went through my checking account, I lost about fifteen hundred dollars. She would write checks and sign my name to them . . . .

I: What did you think she was doing with the money?

R: I don't know. There's nothing to show for it.

Once Kevin recognized and defined his spouse as the problem, he began to look in other places for satisfaction, specifically to his own daughter, whom he began to trust more.

R: I guess I was looking for something. Because I had lost all confidence in the marriage. And I did reach out to [my daughter]....

I: ...Why do you think it occurred . . . ?

R: . . . Because I didn't love my wife anymore. I didn't trust her. Now mind you, it's no mistake whose fault this is. It was mine, but at that time, I think I was replacing . . . [my wife] with [my daughter].

I: . . . Putting your daughter in your wife's place?

R: Yeah. I mean, I could trust [my daughter]. [She] loved her daddy.

Personal Engulfment in Sex

A few men recounted that during the years, months, and weeks before they began offending, they had become privately or secretly engulfed in sex as a way of life. Sexual desire and sexual behavior became their core reality as they thought and fantasized about sex extensively. Routinely, though not in every case, they reported viewing sexually explicit materials on a daily basis for a period that had spanned years. Part of the pattern also included a high frequency of masturbation to orgasm. The men in this group tended to live on the edge, engaging in sexual behaviors that had either an experimental, a thrill, or sometimes even a criminal aspect to them. This included, for example, episodes of exhibitionism (e.g., one offender used to walk naked during the middle of the night through the streets of his town), participating in three-way sex by duplicitously setting the situation up, and participating in homosexual sex out of curiosity.

The men who followed this situational path, sexual engulfment and then offending, seemed to become sexually disinhibited over time. The pattern was similar to what has been labeled elsewhere as a cycle of "sexual addiction."[7] One psychologist, who referred some of the men in this study, called this group of offenders "trysexuals." These men described feeling drawn to sex because they enjoyed the stimulation, the orgasm, the excitement of it, and because sex made them feel good about themselves. At the same time, they admitted to feeling out of control in terms of their sexual desires. Unlike some of the other offenders in the study, they seemed to experience a gradual and lengthy progression of increasingly marginalized sexual behavior leading to sexual offending. Hypothetically, it is possible that the progression would have continued in even more marginalized directions, beyond child molesting, had the men not been caught.

Scott described a sexual history involving the extensive use of pornography coupled with heavy masturbation and sexual fantasy dating back to his early adolescence. At age eleven, he discovered masturbation to orgasm, and enjoyed it so much that he did it daily, often three or four times a day, into his adulthood. He began using pornography to stimulate himself sexually early on, whenever he could find it. He recalled fantasizing about sex with different schoolteachers and about starring in pornographic films because of the access to unlimited sex.

R: I had . . . all these fantasies. I mean at times when I was eighteen or nineteen I used to think about how neat it would be to be in a porno flick or to be part of the porno society . . . . I thought, "Gee, that would be a neat life to be in . . . ."
I: To get paid to have sex?
R: Yeah. *Yeah! I mean just free sex all the time (very loudly).*

Throughout his early twenties Scott made attempts to control his sexual desires and behaviors, but without much success. He vacillated between dedicating himself to God to live a righteous "pure" life and secretly lapsing into a world of erotic indulgence. The religious aspect of his life involved periods of complete immersion in religious thinking and activities. In fact, at one point, before he got married, he decided to become a minister and spent all his free time in Bible study classes, attending church services, and doing guest sermons at a small church. It seemed he was always trying to find something in his life that was missing, and religion, he said, filled that need for him. In his words, religion "was my life. It was everything . . . . It kept me busy. It filled all my void spaces."

The sexual phase of his life, in contrast, involved major surges in the frequency of masturbation, pornography, and sex with women, followed by guilt, blaming women for tempting him, and fear that he was out of control. There was subsequently a period of abstinence and eventually re-indulgence, which became his pattern. There was a sense of moral irony in the sexual partners he chose, given his religious life. For example, there were two women who were married, two women he met at Bible study classes, one woman he smoked marijuana with and then with whom he had "all kinds of crazy sex" during a one night stand, a girlfriend he stayed with for a year for the sex despite not liking her, intercourse with a Catholic girl, and so forth. While he was in the military, throughout this same period, he said he often felt out of control with his desire for sex and masturbation. He actually sought out a military chaplain for help after sex with one woman.

R: I went to the minister and we talked about it. I expressed that that had happened and I sought out help with him to try and get that under control . . . . Because I knew that sexually something wasn't right about me. I mean for some reason . . . I just didn't feel like I had control of my sexual attitude. I mean masturbation was too important to me. I masturbated too much as far as I was concerned.

At age twenty-four, after a three- to four-month period of sexual abstinence and complete immersion in religion, Scott met a woman at his church whom he subsequently married. He stated that premarital sex with her "lighted the fires of passion," and his sexual desire began to take over again. He described feeling like "Jekyl and Hyde," or living a double moral life, preaching behind the pulpit in the morning and then going home and "committing sin." He struggled with his sexual desires and his perceived failure to keep them in check.

R: I still wanted to be that pure person, but yet that drive was there and I lost control . . . . I told her this is wrong . . . . *She claims* I tried to run a guilt trip on her. That wasn't it . . . ; I was asking for help because I'd lost control again . . . . Everything else was still intact . . . on the outside . . . . But that sexual drive was back and in control of me again instead of me in control of it. And we'd have sex and afterwards I'd feel terrible. I'd feel guilty. I'd feel like I was cheating my God . . . . Her line was that she thought it was natural and normal . . . . Anyway that was a real problem in our relationship was having sex before marriage . . . . I was devastated. I just knew it wasn't right but yet I didn't want to stop it . . . . I enjoyed it too much.

Shortly after getting married, Scott labeled his wife a "nymphomaniac" because he felt she wanted sex too often and it was detracting from time with his new stepchildren. She then withdrew from him emotionally and sexually; he in turn got angry because she refused to have sex. He once again turned to autoerotic behavior. In the years before he molested his stepdaughters, Scott increased his frequency of masturbation and use of pornography more than ever. His job kept him on the road traveling and driving, and he would often pull over on the side of the road to masturbate, usually many times a day. He said that as he drove he searched for pornographic materials along the roadside and that he was able to find enough materials to keep his habits satisfied.

Scott was the first to confess that his desire for and interest in sex often dominated his life, and that his sexual urges were more in control of him than vice versa. This was a person who found a great deal of meaning for his life through sex. He had been molested extensively as a child and had constructed the experience as physically pleasureful. The feelings he had while masturbating conveyed his sexual reality.

R: When I masturbated I felt like somebody cared about me. I felt like somebody loved me. Even if it was just myself. At least somebody loved me and cared for me. A lot of times, even in my teenage years, that's the thing that I reached for in masturbation was that feeling of somebody caring for me. And I think it just carried on into adult life.

In the case of Scott, his personal engulfment in masturbation, pornography, and secret fantasy seemed to constitute a pathway into sexual offending. Over a period of years, his interest in sex seemed to win out over whatever moral constraints he tried to impose on himself. Gradually he reached a stage where he was capable of offending, and his sexual interest carried over to his stepdaughter.

R: It became, . . . just prior to the molest and during . . . , sex became my life. It became the thing I lived for . . . . Prior to marrying my wife, God was the primary source of my life. I drew to Him; I drew from Him. Everything that I wanted and wanted to do I wanted it to be centered around God . . . . My marriage choice in my mind was based on selfishness rather than God's will and eventually I separated myself from God's will and lust became my god, so to speak. I lived for sex. I lived for a lustful . . . feeling. I mean it wasn't just an overnight thing; it was gradual. It built up gradually and kind of . . . overcame me. But it was the only way that I could endure real life . . . , by living in a world of lustful fanciful thinking.

A second example of this pattern of engulfment in sex involved the case of Sam, who had a two-dimensional sexual history. On the one hand, he was celibate across much of his life; he stated that he did not engage in heterosexual intercourse until he married at age thirty-two. On the other hand, he reported an extensive homosexual involvement with another boy during adolescence, and from late adolescence through most of his adulthood, he indulged heavily in pornography and masturbation. As he stated, "I got really involved in pornography and reading a lot of weird, weird things." He described traveling a great deal with work, and often holing himself up in hotel rooms to read, fantasize, watch dirty movies, and masturbate. His offenses with his stepson began with mutual masturbation, and he admitted in the interview that he borrowed many ideas for sexual acts from the materials he read.

After he got married, Sam became very sexually active, but in an unconventional way. His wife had an extramarital sexual affair, and when he found out, the two agreed to invite the other male to live with them and form a triad live-in sexual relationship. He suggested the arrangement because he did not want to lose his marriage and he thought it would satisfy his wife. During the triad, Sam became involved in sex with the other male; he stated that he felt turned on watching his wife have sex with another man. As he put it, seeing her have sex with someone else made her seem less virtuous and made him feel less guilty about what he did with her. He believed his involvement in the triad, which in his words had an "immoral" quality to it, made it easier for him to cross the sexual boundary with his stepson.

R: I don't want to sound so stupid that I didn't know it was wrong. But it was the kind of thing that's blocked out, or the kind of thing that's glossed over; rationalized to the point, "Well, it may be wrong, but it isn't hurting anybody." That's the same way we went into this three-way sex sort of thing, "It's wrong, immoral." It wasn't illegal I guess, but it's morally wrong . . . . We really worked real hard to say this is okay. "If it doesn't hurt anybody, it's okay." And I think I must have used the same rationalization with [my stepson], that I saw no hurt.

Sam experienced a progression from adolescent homosexuality, to masturbation and pornography, to a sexual threesome with his wife, to adult homosexuality, and then into sexual offending. Looking back, he stated that he felt as though he was "addicted" to sex. While this was a label he borrowed conveniently from treatment, it seemed to characterize how he became involved in sex with his stepson. Heavy masturbation carried over to the more serious realm.

R: I got so addicted to sex and masturbation that it just became, the masturbation . . . became, just something that I had to do. I'd get home from work
and if I wasn't going to have sex . . . that afternoon, I would have to masturbate. It was a relief. And I'd tell myself I can't relax until I masturbate. I
really feel that I'd been addicted to sex. Somebody told me that's not a good
word about being addicted to sex, but I was a chronic masturbator. And
would masturbate in the office . . . . I had my own office . . . . Never masturbated in public, in a public rest room.

Major Emotional Loss and Collapse

Major emotional "shocks" in the lives of yet other men, life-altering
events that involved extreme feelings of loss and emotional grief, seemed
to represent transition points into sexual offending as well. The most
common type of "shock" event was the sudden and violent death of
someone important: a wife who committed suicide and left a child
behind, two children who were burned to death in a house fire, a close
brother who was killed in a car crash, the experience of seeing buddies
killed and killing the enemy during military combat. Other similar
traumatic events included men discovering they were sterile, discovering
that a partner was nonmonogamous, and/or the experience of getting
divorced. All told, these were events that the men had an extremely difficult time coping with and that subsequently threw their emotional lives
into chaos. Periods of deep depression, heavy drinking and drug use,
suicidal ideation, panic and worry, and loss of emotional feelings were
routine. Typically during this time they befriended or became especially close to the child or children they offended, sharing their problems
with them and looking for the emotional support and understanding
they needed yet could not seem to find elsewhere.

The turning point in John's life occurred when his brother, whom he
was extremely close to, was killed in a car accident. John blamed himself
for his brother's death because his brother drove with a friend to a party
to borrow money from someone else after John had refused to make a
loan to him. It was on the way home that the friend, who was driving,
fell asleep at the wheel. John was racked with grief and guilt. He felt
that if he had given his brother the money he needed he would still be

alive. Extreme depression spanning over a year followed.

R: I went into an unbelievable depression. I mean I seldom ate; refused, absolutely refused to talk to anybody. The girl I was dating tried to come over and talk
to me two or three times and she'd start talking . . . and I'd just walk away
from her. Just refused to even speak to her. At work I'd go in, muddle through
[things], I wouldn't even talk to the guys I was working with. I started drinking real heavy, smoking quite a bit of pot.

Prior to his brother's death, John had separated from his wife, who
was withholding visitation rights with his children. This, combined with
his brother's death, led him to hit an emotional bottom or abyss. During
this period the only pleasant or positive emotion he remembered feeling occurred when he accidentally saw his niece naked.

R: I was separated from my wife and my kids so I was pretty much cut loose.
[My brother] died, was killed, and that was devastating. I mean I had lost
all emotions . . . ; I mean it! It was like nothing in the world mattered . . . ; I
mean I was down to the point where I was actually suicidal . . . . I just did-
n't care anymore . . . . I didn't want to continue the way I was going. So when
it started with [my first victim], that was the first [pleasant] emotion I'd felt
for three or four months, at least, or perhaps longer than that. And the only
emotions that I was feeling at the time was depression and guilt. That's the
only . . . emotion I could actually deal with.

The experience of someone else's death also seemed to devastate and
overwhelm Glenn. Glenn fought in Vietnam as an infantry soldier and
was wounded twice in combat. He admitted having killed people and
also seeing his friends die. Though it had been years since he was in the
service, during the interview he talked as though he was still there.

R: When I first got over there I got friends. I had half a dozen of them. And
after the third month, we got pinned down for several hours and all of them
got killed....
I: Did you see them [get] killed?
R: Yeah (*softly*) . . . . And from then on I didn't have any other friends. I was a
loner....
I: Did you have to . . . go out and kill anybody in 'Nam?
R: Several.
I: Do you think that had any effect on your life and especially the kind of thing
we're here talking about today?

R: I'm sure it did . . . . I'm sorry (*begins to cry and tremble*). I don't think any-body should have to go through what I had to go through. I don't think any-body should have to have three-quarters or more of the people that you're associated with here one moment and gone the next. I don't think anybody needs to go through after being wounded [and] identify . . . bodies.

Glenn's experiences in Vietnam contributed to a general inability to cope with life in the years that followed. After he returned home, the reality of Vietnam remained. He had a very difficult time adjusting emo-tionally and, aside from his marriage, had few friendships. There were lingering flashbacks of combat, and when the war with Iraq began, it brought back upsetting memories. In fact, he began offending soon there-after. He saw his memories and emotions surrounding Vietnam as a pri-vate and permanent fixture in his life.

R: It was real rough when I came back. A lot of nightmares. I talked to coun-selors at the V.A. hospital and I had a rough time. I still have rough times once in a while and the flare-up overseas when we sent all the troops over there, that really bothered me. It seemed to bring back a lot of bad memo-ries . . . . [I've gone] through a lot about Vietnam and it never seemed to go away . . . . I always thought that I was the only person who had those prob-lems, those nightmares . . . . It'll never be right and I'll never be rid of it.

Glenn lived alone in a world of emotional flashbacks. His counselor in sex offender treatment was unaware of this, and the one person who did know, his wife, did not understand, and told him to put his past behind him. He reported years of night chills and trouble sleeping. Then one day, in front of his house, a boy was hit by a car. He was the first per-son on the scene, tried to save the child's life, but he died. After that, Glenn had trouble coping with anything and reported feeling under siege, worrying incessantly that his world was about to collapse around him. In the end, he became overwhelmed by feelings of worthlessness and self-pity. The consequence, as he saw it, was that "everything [got] put into one little kettle and the molest came out."

R: I felt that I wasn't doing a very good job with our marriage. I felt that I was-n't doing good enough at work. I was afraid of the younger kids coming in, [that they] was gonna take my job over . . . . I was unhappy because I was-n't working on cars. I wasn't doing things around the house. I wasn't getting things done. My worth was nothing. I didn't feel very good about myself. I didn't feel anything about myself . . . . I was scared . . . ; I was worried about our marriage. I was worried about [my wife] giving up on me . . . . I was worried about everything in my life. And I do believe that down inside, I wanted some sort of, when I touched my daughter, . . . I wanted peace.

Different men came to feel emotionally devastated as a result of different circumstances in their lives. For some, tracing back to their childhood experiences and pain allowed for a preliminary understanding of their adult anger. Problem-filled childhoods extended continuously into problem-filled and tumultuous adult years with no letup. Brian, as reported previously, was adopted illegally at birth by a mother who was a prostitute, was routinely physically beaten throughout his childhood, worked as a street prostitute by age thirteen, moved in and out of different foster homes during adolescence, and at age fifteen was raped by five males in a group home. As he entered his adult years, he found himself in four different relationships in which the women all had sexual relations with other men while involved with him. The third woman was his first wife, who he caught having sex with one of her old high school friends.

R: I didn't say anything to her. I just closed the door and I laughed . . . . I remembered thinking . . . this had been a pattern with all the girls I've been involved with; . . . I always catch them in bed with somebody else. What's wrong with me? I went out and got drunk . . . . This is, of course, after she had the baby. I was going to work ten, twelve hours a day and coming home and taking care of the baby too. I mean she just got so lazy. I was doing the housework, taking care of the baby at night, and a lot of times I had to cook my own meals. I just had got real tired of that . . . ; I swallowed it all. I mean what good did it do to fight and argue . . . . We'd fought and argued about it. I got to the point to where the heck with it. What good does it do to say anything? She's going to turn around and do it anyway. Here I am working my ass off to give this woman anything she wants and this is how I get treated.

Brian had a son with his first wife, which he learned a few years later was not his, after he had been tested and discovered he was sterile. As it turned out, the child was his brother's. He remembered feeling "devastated." Brian eventually began having a sexual affair with a woman while he was married, divorced his wife, moved in with this other woman, and soon into this next relationship learned that she was sleeping with other men too. His new partner worked at a truck stop and, he said, "she was making it with every trucker that walked in the place." Feelings of humiliation and anger set in and he began to fall apart emotionally and lash out at others.

R: I was angry enough that I wanted to kill her.
I: Did you think about killing her?
R: Yeah. I was angry enough that one of the guys that I saw her getting out of a truck with, I destroyed his truck for him. I popped off the tires. I broke out lights. I scratched the paint, ripped out wires, you name it....
I: What did you do to her?
R: Nothing. Nothing. Why I don't know. I don't believe in hitting women . . . . I was angry. I was hurt. I was tired of putting up with this kind of stuff . . . . I mean, here I took all these years out of my life and I was a father to her boys when their own father wouldn't be a father to them.

When asked to assess his life before he began offending, Brian stated that he was extremely unhappy and that he had reached the end of his rope. It was difficult to disentangle whether he felt trapped in a life he wished he had never lived, which he said he did, or whether the hurt and anger, the emotional turmoil he felt at the major life "shocks" he experienced simply sent him over the edge. When he initiated sex with the son of his involved girlfriend, who was nonmonogamous, he felt his life was a disaster and was contemplating suicide.

R: I was thinking of killing myself . . . ; I was just fed up with the way my whole life had gone. I never seemed to fit in anywhere. I always felt like a misfit. Never could do anything to make any of these women happy, though I tried many things . . . . I just, "This is the way life is, the heck with it. Who needs it?" I'd be happier dead. And one of my particular ways I was going to kill myself was get in a car and drive at a very fast speed and slam into a wall somewhere. And then I'd always think, "Well, if you do that, you might not die anyway. You might end up in the hospital as a vegetable and you'll still have the same old problems."

Buildup of Sexual Problems

Finally, for some respondents, the emergence and magnification of major sexual problems with their adult partners seemed to represent a key stage leading up to sexual offending. The most common sexual problem mentioned was impotence, the inability to achieve an erection. On an emotional level, the result was a loss of sexual confidence. There were a range of other sexual problems as well: concern about penis size, worry over a lack of sexual experience, aversions to vaginas, guilt over homosexual behavior, fear of sex in general, and emptiness after sex. The proportion of offenders who reported sexual problems is not atypical or high compared to men of various sexual preferences.[8] In the cases here, however, the problems seemed to interfere with the men's routine outlets for sexual contact and to open the door more to the possibility of sexual contact with children.[9]

George experienced the onset of sexual impotency a year or two before he engaged his stepdaughter in sex. He had been married four times when he was interviewed and stated he had had sex with around 150 women. In telling his sexual history, George shared the view that he always felt he was competent "as a man" and that this was a critical aspect of his sexual identity.

I: You said you thought you were pretty good; what did you mean by that?
R: . . . I could get an erection pretty regular.
I: Pretty regular; what do you mean?
R: Sometimes a couple of times a night and about every day so . . . ; I didn't think I was superman, but I thought I was a good man . . . . The sex I had, I was taking care of them.

It is impossible to know whether George would have molested his stepdaughter had sexual impotency never occurred. He was in his early fifties when the problem began, and alcohol might have contributed to the situation (he said he drank a case of beer a day for twenty years and then began to drink a fifth of whiskey at a time as well). His situational impotency occupied his attention: "I just worried about it . . . ; I was too young to be having problems like that." Being eleven years older than his wife, he feared her leaving him for another man. He began offending after experiencing an erection while rubbing the back of his stepdaughter.

R: I started, just the last few years I started losing, I mean . . . , I had trouble getting an erection here in the last, oh before the molest.
I: How long before?
R: Probably a year, two years maybe.
I: . . . Ever a problem before that?
R: No.

I: How often were you sexual?

R: I don't know, it seemed like for a long time it was four or five times a week . . . . And I don't know if the alcohol got to me or age . . . ; I definitely slowed down a big bunch it just seems like overnight . . . . It kept bothering me, a lot. In fact, when I went and molested her, I got excited again, and I felt young again. I had kind of lost part of that.

Ken experienced the same problem, sexual impotency, beginning with his first attempt at intercourse. The impotency spanned his life and left him with feelings of sexual inferiority and inadequacy. He believed that being impotent was central to his career as an offender.

R: What's important to all this as well is the long-term impotency I've suffered most of my life, but never more so than after my marriage to [my second wife] . . . . Girls frightened me. I think my fear came from a lack of knowledge about females . . . ; about sex, female relationships, what they [females] were like . . . . My first intercourse was when I was twenty-four in the service with a prostitute in Italy. That didn't go well. This woman had very large breasts. I was taken by them, so much so, I couldn't get an erection.

Impotency, for Ken, was a problem with women he dated, with his first wife, who drank herself to death at age twenty-nine, and with his second wife, who was seventeen years younger. He was never in his life able to sustain a problem-free period of sexuality. Before his first marriage, he broke off relations with one woman he dated because he could not get an erection and decided that, "It was almost as if I failed because I had a fear of failing." Before his second marriage, he dated scores of younger women; again it was always the same story. When asked why he kept dating younger women despite his troubles, he answered, "I guess I thought maybe the next one would be successful." It was at this time, between marriages as his sexual problems surged, that he entered into an initial wave of sexual game playing with his biological daughter and three of her neighborhood friends.

Over time the sexual activity with his biological daughter stopped and Ken remarried. He admitted, however, that his second wife was reluctant to get married because of a "lack of satisfying sex" between them. "She thought it would get better after marrying," he noted. "It never did." His problems with impotency continued and eventually reached a crisis point with his second wife when sex between them ceased altogether. At this time Ken began reoffending much more extensively than before by having sex with his stepdaughter and also three other neighborhood children who were friends of hers. He remembered the point when sex ended with his wife.

R: When I was on [a business] trip in Europe, [I] had [arranged for] my wife to fly over and meet me . . . . [I had] been there two weeks, had a nice room . . . . [She] came over and wasn't interested in sex. [It was] like she was mad at me . . . . [It was a] bad week. [I was] disappointed. [There was] no sex the rest of the trip. In bed [back home a] couple weeks later, we were trying to have sex and she looked at me and said, "You're impotent!" . . . It made me feel inferior, put down, disgraced. We never had sex again.

In a final case, Sam reported a range of sexual problems, the most salient being feelings of sexual inadequacy and incompetence with women, because he believed he had a small penis and was sexually inexperienced, both of which were intensified by an admitted heavy use of pornography. His problems initially surfaced in late adolescence and continued into his adult life.

R: I had no sexual experience prior to my being married . . . . I had relationships, but I never could come to . . . actually having sex . . . . I was afraid, embarrassed, . . . that I really didn't know what I'd be doing . . . .
I: What were you embarrassed about?
R: . . . I anticipated from all of the things I read that I would not be able to perform. That my penis was not as large as it should be. And of course in so much of that pornography it elaborates and exaggerates so much that I couldn't live up to those sort of things.

Sam noted that he had almost always been attracted to and nearly always had dated women with more sexual experience than he had, for example, "divorcées," which contributed to his feelings of incompetence and inadequacy. While he did have a history of some sexual contact with women (e.g., petting and oral sex), he did not have intercourse until he was married and in his thirties.

R: The girls that I was involved with, that I really cared about, again were always girls that . . . had sexual experience. And it seemed to me I was attracted to those and then that would just . . . put a squelch on everything because I felt all the more uncomfortable being with somebody who had already had some sexual experience . . . . But I could just never bring myself to have intercourse.
I: How did you feel about that?

R: Well, I wondered what was wrong with me. I kept thinking, well, it would all straighten out someday.

Though he always hoped his problems would go away, they continued across the course of his marriage. Despite a very extensive sexual involvement with his wife, he remembered constantly feeling inadequate.

R: And then what do I do, I marry a woman who's been divorced and those same things come right back to me. I just feel totally inadequate and unable to . . . . I was married until the divorce for . . . sixteen years. And it wasn't until the month of the divorce that my wife told me that I had . . . satisfied her sexually . . . . That was a significant thing in my life.

Complicating the situation further was the fact that Sam developed a general aversion to his wife's genitals. He stated that his wife had chronic yeast infections, which might have contributed to this feeling. When he had intercourse with her, he claimed his penis hurt and he did not enjoy it. His aversion put serious boundaries around what he was willing to do with his wife.

R: I was never involved in very much foreplay with my wife as far as fondling her vagina and that sort of thing. That was always a bit repulsive to me. Usually . . . we would use some sort of jelly . . . to facilitate penetration . . . . And even the whole . . . idea of intercourse was, . . . I'd be repulsed by it . . . . Nasty, dirty.

The sexual problems Sam felt with his wife were eventually mixed with renewed homosexual activity—which occurred for the first time since his adolescence—and which he said he enjoyed a great deal. He and his wife were involved in a communal sexual relationship with another man that facilitated the homosexual activity. This was later followed by sexual contact with his eleven-year-old stepson. Sam seemed to fade out of a desire for sex in one realm and into it in another. There was a major change in his life, a marked transition in the direction of his sexuality and the rediscovery of homosexual sex, that had a profound impact on what he did.

Conclusion

Offenders experienced six core types of transitions before their involvement in sexual contact with children unfolded. These included feelings of being trapped in an unfulfilling marital, parental, and/or career role; the erosion of sexual happiness with a significant partner in terms of both the quantity and quality of sex; the perceived loss of male authority if wives took over decisions or advanced further in their jobs outside the home; extreme engulfment in masturbation, pornography, and other taboo and risky forms of sex that had a disinhibiting effect; major emotional life shocks and subsequent emotional collapse to the point where feelings shut down or the desire to escape evolved; and sexual problems that resulted in acute performance anxiety and feelings of sexual inadequacy. Most men reported multiple types of transitions in unpredictable combinations. In general, these life realities constituted a stage in the offending process characterized by emotional disconnection, personal unhappiness, and the desire for change. As we shall see, the more such feelings persisted for the men, the closer they drifted toward engagement in the unspeakable.

FOUR

Shifting into an
Offending Mode

The distinction between "situational" versus "fixated" offenders is wide-ly recognized in the literature on child molesting.[1] The sexual prefer-ence of the situational offender is primarily for other adults, while that of the fixated offender is directed exclusively at children. In this study, 97 percent (twenty-nine out of thirty) of the men classified themselves as situation-based offenders. That is, they reported either a history of sex with other adults, or if they had not yet had sex with someone of legal age, as being attracted to and interested in adults, prior to their involve-ment in sex with a minor. These same twenty-nine also stated specifi-cally that they had a sexual age preference for adults. This profile, of course, as described earlier, was part of my sampling criteria. Situational offenders, then, are people who experience a shift in preference toward a minor child as a sexual partner. The question I take up now is how this shift in desire occurs. What types of situational events and inter-pretations move men who had previously been interested in other adults toward thinking about and approaching someone underage? Where does the idea to have sex with a child start? How does the interest surface and become activated? These were adult men who essentially claimed to have never thought of anything like this before. So what happened to change things?

While the background experiences or the prior events in the lives of the offenders I interviewed shaped their readiness or openness to act as they did, in turn, it was the more immediate experiences, or the feelings and definitions that emerged during interaction, that focused their interests and behavior in specific directions. Jack Katz has convincingly argued that prior biography alone cannot explain why people commit one type of crime over another, why people who commit crime act at the exact moment they do, or why people without the right mix of preceding life events engage in the same crimes as those with them.[2] From this, it can be asked, Why do people choose sex with children and not other sex crimes such as peeping, exhibitionism, prostitution, rape, or other personal crimes like spouse battering or homicide, all of which generally derive from background histories similar to those in this study? Why do people who have been molested during their childhood or who experience sexual failure for years suddenly commit a sexual offense at age forty or fifty? Why do men who were not molested or abused as children engage in the same behaviors as those who were? The answer to the puzzle about why men molest children requires that we analyze what happens between victims and offenders and what offenders think and feel in the critical moments when offending unfolds. To explore this question of a sexual reality shift, I asked my respondents to reconstruct their first thoughts or actions with each child they molested, whichever came before the other.

Noticing and Sexualizing

The transition into offending began for many men because they started noticing the physical appearance of a particular child whom they subsequently molested. The men mentioned a range of bodily attributes they attended to: the presence of breasts—especially developing breasts— on girls, the overall contour of the body or the shape of the buttocks on a child of either sex, or the presence of a muscular or firm build on boys. This was coupled with a definition of the parts of the body in erotic terms. A number of men described feeling a degree of excitement, interest, or titillation seeing a particular child. Still others commented that the child they were becoming interested in simply looked good or had a nice body for someone so young. Noticing and eroticizing thus involved a shift from a nonsexual to a sexual frame of interpretation as a result of becoming aware of and turned on to the way the victim looked.[3]

Some men were able to pinpoint a single event during which their view of a child shifted in a sexual direction. In these instances, the men described looking and then being, in their words, "caught by surprise" by how the child had matured and developed physically. Actual sexual contact usually followed quickly. Other times the transition was more gradual, involving many episodes of what was characterized as casual observation lasting a period of weeks or months. This was combined with sexual fantasy about the child while the offender masturbated. After a period of sustained watching and fantasizing, the men reported eventually making the construction that the young person, as they saw it, was a sexual being. Men noticed the victim's sexuality after they had seen the victim getting dressed, for example, or taking a bath, using the rest room, or walking around the house in nightclothes or underwear. Men who started offending in this manner often mentioned being heavy drinkers as well.

George, aged fifty-two at the time, initiated sexual contact with his fourteen-year-old stepdaughter within hours after first noticing and eroticizing her breasts, which he described as large. The situation began when George decided to use the rest room while his stepdaughter was taking a bath and he saw her naked. George was unable to recall any sexual thoughts about his victim prior to that moment.

R: First thing I remember that excited me about her is that, wasn't nothing, but she was in the bathroom. We just had one bathroom and I knocked on the door and asked her if she would hurry up . . . ; I had to use the bathroom real bad. And she hollered back, "Well come on in," says, "Go ahead and use it if you got to go that bad." And well, I went ahead and did it. I was drinking quite a bit but I still remember what I was doing there. I use that for an excuse.

I: . . . What was she doing in the bathroom?

R: She was taking a bath . . . . And I saw her breast . . . . She even tried to hide herself. She's not a backwards person . . . . But I was surprised . . . ; I didn't realize she had filled out as good as she was. She's a big-busted girl really . . . .

I: And what did you think?

R: I was noticing, I thought she looked . . . good. I was excited and I was surprised. I didn't never think of her before as being grown up. But well she's grown up now. I mean big, big breasts and all. I couldn't believe it! I just never did think about it before then . . . . I guess it got my attention.

Leon engaged in sexual contact with his stepdaughter when she was between the ages of eight and nine and he was forty-three. He experienced a gradual shift toward a sexual frame of reference over a period of six months. Unlike the case of George, there was a greater lapse of time between looking and acting. Leon too was adamant about never having had any prior sexual interest in minors.

R: I noticed her bare buttocks . . . . She's a very pretty girl and she was a very . . . well-proportioned girl even at eight years old. Not that she was developed to the point of having breasts or anything like that. But she was very shapely and she had a very nice rear end on her for a little girl.

I: . . . Were you physically turned on in this period?

R: It was a gradual progression, . . . it wasn't like one day I didn't pay any attention and the next day I did. It was very gradual. And I would see her dressing or she wouldn't close her bedroom door and she'd be maybe running around in there . . . after she took a bath, naked. But she would leave her door about half open and yeah, it aroused me. And . . . that went on for several months when I just observed her.

I: . . . Was there a point you just started noticing her?

R: Yeah, sort of. It was like as if one day I viewed her as a little bitsy girl, because she was four years old when we got married, and then it was almost like as if I didn't pay any more attention to her until all of a sudden at eight here I noticed that she was a sexual being.

In the case of Leon, the experience of noticing spilled over in time into sexual fantasy about the victim and occasional masturbation, which then progressed into genital fondling. There was thus a period of sexual observation that got the process of offending started.

R: I would think about what sex would be like with her. And I would think about I would like to touch her . . . . I just remember that I fantasized about her, after I would see her I would think about her. Sometimes I would masturbate.

I: What would you fantasize about?

R: About her being naked and about having sex with her and about touching her vagina and rubbing her buttocks and things like that. And that went on for six months . . . ; I enjoyed looking at her vagina and I enjoyed looking at her buttocks.

I: I don't want to lead you, I'm just wondering if there's a particular reason why?

R: She was a girl, I don't know.

In Tom's case, sexual offending also unfolded from a process of noticing and sexualizing. He observed and fantasized about his stepdaughter for several months, too, before instigating sexual contact with her when she was eleven. In this case the victim was again a girl, and again it was the development of her breasts that, he said, stimulated him sexually. The offender in the account below seemed to glorify and become infatuated with the physical appearance of the victim, defining her as beautiful. He began molesting her when he was thirty-two.

R: She was a early maturer . . . . Throughout her entire life she has always been
   [a] . . . very nicely contoured girl. She had never been the bony type of thing.
   And I think I appreciated her aesthetically . . . . And I think you add . . . the
   appreciation . . . with the narcotics and stuff, I think I began, . . . I know I did,
   I fantasized about just taking that route and touching her . . . . It was . . . her
   grace, . . . her lines, . . . her beauty. . . .
I: What features . . . did you attend to? What turned you on?
R: Oh her breasts . . . . When it started they were very small. They were lovely
   to look at. She was lovely to look at . . . ; I saw her body as perfect, and I
   wondered about that for several months.

Men who reported noticing and sexualizing a particular victim commonly stated that the victim, if the child was a girl, began to remind them of the way their wife looked, or used to look, at a younger age. The child represented a newer, updated, and more erotic version of their spouse. This was what Corey, aged thirty-seven, said about his thirteen-year-old biological daughter, whom he molested much more frequently than his other two children. His other daughter, who looked more like him, was apparently not as appealing.

R: It was more with the oldest than it was with the other two.
I: [The] reason for that?
R: She was the oldest. She was more developed than the other two; than her
   sister.
I: Were you more attracted to her?
R: Yeah. Because she's the spitting image of her mother. The middle one is the
   spitting image of me.
I: . . . So it was the way she looked . . . ?
R: It was just . . . her moves, . . . just little things I remember back when my ex
   was seventeen or eighteen years old.
I: What kind of moves?
R: Just sexy moves . . . . The look in her eye. She just has her mother, . . . everything her mother [had].

Yet another dimension of the noticing and sexualizing sequence was that some men mentioned that they either fantasized about or visualized the victim as grown up, as an adult physically and even mentally, instead of as childlike. Mark, around twenty-nine at the time, said he thought about his six-year-old stepdaughter (he estimated the victim as two years younger than the official record) in these terms during the immediate period before he began offending.

I: What would you fantasize about? What was involved there?

R: I just see her like a grown-up. Like myself. I resented the fact that she was a child. And I started to visualize her as a grown-up individual.

I: What do you mean? I don't understand.

R: Well, she had everything except she didn't have no breasts, nothing at all. But from here down (*indicates the waist*) I was seeing a full-grown woman.

I: [Again], what do you mean?

R: . . . I was seeing a female with a vagina. Something that I would—I love sex—I would really, really like. I wanted to be satisfied at that time.

Reacting to Perceived Cues

If there is one unanimous opinion in the range of literature on sexual crimes against children, it is the view that young people do not initiate sex with adults; rather, it is the adult who initiates. It is not the intent here to challenge this reality, for the reports of vast numbers of victims confirm that this is the case. However, this does not dismiss the testimony of some offenders who stated that sexual contact unfolded after the young person either made *what they interpreted to be* a deliberate sexual overture toward them, or unwittingly expressed *what they saw as* an interest or openness to sex in some way that led them to think they could do more. It was the *perceived* actions or reactions of the child that seemed to spur the offender to try something he had apparently not thought of before.[4] Thus, to borrow a phrase, what the men came to define as real was real in its consequences.[5]

Carl, twenty-two years old when he offended, was arrested for fondling and fellating three boys aged eight, ten, and thirteen all on the same evening at the home of a couple who were close longtime friends. His initial interest surfaced when the father of the boys, a minister at a church where Carl was a gospel singer and member, told him that his eight-year-old son had been caught having oral sex with another boy. A closeted homosexual who dated women as a front, Carl remembered feeling interested.

R: When I heard that, it was kind of like "Hmmmmm." I couldn't believe it at first. That's when I very first . . . wondered what it would be like with him.

A number of months later, after his feelings had long since passed, the transition into offending resurfaced for Carl. One day he encountered the victim in the rest room at the church he attended. That same night, he was staying at the home of the victim, with his minister friend and his wife, something he had done many times before. According to Carl, the youngest of the boys had asked his parents for permission to sleep with Carl that night, and the parents agreed. The perceived cue in both the rest room scene and while sleeping with the victim was that Carl came to believe the child expressed an explicit interest in seeing his penis.

R: I was using the bathroom in the church the day before and [he] kept putting his head beneath the stall and [saying], "Let me see it; let me see it." I kept saying, "Get out of here!" And he kept saying, "Come on, man, let me see it . . . ." And I'd say, "No . . . get out of here. I'm going to holler for your dad if you don't get out of here." As he left the room, I realized I had an erection. His saying that to me excited me. He wanted to see it. And he would have crawled up there with me if I would have let him. I kept telling him, "no, no, no." So . . . that night he slept with me . . . . We were laying there and he started talking about penises . . . . He just started saying, "How big is yours?" I said, "I don't know, go to sleep." Because I kept saying, "You can't do that. You just can't do this." . . . He just kept being real persistent. "How big is it? Come on, show it to me. Please just show it to me." . . . I kept telling him to be quiet, "Just shut up and be quiet." But then he'd sit there and I could tell he was playing with himself. You could tell because the covers were moving. He'd say, "Please, just show it to me." By that time I had an erection. And so I showed it to him.

As his involvement in offending unfolded, Carl remembered feeling caught up in the heat of the moment, something he later came to regret quite deeply. There was a sense of spontaneous transition from outside to inside the phenomenon of sex, which later came to take on the meaning of a sexual offense to this offender. He admitted knowing what he did was wrong, but he lost track of things, simply reacting to cues as he decided he received them.

R: Then it was like I didn't care anymore. Just kind of [got] caught up in the moment . . . . It wasn't a planned thing at all. It was more of a thing that he just kept saying, "Come on, come on, please show me; just show me it. . . ." And before long I thought, "Well, that might be fun to show him. . . ." The enticement became too great and I did it. It was one of those things where, most people that go to church know that premarital sex is wrong, but hey, when you're in the backseat of a car in the heat of the moment, you don't care. It's just one of those things.

Sidney was thirty-two when he began offending. He exposed his genitals first accidentally, then deliberately, to his nine-year-old stepdaughter. The girl, according to Sidney, reacted with indifference, which was subsequently taken by him as a cue to proceed. As he saw it, the fact that she did not react negatively to a situation that he saw as sexual in content suggested to him that maybe the child was open to sex on some level and might even condone or permit sexual relations. Her perceived actions, from his standpoint, stood as an unspoken overture and cued him to the idea of sex. There was no apparent interchangeability of standpoints. By his own admission, he constructed an invitation to act where none realistically ever had existed.

R: The first time was a situation where I had accidentally exposed myself and she didn't make a big thing out of it and I didn't make a big thing out of it . . . . That was the beginning. . . .
I: What happened there when you accidentally exposed yourself?
R: Well, at the time I was wearing . . . boxer shorts. And it was pretty common for me to run around the house in my shorts and T-shirt. And we were at breakfast one morning and . . . it just so happened that the way the shorts had arranged themselves on me that a part of my genitalia or genitals, or whatever you want to call it, were exposed. And I noticed it and said something to her but she didn't make a big deal out of it. Then I think it was like two or three weeks later when I did it intentionally and once again she didn't make a big deal out of it. And it just sort of progressed from there.
I: What did you think . . . why she didn't make anything out of it?
R: Well, I think I was operating on . . . kind of an immature level . . . . I took her for not making a big deal out of it, first I think as an acceptance of it, and then possibly as an endorsement . . . . I was putting her on a level that she wasn't operating on. I was having her operate on an adult level . . . . I was thinking of her in that way.

Sidney related that the apparent cuing experience he underwent with his victim tapped a type of primal sexual urge, one that was strongest for him when he woke up in the morning, which was when he committed his offenses, after breakfast. As he remembered, he basically just reacted; he did not give what he was doing enough thought in light of the consequences for him.

R: I don't know if there was a lot of thought involved in it. I sometimes . . . get the feeling that if I had thought about it, it never would have happened. It was more primal than that I think. It was more like operating on instinct . . . . In the mornings when I wake up, first of all my brain doesn't seem to kick in right away. And second of all . . . I seem to be more sexually oriented.

In the case of yet another offender, his interest in the second of his three biological daughters, all of whom he molested, emerged in part from what he perceived as a distinct indication of sexual initiation and responsiveness on her part. Ian had been napping one afternoon on the sofa in his home. His daughter, aged eleven, climbed up on top of him; he was on his back, and she layed down face-to-face and fell asleep. This was something all three daughters had done since they were very little without any sexual consequences. He then said he woke up, noticed she was there, tried to go back to sleep, but realized he had an erection. At that moment he suddenly came to believe his daughter was deliberately rubbing herself against him, which stimulated him. He attached sexual meaning to her actions, which led him to try more with her rather than stopping. He was in his mid- to late thirties when this episode occurred.

R: I think I had an erection. And I sensed that she thought that. And . . . I thought she was rubbing against me. And up to that time . . . there wasn't . . . anything that I'd ever done with her . . . . The sensation I had of her was that she was rubbing herself on me, getting aroused, and pushing against me . . . . I don't know if I put my hand down there to touch her on the vagina . . . ; I either did that or I might have grabbed her tush and pulled her closer to me . . . to get more stimulation . . . . And all this time I was convinced, and I couldn't believe it, I'm sitting there and thinking, "Oh my gosh, this girl is sexually responsive here." And I couldn't believe it was happening . . . . And the bad part of it, I wasn't horrified by it . . . . It was a situation that almost seemed like it was . . . my good fortune. Instead of being disappointed in her, or taking the attitude of "Hey, stop this right now!" . . . I tried to encourage more is the bottom line . . . ; I tried to get more activity going. And I was convinced as anything; the movement she had was pretty obvious . . . . I mean she was moving her hips rhythmically . . . . There was no doubt about it in my mind. And I just went, "Wow, what's happening here?" And instead of doing the right thing, I just tried to make it worse.

Like other men who got involved the same way, when it came to the moment of offending, with each of his daughters, Ian seemed to act without thinking, reacting to what he believed were sexual cues. In each case, as he put it, "It was spontaneous, and then once it occurred, then the interest was there." His interpretation determined what occurred.

R: The idea that a molester always seeks his victim out, he knows what he's doing, it's never spontaneous, it's planned in advance, I don't agree with that. These things just like clear out of the blue happen. No desire built up in advance. Now once that happened, yeah, then you try to get yourself in a scenario, or try to get the circumstances right to remolest. But initially it just happened. And being there with the child, and just one thing leads to another, and touching, and then maybe a day or two later you're doing a little more touching . . . . But the initial part of it wasn't planned; it just bingo, it happens. With me!

Whatever the type of perceived sexual cue, as the previous examples have shown, the men who reported this type of transition said they reacted to the victim without thinking about the consequences of their actions. The transition into offending was described as unplanned, spontaneous, and not rational. Both Randy and William, forty and thirty-four years old in the episodes below, insisted they began offending after reacting to what they interpreted to be explicit sexual advances by their female victims, ages fourteen and fifteen at the time, respectively. In the case of William, the second example, the shift involved remolesting his own daughter after he had been arrested and had spent eighteen months in sex offender treatment.

I: Why did you go ahead and touch her? What were you thinking?
R: . . . There was no thought to it. It was almost like a reaction type of thing, but there was no thought to it. It wasn't like I thought it out or planned it, it just happened . . . . And I mean . . . at that first particular time I was still 70 percent asleep when it happened . . . ; it was almost like this happened but it didn't happen . . . . And then it was like I just came out of a fog.

R: This incident was like stepping in front of a freight train. It was not something I planned. I didn't think of the consequences. It just occurred so quick. It's like if someone comes up to you and draws back to swing at you and you swing at him. It is a reflex, and not one that is given much thought. And that night it was like a reflex. I didn't say, "Let's stop and think about this thing." It just didn't happen. Because of incest being kept in the closet as much as it is, one seems to be dumbfounded how it could occur without consequences being considered.

Getting Aroused from Nonsexual Contact

A third pathway into sexual offending was followed by men who became physiologically aroused during the course of incidental physical contact with the young person they subsequently victimized. The type of incidental contact that served as a source of stimulation varied from case to case: a child sitting on the lap, an accidental brush of one leg against another, rubbing the shoulders of a child to relax him/her. Routinely, the men said they had experienced the same or similar types of physical contact on many occasions with no prior sexual interest. Then suddenly and (as they described it) unexpectedly, they felt aroused. The shift from a nonsexual to a sexual framework usually was signaled by the presence of an erection. From there, these men initiated sexual contact with the child typically quite abruptly.

Larry engaged in various sexual activities with his stepdaughter, culminating in attempted intercourse, beginning when she was seven. His career as an offender began at age twenty-two after he experienced an erection when his stepdaughter sat on his lap. He claimed to have had no prior sexual thoughts about the girl and no prior sexual contact with her or any other child.

R: The first time it happened [she] came in and it was . . . kind of innocent . . . . She came in and sat on my lap. She just kind of sat down, rolled around, and I just had some strange feelings and all of a sudden I had a hard-on. And at first, all it was was just a touch, a rub, a brush.

I: A brush of what against what?

R: An arm against her, between her legs, or up on her chest. . . .

I: . . . When did you think about sexual attraction or sexual [arousal]? At what point?

R: As soon as I started getting a hard-on.

The shift into offending also occurred for Earl through incidental touching. He was forty at the time of first sexual contact; the girl, the daughter of his long-time live-in girlfriend, was thirteen. (He referred to her throughout his interview as his stepdaughter.) Earl was used to sexual privilege. You will recall that he reported having had sexual intercourse multiple times every day with his girlfriend for roughly ten years, whether she was interested or not. He allegedly became sexually aroused after the victim accidentally brushed against his genitals when she jumped up in bed to wake him up. He acted without thinking.

R: My stepdaughter, we let her sleep in the room with us . . . . One time she hopped up in bed and she put her feet over on me and . . . from that moment on something happened . . . . There was no desire before.

I: . . . She put her feet on you. How so?

R: Well, just her feet rubbing up against my legs. And then from then on out I think her foot touched me, I know she touched me accidentally, kind of hit my groin area. When that happened there was just something in my head that wasn't there before . . . ; I just reached over and grabbed her by her breast.

I: . . . Was it a physical turn-on kind of thing . . . ?

R: I think it was a sexual turn-on. But being aware or not aware . . . , I believe I was aware of it, but not under control.

I: Did you have an erection when she touched you that first time?

R: I believe so . . . . The playing around, the jostling around and all that did lay it on . . . ; it led on to more touching.

Another example is George, who previously described noticing the breasts of his stepdaughter while she was bathing. While rubbing her back, something he had done numerous times without sexual arousal, he began to experience an erection. It was this physical contact and the presence of an erection, in conjunction with his prior noticing, that put him over the line. After this incident, the offending sequence picked up in the weeks that followed. The victim was fourteen.

R: Her mother would come in and lay on the couch sometimes. I'd rub her back for her. When all the girls come home they'd want me to rub their backs . . . . [My stepdaughter] had come in that evening, laid down on the couch and I rubbed her back after I'd seen her in the bathroom . . . . I rubbed her back a lot of times, and I don't remember ever anything happening. But this time when I rubbed her back I started getting an erection. I hadn't been getting one much before. I was having a lot of trouble. [Earlier the respondent had reported recent problems achieving erections with his wife.]

I: . . . So you were rubbing your daughter's back and . . . ?

R: And I moved my hand down over her butt instead of rubbing her back. And I think that's when I started getting an erection.

I: What did you think when . . . you got the erection?

R: I began to think there's something wrong with my wife instead of me then at that time . . . because she wasn't exciting me.

Becoming Curious and Fascinated

In the cases of still other men, their initial interest in sexual contact with a child emerged from feelings of curiosity. This occurred especially in relation to prepubescent girls. Brief observation of the genital area of a child—for example, while changing a diaper or tending to a medical problem in the genital region—stirred recurring questions about what the child looked like, whether the child was capable of physical arousal, or what it would be like to touch the child. These men described feeling an overwhelming, unrelenting desire to find the answers to their questions. They were on a quest for knowledge and decided to become explorers. Their offending typically had a bizarre quality to it: genital inspections or masturbating a two-year-old. The focus was on studying and gaining information. To this type of offender, the source of their pressing curiosity was usually mysterious; it seemed to come out of nowhere. But when pressed to think of a source, they were able to recall nonsexual events during which they saw the vaginal region of the victim, from which the interpretive process emerged.

Steve's sexual offenses involved going into his stepdaughter's room at night and peering and poking at her genitals with his fingers while she was asleep, using a flashlight so he could see. At the point of onset, the girl was eight years old. Steve was thirty.

R: Something came upon me, I'm not sure exactly where it came from, why I felt I had to do this . . . ; I just had to see what [my stepdaughter] looked like. What does this little girl look like . . . . She was like nine, ten maybe at the time.

I: . . . Do you remember where the thought initially came from?

R: Nope. I do not. I just know I remember this feeling coming over [me] like, almost like your body being invaded or your mind being invaded. "You must do this; you just have to do this," and satisfy that particular curiosity, need . . . , urge . . . . The first time . . . I looked with the flashlight.

Despite initially claiming to have no explanation about how this curiosity started, at a different point in the interview, Steve described an event involving him, his stepdaughter, and his wife, that did seem to be the genesis of the process. His wife asked him to inspect a rash near the child's genitals, at which time he focused in on her vaginal region.

R: I remember one time, . . . I don't know if she had a rash or hives or something . . . ; her mother had her basically drop her pants in front of me.
I: Do you remember thinking anything at the time when she did that? . . . Any sexual thoughts go through your mind?
R: No, I don't remember having a sexual thought. Maybe I suppressed it, I don't know. But I do remember being fascinated.
I: Fascinated with what?
R: What I saw. Basically, well obviously she didn't have pubic hair . . . . Of course then it was a quick event and she went on about her business. But it must have triggered something.

Glenn too described pervasive feelings of curiosity surrounding the bodies of his three adopted daughters, but said that his feelings mounted over a period of years of intermittent observation. The process began when he was a soldier in Vietnam and saw a naked East Asian woman. He believed that this experience carried over to his situation later.

R: In Vietnam . . . one time I was downtown with some friends and I went back of the hootches which are made out of grass and I was taking a leak and I looked and this lady came out of a hooch into a wash basin . . . and she was washing herself off. And I noticed at that time that she did not have any hair and it just stuck in my mind . . . ; I was surprised that God didn't give them hair or that they didn't have some of the things that American women [got] . . . .
I: How did that tie in later?
R: I think that I was curious what the girls looked like through their stages of development.

Glenn remembered being curious about what his daughters looked like physically from the moment they arrived in the house, beginning at ages three, five, and six. Over the years, he said, it was the biological changes the girls passed through that continually caught his attention.

He studied their physiological development for nine years. He thought seeing the changes was interesting.

I: What were you looking for or watching?

R: . . . Physically their bodies changing. And I wouldn't just do it day in and day out. Maybe a few months go by and I mention it to my wife "Oh, their nipples are starting to grow." "Yeah, well I wish you wouldn't look at that. That's not right for you to look at that." I said, "Well, I'm not doing nothing. I just made a comment. . . ."

I: What was your feeling in seeing . . . the physiological change?

R: I thought it was neat . . . that they were becoming young ladies. When they started getting hair on them, the first couple times I saw them, it was a big deal.

For Glenn curiosity was a stepping-stone. He believed that one thing, seeing his daughters develop, led eventually to another, his desire to touch.

R: I believe that the seeing as they were growing up and the point where they started developing, where the hair started, their behinds started getting a little larger, their boobs started developing, their nipples were spreading out, I believe it just led, I think it was one step right after another. And I think, I guess, I wanted to see what it felt like. I feel it just led right into it.

As Glenn began sexual contact, his curiosity carried over into the kinds of acts he committed. For example, he reported making biological comparisons between his wife and his middle adopted daughter, who experienced the bulk of his sexual advances, wondering specifically whether the vaginal region of his daughter looked the same as that of his wife. So he inspected the genitals of his daughter to find out. There was one specific incident, however, that involved the shift from looking to becoming more interested in touching. He had taken it upon himself to try to show this same daughter an aspect of feminine hygiene. He was forty-two and she was just twelve when this happened.

R: And the girls were having problems . . . with becoming young ladies. They started the . . . monthly cycles, and my wife wouldn't show them how to use the different things. And I'd get the box out and read the directions and I said, "You have to do this because they wanted to use a tampon to go swimming." And I'd ask my wife, I said, "Would you show them?" [She said,] "They will learn. They will learn how to put it in." I'd get the box out and I'd read them directions and I'd show them how to angle it—I didn't mess with them. That probably led to me messing with them, but I didn't mess with them at that time.

I: Did it spark your curiosity, doing those type of things?

R: Yeah it did. It did. And I know, with my middle daughter, I was wondering what it was like to rub through there after I had already helped her with her tampon, which I wish I'd never did now.

Phil claimed he never had a sexual thought about a child ever at any time in his life, but then one day, at age twenty-seven, when he was changing his two-year-old biological daughter's diaper and putting powder on her genitals, a feeling of curiosity overwhelmed him. He wanted to find out whether his daughter was responsive to sexual stimulation. So he masturbated her to see what would happen. Four years of offending followed.

R: I think the molest began as a curiosity and became an obsession . . . . Wanting to see what my daughter, how she would respond to sexual stimulation. I mean that's what . . . started it.

I: . . . I would like you to describe what happened beginning with your first thoughts . . . or actions.

R: Well, my first actions . . . occurred when I was changing her diaper and applying some medication for a rash . . . . And then I fondled her on her genitals, to see how she would respond . . . , and if it had any effect on her . . . . I was wondering how she would respond, if there was a response from her.

I: You had used the term "curious." What does that mean?

R: Well, I wanted to see . . . ; I wanted to find out what it would be like for her.

Curiosity also motivated the transition into offending for Corey. This offender molested all three of his biological children, two daughters and a son, starting, as mentioned earlier, when he was thirty-seven. He had been heterosexual all of his life, and he had sex with both biological daughters first. Later he molested his nine-year-old son. During the interview, he was asked to explain the shift from his girls to a male child. The shift seemed out of character, given his pattern of offending. Corey related that his interest in sexual contact with his son developed largely tangentially to the situation with the girls; he commented that he had done it with them so he figured he should include the boy. This was coupled with feelings of curiosity about what homosexual sex might be like. As he put it, "Maybe it was . . . just a curiosity. My curiosity . . . . What it was like to touch another man . . . . I had the opportunity, so why not try it?" Corey had a try anything or a "trysexual" view of sexual reality. And when the opportunity for sex with his son arose, he went ahead with it. Thus curiosity was mixed with opportunity and indifference.

Merging Sex and Affection

Among another subgroup of men, sexual interest in a minor child seemed to emerge from the context of parental love or closeness. As has been suggested by Kevin Howells, it may be that the boundary between parental love and sex is vulnerable to misinterpretations: "Children appear to elicit strong emotional reactions in many people, reactions usually labeled as parental or protective or affectionate, but potentially definable as sexual love."[6] In this respect, some men were unable to separate emotional closeness, or their need for it, from feelings of sexual arousal. They either saw sex as a way of getting closer or felt extremely close to a particular child, which led to sexual desires. This boundary between emotion and sex seemed to get blurred and merged by men who spent a great deal of time around a particular child in a nurturing role, who described being distant from their spouses, and who felt that one of their children was not receiving enough love from their mother or stepmother. Usually they described replacing an adult partner who was often absent with a young person who was routinely present in their day-to-day lives, or trying to provide love to the victim that they felt was not freely given from others.

This pattern was reported by Larry, who earlier described becoming turned on to his seven-year-old stepdaughter when he got an erection while she sat on his lap. Later on in the interview, he was pressed for more detail about how the process of offending started for him. He provided an account in which he turned to his stepdaughter for emotional intimacy, in part because his wife was never around, and sex emerged from this context. He saw sex as a way of getting closer. He remembered thinking that there was a kind of role reversal between the child and his wife. It is important to point out the scripted nature of the account by Larry below. Though asked to separate his feelings at the time from what he had learned in treatment, it seems that some of the language of treatment carried over. To Larry, whatever the language, the experience still appeared to be real. He was only twenty-two at the time.

I: Was it a sexual attraction thing, would you say, or an emotional attraction?
. . . In terms of the way it started . . . ?

R: Somebody to be close with . . . ; because [my wife] wasn't hardly ever around.
And . . . I guess I thought because it's somebody that I . . . could be close to,
I guess I thought I had to be sexual.

I: . . . In order to get emotional intimacy you thought you needed to be sexual?
Is that . . . a fair summary?

R: Yeah . . . . I couldn't be sexual with my wife. I couldn't be close with my wife
because she was never around. [My stepdaughter] was always around and
[she] was always: "Daddy can I do this for you? Daddy can I do that for
you? Daddy let me rub your back . . . . Daddy let me do that." And it was
more like . . . I'm trying to stay away from it but I can't help it. But it seems
like that [she] ended up taking the mother's role. And [my wife] took the
daughter's role . . . . And what I wanted [was] not sexual intimacy . . . but just
somebody to be intimate with. It turned out to be [my stepdaughter] because
she was always there. She cared about what happened . . . . And it wasn't a
preplanned thing.

William, thirty years old, had sex with his two biological daughters
beginning when they were eleven and thirteen. In his personal reality,
emotional bonding and sex were closely linked, the second evolving
from the first. As he put it, "I took sexuality as a way of being able to
show my love and have it accepted and returned in the same form." As
with the previous case, the offender described replacing his spouse with
the victim. William too sounded scripted. While in prison, he spent considerable time in counseling. Yet William seemed sincere in the interview and claimed that what he said reflected his feelings at the onset of
offending and was not programmed into him.

R: The sexual part of the relationship itself was only minor compared to the
emotional relationship that bonded my daughters and I together.

I: The molest helped to cement that bond? To deepen that bond?

R: Yes. But that was not why the molest happened. The molest was a result of
the bond deepening more than the bond deepening was a result of the molest.
I feel before the molest occurred, the boundary was crossed between parent
and child, to an emotional feeling of love between male and female. And this
allowed the molest to occur . . . . The point is, at the time, the relationship was
deepening, and then the fondling began.

I: . . . On a gut level, at the time, why did the molest occur?

R: Replacing my wife's love on an intimate and sexual level through my daughters out of hurt, anger, loneliness. And I think I wanted to somehow make up to my daughters the love that I felt was missing from their stepmother. I really felt responsible. I felt very bad about the different affection level accorded them versus our son. And I really believe that in trying to balance that I overextended myself emotionally with them. And that overextension progressed into a physical and sexual involvement . . . . I reasoned if in a relationship between a man and a woman, who are in love, that sex is the ultimate expression of that love, that by acting sexually with my daughters, I was giving them the ultimate expression of love I could give them.

Tom is a third example of the way some men crossed from an emotional to a sexual realm. Unlike the previous two cases, Tom described a problem of emotional distance between him and his stepdaughter and said he wanted to be accepted and liked by her. He came to see touching her and sexual contact as a solution to this problem. An emotional rift with his stepdaughter emerged around the time she was ten. She wanted to go on a date with a boy and Tom thought she was too young. He refused to let her do so and grounded her. After that point, Tom recalled a troubled relationship, which he felt he had caused by his actions in disciplining the girl. Tom described himself as emotionally needy, and his desire to be close to his stepdaughter was partly a consequence of his biological sterility and thus his inability to have children of his own. He felt an urgency to have a meaningful relationship with the victim. Sex seemed the way to do it. She was eleven, he thirty-two, when sexual contact actually began.

R: There was sort of a cold war going on between [my stepdaughter] and I and it was very painful for me. I was very afraid and sensitive to her not loving me. I had adopted her . . . . It just hurt me . . . . I wanted to love her, to feel important to her. I also felt afraid of her. [She] was very cold and aloof. [I wanted to feel] that I meant something to her. I also felt very responsible for how she was feeling, that it was, somehow it had something to do with me, that I made her cold. I felt very bad about it. Her approval became more important than anything. Her acceptance. My ex-wife, she even asked my daughter if, she'd say: "Why are you being cold to Tom today? Why are you being mean to Tom today?" I'd cry; I'd be real upset about it . . . . [So] I told her, one afternoon, . . . three months before the incest started, I told her that I wanted to touch her . . . ; I believed that if she were to allow me to do so, that would mean she really did love me, or that she would grow to love me. I believed if I could touch her (*pauses*), I had all these feelings of wanting to caress, to soothe, to neutralize the animosity through touching . . . . I thought the touching would make everything okay.

Finally, Harry too admitted crossing the affectional-emotional boundary he shared with his girlfriend's seven-year-old daughter, whom he ended up molesting. In this case, the offender spent a great deal of time with the victim in a nurturing, parental role. Her biological father seldom showed up for visitation, and Harry picked up the emotional slack by talking with the girl and holding her while she cried herself to sleep at night. Over a period of months, a deep emotional bond began to form. Given his own abusive and violent childhood, being in a parenting role began to help him symbolically fill a part of his life that to him had been missing up to that point. Eventually the relationship built to the level of emotional dependence. As Harry said, "I really depended on her emotionally. And she did me too." And "I really needed . . . love, I guess . . . and didn't know how to get it." Ultimately, in his late twenties, Harry crossed from the emotional to the sexual realm because he linked sex with the desire for closeness.

R: For me it was like a desire to be close with someone.
I: You were thinking this at the time?
R: No, I was feeling it. There's a little bit of difference. It was like a need that you feel. Like when you're hungry, you don't think, I'm hungry, [rather] your belly starts growling and you say, "Oh I feel like I'm hungry so I must be . . . ."
I: Was sex a way of feeling close . . . to her?
R: Yeah. Not so much close, but connected . . . . The less I felt the closeness, if I felt us getting further apart, the more I felt I needed to do that in order to bring that back.

The men above indicated that they were looking for love and that they had become emotionally dependent on the victim. In contrast, Earl indicated he was not used to receiving nonsexual affection. As a child, he and his brother had been molested extensively by an older female relative. He had also had hundreds of female sexual partners and said he and his common-law wife (yes, this case again) had sex numerous times a day for about ten years at the time he began molesting. Almost all his relations with the opposite sex involved sexual encounters. When it came to his stepdaughter, he seemed unable to distinguish the situation as different. He saw her daughterly affection as a sexual come-on; he merged sex and affection into one reality. The girl was thirteen at onset. As I reported earlier, he was forty years old.

R: I wasn't used to being shown a kind of affection. I just really, if anybody asked me, I couldn't handle it.

I: The girl showed you a lot of affection?

R: Oh she, yeah . . . as a daughter, yeah. I personally, at the time, if I had to read, well I read hers as a sexual, as all the women in my life, as a come-on.

Lashing Out in Anger

The vast majority of men who made the transition into offending did so on the basis of interpretations they formulated about specific children. Such interpretations had to do with the way a given boy or girl looked or acted or with the blurring of emotional boundaries. Another pathway into sexual contact had to do with interpretations that were made in relation to a third party, someone else besides the victim. Some men targeted or lashed out at a particular victim because of feelings of anger and betrayal involving another person. Either the other person was the victim's mother, and the offender specifically targeted the victim to exact retribution; or the other person was the offender's wife or an employer the offender was angry at for various reasons, and there was a spillover effect to the victim. Thus, similar to findings on adult rapists, anger and/or the desire for revenge against someone else were central realities that shifted some men into sexual offending against children.[7]

Brian, who was twenty-seven, performed oral sex on a six-year-old boy while parked in his car on the side of a dark road on one occasion. At the time he began offending, he was angry at the mother of the victim, the girlfriend he lived with, because he discovered she had slept with other men, men who were customers at a restaurant where she worked. His anger quickly transformed into a desire to get even.

R: I never had any history of anything like this . . . . At the time . . . I was very hurt. I was very angry . . . . I was to the point of wanting to hurt her bad, even kill her maybe. And at the same time I still loved this woman . . . . I kept going back to her after all this stuff was going on. And her kids and I had become very close . . . . The older one went everywhere with me . . . . So I just decided that's the only way I could get her love is through him. At the same time, I could pay her back for what she's done.

I: How would the molest serve getting her love?

R: That's her son. That's her baby. She loves that baby . . . . It was like her. I could . . . receive some of her love through him. At the same time, anger, pay-back, revenge!

Before he molested the victim, Brian had gone on a destructive rampage, nearly destroying a semi truck owned by a man who slept with his girlfriend, a man he did not personally know. Apparently that did not quell his anger. When asked why he did not lash out directly at his partner, as you will remember, he said he did not believe in hitting women. The boy Brian targeted seemed to represent a symbolic extension of the girlfriend at whom he was angry. His feelings appeared confused and complex. On the one hand, he believed molesting the boy was a way of vicariously holding onto someone he loved but was losing. On the other hand, there was a stated premeditated desire for revenge. He felt that by hurting her son he would really be hurting her. In the end, the child became the target because, as he put it, "He's the closest thing to her."

R: By the time I tried it the first time, I had ruled out everything but revenge. I wanted revenge more than anything at that particular time and I was going to get it and that's how I was going to get it. Because I knew that would get to her.

Feelings of anger in the case of Brian more or less took on a life all their own. They seemed to consume him. He admitted having contemplated for nearly a month about where and how he could molest the victim. He mentioned knowing how the mother of the boy trusted him with her children. And he conveyed in a sad tone at one point that his actions "hurt the child's mother," which was what he intended. He acknowledged that he had always considered behavior like that he engaged in to be wrong, but he tossed his morality out the window. Tunnel vision and the desire for revenge reigned.

R: I totally obliterated every moral thought I had when I was doing this because I was doing this for me. And me was the only thing that counted at the time. I didn't care who, where, why, how come, what, how I did [it], [or] who I hurt to do it. As long as I got [revenge], I got it.

Sometimes the basis of anger that carried over into offending did not seem to match the seriousness of the act inflicted on the victim. Larry shifted into offending initially after getting turned on from incidental physical contact. There were other times, however, when other reasons seemed to emerge and continually refocus his interest back on the victim, his stepdaughter. He admitted to sometimes getting back at his wife because the house was routinely dirty. He was in his mid-twenties; the girl was seven at the onset, twelve by the time the offending stopped.

R: There was a few times that I molested [my stepdaughter] out of being mad, . . . and not at [her]; it would be at [my wife]. It was kind of like a get even thing, but again I was drunk when I did it. And it was like the more I drank the angrier I got . . . ; and then I would molest my daughter.
I: . . . What would you be mad at your wife for?
R: Not cleaning the house. Letting the dog shit on the floor and nobody cleaning it up.

The way his wife spent money was another irritation; it precipitated a turning point. The shift into offending occurred because he was trying to balance the ledger, so to speak. It was as though two wrongs made everything right. The victim was a convenient target since he had already been sexual with her.

R: We had . . . money problems. [My wife] wanted to spend money. I wanted to save money. If I . . . had $10,000 . . . she could . . . spend $10,000 and then bitch because the bills aren't being paid . . . . "Well, what happened to the $10,000?" "Well, I had some things that I needed to do. . . ." "Well, fuck your things. Pay the fucking bills first." . . . I'd almost be willing to say that a few of them . . . , a few of the molests were probably over money. I was . . . a tightwad. . . .
I: Connect for me, if you could, the relationship between money and the molest. Why would the money lead to the molest?
R: It was almost like I got even with [my wife] for spending the money that she had no right to. No right to because that was bill money.

John also initially shifted into offending for reasons other than anger. In particular, he described a process of noticing and sexualizing the first of two children he victimized. But his life was in general characterized by feelings of hostility, especially toward his ex-wife. He wanted to reunite with her and have sex with her but she did not feel the same way. The result was tremendous anger, and the victim, his niece, just happened to be in the wrong place at a time right for the offender. He admitted trying to degrade the girl. Anger thus was blended into the process of offending, after numerous offending episodes had already occurred, and became a new situational catalyst of sorts over time for this particular offender. John was in his early thirties. The girl was thirteen in the episode he describes here.

R: The last two incidents I actually placed my penis inside of her mouth . . . . Both times happened where I was actually trying to degrade her . . . . The first of the two I had had an argument with my first wife. I was very angry and actually the argument was over whether or not she'd spend the weekend with me. We had got back together and separated again this time for about six months and I was angry that she'd denied me. I mean *really* angry . . . . I needed some money so I went to mom's house to see if she'd loan me ten dollars. And mom wasn't there and [my niece] was. And [she] of course started talking to me and asked me . . . what I was mad about. I remember telling her just don't worry about it. And I walked up to her and I . . . stuck my hand down inside of her blouse and began to fondle her breast and she asked me to stop. And this was the first time she'd ever . . . denied me in any way, and it just *infuriated* me (*very loudly*).

The last episode with this same victim, which also started, John said, out of anger, had more to do with his employer than his wife. He molested his niece after a bad day at work when he had been fighting with his boss. When his niece said something he did not like, it sent him over the edge. He was like a ticking bomb; again the victim was someone he could control and the timing happened to be right.

R: It was about a month later we were basically in exactly the same position again. I was pissed off . . . . It was just a *real* bad day at work. Me and the boss had got into it—arguing, fighting . . . over something that I was doing that he didn't like. And I was still trying to talk my ex-wife into moving back in with me and not having a whole lot of success. And I'd went over to . . . see [my brother] . . . . And mom and [my niece] were there and [my niece] went upstairs and I went upstairs to use the rest room. And [my niece] was sitting on the bed. I walked up to her and put my hand on . . . her shoulder, was talking to her. And she kind of shrugged it off and it angered me. And basically it was the same thing . . . again where I felt rejected.

The level of anger John felt toward his employer and about life in general is worth noting, given that his emotions seemed to spill over to, and get played out with, his niece. He recalled reaching a state of wanting to do violence to someone in general and of having fantasies of raping his boss's wife. He got caught for child molesting before he acted on his fantasies.

R: I was very close, *very* close to the point of committing a major violent offense. Extremely short-tempered. . . .

I: Did you ever think about, for example, rape?

R: Yeah. Like I said, one of the fantasies involving my boss at the time who was really getting down on me was . . . being sexual with his wife . . . . I think it was the thought of raping her . . . , grabbing her and eventually she would come around to enjoying sex with me and . . . he would find out about it.

Taking the Easy Path

Perceptions about the relative accessibility of a given child for sexual contact and the relative unavailability of other adult partners seemed to shape the interests of many men in this study as well. That is, perceptions about sexual opportunity were pivotal. Some children were seen as more likely than other children to acquiesce to sex or as being generally approachable for sex because of their personalities, for example, immodest or passive. And children who became targets were routinely said by offenders to be around more, making them the most readily available sexual outlet regardless of age.[8] In turn, avenues to sex with other adults were often said to be blocked or closed off because of anticipated difficulties with finding willing partners and hiding sexual affairs, or because extra-relationship sex, ironically, was seen as immoral and thus not an available option.[9] Whatever the type of construction, the men stated that they followed the path with the fewest obstacles, that they took the easiest path available, when it came to making the decision to engage in sexual offending.

Leon, forty-three at onset, had two stepdaughters but molested only one of them. His choice of victims was in part a matter of perceived accessibility. He felt the opportunity was there with the girl he approached much more so than with the other because she was more immodest. The girl he touched was eight years old at the start.

R: I never molested my oldest daughter and there wasn't that much difference in age . . . . There was a difference in personalities . . . . The older one was . . . very modest. You never saw her running around with her pants down or her door open . . . . She was not very affectionate. She wasn't a hugger and a kisser and getting close to you all the time. . . .

I: So why one girl versus the other?

R: . . . The opportunity was there with the younger one because she was immodest, because she was very affectionate . . . . She was just constantly there.

Sam had four children, three of whom were biological children, but engaged in sexual contact only with his stepson, starting when the boy was eleven and he had recently turned forty. He saw his stepson as being an easier mark to manipulate because of his timid personality. Plus, ironically in his reality, his other son, whom he could have molested, was too young for sex.

I: Why your stepson?

R: Well, he was there, he was the oldest, and he was I think the most vulnerable. I don't think I would have molested the other boy because he was too young at the time the molest started . . . . He was not someone who could be manipulated, the younger boy.

I: He was more strong personally? How so?

R: . . . Just the personality. The way he was . . . ; he was not vulnerable. [My biological son] was always strong and outgoing and [my stepson] cried a lot and was timid and was just an easier mark.

Gary, too, said his interest in his seven-year-old stepdaughter emerged partly as a response to her personality. If he asked her to do something she always did it; the girl was not disobedient like his ex-wife. This led him to feel close to the victim as a consequence and to think that "it would be okay to have a limited sexual relationship" with her. Most critical, though, was that to him the girl was not shy and was openly affectionate. He figured that if he initiated sex she would cooperate. The victim, it should be noted, was physically handicapped and had trouble walking. At the time, Gary was twenty-nine.

R: Her personality, she's always been very bold, . . . never afraid . . . . She was always a very affectionate girl . . . . Never shy to come up and give . . . a hug or kiss or whatever. She likes that. She's always liked closeness . . . . I knew that I felt secure that she would do it. It's kind of like electricity or water, it takes the path of least resistance.

Conrad had sex with his biological daughter starting when she was eight. He admitted that when he began offending he was seeking some type of sexual gratification, in part, he claimed, because his sexual relationship with his wife had become unsatisfying. The specific reason he chose his daughter, however, was that sex with her seemed to be an easier and more practical alternative than an extramarital affair. The latter was too difficult, he said, for him to create and hide. Conrad was thirty.

R: I didn't want to go outside the marriage for a lover because of, . . . it's going to sound kind of crazy (*laughs lightly*) when I say it, but I couldn't lie well enough to hide an affair with an outside person, but I could lie good enough to hide an affair with my daughter.

I: . . . Why would it have been harder to hide an affair with an adult?

R: Because I couldn't account for my time away from home. And the opportunity outside was harder for me to create. I mean it was already there and ready-made. So that was another reason I turned to my daughter.

Ironically, Harry and Scott, both in their late twenties, each reported that their belief that extra-relationship sex was wrong made sex with their stepdaughters easier and more viable and closed them off to other alternative sexual outlets. In the first case, the victim was only seven at onset, in the second she was ten.

R: Even if I had the desire to fulfill my needs with someone else my age, I wouldn't have because I believed that you just don't do that. . . .

I: So you would never have sex outside of the relationship?

R: . . . I guess I didn't believe that was having sex outside of the relationship. Because it wasn't with another woman, so to speak. I guess I considered that to be less threatening to our relationship.

I: Why not other adult women?

R: . . . Because I was running in a very strict Christian circle and I felt those . . . strict Christian designs. I mean I believed in those. And adultery . . . just was not something you do. The opportunity wasn't there either. Maybe had the opportunity been there I might have pursued it.

Brian stated he molested the six-year-old boy he did because of two interrelated factors. First, he said he spent a great deal of time alone every day with the child. As he put it, "I was around her boys a lot. We became very close, particularly the older one and I." Thus, in his reality, the child was around for the taking. And while partly targeting the victim out of anger, partly admitting that he was seeking gratification because of a period of sexual deprivation, and partly confusing sex and closeness, Brian also believed that sex outside his relationship with another adult was not an available option. The reason, he said, was that he felt inadequate because his girlfriend had cheated on him. Brian was twenty-seven.

R: I was feeling inadequate. I felt, well . . . , "How can I cheat on her . . . with another woman if I can't even keep her home? Can't even keep her interested in me? What other woman's going to be interested in me?" . . . I had such a low opinion of myself I didn't think that any other woman would want me or want to have sex with me. So this little six-year-old boy doesn't know any different, easy pickings. That's what I thought.
I: . . . Why do you think the child that was involved . . . , why do you think it was a boy, not a girl . . . ?
R: If it had been a girl I'm sure I would have molested her.
I: So the sex [gender] had nothing to do with it?
R: Not really. He was there! He was a boy.

Similar to Brian, Bob felt that children were simply easier to approach for sex than other adults, though his reason differed somewhat. Other adults, he explained, had a lot of hang-ups about sex. Children, however, did not. Bob was a closeted homosexual who was looking for same-sex activity wherever he could find it. He molested two boys, a nephew and a neighbor, each aged eight at onset, starting when he was thirty-seven, married, and had children of his own.

I: Any idea why you chose children as opposed to adults as a sexual outlet?
R: Children were more approachable than adults.
I: In what way?
R: Most adults have fixed feelings, especially when it comes to sex . . . . I don't think children have that fixed standard. Also, most adults are inhibited in some way. In here, in prison, you call them closeted people.

Finally, the desire for sex among some men, such as Sidney, who was thirty-two, became so strong that the choice of target boiled down to whoever happened to be in the wrong place at a specific moment. It could have been any child, or any adult female for that matter; it was simply the result of sheer physical access. In this case it happened to be his stepdaughter, who was nine when he molested her.

R: I felt a need for, among other things, a form of sexual satisfaction, and that required a female. And she was the person there at the time. I don't think there was anything specifically about her that I found attractive, not that she's unattractive.

Idiosyncratic Transitions

There were also idiosyncratic types of interpretive realities involved in the situational transition into sexual offending. These idiosyncratic factors were usually, though not always, mixed with other constructions about the victim outlined previously. They seemed to contribute to their involvement rather than being the predominant reason for it. In particular, the men mentioned the following as relevant in their cases: being turned off by adult genitalia, blacking out, noticing the way a child smelled, or feeling attracted to the personality of a child. Thus, not every offender fit neatly or cleanly into a distinct category.

With Tom, who was thirty-two at the onset of offending, the sexual interest in his stepdaughter seemed to emerge at least partially as a consequence of sexual aversions toward the genitalia of adult women, which became more severe while he was married to his wife. He described the vaginas of adult women as unpleasant and malodorous, and saw intercourse as dirty and foul. Menstruation, he said, was a major sexual turn off for him. His stepdaughter, in contrast, fit his image of the ideal sexual partner on a physiological, developmental level, primarily because she was too young to menstruate. His interest, he recalled, began initially to surface when she was just eight, though actual sexual contact did not occur until three years later.

R: Part of what was appealing about her was that . . . [the] appearance of her and . . . [her] age meant that she was not menstruating, even though the incest continued throughout the time that she started. But I was telling myself, it's like, maybe there's something in me that's got a real problem with that, [a] real problem with women's genitals . . . . And if I . . . had to create an ideal woman, . . . she would be adult height, adult mentality, adult emotions, nice breasts as opposed to sagging things, okay, but . . . she wouldn't be menstruating and she wouldn't have any pubic hair because the pubic hair represents an age where menstruation occurs.

Kelly said that much of his interest in the girl he molested, the daughter of his live-in girlfriend, had to do with the fact that he liked her personality. He saw the victim as inquisitive, alert, and smart. This offender also indicated noticing the physical appearance of the child and claimed that the girl cued him at times that she was interested in sex. Still, her personality seemed to matter more. To him, she was the right "girl," so to speak, at the "right" time; the kind of "girl" he was looking for. The victim was only four; Kelly was twenty-two.

I: Why didn't you turn to someone else?

R: . . . I think I would say I was more infatuated with her.

I: Than somebody outside?

R: Yeah. She just had a real nice personality. She's really different. She really is. To me she is . . . ; she's on top of it. I mean she knows. You can tell her something. She asks you questions. She'll remember it. It's like a computer bank . . . . She's really alert.

I: So there was a part of you that was impressed with her?

R: Yeah. She always want[ed] to go places. She wanted to learn new things.

Corey and Gary also stated that the personality of the victims they molested was partly the basis for their sexual interest. Each one said that there was something "special" about the victim that drew him. The children were thirteen and seven, respectively, at the onset of offending. Corey was in his late thirties, Gary in his late twenties.

I: You were attracted to her personality? . . . What was it like?

R: Pleasant. Fun. We got along great. We talked a lot, the two of us did . . . . She was the first one. She was more special than the other two . . . . She was special because she was first. But her and I could talk.

R: There was something special about her that kind of, I don't know what it was, but kind of drew you. Some kids have just got a certain charisma about them that attracts anybody really.

Equally as important for Conrad, when he related why he molested the daughter he did, was his account of why he ruled out the idea of sexual contact with another of his other two daughters. As he put it, it was basically the way she smelled. Sometimes there was a very fine line that kept men from crossing the boundary into offending with a particular child.

R: This is something I've never told anybody. I thought about it with her other sister, the next one down . . . . One day I was holding her and that thought crossed my mind and I just explored it . . . and it just didn't seem right. And so I didn't . . . . It seemed okay to do it with the oldest one, but the other ones, there was something wrong with that . . . . It was like it was taboo. Something went haywire with the oldest daughter. . . .

I: You said you explored the idea. What did you think about?

R: . . . I remember . . . when I thought about it was when . . . I was sitting on the couch . . . in the living room and I was holding her. And I could smell the smell of her body and just something about that said no don't do that. Just something about it turned me off.

Another man, Michael, aged twenty, the youngest offender in the sample, stated that his transition into offending occurred in the context of blacking out. He claimed to have no memory about what he did at the time he did it. When he was confronted and told what the victim alleged he had done a few hours later, he admitted his involvement because he experienced flashbacks and began to remember things. He reported the loss of a period of time or a gap in his stream of consciousness. Importantly, this respondent was severely and repeatedly sexually abused as a boy by five male relatives. Memory of his own victimization was sporadic, suggesting a pattern of dissociation. He also consumed large quantities of alcohol. The victim was his seven-year-old second cousin, whom he was baby sitting.

R: I don't remember anything about thinking about something like that. I don't remember even beginning, anywhere in my mind, of thinking of doing something . . . . I mean, it was not planned . . . . And I just keep thinking, and I can't even remember when I first blacked out. From as far as I know the last thing I can remember is my girlfriend leaving and that's all I can remember . . . . I can't remember the rest of the story. I mean, at the time that they asked me, then it all came back. But I can't explain how it was . . . ; I just didn't know what I'd done. I don't know if they call it a blackout or what.

Conclusion

Nearly every man in my study was able to pinpoint a specific moment and set of circumstances in which his interest in a particular victim initially emerged. Seven types of transitional, reality-shifting experiences were documented, listed in descending order of prevalence: noticing and eroticizing, reacting to perceived sexual cues, selecting easy targets, becoming curious about biological changes, merging or confusing feelings of affection with sex, getting aroused from nonsexual touching, and targeting out of anger. Each type of shift into offending occurred situationally through interaction with the victim. Rather than a single experience, most men reported more than one pattern of shifting, sometimes three or four in different combinations. For example, noticing and sexualizing, arousal from incidental contact, and merging of sex and love surfaced together in some cases. Thus the pathway into sexual offending is, in fact, more complex than the categories indicate. This reframing process in which sexual interest emerges and the methods by which it unfolds constitutes the critical bridge between the background factors reported earlier that increase the likelihood of becoming an offender and the subsequent onset of sexual contact with victims. Without this interpretive bridge, the crimes reported by the men here would not have occurred.

FIVE

Approaching and Engaging the Victim

Research and media coverage on intrafamilial child molesting since the late 1970s have revealed a dramatic image about the ways children are victimized. In particular, studies have shown that offenders employ a range of tactics to gain sexual compliance, tactics such as verbal coercion and intimidation, seduction, misrepresentation of sex as a game or as something innocent, physical force or blitz attacks, or the use of enticements like money or candy, to name a few.[1] Most discussions of this topic, however, provide only a cursory profile of tactics. Surprisingly, there has been no real effort to look closely at what offenders themselves state they did when they offended. In the interviews I conducted, I carefully documented the ways offenders approached and initiated sex with their victims, focusing on the strategies they used to gain sexual access along with the reasons they had for the type of approach made. What follows is a survey of the range of tactics that were reported along with various detailed illustrations of each. Extending the analysis further, I also focus on the perceived reactions of the victim, as offenders saw things, from acquiescence to resistance. I show how offenders often monitored their victims and continued or adjusted their method of access, in a much more dynamic sense, depending on the apparent reactions received.

Since most of the offenders in this research were involved in numerous sexual acts, sometimes with multiple victims, it was usually impossible to get a complete description of every offense any one person committed. Thus, I asked my respondents to reconstruct what occurred during the first episode of sexual contact they engaged in with each victim, or the first episode they could remember in detail. In particular, I probed for information about how the victim or victims reacted as the situation unfolded, what words were exchanged, and whether any physical force was used. I also asked the men to describe any changes in the way subsequent episodes occurred, and to provide additional examples of later encounters that stood out most clearly in their memory. In my sample, every offender always acted alone, never with an accomplice. Usually, they approached their victims individually, though some offenses did involve multiple victims simultaneously. There were two general groups of tactics reported—surreptitious approaches, when victims were not aware of the offenders' intentions, and explicit or direct approaches, containing some element of coercion, when they were aware.[2] Offenders who encountered little or no perceived resistance from victims continued to use the same approach tactic repeatedly. Those who did report resistance routinely switched between surreptitious and explicit tactics, depending on which of the two they had tried first, or scaled up their use of more overt force or manipulation.

Seducing and Testing

One type of offending transaction common among the men in my sample consisted of the extension of affectionate touching to a sexual realm. This tactic depended on the existence of an already established routine of nonsexual touching with the child who was molested. For example, some men described how a particular child liked to sit on their lap and watch television with them at night before going to bed. Or they told about how they used to enjoy rubbing or softly tickling one of their children as their way of showing fatherly affection. Sexual contact then was added on in these interactions. The offender transformed the situation in a sexual direction, touching the child in increments, testing for a reaction, and then continuing if no overt resistance was observed. The transaction took on the form of a seduction. The strategy was to try and introduce sex before the victim could really figure out what was going on. Then, because sex was something that naturally felt good, it was presumed the younger person would want to continue.

Leon first molested his youngest stepdaughter when she was around eight. He admitted to roughly sixteen episodes of vaginal fondling spanning about four months. The sexual contact occurred while the two sat in a recliner chair together and watched television in the evenings before she went to bed. Every offense occurred in the same place and the same way. He began with affectionate holding and caressing.

R: This would be after a bath so she would have a nightgown on . . . ; and she would have panties on, okay? And she would come and sit on my lap and we would watch television . . . . Several times when we were alone like that I would rub her leg or rub her stomach while she was sitting [there]. I mean affectionate rubs and pats, at least that's the way I viewed it.

I: Were you thinking sexual thoughts at that time?

R: Yes, yes I was. And I guess I was trying to get her accustomed to that so that it wouldn't be a surprise if I did touch her vagina or whatever. I thought I was getting her used to it and that by her silence that she . . . would just go along with it.

The method Leon reported using involved a slow progression toward touching the genitals of his stepdaughter. He never forced her to sit on his lap. When she did, then he would touch her. The goal was to introduce sex without the victim really knowing what was occurring until it was already happening. He described testing her to see how she would react.

R: I smoke. Well, she doesn't like to be around smoke, okay. So if I smoked, . . . she would get up and go lay on the couch. Sometimes she would stay over there the rest of the night. Sometimes she would come back and sit on my lap . . . . I let her control that. I didn't want her to think that I was overanxious. I didn't want her to realize that I wanted her sitting on my lap, see? . . . So . . . after I would get more courage, after a few times of doing this, . . . I would rub her leg and . . . her buttocks through her clothes, and I would keep moving my hand in between her legs, not necessarily down as far as her vagina but just a lot of movement . . . . And she didn't move or say anything about it.

I: Sounded like you were testing her limits?

R: Yes, exactly. And . . . I kept telling myself, "If she says no I'll stop and won't do it again." I don't know if that was true . . . because . . . she never did say "stop."

Eventually the situation involved full-fledged fondling of the genitals. With each episode, there was no explicit negative reaction from the victim that he could see, and his response was to continue with what he was doing. Watching television together served to distract the attention of the victim.

R: I would keep working around and I would try to get my hand up her night-gown and I would rub her buttocks and her thighs because she didn't neces-sarily sit with her legs spread open . . . . And then I would take my finger and go around the edge of her panties and . . . I would stick it in the crotch of her panties and I would rub her vagina. And she would never look at me or say a word or show any fear or act that anything was . . . different. And I always kidded myself thinking that meant she liked it.

Ian initiated sexual contact with all three of his biological daughters starting at about the same age with each, around eleven. His offending with all three spanned intermittently over a ten-year period. It was the biological development of their breasts that triggered his interest. In the case of his third daughter, whom he molested most extensively, once he began noticing her, he quickly progressed from nonsexual touching to the point where he fondled her breasts.

R: [It was] one of those kinds of occasions where she is watching TV, . . . she crawls up, . . . plops in my lap . . . . For some reason I began to touch her, and just like you hold somebody, . . . then beginning to caress her. Well she loved to have her arms . . . and her legs and her feet tickled . . . . And . . . you start with the arms, then for some reason . . . , it just started with her breast. And she liked it and didn't say anything about it.

In explaining his strategy of offending, Ian drew a parallel to the days of dating in high school. The reaction of the girl shaped the boy's sub-sequent actions.

R: I guess maybe it just was a lot like high school, where you go out with some-body, and the girl, you just reach over and you kind of hold your breath when you touch her, and if she doesn't resist you keep going. And if she resists, why it stops your hand and you pull it back and that's the end of it. Or the next date you try again.

There was always one activity that spread over into another: rubbing his daughter's feet, her watching television on his lap. Nonsexual contact of this type was said to be a way of preparing the victim, of getting her used to being touched.

R: Maybe she had taken a shower after being out in the yard . . . and I'm watching TV. And she'd come down and sit in the chair in my lap or maybe . . . cuddled up to me. And one of the things . . . that she liked was her feet being tickled. She just enjoyed that. So oftentimes she'd sit on the floor in the family room and put her feet up in my lap and want me to do that, and I would relax her and make her feel good. And then maybe she'd get up and sit in my lap, and I kind of prepared her.

With Ian, the sequence of testing and seducing involved watching and reacting to the victim each time he was sexual with her. As he approached her, he wondered what she might do. After he touched her, he noted a physical cue of enjoyment and no explicit requests to stop. As a consequence, he continued.

R: One time . . . I was caressing her on the neck and the cheeks and just wondering as I went down in her shirt what her reaction would be. And instead of putting a hand up there and saying, "Hey, stop" or something like that, which I wish she had, . . . there was no stopping, and I continued as far as she allowed me. And I remember touching her breasts at that point. And . . . immediately, her nipples got hard.

The seduction of his third daughter unfolded over a period of roughly two years. There were multiple episodes of touching and testing that eventually led to genital contact and later to attempted intercourse. Over time an unspoken understanding of how sex would proceed developed. He admitted to at least a hundred molest episodes with this particular daughter.

R: A lot of times . . . , especially later on as it progressed, you could do that for her [tickle her feet] and then you just move up the leg and you just keep going until there's some resistance. And there'd be no resistance, or she would pretend to go to sleep.

John, likewise, described the seduction of his half-sister, aged thirteen at the time, whom he admitted he had sexual contact with twice. He began by caressing her legs and moved quickly to touching her genitals. Eventually he got to the point where he placed his penis against her vagina and ejaculated. He also molested a niece much more extensively, using a different approach. This was not his only tactic.

R: She was laying there and the only thing she had on was a . . . nylon nightgown . . . . She kind of lifted her leg, one leg up, and that was when I noticed that she didn't have any underwear on . . . . I was laying there and I kind of casually put my hand up on her knee and she didn't say anything. So I just began stroking her knee and basically just worked my way up her leg and began to fondle her vagina . . . . After a few minutes I got up and laid down beside her on the couch and began to fondle her breast and kiss her on the neck . . . . And I unzipped my pants and took my penis out and placed it between her legs . . . . I actually ejaculated and I got up and . . . got a wash-cloth and cleaned her off . . . . I don't think we said three or four words to each other the entire incident. In fact after it was over she continued to lay there and watch TV.

As with the other men above, critical to the seduction process was the perceived reaction of the victim as the touching progressed. John stated that his half-sister began to respond physiologically when he touched her. This interpretation of the victim provided the basis for the offender to continue with the situation as it unfolded.

R: She became sexually excited both times.
I: What do you mean?
R: Lubrication in her vagina area and rapid breathing, or breathing increased. And as I was kissing her on the neck, she'd make it more accessible . . . . And she actually fondled my penis.
I: . . . What did that symbolize to you when she did that?
R: Oh . . . in my own mind I was thinking that she was enjoying it and wanting me to continue.

Catching the Victim by Surprise

A second method of making sexual contact, one not quite as frequent as the first, consisted of catching the victim off guard or by surprise. In these instances, the victim was approached either while asleep or while involved in or distracted by another activity or task. Sometimes the offender set the situation up by asking the victim to do something to put her or him off guard. More commonly, the offender had been looking for an opportunity to initiate contact, but had been frustrated in doing so because of situational problems—too many people around, not home at the right time, the victim had resisted with other methods—and so the offender seized the first opportunity that presented itself. When the victim was not looking, was unaware, or was not awake, the men acted, most often by grabbing at the breasts or genitals of the younger person or by taking the hand of the victim and putting it on their genitals.

Brian molested the six-year-old son of his girlfriend while stopped in his car along the side of a road. He admitted that he planned for some time to have sex with the boy but had been unable to initiate contact. Still, Brian stated that he did not set the victim up per se. Rather, the decision to act was spontaneous. The boy had just gotten back into the car after urinating on the roadside when Brian grabbed his penis. This was the first and only molest episode Brian acknowledged.

R: We went to the grocery store. Went into the store, got the things we needed for dinner, come back out. I started the car and drove around the parking lot to a dark secluded place . . . . The child had to go to the bathroom . . . . So I just told him to step outside and go. When he got back in the car he could not zip up his pants. That's when I took advantage of it. I pulled his pants down and started fondling his penis.

I: . . . Did you have any thought about doing this to this boy prior to this?

R: Yeah, I had. I had thought about where I could do it and when, how I could lead up to it. But I never had the opportunities because there was always too many people around the house. Or I was coming in from work or I was going to work . . . . So my first chance was then and there in that parking lot and I tried it.

Gary approached his stepdaughter when she was seven by catching her by surprise as well. The first time he molested her he was sleeping with his biological daughter and stepdaughter in sleeping bags on the floor in the living room of his house. In the middle of the night, Gary said, he took the victim's hand while she was asleep and put it on his penis. When she woke up, he told the victim to masturbate him. There was no time for the victim to think. He said she acquiesced. There were three other episodes over a two-year period with this victim. Each subsequent approach became increasingly direct and up front, eventually resulting in requests for the victim to perform oral sex, without the pretense used here.

R: I had been laying there . . . . So I went ahead and I took her hand, . . . I [had] obtained [an] erection, and I placed her hand . . . on my penis, . . . and in a gripping form. And then . . . she woke up but it wasn't a startling wake . . . .

I: So she was asleep when you took her hand and initiated it.

R: Right, and then she woke up . . . . And as she woke up, I thought, "Oh boy,

I'm going to scare [her] . . . ." I know I said words to comfort her, to let her know that I wasn't some stranger . . . , because she had her back to me . . . . Then I asked her if she would pull it for me . . . . So she went ahead and did it . . . . She couldn't have understood what sex was . . . . Like I said, I never had any problems getting the kids to do anything . . . ; I always ask[ed] . . . and they'd do it . . . . The reason why I went ahead and took her hand while she was asleep, instead of asking her when she was awake, is because I weren't sure if she would or not.

Scott, a third example of an offender who used surprise, started noticing and observing his oldest stepdaughter over a period of months. He also had exposed himself to her numerous times to try and arouse her, but to no effect. On two occasions, Scott acted abruptly without pretense, grabbing at the victim's genitals and breasts. Both times his stepdaughter rebuffed his advances. The girl was eleven at the time. He soon turned to molesting his other, younger stepdaughter, which I describe later.

R: The first time I ever touched her I was putting her up in the attic . . . . She was dressed in a jogging . . . outfit, it wasn't shorts or anything like that . . . . I had just been thinking about touching her to see if she felt like a woman is I think what was running through my mind. And when I was lifting her up in the attic I put my hand between her crotch, up in her crotch. And it made her uncomfortable because she looked down at me and she says, "Daddy!" She knew . . . there wasn't something right about it. And I just kind of puffed it off like, "Oh I'm sorry, it was an accident," and I moved my hand real quick . . . . There was only one other time when she was sleeping. I went to wake her up and instead of reaching for her shoulder, I touched her breast as she was laying on the couch sleeping. And she opened her eyes and gave me this dirty look like, "Don't do that." And I just walked away. I just told her, "Hey, it's time for dinner."

And then there was the case of Carl, who gained sexual access three or four times to one of three boys he molested, during a three-year span, beginning when the boy was ten, by trying to teach the child how to drive. He would have the victim sit on his lap when he drove, and let him steer the car, at which time he would fondle his penis. The tactic was a setup, something he planned.

R: He would be riding on my [lap]; I would let him drive my car and I would fondle him. I put him on my lap . . . . He was an extremely cute little boy . . . .

I: He was steering?

R: Yeah . . . . He had jeans on and I fondled his penis through his jeans . . . .

I: Did he ever say he didn't want you to do that?

R: No. One time I did notice some resistance. I offered to let him drive my car and he wouldn't . . . .

I: When you asked him to drive your car . . . , was touching him part of your idea?

R: Oh yeah! Yeah . . . .

I: It was almost like a setup . . . ?

R: Oh yeah!

Sneaking and Spying

A few men instigated sexual contact by sneaking up and spying on their victim while the victim was actually or allegedly asleep. Generally the offender would get out of bed in the middle of the night and tiptoe into the victim's room or go to check on the children in their room during the evening after they were in bed. The offenses typically involved lifting up covers, removing or pulling open underwear, looking at the genitals, poking at the genitals with fingers, and digital-vaginal insertion. Fondling of the breasts and even oral-genital sex occurred in one case. With this method, the strategy involved trying not to wake the victim, to offend covertly without the other person ever being aware of the situation. By touching the child when he/she was asleep, the offender had no negative reactions and consequently no resistance to face; thus it was easier to complete the transaction.

Scott, who attempted to molest his older stepdaughter, as mentioned previously, by making surprise advances toward her, used a different tactic with his younger stepdaughter, who was ten. Scott approached and initiated sexual contact many times with this second stepdaughter while she was asleep. Although he did not admit it, he may have decided on this course of action as a consequence of having encountered stiff resistance from his first victim. He went on to molest her over a hundred times for a period of over three years.

R: One night . . . I thought about . . . [my stepdaughter] being in the room and nobody being home, and I took the opportunity and I went in and I pulled her panties down. Well first I grabbed her arm or just picked it up and dropped it to see if she was asleep and it was like she was . . . ; I don't think she was but I convinced myself she was, let myself believe it anyway. And I pulled her pants down and just kind of looked at her vagina and rubbed it a little bit. And that was really about all the first time and then I just put her panties back up and covered her up and went off in our master bathroom and I masturbated and I went to sleep.

Steve, too, spied on his stepdaughter at night while she was sleeping. He would sneak into her bedroom while his wife was watching television at the other end of the house. Another stepdaughter, whom he did not offend, was always asleep in the same room as the victim. He said he used the same method of offending in every instance. There were ten admitted episodes over a two-year period, starting when the victim was eight.

R: I had . . . a little hand flashlight. I went into the bedroom and would just like lift her underwear or if she had pajamas on or whatever, and kind of look and see what was there . . . . During all the incidents she was asleep. There was no coercion. As far as I knew . . . she was asleep. She wouldn't know it was happening and I could justify the behavior by that . . . . [I'd] . . . go to the bathroom or whatever I had to do. Or in one case my wife would be up watching TV and they had the room downstairs. And I have an office down there, see . . . . Well of course . . . , the urge would come on, and I'd sneak down there . . . .

I: . . . In terms of the sequence of actual behaviors, the first time you pulled her panties down and just looked at her?

R: I think I might have lifted them up, along the leg area, just lifted them up and looked . . . . It was usually a case of lifting them up, whatever was easiest to do. You can't pull the pants down . . . without moving their legs and all that. It had to be, what's the word I want, not easy, but . . . with the least . . . chance of waking her up, I guess . . . . So whatever is easiest. And so I'd touch her and look with my flashlight.

Ordering and Physically Forcing

Other men either verbally ordered and commanded their victims or used deliberate and explicit physical force to complete sexual transactions. The kinds of force or commands used included pulling off clothes, trying to force open mouths, holding the victim down, telling the victim to perform fellatio, or yelling at the child. Physical force, in particular, was not common among the men in this study, and when it was used, it was typically of low severity.[3] This is not to minimize the impact of the use of physical force on a victim. It is just to say that it seldom escalated to extreme levels. Specifically, none of the men used weapons, and according to their accounts, none left physical injuries on the victim. When physical force was used, the men tended to minimize its severity, by claiming that they could have been more physical than they were, believing they had not crossed the line into brutality. Verbal intimidation, in comparison, was more common. Sometimes both methods of controlling and engaging were employed together.

John, who I reported above used a seducing strategy with one victim, molested a second victim, his niece, around twenty-five times when she was between the ages of eleven and thirteen. One time when he attacked his niece, he had asked his wife, from whom he was separated, to have sex with him, but she declined. Later, while staying at his mother's house, his niece came into his bedroom to ask whether something was wrong. Still angry at being rebuffed by his wife, he ordered her to have sex, to perform fellatio on him. The more she resisted, the more insistent and intimidating he seemed to become. Being at least six feet and two hundred pounds, John was too formidable to fend off. He admitted that he treated this victim, as well as the other girl he molested, like "inanimate objects" and as "a possession . . . that was mine to do what I wanted with." He said he never gave any thought to how the younger person might have felt. The episode quoted here began when John stuck his hand in the victim's shirt and she told him to stop.

R: I remember saying words along the effect, "You want me to stop?" And she said, "Yeah." And I said, "Well okay fine, I want you to do something for me." And I told her what I wanted and she said, "No way." Refused. And I said, "Fine, then I'm not going to stop . . . ." Eventually she said, "Okay, I'll do it for a few seconds." And she did. I placed my penis in her mouth . . . for maybe thirty seconds. And she pulled back and said that she was getting ill. I said, "Fine, I don't care."

Conrad admitted that, with his biological daughter, who was eight at the start, he initiated contact early on by verbally ordering her to do things, in particular to take her clothes off. When she tried to resist, he told her that her efforts were fruitless, and he would use whatever physical force was necessary until she acquiesced and started to cooperate. Usually it did not take too much force to get her to submit to his will. There were over three hundred episodes before things ended for this victim when she was thirteen.

R: I'd tell, "Why don't you take your clothes off?" "No, I don't want to do that." Well I'd say, "Come on, take them off!" and I mean "We're going to do this so . . . it's not going to make things any easier on you if you resist." That was the message that was given. And, oh the first months and so, I would have to take her clothes off myself. But then as time went on, I'd get her to take them off. I'd say, "Take your clothes off!" and she would just comply. But like I would (*sighs heavily*), I would take her nightgown off. And then she'd have her panties on. As I'd pull on her panties, she would tug on them to try and prevent me from, telling me no, she didn't want to do that. So I'd say, "Come on, let's do it."

I: So she'd try to hold her panties up?

R: When she'd try to hold her panties up, I kept pulling them down, and then she would just give in. And I'd take her pants off, her panties down. And then after that, after I got her undressed, well then she just basically did what I [asked], that was the end of her resistance.

Sidney used verbal force on his nine-year-old stepdaughter during the six times and three months he said he molested her. He was also formidable physically, described previously as roughly six feet and three hundred or so pounds with tatoos on both arms. In his scheme of reality, he never used physical force.

R: I didn't have to become physical. I'm not sure I would have ever become physical . . . . It never came up so I don't know . . . . It was simply a matter of telling her yes, do this and do that.

I: She didn't want to participate?

R: Most of the time she said no, or "I don't want to." That wasn't constant. I think that was like the first two or three times. Then I think she realized that it wasn't going to get her anywhere and so she simply didn't resist . . . .

I: What kinds of things would you say to her . . . ?

R: Well, it would be almost direct commands. "Undress." I'd show her how I masturbated and say, "Now you do it." . . . There was no subtlety to it. There was very little subterfuge. It was simply direct, "Do this, do that."

I: Did you threaten her in any . . . way?

R: . . . I never threatened her, "If you don't do it, I'm going to do this to you." . . . I mean if she said no and I said, "Yes, do it," she did it. So there never was an instance where I had to say, "Do this or else."

Scott used a low level of force when he engaged in sexual contact with his ten-year-old stepdaughter. Usually he approached the girl while she was asleep, as I reported earlier. Sometimes, however, he acknowledged that she was actually awake, but pretending to be asleep, and that she resisted his advances. He would continue with what he wanted to do anyhow. Scott minimized his efforts, admitting to using physical force, but denying that it reached a serious level.

R: As she was laying there . . . I physically opened her mouth and physically inserted my penis. She kind of allowed that to happen because she didn't know what was going on. After that I could never get her mouth open . . . . But I tried a couple of times . . . . One time she wouldn't and I just said, "the heck with it." Okay? One time she wouldn't and I tried anyway just to like put my penis up in her mouth . . . .

I: Did you force yourself? In that instance?

R: Yes, . . . I forced myself on *her*, yes I did (*very loudly*).

I: Did you physically open her mouth and insert your penis?

R: No, I didn't. I put my penis on her lips but I didn't put it inside her mouth because she . . . just wouldn't let me. And I wasn't going to get . . . brutal; I mean if I could have done it easily I would have, but I wasn't going to be brutal, that wasn't my goal.

I: You never got brutal?

R: I never got brutal.

Taking Over from the Victim

Rather than initiating sexual contact with their victims, some men insisted that their victims actually initiated sexual contact at times with them. They said they carried on with offending after the child got things started, that they simply failed to stop themselves from continuing. Men who reported this pattern were also the ones who typically insisted that their initial interest in offending emerged from sexual cues given off by the younger person, but not always. They sometimes argued, sometimes suggested, that the victim set them up, was sexually aggressive, even pursued them, or used sex to get money. Do these types of accounts reflect distorted perceptions on the part of offenders? Are they a way of blaming the victim? Are the men lying? The accounts speak for themselves. They are reported here because the mission of the research is to let the men tell their version of events. It is up to the reader to decide whether they might be true.

Larry stated that there were several occasions later in his involvement in offending when the victim, his stepdaughter, began acting sexually with him and, then taking over from her, he continued with the situation. In the following example, Larry said he had to get up during the night to attend to one of the children. The victim's age ranged from seven to twelve during the period of contact. Overall he admitted twenty to twenty-five episodes with her.

R: I would have to end up getting up. I'd be pissed off because . . . somebody woke me up . . . . Well, I'd go in the living room and I would catch [my stepdaughter] in there laying on the couch . . . . The first time I didn't . . . know it was [her]. So I walked over and I touched her and I went to shake her and she was naked. And I started to draw back and she grabbed hold of me. And she wanted a kiss. And I asked her, I said, "What are you doing in here?" She says, "Mommy told me I can sleep in here." And I said, "I don't think she told you you can sleep like that." And she said, "Mommy don't know." And so it was kind of like I was being set up.
I: What happened then, in that episode?
R: Well, . . . we ended up by the fireplace. And I was rubbing my penis on her vagina.

Larry acknowledged that most of the sexual episodes were initiated by him. He also admitted being responsible, that he was the adult and should have stopped himself. Larry insisted, however, that in a few instances the victim acted back, the reason being that he groomed or programmed her, inadvertently, to be sexual. He figured she learned that sex was a way of getting his attention, which she seldom otherwise received.

R: I touched her on her . . . bare skin first. Okay. And I guess she just kind of copied what I did. I touched her so she's going to touch me. Okay. And then it got to the place . . . where I didn't have to touch her but she would touch me just for the attention . . . . I'm really getting worried about this because it's sounding like I'm blaming it on her and I don't want it to . . . . Because . . . I started it . . . . You can kind of say I taught her what she needed to know . . . . And I really wasn't thinking that that's what I was doing at that time. But that is in reality what I did.

Randy was one offender who insisted that the victim, his fourteen-year-old stepdaughter, initiated things with him pretty much every time they had sex, and that he carried on with her from there. He reported between twelve and fourteen separate offending episodes over roughly three months. Early on, he claimed that many times the girl came to his bedroom wrapped in a towel and would ask him to rub her back. He described the second time he had sex with her.

R: Same situation. She come in and came to bed with me. And I allowed that to happen. Whether I intentionally allowed it to happen, . . . I don't know . . . . But she came to bed with me . . . ; she came and got under the covers . . . . She asked me if I'd rub her back . . . . I think she turned over and I continued to rub and then that time I actually touched her vagina . . . , the clitoris . . . . I actually tried to stimulate her that time . . . .

I: Did she respond to your touch?

R: Yes . . . . She turned over and put her leg over me and took a hold of my penis.

Over time, he reported, the victim became increasingly aggressive, to the point that she began asking for money; from his standpoint, she used sex to get it. When told that the account seemed unbelievable, he insisted it was true.

R: Somewhere like probably the fifth or sixth time . . . she actually tried to get on top of me . . . ; I just got out of there . . . . The next episode she wanted . . . , she needed thirty dollars for something. She'd ask me for money and then she come lay down with me and all the episodes were basically the same.

I: . . . Did you pay her then?

R: Yes, well, I gave her money . . . ; I wasn't thinking the thirty dollars was for her doing anything . . . .

I: You described the child as taking a lot of initiative here. People throughout the literature write that that is not the way things happen . . . . What do you say to that?

R: I say they're full of shit! . . . That's exactly the way it happened.

Randy claimed that his stepdaughter encouraged more and more and that he obliged her and was just going along with things. He seemed to see himself more as the victim than the perpetrator.

I: Did she ever resist in any way?

R: No. She even asked me to continue.

I: . . . Was that the episode in the truck?

R: Yeah. She got on top of me and wanted me to insert my penis . . . .

I: How did you react when she asked that?

R: Shocked . . . . I knew things had got totally out of hand . . . . I know you told me . . . that clinically a girl doesn't become aggressive . . . . That's bullshit! In this particular circumstance, she was aggressive.

I: She wanted to have intercourse?

R: She even asked me to eat her!

As Randy saw it, he was the instigator of sexual contact to the extent that he carried on with things once they had gotten started. He hinted that maybe he encouraged the right circumstances for contact to occur by agreeing to go places alone with the victim.

R: She kept wanting to drive. I had taught all the kids to drive. And . . . we had stopped to switch sides. And she scooted over next to me and she asked me for the money. And she put her hand down on my leg. And that's when I gave her the thirty dollars . . . . I ain't going to keep saying she initiated it because for the simple reason that I did it . . . . I just carried it on that night from there . . . . I probably set the situation up to where we were out totally in a place and an area that I knew that it could happen.

Bob was yet a third offender who claimed that the victim, one of two boys he molested, aged eight at onset, initiated sexual contact with him. The episode below was the first time he was sexual with the boy, but he added that the boy took the initiative to keep coming back and do more. The situation with this boy and his other victim spanned around three years and over a hundred sexual episodes. He painted the boy as the aggressor, claiming he had asked for money and cigarettes. Bob, of course, might have fabricated this account to mitigate any feelings of shame he felt at having been arrested, convicted, and sentenced to prison.

R: At first he just sat on the bed . . . . Then he laid down on the bed. And then he just got under the covers with me . . . . First we had oral sex . . . ; he performed oral sex on me.

I: [Did you] request for him to do this?

R: No . . . . That was all there was to the first time . . . . The more often he came back, the more involved it became.

I: He came back?

R: To the house. Wherever I was.

I: Did you request that of him?

R: No . . . . There were times when . . . he'd ask me for money.

I: And did you give it?

R: Yes. There were also times when I'd give him cigarettes.

I: He asked for them?

R: Yeah. There . . . was never large sums of money, just a dollar here, a dollar there. I don't know why he asked for the money . . . ; his parents gave him an allowance.

When pressed that others might not believe his account, Bob defended himself. He gave his own account about why the boy might have initiated.

I: . . . What can you say to convince me this account is accurate?

R: The only thing I can say is why would I lie? I have nothing to gain . . . . I voluntarily gave this information . . . .

I: The account makes you look less villainous.

R: I'm not a villain. Society has a picture of me as some evil monster and I'm not . . . .

I: Why do you think this boy initiated sex with you?

R: . . . Because he wanted to. He had been involved with an older male.

Finally, William stated that most of the five or six episodes of intercourse he engaged in with the older of two biological daughters, both of whom he molested, began after the victim initiated sex with him and he then took the situation over. He said that the victim sometimes came into his bedroom, got undressed, and climbed into bed with him without his having said a word. He said that his older daughter "became like a mistress" and that he was culpable as an offender for "allowing it to happen." Reported below is the final episode of offending he was involved in with her when she was fifteen.

R: I was sitting on the couch . . . alone watching TV. I had on a pair of gym shorts and a T-shirt. My oldest daughter came in around eleven that night, laid down on the couch, and had her feet in my lap. She took her feet and began playing with my penis, rubbing it between her feet. This gave me an erection. I ran my hand down her leg . . . and placed my finger inside her vagina. Then I laid down beside her and rubbed her breasts. She was still rubbing my penis, now with her hands. I entered her with my penis from the backside and had intercourse. There was absolutely no communication between us this whole time.

Like the other men who reported this method of engagement, when asked to remark about the truthfulness of his reply, William reaffirmed that it was accurate. When asked if he felt he misinterpreted the actions of the victim, he attached a degree of culpability to her.

I: You described your daughter initiated first contact . . . ; that defies accepted beliefs.
R: Nothing about incest is acceptable so it should.
I: She climbed on the couch with you?
R: She sat on the couch, put her feet in my lap, and began playing with my penis with her feet . . . .
I: How did you know your daughter's actions, . . . that this was sexual in intent?
R: It's obvious when a person takes two feet, wraps it around something, and moves those feet up and down; I'm sure she was fully aware of what she was doing.

Again, there is no way of confirming whether these offense scenarios bear any resemblance to what actually happened, except to talk to the victims and listen to their accounts, which I was unable to do. Offenders, of course, have every reason to lie. Transforming the victim into the instigator, which is what may be occurring here, is a powerful way of protecting and preserving both the inner and outer dimensions of the self. Still, even supposing these depictions unfolded as described, the ultimate responsibility for what happened falls entirely on the shoulders of the adult. These are men who could have stopped themselves but who decided otherwise.

Using Emotional and Verbal Coercion

One of the most common methods of gaining sexual access to victims was verbal and emotional manipulation. There were different ways this occurred: trying to talk the younger person into sex, acting disappointed or upset if the victim refused, easing off on discipline or doing favors in exchange for sex, threatening to molest friends if the victim did not comply, and so forth. The key to this approach was that offenders persuaded and pushed the child to the point that his or her back was against the wall. The outcome was based on a one-sided negotiation that always favored the older and more powerful person. The degree of manipulation varied in intensity, regularity, and explicitness, depending on the degree of resistance.

Glenn admitted to two episodes of sexual contact with his then twelve-year-old adopted daughter, one of three adopted girls, with two months in between. The acts involved stroking his penis on the victim's vagina. In actuality, he approached all three of his adopted daughters for sex by walking in on them and asking if he could hug or touch them routinely when they were getting dressed. All three adamantly refused. When they refused, he would act angry, "sulk," and leave the room. Two of the girls just ignored his reactions. The daughter he offended more seriously felt sorry for him and reengaged him. According to Glenn, she reluctantly agreed to sex because she was trying to make him feel better. He admitted to deliberately playing on the emotions of the girl to make her acquiesce.

R: She came back and she felt sorry that I was down . . . , "Don't feel bad dad. Don't feel down. It's okay." And I can remember her saying that several times through the times I touched her.

I: When she said that, did she then agree at that time to . . .

R: Yeah. "Go ahead if you want to. Just a little." . . . She didn't want me to do it.

I: . . . She resisted and then would say go ahead?

R: Yes . . . . And every time I had something that I did to her, almost every time, it was that she came back. That was my doing, that wasn't hers. I finagled her into that . . . ; I knew that she would . . . . I manipulated her into those [behaviors].

During the first episode of penis-vaginal contact, Glenn spoke to the victim as he touched her, basically talking his way through the situation. His words seemed almost sensitive, intended to soothe the victim and to soothe himself, and to convince her to continue with him. He acknowledged that what he was doing was wrong and asked her again to say no if she did not want him to touch her. He proceeded anyway, overpowering the girl with his words.

R: I put my arms around her, . . . she came over to me . . . , I rubbed my hands up and down her back. I told her . . . , "This isn't proper for me to do, but I hope you don't mind. I just want to touch you."

I: You said it that way?

R: I said it that way. And I said that, "I know it doesn't make it right" and I says, "If you don't want me to, just say so . . . ."

I: When you were going on with it, was she hedging . . . ?

R: Yeah, she was really hedging.

A subsequent episode, the last Glenn initiated, occurred the same way. He asked to touch her, she said no, he sulked and acted sorry, she acquiesced to appease him.

R: It was about a month later, the opportunity came back up and I walked in [the bedroom]. She was laying on the bed and I asked her if I could touch her. And she said, "No dad!" and I said, "Okay." I had a habit, if I didn't get my way, I would sulk. And she knew that and she said, "Oh dad, go ahead, if that makes you feel better." . . . She wanted to please me. She didn't want to see me unhappy whatever the unhappiness was and she said, "Dad, go ahead and touch me."

Sam, as will be described later, engaged his stepson in sexual contact in a variety of ways, including paying him large sums of money, beginning when the boy was eleven. The situation spanned roughly nine years and involved hundreds of sexual episodes. One approach Sam used as the situation with his stepson progressed was verbal and emotional pressuring. He would call his stepson on the phone, give instructions about what he wanted to do with the boy when he came home from work, and then suggest to the boy that going out with his friends was contingent on his doing what Sam wanted. If the boy did not go along with the situation, Sam too said he would pout and become very difficult and irate.

R: I would set up the situation by telephone to home . . . ; to [instruct my stepson] to do this or to do that . . . ; to be with me or to suggest that [my wife] go off somewhere or whatever . . . .

I: . . . You'd actually get on the phone with your stepson and tell him that you wanted to do this . . . and what he should do?

R: Yeah . . . . I'd say, "Now . . . what's your plan for tonight? . . . What are you going to do? You're going to go down to a friend's house? Okay. Well, I'll be home at . . . five thirty and we'll go out to the barn and then . . . you can go." And he'd say, "Okay." . . . If he would not follow through on the plan, I'd be really upset. And he would know I was upset.

I: What would you do?

R: Well . . . I would pout I guess to put it . . . ; I would just . . . show my displeasure by being a bit disagreeable, but never yelled at him. Never . . . punished him by taking something away.

I: You never physically threatened him in any way?

R: No . . . . Nor did I ever say, "Well, now you weren't here when I wanted to see you and now you can't go out." . . . I tried to make him want to do it, want to be molested rather than be forced.

Ian was a third offender who used emotional and verbal coercion to start and complete sexual contact. As reported previously, he admitted having sex with his three biological girls over a ten-year period. With his third and youngest daughter, there were two phases to the activities. In the first phase, when the victim was younger (eleven), he initiated contact through a process of testing and monitoring and received only passive resistance. The second phase, when the victim was around fifteen, came after his wife, the victim's mother, had died. It was at this point that the child started to actively resist his efforts. One thing he then did, to try and sustain the situation, was trade off household chores and tasks in exchange for sexual privileges.

R: I mean this kid . . . , even her mother had trouble with getting her to do things . . . . Brilliant girl, but very lazy . . . . And I used a lot of things that, what her responsibilities were considered to be, and I would trade off sexual favors for doing it. I would complete some of her tasks in return for [sex]. Whether it was coercion, or blackmail, or whatever.

I: . . . Was this through[out] the relationship that you would do these things?

R: Yeah, on and off, but mostly towards the end there, because the responsibility of the house came down to the two of us.

The culmination of his offending involved engaging the victim by trying to talk her into having sex with him. Ian had taken his youngest daughter on a vacation to a condo he rented. The second night there he asked his daughter to take a shower with him and she refused. The night after that, he took her out to dinner at an expensive restaurant. During dinner he offered her a deal if she agreed to have sex. There was deliberate and explicit emotional blackmail.

R: I . . . told her that . . . , "If you go along with me this one last time," that "I'll never touch you again. I'll leave you alone." And that was the deal.

I: . . . How did she respond when you told her that?

R: Whewwwwwww, like she had a deal, like "Okay, great." It wasn't that she was looking forward to it. It was like she wanted to get it over with. And so . . . we got cleaned up from dinner . . . . We went back and probably watched a little TV . . . . And then it was time to go to bed . . . . And when it came time to take our clothes off, . . . she went to her room like she would normally do, and I said, "Haven't you forgotten something?" I guess like she was trying to avoid it . . . . I then led her back to my room . . . and disrobed and said, "You're sleeping here tonight, remember?" And she says, "Oh, whatever, I'd thought you forgot." Obviously I wouldn't forget it . . . . We just got into bed naked together and we just cuddled all night long. And she, much to my surprise, enjoyed being masturbated.

Harry molested seven children—his girlfriend's two daughters, four girls from around his neighborhood, and his girlfriend's niece. One girl, the oldest of his partner's two children, aged seven at onset, was the primary victim. He admitted fondling her genitals eight times over a one-year period. After four or five sexual episodes where he approached the victim in other ways, he said the girl began to vigorously resist his advances. Still wanting to continue, he molested the six other children involved, each one time, to try to get the first victim to acquiesce to his requests. Again, the tactic was emotional blackmail.

R: Her sister was asleep next to her. They slept in the same bed . . . , the three-year-old. And I said, "Well she loves me," and I scooted over there, and she was asleep, and I touched her . . . . The first time that didn't work. It didn't change her mind. She still didn't want me to touch her. And the next time was when she had these friends stay all night. She was having . . . a slumber party. I did that then and that night it did work.
I: . . . So you were touching the young[er] child as a way to try to get her [the primary victim] to respond to you?
R: To agree. To let me do that. To fondle her. And that also was the case with the other children and that night she did agree to it . . . . She didn't want to, but she did that because I touched the other children, and as soon as I touched her she got angry with me for kind of forcing her into that situation . . . .
I: Did you think you had forced her into it?
R: Yeah, I knew I did. I was trying to manipulate her into doing that . . . , "If you don't love me, she does," it was kind of that kind of thing.

Masking Sex in a Play/Game Context

Still another strategy of approaching and engaging victims involved masking or camouflaging sexual advances in the context of a fabricated game or play scenario. Some offenders started by tickling or wrestling extensively with the younger person and then introduced sexual behavior into what they were doing. As with other tactics, the victims involved were allegedly unaware of the real purpose of the exchange. The approach differed from seducing because it was more surreptitious—playing was enacted as a diversion. A few men, too, instigated more elaborate sexual games whose goals, which were sexual in nature, were specified or described in advance. This typically involved a dare of some sort to a particular victim to try something, to play along with what the offender wanted to do. Use of a game or play strategy, in general, allowed offenders to instigate sex in an apparently less threatening and nonforceful way, in a manner that to their victims probably appeared to involve an element of fun. And, because this tactic was employed more often with younger victims, the game most likely was not interpreted as specifically sexual in nature.

Tickling and wrestling were most common with victims who were younger than twelve. Kevin played a tickling game with his biological daughter during which he began to fondle her vagina and she seemed to copy his behavior and fondle him. The victim was six at onset, and there were four or five episodes of sexual contact over six months that occurred the same way each time.

R: I was tickling her. We were playing on the floor . . . . I'd tickle her on her stomach and then she'd tickle me on my stomach. I tickled her on her legs. She tickled me on my leg. And then I went down underneath her underwear a little bit and tickled her just north of her vagina, so to speak. And she tickled me.
I: . . . In the same area she'd tickle you?
R: Uh huh [yes].
I: And then you . . . what, you just kept going then?
R: Uh huh [yes] . . . I kept going and . . . at that time I thought she liked it.

Every time Phil offended he did it by tickling the victim too. He began when the victim was two, tickling her vagina while changing her diaper. As the victim grew older, genital tickling became a routine game. The mood to Phil always seemed to be one of playful fun. He ended up touching her fifty to sixty times over the next four years.

R: I would ask her if she wanted me to tickle her on her genitals, and a lot of times I would get a yes response.

I: And this would be where?

R: Either in her room or in the bathroom . . . . And there's been a couple times when she has asked me, too.

I: And what would she ask?

R: She would ask me to tickle her wee-wee.

I: . . . Could you characterize the situation?

R: . . . I'd ask her if I could tickle her. And it'd be after I put her to bed. And then I would reach my hand down and start touching her . . . around her legs and the insides of her thighs. And then I would reach in and fondle her on her genitals.

With Scott, tickling was a fourth method of offending, illustrating the wide-ranging tactics sometimes used by offenders who were determined to do what they wanted. He had tried to molest one stepdaughter by catching her by surprise. He had successfully molested his second stepdaughter through a method of sneaking and spying and then using explicit force. Later in his offending, after a lengthy period of nonoffending, and after concluding that the latter victim was really awake when he touched her, he turned to tickling as a front and lead-in to fondling. The victim was around eleven at the time.

R: She'd be in bed, she went to bed earlier than her older sister, and while I was tucking the boys in, I'd stop in and joke around with her a little bit. And the joking led to tickling and from tickling it led to touching her vagina . . . . She was fully awake and actually seemed to enjoy it . . . . We'd be laughing and giggling and like well, for example, . . . I would like tickle her between her legs and work my way up to her vagina. There were times when she was very moist, which led me to believe she was excited by it.

Keith touched the breasts of his niece, aged eleven at onset, while wrestling with her and her father, his brother. He claimed that he used to wrestle with his brother growing up, have "free-for-alls" with his father and six other siblings. It was in this context that the offending occurred. He said that his hand accidentally slipped under the shirt his niece was wearing and grabbed onto her breast. His hand seemed to have a mind of its own. This offender admitted to only one sexual episode. I suspect there were many more, given his use of the term "a lot" in describing the loose-fitting clothes his niece wore. In other words, he indicates a great deal of opportunity. Why this choice of words if there was only one episode?

R: We used to wrestle around a lot. Me and her dad. And then she'd get in on it. And that's when everything happened . . . . The only thing I ever done was touch her breast . . . . We'd be wrestling . . . around on the floor . . . .
I: You and the child and the father? All of you?
R: Yeah. Like a big free-for-all . . . . And [my] niece, a lot of times she'd have on like a loose-fitting top.
I: And what would happen? What would you do?
R: Well unavoidably . . . , that's when I got hold of her breast when she got in that free-for-all with that loose top on . . . . My hand got up under her . . . blouse and touched her breast.

The games the men played were sometimes much more elaborate, and much more straightforward, than tickling and wrestling. Ian tried to initiate sexual contact with his youngest daughter by, among other means, asking her to play strip poker. She was fifteen at the time. This tactic came toward the end of the six plus years he spent molesting this particular victim. He too was another offender who continually invented new tactics such as this to keep things going.

R: I was stupid enough to suggest playing a game of strip poker. I had a deck of cards . . . . And she had not been very accepting of any of my initiations or attempts for some time. And so she was very much in favor of it. I was shocked. I was surprised. She jumped at it. I thought it was terrific. "Well okay." And we participated in that. And I don't [think] we ever did anything like that before. And I was aroused by that. She's fully developed, a beautiful body, which was readily apparent.

With his oldest daughter, Ian played a game that involved going into a darkened room together and trying to find each other by touching. During the game, he fondled her breasts. In this instance the game was deliberately played for the purpose of sex. The girl involved was eleven. He claimed only ten episodes with this daughter.

R: There was one time in the bathroom she got aroused. And we were in the dark. We used to play these games where you could find each other in the dark somewhere and crawl around and so forth. And it started when the kids were real little. And we had this large bathroom that had no windows to it and you closed the door and it was totally dark in there. And one time we played that game after all this started and I remember caressing her on the breasts and she did like that.

Another offender, Kelly, turned to the use of whipped cream to engage his victim. He would put whipped cream on his penis and then have the four-year-old girl who was involved perform oral sex. The tactic seemed to be a type of game, something the offender believed was fun for the victim. There were seventy-five episodes in just three months involving the same or similar tactics.

R: Well, what I would do is we had a bowl of [whipped cream] in the refrigerator. And I['d] go, "Well, I'm gonna put this on here." And she goes . . . , "I like that."
I: I take it you took your clothes off?
R: Yeah . . . . She goes, "Put some more on." And basically that's how it happened . . . . And then she would, I don't know how to say it, [a] blow job, I suppose you would say.
I: . . . Did you ask her to do that?
R: Sometimes I did; sometimes I didn't. One time I was sitting in there [the kitchen] and her mom was there and she came and says, "I've got the [whipped cream] daddy!" I went, "Oh boy!" you know. And she didn't catch it and I said, "That's nice."
I: . . . How did the child respond to the sexual touch?
R: It was like giggles and laughs . . . . Obviously she wanted me to keep doing it. That's the way I took it.

One offender, in particular, designed a variety of sexual games that involved two or more children at a time. Ken played sexual games with his biological daughter, his stepdaughter, and six of their neighborhood girlfriends, actively offending for roughly eleven years, when all were between the ages of nine and thirteen. This offender admitted a minimum of a hundred episodes, but said the number was impossible to guess. All the games he played involved an element of exhibitionism. There was also a degree of kinkiness involved. In the next two examples below, Ken refers to behavior involving his biological daughter.

R: What I would do . . . was take a nap, where I would pretend to be asleep, and then prior to having taken a nap, I would impress upon [my daughter] [who was with] a girlfriend she had who would come over [what we were going to do]. I would be in bed with a blanket over me with no clothes on . . . . [The girls then pulled the blanket off, and while lying on the bed nude] . . . , they would cover me with shaving cream. On one occasion they even shaved my pubic hair off. Another friend of [my daughter] painted my feet purple . . . . That type of activity went on for a year and a half.

Routinely there was an element of risk as well. The games commonly entailed going outside in the nude. To get the children to play the games, Ken typically couched them as dares. This was sometimes coupled with promised rewards of one sort or another.

R: I challenged them to get me to a churchyard across the street and back without any clothes. [During the activity I was] pretending I was asleep. [As an incentive], I offered them a dollar. It was eleven or twelve at night. [When they got me over there], I put my initials on the goalpost. They got the biggest kick out of it, laughing and having a ball. So that was the basic type of activity between the kids and I . . . . [On another occasion] they tied me to a tree, to a post in the snow, then began throwing snowballs at me. They [thought, what] a great old time. Then I got away and went back into the house.

Whatever the game Ken instigated, there was almost always an element of coercion involved. He used his two daughters to create setups or planned meetings for the other children who came to his house. Ken would tell either his biological daughter or his stepdaughter what they were supposed to do when they came home from school that day and had a friend with them. He gave an example of a game he used to play that involved pulling off his own daughter's pants.

R: The things that took place were not of the kids' origin. They were things I would think of and pass on to my daughter, who would then carry out the activity with the other child. There was no physical force used, but . . . there was parental coercion . . . . I strongly urged her to participate . . . . I would tell [my daughter] when we got to wrestling, I wanted her to pull down my pants. Then she would. I'd pull them back up, she'd pull them down again, I'd pull them up, she'd pull them down, then maybe the other kids would too.

Ken insisted that "sex" was not a big part of the activities that occurred, but he did admit that he added on sexual behaviors to the play scenarios he constructed, thus introducing a more serious level of contact, but in what to him was a less threatening manner. He did this primarily with his stepdaughter and her friends.

R: Oral contact occurred relatively infrequently, but it did occur with the kids. Similarly, with the fondling, that occurred occasionally . . . . It was my perception that the kids liked to cuddle without clothes on. I don't recall ever asking them to take their clothes off. It seemed to be just a part of the games we were playing. But the fondling aspects were two-way in that the kids would touch me and I'd touch them. There were occasions when I performed oral sex on them . . . . Also at night, on weekends, when my wife was away, the kids would sleep with me, and all of us would be without clothes on . . . . The kids would not freely fondle . . . . So occasionally I would put their hand on my groin.

Turning the Victim Out

The most methodical and deliberate tactic of initiating sexual contact involved a process of turning the victim out by introducing the idea of sex and actual sexual behavior in stages, slowly building toward more serious levels of genital sexual contact. While there was a process to every tactic that was used, in this approach, it was much more extensive and premeditated, spanning months or years. The turning-out process began with offenders displaying themselves in the nude. This was followed typically by their fondling the targeted victim or having the victim fondle them. Then there was a period of verbal praise and rationalizing that sex was okay. Sometimes there was a stage at which pornography was introduced. Later the offender asked the victim to perform more serious sexual acts such as fellatio, at their suggestion, instruction, or assistance. Characteristic of this method of offending was that eventually the men began to offer rewards such as money, cigarettes, or greater social freedom in exchange for sex. Over time, the child became groomed or programmed to engage in sex more or less automatically, if requested, without force or resistance.

Sam admitted, as mentioned previously, to hundreds of episodes of fondling and oral sex with his stepson from the time the boy was eleven and continuing until he was around twenty. In the first episode, Sam said he grabbed and fondled the victim in the bathroom, using the tactic of catching the victim by surprise, after the boy had finished taking a bath. It was at this point that Sam backed off and began a more deliberate strategy of initiating sex. The first stage involved displaying himself nude in front of the child.

R: I would arrange to start being with him . . . in the bathroom and eventually I began to take showers with him [in there] and to have him see me nude. And I did it . . . in a very methodical, [in] well planned out situations, so that there was never any threat, never any pushing, as I would say, on my part . . . . [I] tried to make it seem as a very natural thing and eventually I'd have him see me with . . . an erection.

In the second stage the offender asked the boy to fondle him. The sex was one-way.

R: Then . . . I asked him if he wanted to touch me and he did. I don't know whether he "wanted to," but he did. And again . . . it was not a rush situation . . . . In fact . . . , I would say it was . . . several months after a dozen or more contacts before we touched each other at the same time.

In the third stage, after a period of initial touching, Sam took the role of a teacher and explained sex to his stepson. He mentioned trying to make the boy believe he was helping him with women.

R: Then I took the tack of explaining sex to him . . . ; I was telling him why this was okay . . . . I was teaching him about sex and how to have good sex and what he should know about women. And trying to make him think that what I was doing was helping him.

The next stage involved looking at pornographic pictures with the victim and beginning to praise him about his physical prowess and appearance.

R: It eventually got to where we would look at pictures and that sort of thing . . . . I would then lavish praise upon him about his body development . . . . I'd say how good he looked, . . . he was muscular, big penis. That he was going to be very attractive to women . . . ; and . . . that I was helping him to do that.

After approximately a year, the fifth stage evolved, at which masturbation of the victim became a routine occurrence.

R: It became just so commonplace, . . . the masturbation was. We'd just say, "Well, you want to do it now?" That type of thing . . . . We'd go either in the basement or out to the barn. Or I would help him study and we'd go into his room.

Eventually, in the sixth stage, the offender began to push the victim to perform oral sex on him, to get the victim to do something back.

R: He always ejaculated first, and then . . . it was sort of . . . , "Well, I'm at this point. Now you've got to do . . . ." I don't know that he was . . . all that willing if I look back . . . ; it was always sort of . . . a forced situation. "Well now you owe me. You owe me because I did this pleasure for you." Which of course it was my pleasure.

This was followed by a seventh stage, in this case, in which money and gifts were offered in exchange for sex. The amount of money that changed hands added up to roughly six hundred dollars a month before the situation ended.

R: As he got older . . . I literally made him into a prostitute. Because . . . I was paying him money.
I: How much money are we talking?
R: Oh, about fifty dollars at a time . . . ; I always gave it to him after we had a sexual contact. And we'd do it three times a week. That would be $150. I had plenty of money so it wasn't . . . a problem. I bought him a truck, a car, and a motorbike.

Looking back, Sam stated that he felt he had programmed and conditioned his stepson to engage in sex with him whenever he wanted, to the point of being brainwashed.

R: I trained him like a dog . . . . (*sighs*) . . . You train a dog by giving him food by rewarding him for some little trick that they do. That's just the way I felt. I really just . . . used him and abused him; . . . I was really bending his mind. Training him. Brainwashing him.

Corey also used the tactic of turning out. This offender molested his three biological children (two daughters and a son) between fifty and a hundred times off and on over five years. His two daughters were ten and thirteen, his son nine, when things began. In the first stage in his offending, he walked naked around the house regularly.

R: I . . . started running around the house when their mother wasn't home in the nude all the time . . . . And I asked them, I said, did it bother them? They said no. I said, "Great. All right." . . . I felt . . . there was nothing wrong with nudity. There's nothing to be ashamed [of] about your body.

That carried over to the second stage, when he began wrestling with his daughters while he was nude and positioning himself so they would touch his penis in such a way as to think it was accidental.

R: As it went along . . . , I would start wrestling with them. The two girls. And I would feel their breasts, play with their vaginas, on the outside of their clothes . . . ; and accidentally have them touch me on the penis . . . . That's in the mind, okay . . . . (*sighs*) . . . I would work myself around where . . . their hand would hit it, [it would] rub against their arm.

In the third stage of his offending sequence he undressed his oldest daughter, thirteen at onset, in his bedroom alone. He began fondling at this stage.

R: I took my oldest in the bedroom and at the time I was already nude and I would have her undress.
I: What would you say to her?
R: I just told her I wanted to see what she looked like, how she was growing. And I would feel her breasts and touch the outside of her vagina and have her . . . rub my penis. Then I'd have her dress and leave; then I would go in the bathroom and masturbate.

Then came yet a fourth stage of showering with his two daughters. He added on the second daughter in this stage, and the victims began to fondle him. He would take the victim's hand to get things started.

R: From there it went to the girls taking a shower; I would go in and take a shower with them . . . . It started out, "I'm going to wash your back, wash your hair." Start washing them, rub them all over, . . . and I would always have an erection and I would press my penis in their back . . . . And I'd take their hand and have them masturbate me . . . . Sometimes . . . I'd masturbate while they were in there where they didn't see. I had my back to them.

Eventually Corey included his son, age nine, in sexual contact, because, as he put it, "I was trying to keep him in with the program." He kept his activities with his son separate from his offenses with the daughters. There was initially nudity, then fondling, and the use of nude magazines.

R: I would have him, when the girls weren't around, I would have him undress and run around in the house in the nude. I would play with his penis, and that would be about the size of it . . . . I'd show him all my Penthouse and Playboy books. I'd go skinny-dipping; we had a pool.

As he saw it, Corey never explicitly used money or other rewards in exchange for sexual favors. What he did was relinquish practically all restrictions on places the children could go, which was very out of character for him, since he was a former military drill Sergeant. He figured that this was, in part, a way to keep them from telling their mother about what he was doing. The implicit message, however, was one of sex for freedom. In addition, he admitted sending the message over and over to the children that what he was doing was good for them: "I kept telling them it was for their education." And in summing up his method of offending, he acknowledged that there was a process involved, using nudity as an introduction to build to more serious behaviors, trying to reach the point at which the victims performed sexual acts back.

I: How did you go from nudity was okay to sex was okay?
R: I guess it [was] just a process . . . ; I was using that as a stepping-stone, running around the house nude. I'd start fondling them and then they'd start fondling me.

Conclusion

Offenders used a variety of tactics to engage their victims in sexual contact. The most common tactics included seducing and testing, which involved slowly introducing sex by adding it on in instances of otherwise routine affectionate contact; masking sex in the context of play or game situations that were surreptitiously initiated by the offender; using verbal and emotional coercion to pressure the victim into sexual compliance; or taking over from the victim when, offenders alleged, the other person approached and engaged them in sexual contact and then they took control of the situation from there. Less common strategies for initiating sexual contact consisted of catching the victim by surprise, which involved grabbing at victims at times when they were busy with something else; sneaking and spying on children in the middle of the night while they were allegedly asleep; commanding or physically forcing a victim to submit or acquiesce to sexual advances with no pretense; or turning the victim out in stages that involved displays of nudity, use of pornography, praise about physical appearance, and monetary or social rewards to try and groom the younger person to want to be sexual back. Most offenders used multiple methods of approaching and engaging their victims. Whatever the strategy of engagement utilized, the offenders often monitored the reactions of their victims and adjusted their approach accordingly. They usually locked into those tactics that were successful in gaining the victim's compliance, and tried new tactics if their approach was unsuccessful. Some offenders strung together a range of tactics the longer their offending careers continued.

SIX

Snowballing from One Act to Many

It is generally accepted in the literature on sexual abuse that men who molest children do not stop their behavior after one sexual episode unless they are caught. When offenders know their victims, especially if they happen to be parents, relatives, or family friends, the same victims often are molested multiple times.[1] This pattern of repetitive victimization of the same person or persons is the one dimension that makes sexual abuse in or around the family unique compared to most other types of crime. So far, I have attempted to explain how men initially become offenders. Equally important is understanding how they become repetitive offenders. Focusing on this question, I asked the men I interviewed what they remembered thinking and feeling about their behavior, themselves, and the children they molested from one sexual episode to the next. What goes through someone's mind while they are molesting a child? Do offenders feel good, bad, guilty, or indifferent afterwards? What range of emotions follow? How do offenders view their behavior morally? What kinds of rationalizations do they assemble about their victims? How do they cope with strong emotions if they have them? Finally, what exactly triggers the thought or desire to do the same thing again?

More technically, my concern at this point is with the subjective reality of involvement in regular offending. There are two related meanings to what I describe here as subjective reality. In one respect, I explore what can be referred to as the "moral career" of offenders. The moral career has been defined by Erving Goffman as "the regular sequence of changes . . . in the person's self and in his framework of imagery for judging himself and others."[2] Thus my focus is on the construction of self offenders formulate, or how they view themselves, in light of the morally condemned nature of their actions. In a similar direction, I also look at the specific definitions and interpretations offenders attach to the offending experience, and how the desire and motivation to offend again emerge over time. I draw a parallel to what Howard Becker has stated about regular marijuana use, "instead of deviant motives leading to the deviant behavior, it is the other way around; the deviant behavior in time produces the deviant motivation."[3] In short, I analyze the internal stages of the offending career that unfold once sexual contact with a victim has been initiated.

Feeling Good at First

It goes without saying that people tend to do things again if they define what they do as pleasureful. Participation in banned behavior is no exception. Thus, it could be said that continued involvement in morally condemned conduct depends in part on whether the person who engages in it is "turned on" rather than "turned off" by the experience, if they see what they do as pleasureful in some way.[4] When asked what the experience of offending was like as it was occurring, what offenders were thinking while they were interacting with their victims, nearly all the men in this study said they remembered "feeling good" at first.[5] They routinely mentioned that sexual contact involved the feeling of a *quick high*, a sudden intense rush or release, on a variety of emotional and personal levels.

Sex crimes have long been defined as acts of violence, exploitation, and domination, not crimes of sex.[6] Contrary to this view, many men said that they enjoyed the act of offending on a sexual level. Frequently they described liking the sensation of touching their victims and the gratification of reaching orgasm. Three men, among others, Conrad, Sam, and Tom, reported this reality.

R: The pleasure came from the sensation of touching, of feeling her flesh against me, my flesh. The contact of our genitals. The intercourse itself. The ejaculation. All of those sensations were pleasureful. And they had a very strong . . . feel good message.

R: I like the contact with the male body . . . . I like to feel a muscular body. It wasn't just grasping a penis.

R: At times it would be intensely sexually stimulating . . . . I mean . . . she was nude and I would start caressing her and the friction against my jeans, that alone triggered an orgasm . . . . There's something about that experience that makes all prior sex seem like an empty ritual, when it's your [step]daughter.

Other men did not so much emphasize the experience of orgasm or tactile sensations; rather they talked about feelings of sexual excitement and sexual arousal in general. They were turned on sexually because they were doing something different for a change, it was a new experience, or simply because they were having sex, period. Scott and Leon admitted they had feelings like these.

R: In the early phase it was something different, something to raise the excitation, or the . . . sexual arousalness . . . . It was . . . somebody else. Somebody else's hand was touching me . . . . I was getting some interaction even though it wasn't a willing interaction. There was something else touching my penis that was making me more excited than myself.

R: It was very exciting . . . . It was a regular sexual feeling . . . . I was erect and I wanted to touch her and feel her like you would anybody, or any woman, or if that's your fancy. I felt the same as I would have [with] any woman, especially in the first several times when it's very, very exciting. When it's all new. It was exactly like that.

For some men it was difficult to disentangle the sexual dimension of the act from the thrill they experienced. The term "thrill" has been defined as the excitement a person experiences getting away with something which could have serious consequences if caught.[7] Leon and John recalled the quick charge they felt knowing they were doing something that could have cost them a lot.

R: It was very exiting to me. It's like as if you're doing something that you're really not supposed to but you'll never get caught at . . . . I remember once stealing a hubcap when I was a kid; . . . that was very exciting, the heart was pounding and exhilarating. And it was like that; it was something wild and exciting that you're not supposed to do but that you're getting by with. And I thought, well, I was a lot smarter than she was and there was no way that I could get caught.

R: It was basically I was doing something that I . . . knew was wrong . . . . There was the excitement in doing something that I shouldn't have been doing . . . . The excitement was mostly just in doing something that most people wouldn't do.

While one type of thrill revolved around the situation of risk and getting away with the act, a second type involved the thrill of discovering something unknown. Some men described feeling euphoria or an overwhelming exhilaration when they saw and touched their victims. Initially interested by profound curiosity about the biological development of a particular child, these men felt they were exploring uncharted territory and had "traveled where no human being had gone before."[8] Phil fondled his two-year-old biological daughter to see whether she was sexually responsive. He recalled being overcome with euphoria. Steve inspected the genitals of his stepdaughter at night with a flashlight. He seemed to relive his thrill describing how he felt in the interview.

R: A wave of emotions came over me . . . ; arousal and . . . my heartbeat. I don't know how to explain it. It was like . . . a wave of anxiety and emotions.
I: . . . Okay, this wave of emotions. Can you clarify it any more?
R: Yeah, it was like a pressure sensation, or . . . like a rush . . . internally inside, I guess as some people would say like a high.
I: Did you experience that as pleasureful or unpleasureful?
R: I don't know. It was a unique experience. I had never been with somebody [who] was [so] different from me.

R: I can remember there being a very pounding heartbeat. Just like in anticipation of something . . . . I was so fascinated, so fixed on that. It was like it was a sex object. I didn't see her face. It's like this little thing here is her vagina, that's what I was fixed on! How it looked, what it looked like . . . ! So it was an object of fixation . . . . As it progressed, she was starting to get pubic hair. Of course that was fascinating too! Geez, I remember that, *aw geez!* (*very loudly*) . . . What I was seeing was her sexual organ and what that particular behavior would get me, a quick high.

Child molesting has been described clinically as the sexual expression of nonsexual needs.[9] In contrast with this view, many of the men in this research stated that they received sexual gratification from what they did. However, other nonsexual factors were also reported as part of the high from offending. Some men, in particular, said that as they were molesting their victims, they felt they were escaping from the pressures and strains of the larger world. The sexual contact allowed them a brief period to forget their problems. For Glenn, Bob, and Scott, having sex with a child was a way of taking a time-out from their lives, a respite, if only for a moment. Ironically, such extreme boundary-violating behavior is actually relaxing for some people.

R: It just was relaxing. I didn't have to have an orgasm in order to make me relaxed. Holding on to her and feeling her, her skin was soft . . . .

I: What else do you remember feeling about that situation?

R: . . . I wasn't worried about work. I wasn't worried about [things]; I was relaxed. Usually, I'm so tensed up . . . . I felt, just relaxed. I felt that I was at ease.

R: It relieved tension, but . . . only at the moment . . . . The everyday stress of working, just putting up with life in general.

R: It gave me the strength in a way emotionally to deal with the garbage that my wife and I were going through. I mean it was like . . . an escape from reality . . . . It was just a fantasy world that was *real* all of a sudden. There was somebody touching me in my fantasies. My fantasies were not just fantasies anymore, they were actions . . . . As life got more miserable the drives got stronger . . . . To me I feel like *it* was my escape from all the other junk that was going on. It was my way of saying, "I can't deal with that. I don't want to deal with that. I'll choose this."

A few men, not most, said they enjoyed sex with the children they molested because the experience made them feel suddenly young again. They seemed to live vicariously through their victims, trying to relive a part of their past that had at one time been exciting, or that they felt they never had. Steve said he remembered thinking he was in high school again. Sam too remembered drifting back twenty-five years; he said that during sex with his stepson, he was symbolically reliving his lost youth.

R: I felt like a boy in a man's body . . . . I had the education and the intellect, but from a maturity standpoint, I was a boy in a man's body. Still being high schoolish . . . . I do recall at the time, . . . the first time I actually touched her, I felt like I was back as a boy again.

R: I found that I was living the life that I didn't have as a teenager through him . . . . I put myself to be on [my stepson's] age level . . . ; that's all. I was living out my childhood that I didn't have . . . ; I would just put myself into his life. At his age.

Some men seemed to enjoy, if only for a brief time, the feeling of power, control, or absolute domination they exerted over their victims while molesting them.[10] They described feeling that they were not respected and that they had little or no control in other areas of their lives, especially the domestic realm. There was a harsh, instrumental quality to the way men in this group interpreted their acts—they report-ed feeling good from manipulating, commanding, humiliating, exacting obedience out of someone who was much less powerful. John admitted that he got pleasure from exerting total sexual control over his niece. He stated, "I was actually getting satisfaction in the humiliation I was causing her." Sam, active in politics, drew a parallel between sex with his stepson and the Nixon presidency. He said he felt omnipotent.

R: I knew that if I wanted her to go upstairs and take her clothes off, she'd go upstairs and take her clothes off . . . . You feel superior when you are abus-ing someone else . . . . It's strange but, it's not so much superior as in con-trol . . . . With [my niece] I knew I was absolutely in control. I knew she was-n't going to give me a hard time or object or anything.

R: I likened it in one sense to the way Nixon's presidency went to pot . . . . At the time you just think anything's possible. You can do anything you want. You're in power. You're in control. Nothing can stop you. If you want to do it, you do it. And yeah, that's the way I feel that I was.

A more elaborate account of feelings of power and control was pro-vided by Conrad. He was married to a woman who often defied his authority. He admitted wanting to be "king of the throne" around the home, but that his wife had a different attitude. When he had sex with his biological daughter, he remembered being in control, which he seemed to like a great deal.

R: Another thing I got out of it, she would cooperate with me. Even if she did-n't want to, she'd still do it. And I felt this lack of cooperation, or sensed it . . . from my wife: "Well, I just do what I want. And if I don't want to do it, well that's just tough toenails."
I: That was your wife's attitude?
R: . . . Yeah. And it wasn't just with sex, but life in general and with the way

things happened in our marriage . . . .

I: But with the child, you're describing the child as?

R: The child was submissive.

Conrad was a brutal physical disciplinarian when his daughter refused to do what he felt were legitimate requests to fulfill everyday tasks and responsibilities. He described how she was more controllable when he demanded sex.

R: That child would defy me as far as a reasonable request like do the dishes or clean up your room . . . . I'd beat her . . . , whip her butt . . . , with a belt. I'd use a broom . . . . It even got to the point towards the end, I'd use broomsticks or coat hangers. And when I give her beatings like that for not doing legitimate parental requests, . . . she would defy me on those things. But when it come to cooperating with me on having sex with me, I mean she'd tell me, yeah, she didn't want to do it, but she would go ahead and do it.

For still other men, sexual contact seemed to generate feelings of emotional connectedness. Sex was an experience only two people shared, and once it occurred, was something that bonded the two together forever, because it was their experience alone. These men recalled feeling especially close as a result of sex and feeling a surge of love for the victim during sexual contact or immediately afterwards. Leon, Bob, and Harry described their molesting as a secretive bonding experience.

R: I felt very close to her when I was touching her vagina . . . . Almost like as if she was a woman or a wife or a girlfriend . . . . I felt very affectionate towards her during those times . . . .

I: Did you feel closer than before this stuff began?

R: Yes, yes, it was almost like as if two people witnessed a murder and that was their little thing, and they kept that with them forever . . . . This was our . . . thing.

R: It was like sharing an intimacy with someone closer than a friend. It was like being able to tell someone something and not fearing that they would tell someone else.

R: In my mind at the time it was a mutual thing and like a secret that we had, that we shared, that no one else had. And it made us closer.

Some men interpreted the sexual act as a demonstration of love. The fact that the child involved had been sexual with them meant that that child loved and accepted them, in whatever form, good or bad. The sexual act itself seemed to have emotional healing properties for the men. They mentioned feeling appreciated as a consequence. William and Tom are two examples.

R: I felt loved by her and wanted by her . . . ; in a way that I wanted to be loved by my wife.

I: How do you know she loved you that way . . . ?

R: . . . The same way you know if your wife loves you if she doesn't explicitly tell you . . . . It was a feeling, not a factual knowledge . . . . It felt good because it gave me an emotional feeling of being needed, of being desired and appreciated sexually.

R: This is going to sound like double-talk . . . ; the motive wasn't sexual. It's like the sexual behavior, . . . I almost felt like a doctor or something. I was performing some kind of ritual that would make her feel better and make me feel better . . . . Her doing this meant she loved me. I could really believe that for some reason . . . . But that was the connection. And continuing with the behavior meant that she continued to love me and so . . . it was sort of like I was being hooked.

With other men, especially those who reported sexual problems as a turning point in their lives prior to offending, having sex with a child felt safer, less threatening, than sex they had experienced with adults. They mentioned discovering that the younger person or younger persons they molested did not have any expectations about sex—what was good or what was bad—easing any feelings of performance anxiety.[11] Tom molested his stepdaughter and Bob had sex with two boys. Both reported feeling pressure to perform sexually with their spouses and at the same time a loss of sexual interest in them.

R: I felt threatened by her before the incest started. I didn't feel threatened by her afterwards. She felt safe for me. I can look at [my] relationship with my wife and sex with her was repugnant to me . . . . It was like me horny you fuck me kind of thing . . . . I always felt when I was with a woman . . . my whole self-worth was on the line.

R: I didn't have to reach any kind of set standard with them . . . . Like if you have sex with a woman you just assume she wants and expects as much out of it as you get out of it . . . . I didn't have to prove anything to them.

A third example was George, who had been experiencing impotency with his wife during sex. When he had sex with his stepdaughter, he remembered becoming excited on a sexual level, but more than that, he indicated feeling relieved that he was still a real man. Sex with the victim felt good to him at the time because it seemed to solve his sexual problems.

R: I got real excited and had an erection . . . . It made me feel good . . . , like . . . I'm still alive . . . . Still a man . . . . She made me feel like a man again, feel younger. At that time my wife didn't excite me anymore.

Finally, for those who targeted a victim out of anger, or who offended while angry in general, sexual contact was a way of letting off steam, venting hostility and frustration. Such offenders described feeling better about things, less angry, and more levelheaded again when they were finished, until of course the same problem that got them angry the last time arose. Both Larry and John said that offending was a way for them to release the anger they felt toward their spouses.

R: It was kind of like a get even thing . . . . And it was like the more I drank the angrier I got . . . . I would molest my daughter. And then I would feel better about the anger that I had built up.

R: I remember after I achieved orgasm by masturbating it was like releasing the anger. I didn't feel angry anymore.

Flooding with Guilt

Often the respondents reported feelings of guilt, shame, and wrongdoing after sexual contact with a victim. There was an intense period of deviant "self-labeling."[12] Most of the men had a sense that they probably should not be doing what they were doing. For the most part, however, moral feelings did not strongly enter into the picture until the act itself was actually in progress, but typically within the first few minutes after its completion. It was generally during and/or afterwards that the men would experience a range of emotions. The offenders commonly described having felt blown away, being in wonderment about themselves, ruminating over and over about how they could have done such a thing, and thinking intently about what might happen if they got caught.

More generally, reasoning was a consequence much more so than it was a precursor to the offenses. If the men had evaluated the morality of their behaviors more strongly before rather than after they acted, many might not have done what they did at all. This is one of the most important findings of the research conducted here. It runs squarely against what is known as the "deterrence" model of criminal behavior, which emphasizes that people rationally evaluate whether or not they want to engage in a course of conduct in the moments before they act.[13] Molesters do evaluate and consider courses of action, but the crux of this activity comes afterwards, especially early on in their involvement. Usually there was a period of days or weeks before another episode, which diffused the effects of whatever moral evaluation had occurred.

This after-the-fact period of emotional upheaval was vividly reported by Kevin, who after each time he fondled his biological daughter was literally overcome with guilt. This feeling, however, came immediately following sexual contact, never before. The guilt dissipated as each new episode neared.

R: I thought, oh God, all kinds of things. Like "God, what have I done? She's going to get to be a teenager and what if she turns into a fourteen-year-old hooker and it's all my fault . . . ." And I thought, "Well, what's going to happen when she gets older and she wants to get married? Is she going to have bad feelings about sex?" . . . I thought, "I'm the worst father in the world. How . . . can a father do this to his own child . . . ?" Before the molest happened this was something I would read about. And the first thing that would come to my mind was, "They ought to take that sucker out and cut his nuts off and kill him. He doesn't deserve a trial." And that's the way I felt. Then it happened to me and that's what I thought about myself. I ought to be taken out and shot . . . . But that didn't stop me from doing it . . . because I done it again and again . . . . It's really difficult to explain if you haven't done it . . . . It's haunting! It really is. To do something like . . . molesting your daughter, and in your mind you know it's wrong, but in your heart you do it anyway . . . . Every time after I molested my daughter all these feelings would come back.

Glenn too was consumed with guilt as a consequence of what he did with his adopted daughter. The emotional surge began during the sexual episodes themselves, at the moment Glenn thought he was going to reach orgasm. The thought of ejaculating during sex with his adopted daughter seemed to be too much.

R: When I touched her the first time on her behind, . . . almost every time I touched her, I said, "This isn't right." I knew it wasn't right . . . . Dads should not be rubbing them behinds. Dads should be taking care of splinters and cuts and bruises . . . . Chauffeuring them here and there. In other words, if they have a question, or a problem arises, help them out. But dads shouldn't be doing things to their body. I was a firm believer in that, but it wasn't strong enough to stop me . . . .

I: . . . In the period when contact is occurring you have this . . . feeling of wrongness. How strong was it at that moment?

R: At the time prior, not very. At the time of actually touching, very strong, because I immediately stopped . . . . I'd just get up and say . . . , "Please go in the other room right now." And she'd go because I'd usually yell at her . . . ; I was really upset with myself.

In the aftermath of one offense, in the case of this same offender, his reaction built to anger and rage. Then he broke down crying. He remembered feeling all alone as a human being. And he recalled being so racked with guilt that he confessed what happened to his wife.

R: I wished I could turn a switch that it didn't happen . . . ; I wished I didn't do it . . . . After the first episode . . . I got mad. I picked a chair up and tossed it across the room. And I said, "I am really mad! This stuff should not happen." And my oldest daughter says, "Well, I didn't do anything." And the middle daughter says, "Everything's fine, dad." I says, "No it's not and I don't know what to do about it." And I went over and I sat down on the stairs . . . . And my middle daughter came over and put her arm around me and says . . . , "It's all right, dad." "No, it's not all right. I don't know why . . . ." I was mad because it happened. I was mad because my middle daughter let it happen. I was mad because I did it . . . . That's the only time I threw the chair. They still remember that. That left an impression on them.

In the case of Phil, feelings of guilt seemed to mount with each successive offending episode. In spite of that, he offended over a period spanning four years. The turmoil that came after was not enough to stop him.

R: More and more as the molest continued, . . . afterwards there was feelings of guilt . . . . After I had committed the molest, say within ten or fifteen minutes . . . , I would start thinking about what I had done . . . . The first episode I took relatively lightly. I [said], "Well, this isn't going to occur again." I took

it as innocent, what I had done . . . . But when it continued, when I molested the second time, the third time, thereafter, . . . the feelings afterwards
became more and more of heavier and heavier guilt and self-condemna-
tion . . . . I'd be thinking to myself, "Here I [am] doing this to my own daughter. My own daughter!" . . . I mean for the temporary satisfaction that I had,
I did not consider it worth the condemnation, the guilt, and all the stuff that
built up afterwards. But then I would still continue and it became worse and
worse within myself.

The guilt men experienced was occasionally magnified by strong
religious beliefs. Phil was convinced he was doing something evil and
was going to go to hell. He reached a stage of private hopelessness. He
quoted the Bible, though he gave his own twist to a particular passage
therein.

R: It got to the point . . . where the feelings . . . that I had afterwards would last
longer and longer. It would be days afterwards that I would think about
it . . . . Well, "What I'm doing is totally evil . . . ." It would be feelings of
total loss. And the scripture [that] would come to my mind would be that,
"He who calls . . . my little ones his thumb would be better for him to have
a millstone tied about his neck and thrown to the depths of the sea . . . ." I felt
guilt, but more than that, I felt hopelessness. I mean I felt . . . there was
nowhere I could go to get help.

Brian reported flooding with guilt while victimizing the child he
molested. A couple of minutes into the act, he remembered, he wondered what he was doing. The guilt was strong enough in this episode to
stop the contact.

R: After I stepped over the line I thought, "What is wrong with you? Why are
you doing this?" which is very strange.
I: How shortly after did you think that?
R: It wasn't very long after . . . ; because I thought, . . . [the] first two or three
minutes, "Wow, this is easy." And then I thought during the last couple of
minutes, "This is wrong!" and I told him to pull up his pants . . . . Like I said
before, I would have been appalled at somebody having sex with a child,
particularly one that young. "He's still a baby. I mean . . . still a little boy.
He's a child. He's a baby." Those thoughts started coming back into my head
and I thought, "Gee, what is wrong with you? You know better. You're sitting here doing it. How can you even be appalled at somebody who's doing

it? . . . You see it or hear about it on TV or read about it. And you're sitting here doing it. What's wrong with you?"

The flooding experience was a private reality for the men who offended. There was no one to talk to about their guilt. There was a lot of talking to themselves. Brian remembered an internal moral debate and self-assessment as he offended.

R: When I'd come back to reality and realized what I was doing, . . . I felt awful. I felt even lower than a dog . . . because, "How can I do this to this kid? This kid looks up to me as a father figure . . . . How can I be doing this? . . . Look at my life, I'm ruining it!" . . . Sometimes I even felt like I was a totally different person. Like I had a split personality because I had this one voice saying, "Yeah, go ahead and do this to this kid," and the other one saying, "No, this is wrong. Don't do this." And it was a constant war.

Men who experienced the flooding process were not always upset with themselves because of what they did to the victim. Occasionally they felt bad because they had cheated on their spouse, or they were afraid that if their partner discovered it, it would really hurt her. Leon is one offender who felt more guilt and shame in regard to his wife than for the victim.

R: The guilt would be even worse when my wife would get home. What I was doing to my wife. I felt more guilty about my wife than I did about my stepdaughter. Her finding out; how it would hurt her; how it would crush her too; and what she would think of me if she ever found out.

Not everyone reported flooding with guilt after sexual contact, or even experiencing any guilt during the period they offended. Some offenders bypassed this stage altogether. The men who reported an absence of guilt commented that they never realized that sex with a minor was wrong or that it was a crime. They seemed oblivious to the fact that such behavior is outlawed and banned in Western society; this was something they had never considered before. Men who fit in this group usually, but not always, had themselves been extensively involved in childhood sex with someone older and had normalized their experiences. They also, as I report in a later section, justified their behavior on the grounds that the victim initiated sex and was a willing participant, and/or that the behavior was wrong only in a relative sense because it is practiced freely in other cultures.

Bob is a case in point. He molested two boys and reported an extensive childhood history of sex with older cousins and uncles, which he did not see or experience as harmful. Despite having heard stories about incest and molesting on the television, he said he never made anything of them or paid much attention to them. He claimed to be unaware of the criminal consequences of his behavior. He did, however, express feelings of guilt after he was caught and in prison. Bob stated that the fact that the victims were not his own children and did not live with him was critical. He admitted that if he had molested his own children, "the guilt and shame would have eventually overtaken me."

I: Did you ever take into consideration that sexual behavior with a child might be . . . something adults are not supposed to do?

R: I never thought about it. I really never even, I felt no guilt. I'll put it that way. Because I think if I'd felt guilty about doing it, I don't think I would have . . . . After I was sentenced, . . . for the first year after I was here [in prison], I felt guilty. It haunted me day and night. I thought, have I ruined those boys' lives?

Harry is a second example. As a child he was molested hundreds of times by his father and was involved in incestuous sex with his biological sister beginning as early as age three and continuing through late adolescence. Many of his relatives, he said, were aware of what was happening to him but never said anything. He had few boundaries about sexual behavior that carried over into his adult life. He admitted that he fondled seven children and never felt a pang of guilt until the very end. Even then, despite repeated questioning, he was unable to articulate why he felt guilty.

I: Did you ever think that what you were doing was wrong?

R: No. Not until right at the very end. When she started saying no, and when she got angry with me, I did then . . . .

I: Did you ever have any feelings of guilt after the episodes?

R: I would say that last time . . . , I felt pretty guilty then . . . . I started thinking . . . that this isn't what I wanted . . . . At the time, I believed I was a good parent.

I: . . . Why did you believe that?

R: Because I felt that I was meeting more of my child's needs than what most parents do.

Making Escape Attempts

Once inside the experience of offending, most of the men in this study were faced with having to preserve whatever they could of their personal identity, while confronting and dealing with the wave of emotions and guilt that enveloped them. What do people do when they believe they have done something terrible? How are such feelings managed? Many of the men reported engaging in "escape attempts," similar to attempts to cope with the frustrations and unhappiness that build during everyday life. By escape attempts, I mean the external and internal places offenders go to temporarily forget the behavior in which they have been involved. The net result is a time-out from the threat to identity sexual offending presents.[14]

Emotional escapes usually meant turning to routine "activity enclaves" such as "games, hobbies, work," or to other children whom they did not offend, often a son if they had molested one or more daughters, and then submerging themselves in that activity or relationship.[15] A few admitted "mindscaping" by turning increasingly to alcohol.[16] Others said they tried to escape by refusing to think about things, by trying to push the thought of what they had done and what they were feeling out of their minds. Whatever the attempted route of escape, among those who did experience guilt, all admitted they could never completely forget what they had done.

Phil pushed the guilt and recriminations to the back of his mind by thinking and doing other things, especially by being with his son, whom he did not molest. His escapes included work and Nintendo.

I: What did you do with these feelings?
R: . . . Just a matter of not dwelling on them . . . . It's like thinking . . . of something else or doing something else that would keep me from thinking about the situation . . . . Anything that could distract me, whether it be doing some work in the yard or going to work. As long as I took my thoughts or separated my thoughts . . . ; then again . . . I was not totally able to bury the feelings . . . . I'd keep my mind busy; I would spend time on the computer, or watch TV or play Nintendo with my son . . . . Something else that would distract me from thinking about what I had done.

In the periods after he offended, Larry buried his guilt in alcohol. He said he often tried to get himself drunk so that if the desire to reoffend resurfaced he would be too intoxicated to do anything. The amount he drank was extensive—one fifth of brandy and one fifth of vodka a night. He also escaped through work and television.

I: How did you get past these initial feelings of guilt?

R: . . . As far as trying to rationalize the whole thing, I think I stayed drunk just because when you're drunk you're . . . not aware of what's really going on. I would pass out before anything could happen.

I: . . . So the drinking helped the feelings of guilt . . . ?

R: No, it disguised [it] . . . ; it was there, okay? And then what I would do through the daytime is I would bury it. I literally buried myself in work. And that way it wouldn't bother me as bad because I had something else on my mind to keep my mind preoccupied to keep it from eating away at me . . . . I was trying to run from the problem through drinking . . . . And for every time it happened, I put myself further into my work and further into the bottle.

Randy described trying to mentally shelve the memory of what he had done and also immersing himself in his work. He avoided coming home to keep anything more from happening and to keep from having to face his wife and the victim.

R: The guilt part is, . . . I call it abusive guilt now, but where you just verbally beat yourself; it would go on for two or three days with me, and then . . . you kind of shelve it . . . ; just stick it in back of your mind. You got to go on about your life.

I: . . . Would you do things to help you forget?

R: . . . Just more work; stay at work; didn't want to come home . . . . Sixteen, eighteen hours a day.

I: . . . Were you working to remove yourself from the [situation]?

R: Yes, I didn't want to go home . . . . I didn't want to be back in that situation again. And I thought that if I disassociated myself, then nothing would happen. And I'd wait till they had actually went to bed . . . [or] . . . to school before [I'd] go home.

I: . . . Were you able to effectively forget it?

R: Well, you never forget it. You never forget it. You just . . . , it can't be a constant on your mind.

Telling the Victim It Was Wrong

Some men admitted talking to their victims immediately after they molested them, telling them they knew what they did was wrong, apologizing, and even promising that nothing else would happen. In part, such accounts seemed to be a way of controlling and ensuring the silence of the victim. But in terms of their implication for the offender's sense of self, they were also a practical method of relieving or symbolically *cleansing* themselves of guilt, a type of "purification" strategy.[17] By defining their actions as wrong, these men appeared to be attempting to elicit forgiveness. They were in a sense trying to repair the wrong they felt they had committed. It was their way of setting the record straight, redefining themselves as moral people in the face of actions that suggested otherwise.

Scott, who over time became more forceful with his stepdaughter, was driving with her when he pulled over to the side of the road twice and tried to force his hands down her pants. The girl successfully resisted each advance by balling herself up in the backseat where she was lying and pretending to be asleep. A few minutes later, after getting upset with himself, Scott forcefully sat the victim up and started apologizing. On the one hand, he seemed to be trying to control the victim by convincing her she was "safe." On the other hand, he seemed to be seeking forgiveness and trying to reestablish a sense of morality and self-control.

R: I told her . . . , "We need to talk!" And she just kind of looked at me like "Yeah?" And I said . . . , "What I've been doing is not right." I said, "What's been happening is wrong. You know what I'm talking about, don't you?" And I wouldn't mention it directly but . . . she said, "Yeah." And I said, "That's not right." I said, "What I've done is something that should be done between a husband and a wife and not between a father and a daughter." And I tried to explain . . . that it was all my fault and . . . that I wouldn't do it anymore. And I prayed with her about it and told her at that time that someday she was going to need to talk to *some*body . . . . I was hoping that it would be me that she would choose to talk to so [I] could explain it out, because at that time I felt very sincere in my effort to stop this . . . . But of course that wasn't to be. She didn't open up . . . . I molested her a couple of times after that.

Gary molested his stepdaughter on four occasions and said each time he told the victim that what he did was wrong. As he put it, "I felt like that was the least I could do. I owed her that much." He was afraid his actions might negatively affect her future and how she felt about him years later. He said he wanted to soften the impact of the experience when she realized years later what had occurred. To Gary, who experienced heavy guilt in the aftermath of offending, it was his way of doing the right thing.

R: I always explained to her that it was wrong, because I didn't want her to think it was right, and then all of a sudden when it does stop and someone does explain [things] to them, there'd be this big shock, or traumatic changing of her feelings towards me.

I: So . . . telling her it was wrong was a way of protecting her from what other people might tell her in the future?

R: Yeah, trying to soften the blow . . . . Because you always know that one day she's going to realize, she's going to learn, she's going to understand what it is about. And I just kind of wanted to get this in her head, so that she doesn't go through life, later on maybe thinking that it's okay just to go around and then do this with just anybody. Maybe turn out to be a prostitute or something. I mean . . . there's a lot of things that run through your mind . . . . And if you do care about them, . . . I felt that I should say something to her.

Attaching Permission to the Act

Men who became repetitive offenders did so, in part, because of different "neutralizations" they attached to their behavior, themselves, and their victims. Neutralizations are accounts that diminish feelings of wrongdoing and shame by providing a defensible basis for behavior.[18] Some people neutralize their behavior by making "excuses": they admit that their actions are wrong but do not see themselves as responsible. Other people invoke "justifications" for their actions: they interpret their behavior as less wrong, or not wrong at all, in the face of more common beliefs.[19] In this section, I focus on the second type of neutralization, the justifications men formulated that led them to think their conduct was permissible.[20] The neutralizations men admitted making reveal how they were inattentive and oblivious to their victims, and how major sexual boundaries that might stop many of us from acting were easily reformulated to fit more momentary needs and desires.

Some men rationalized that they were helping, not hurting, the children they molested, by having sex with them. They saw themselves as teachers, preparing their victims sexually so that they would not have sexual problems as adults, and helping to increase their sexual confidence. Or they claimed that by having sex, they could provide firsthand knowledge about birth control and possibly prevent early unwanted pregnancy; or in the case of girls, they claimed that they were reinforcing why it was important to learn to say no to boys who propositioned them for sex while dating.[21] Such accounts show just how far some men were willing to stretch the boundaries of their sexual morality. Ian and Stuart reported justifying their behavior in this way.

R: Sometimes I speculated or rationalized that maybe I thought I was doing my daughters a favor by preparing them sexually. So they don't go out in the world and be like their mother was, taking years to [have an orgasm]. Because most men wouldn't have put up with what I did.

R: I was teaching my [adopted] daughter something that she might not be learning the right way at school. I was showing my daughter sex, what it was about, trying to show my love towards her, letting her know things, sexual things . . . . I knew it was wrong but I felt like she needed the knowledge because of the way things are today. She was born out of wedlock, [her aunt] . . . had two kids out of wedlock. I didn't want her to have any [that way].

A related neutralization made by one man, Sam, that he was helping and not hurting, involved the belief that sex with his stepson would improve the boy's self-esteem. He searched out literature about adult-child sex for evidence that such behavior could be beneficial and eventually found something that told him what he needed to hear.

R: I searched out as many articles and magazines and so forth as I could about it, trying to justify to myself that I was not hurting my victim. And I finally found a book that said . . . it helped the boy's self-esteem . . . . And I read a lot about Greek history and that sort of thing to justify, I'm sure as I look back in my mind, that what I was doing was not as horrible . . . as it was. And I never really thought that I was hurting the victim at that time.

A second type of neutralization emerged directly from the context of offending and carried over to each subsequent episode. Some men reasoned that no overt signs of resistance, no explicit requests to stop, no obvious indicators that sex was unwanted on the part of their victims meant that their actions were not causing any harm, that the victims were enjoying things, and that what they were doing was all right. There were often "disclaimers" by these men, qualifying statements, that they would have stopped what they were doing if they thought the victim was being hurt in any way.[22] The onus of responsibility was on the victim, despite being very young, to clearly and explicitly say no, and any reaction that deviated from this script as such was taken as a tacit sign to proceed. Tom, Scott, George, and Leon admitted that they saw their behavior this way.

R: I kept wondering about whether or not I was harming my daughter, but I would look at what was going on and her responses and I would think, well, if I were, she would be telling me about it. And she wasn't; she wasn't saying no. She was saying yes.

R: In my mind I wasn't out to hurt. I wasn't out to steal something that didn't belong to me . . . . [My stepdaughter] didn't seem like she was resisting. And the fact that she wasn't resisting, I guess I just assumed that meant she didn't mind, that she didn't care.

R: She didn't stop me and I thought it was okay . . . . She acted like she enjoyed it each time . . . . She didn't fight me . . . ; I never did force her to lay down on the couch with me . . . . I just thought it was exciting her . . . because I was getting excited.

R: I thought she . . . enjoyed it and that she really knew what I was doing . . . . Because she didn't move my hand, . . . she didn't say anything, she didn't wince or make any jerky movement . . . . All there was was just her sitting there and allowing what was going on. And I took the allowing to mean that she liked it and wanted me to do it.

This kind of rationalization, no reaction interpreted as no harm, extended in one instance to a victim who was asleep. Steve figured that because his stepdaughter was not awake when he touched her, she too was not being hurt, and thus what he was doing was okay.

R: I remember rationalizing, "Well, she's asleep, she'll never know," feeling guilty as heck, but I'd say at least she's asleep, and won't know this is going on. And I believed that. That's the crazy thing . . . . So as long as I continued believing that she was asleep and didn't know, then I guess it made it easier each time.

A corollary construction was the belief by some men, such as Tom, George, and Bob, that children could make their own decisions about sex. They lost track of the fact that children were children, not adults.

R: I think in ways I was just sort of seeing her as an adult and looking for adult responses.

R: I felt like she was grown up enough to know what she wanted to do . . . . Somehow or another, I lost it someplace, the fact that she was still a kid.

R: I felt like he was old enough to know if he wanted to do it or not.

In other cases, some offenders deliberately monitored their victims in the days and weeks after sexual contact occurred to see if there were any signs of harm. These men routinely mentioned that they did not see any changes in everyday behavior, that there was no change in grades at school, and even that the victim they were monitoring seemed happier, more content, and easier to get along with. The absence of any obvious, more general negative aftereffects seemed to decrease any feelings of guilt and to bolster the willingness of offenders to continue. Sidney, Bob, Scott, and William were four such cases.

I: What happened with that guilt from the time right afterwards to the time it happened again?

R: It dissipated. It became diluted. It became weak. I saw no visible signs of any harm done. I saw no proof that anything I'd done had caused any genuine effect on my daughter's life or the way she was acting or the way we were interacting.

R: They spent more time, not necessarily with me, but around the house, wherever I was at. They seemed to be happier. They laughed more. They worked harder . . . [at] . . . their studies, their chores. They seemed to be more active in playing with the other neighborhood kids—softball, swimming.

R: I watched my daughter very closely, watched for signs of shying away from me, signs of being afraid of me, signs of hatred, signs of dislike, signs of discomfort around me and I didn't see any. We clowned around a lot. We joked with each other.

R: It did not seem to affect their personality or school grades. I did not see a difference in their behavior from having it. They still had their friendships, did excellent in school, still enjoyed the activities they were involved in. I saw no change; everything seemed normal . . . . It seemed to alleviate the tension that existed within the family and the family situation seemed more stable from it. There was less dissension between my children and their stepmother, between my wife and I.

Other men convinced themselves that the children they had sex with were active and full-fledged participants in what occurred, and in the extreme, that they initiated sex. Any expression of interest or enjoyment, however unintended, either verbal or physiological, indicated a lack of harm and apparent permission to reoffend later.[23] Sam, Ian, and Kevin defined their victims as participants.

R: I didn't want to admit that I was doing anything wrong. I always wanted to convince myself that he wanted to do this. And of course . . . as he got older then I could quite easily convince myself, because he would initiate it.
I: And that . . . symbolized what?
R: That what I did hadn't hurt him. That he was not angry. That I think helped to alleviate any pangs of conscience that I was having.

R: It was like she enjoyed it. You could tell. The breathing got heavier.
I: Even when she was acting like she was asleep?
R: Oh yeah! . . . It was a little silly game we played. I knew she was awake. And she knew that I knew . . . . And this girl at that age then, twelve or thirteen, would get orgasms. And very easily . . . . And then after a while it got to the point where there was no point in pretending. I mean she was an active participant and she enjoyed what was going on. And then she . . . would initiate but . . . in a very quiet way . . . ; like letting the sleeve in her robe open up.

I: You said you "thought she liked it."
R: I had convinced myself that that's what she wanted.
I: . . . What was she doing that made you think that?
R: . . . She would put her nightgown on. She'd take her panties off and she'd come in and sit down on me.
I: . . . How did you read that when she did that . . . ?
R: I just thought, "Well, if that's what she wants, okay." I didn't see anything wrong with it . . . . I'd convinced myself . . . that this is what she wants . . . . That [was] my way of making myself feel better, I guess. Ease my own pain.

A few offenders reframed their victims as having been sexual with others before them, in particular with other age mates, which then stood as an indicator of a general willingness to have sex.[24] Both Bob and Carl, who each had molested boys, and Kevin, who had sex with a girl, justified their behavior in this fashion. These men did not seem to see the difference between exploring sex with peers and being approached by an adult.

R: He told me that he had had sex with one of his older brothers, which seemed to make it easier for me . . . . I knew then that he was willing.

R: This kid had had many little boy partners. I know he had. He told me he had.

R: I honestly think that she had also got some other type of coaching some-where else. Because I had never had sexual intercourse with her, yet when she took my finger and put it inside of her, her hymen was already broke.

Still others seemed to cope with and deflect their guilt by defining their actions with children as different from those of other sexual offend-ers. Child molesting was one thing—hanging out around school yards, pulling a child into a car and driving off, using force to gain sexual access, committing rape or having intercourse with a minor—what they did was another! They saw their own behavior as less wrong, more acceptable, and often not criminal because they had sex with one of their own children and not somebody else's or because they saw themselves as nonviolent. As long as they were not really molesting, what they were doing seemed to be okay.[25] This was a type of "deviance disavowal,"[26] a denial that one's self or behavior is abnormal, which occurred as part of the process of offending, not as an aftereffect of being caught and try-ing to cope with being discredited. Neither Ian, Tom, John, nor Harry ever considered themselves child molesters, for various reasons.

R: *The day I got arrested (very loudly)*, there was a big article in the paper . . . , a write-up on a guy . . . who was the fire chief . . . , who was arrested . . . for child molesting . . . . And the reaction was . . . *(very loudly) nothing like that could ever happen to me!* . . . I remember being somewhat appalled and think-ing, "Geez, a guy like him? . . . Why would?" Like most people would prob-ably think. But never relating it to myself that I was doing the same thing. And my way of looking at things, . . . I never thought of myself . . . as a child molester.

R: I didn't see myself as a sex fiend or a sex criminal or a deviant in any form. I saw myself as trying to genuinely connect with someone I genuinely loved. And so therefore, if that does it, that's okay.

R: I thought of it as being wrong . . . , but I didn't think of it as being illegal, that I might be arrested for it . . . . I thought the worst that would happen to me was mom would find out or somebody would find out and they would . . . ignore it . . . . I mean it was part of a family thing . . . . I've seen things in the paper about people going to jail for molesting children, that sort of thing, . . . but I always thought that they were going out and grabbing other people's children and molesting them.

R: The entire time I was doing that I never considered myself to be molesting. I didn't call it that . . . . I knew that molesting was a crime. I didn't believe what I was doing was molesting. Especially at first because I wasn't . . . sexually aroused. It wasn't like that . . . . My opinion was of a stereotype molester—hiding in the park . . . , someone they didn't know abducting them . . . , someone that didn't care whether or not the child was hurt. There was a lot of things I believed was a child molester that I wasn't. That's why I didn't consider myself a child molester.

Every offender seemed to measure his behavior against something more extreme to discount what he had done. Eric, still thinking in the present tense because at the time of the interview he had just started treatment, did not see himself as a sex offender either, despite admitting to sexual relations with over a hundred boys over the years. This offender was the one man in the sample who was not clearly a situational offender, though he did admit to sex with adult men in his adult life.

R: I feel it shouldn't be against the law. I don't feel there are any victims to my crimes. If I force myself on boys, then I should be put in an institution. Just like a male who rapes women . . . . [Or] if I seen some boy I wanted to mess around with and grabbed him, tied him up, and took him into the bushes. But I'm not interested in that kind of sex. That kind of guy should be put in an institution.

In reality, rather than using a single method to free themselves emotionally such that they could continue offending, most men used many. Ken, for example, at different moments in his offending career, seemed to use each of the methods presented above to interpret and define what he was doing. His involvement in offending spanned eleven years, which expanded his recipe box of rationalizations. An added neutralization was his belief that he was not really having sex because his penis was flaccid most of the time and he did not engage in intercourse.

R: There was never any sex, never any sexual intercourse . . . . At no time did I go into the street and entice or solicit anyone to become involved . . . . No one forced these kids to participate. They participated on their own, though I did bring parental pressure to bear . . . . I rationalized I was teaching these kids about sex, and better they learned it from me than some other kid . . . . I've never hurt anyone in my life. If I knew I had hurt the children, I probably would never have done it . . . . My perception was the kids were enjoying what we were doing. They were laughing, having fun . . . . They seemed to come to the house willingly . . . . There did not appear to be outward animosity or hostility. I even thought the relationship between [my stepdaughter] and myself was improving.

There was a small group of men who rejected conventional morality altogether and justified their behavior to varying degrees on the grounds that sex with children in general was not really bad or harmful. A type of moral relativism prevailed. The more the men offended, the more they began to restructure and reformulate what they really believed, realigning their morality as best they could with what they were doing. In the extreme, they began to see society as the real source of harm and damage.[27] These men typically invoked knowledge of adult-child sex in other cultures or other historical periods as evidence that harm is a matter of definition. As a group, they reported the most extensive and most serious levels of sexual contact of all the men in the study. Conrad, William, and Eric all adopted this stance toward sexual relations with the children they molested.

R: The moral aspect of it depends on a person's point of view . . . . For example, person A says it's okay to have sex with children. And person B says it's wrong . . . . Who's to say who's right and who's wrong? . . . I thought it was okay to have sex with a child; [that] it could be presented in a way that would not be harmful . . . . The thing that was harmful is not the fact that I was having sex with her, but the conflicting messages that were coming from . . . the outside. I actually believed . . . if people would just mind their own business, not meddle in our family affairs, that she would come through the experience okay, without having any damage . . . . It was a belief that enabled me to go ahead and participate in this activity.

R: I have always wondered what it is other than society's standards that is actually wrong about it. I realize that there are certain physical aspects that are not possible when children are very young. But I have always wondered why certain areas of one's body is considered dirty, wrong to touch, and prohibitive, when other areas are okay. I have always wondered why society dresses its adolescents with clothing that is revealing of these areas, why society glamorizes in books and in movie teenage sexuality, and then passes laws prohibiting that which it glorifies. In the 1800s people married in their very early teens, had children in their very early teens . . . . I feel today we have a double standard, of life the way it is, and of laws . . . saying how it should be.

R: In this country, we're puritanical when it comes to sex. Others don't look at it like we do. Like in Sweden, eleven is legal, eleven or older. I don't know about other countries. It's looked on differently elsewhere . . . . If a twelve- and fourteen-year-old boy jack off [together], it's okay. But if I do it with them, then I should go to jail or be put in an institution. It's the same thing . . . . No one wants to make an issue of it if it's just boys having sex together. But if a grown man is involved, they think you "molested" them . . . . I get made the scapegoat . . . . People are weird. There's so much hypocrisy in life. It's historical fact that [different] popes in past times have had harems in the Vatican.

Drifting out of Sexual Control

Following the first episode of sexual contact, there was usually a lengthy period before a second episode began. Three men never made it to a next episode because they got caught the first time, but the rest did. Typically within a few weeks to a month, there would be another offense, and another. In the aftermath of each occurrence, the guilt and personal upheaval that were experienced began to fade, while the desire to repeat the act seemed to build and dominate the day-to-day reality of the offender. Eventually most men described feeling overcome by the desire to repeat the sexual experience; they said they had lost the ability to control themselves. Many described waging an internal battle that, no matter how hard they fought, they always lost. The men seemed to get caught in a process that developed its own momentum.

Steve said that his feelings of guilt and despair stopped him from reoffending for a while, but with time the urge to offend again simply became too strong. Even while struggling with an internal tug-of-war, wanting to act and feeling bad afterwards, he continued to molest.

I: You had this feeling that what you were doing was wrong . . . ; did that feeling stop you from doing it again?

R: No, it never stopped me from doing it in a subsequent time. It might have stopped me from doing it for a while, but eventually I would just finally give in. The urge to do it, to have that high, that feeling, . . . would outweigh and I'd say, "Aw [the] heck with it, go ahead." And I can remember saying, "Oh, the heck with [it], just go on. Just let go of [it]." Instead of keep[ing on] fighting it, fighting that urge, I'd just let go . . . . And then the pattern started again, the guilt and the low feeling. It never stops.

Gary felt overcome by urges as if he was being pulled by forces he had no power to stop.

R: It's almost like being sucked into a trap. When you start getting those urges and feelings, . . . it's like . . . something's just pulling you . . . . It's like you can't stop it . . . . This urge is a killer. I mean it's just so overwhelming . . . . I say it's almost like . . . a cannonball shooting out . . . ; you can't stop it. It's just too strong.

Scott described a similar process of losing self-control. Sexual desire seemed to overpower the feelings of guilt he experienced. A type of momentum to reoffend emerged.

R: A lot of times what happened, and this is the scary part to me, is I'd say to myself, "this isn't right, you can't do it." But the desire for the fulfillment, for the sexual excitement, for the sexual feeling was just like . . . , you block out the world, you block out life, you block out everything that you know and believe in and feel for. And you *allow* that to rule you . . . . I *knew* that it was wrong (*very loudly*). Obviously I knew that it would cost me everything that I cared for if it were found out, at least at first. But it was just more dominant, more important to me than anything else. And progressively got more important. I mean progressively got stronger and stronger as a driving force.

Randy felt he was another person when he offended, someone separate from himself. He reported strong recriminations each time he offended, but just before each new episode, nothing seemed to matter to him.

R: Once you're in that situation, I think you allow yourself just to continue with it . . . . I don't think you're in a right state of mind as far as saying, is this right or is this wrong . . . . A lot of times it was . . . almost like it was surreal . . . ; it wasn't really happening to me . . . . It wasn't a situation that you wanted to stay in. But it wasn't a situation that you really want to break . . . . It's almost like being locked in this situation . . . . It was like another person doing it . . . ; it was like it wasn't me. I now know that . . . it was me and I know what will happen, but at that very particular minute it was like I could just switch a switch off and just turn into somebody else.

Conrad too described how the desire to get off sexually overpowered any feelings of shame he experienced. Over time, the shame began to disappear and he admitted he did not even try to stop after that point.

R: I didn't understand what was happening inside of me . . . . I did feel the
shame. And I knew that I had this strong desire to do it. And when the desire
came up, then I would give into it . . . . When the desire was present and
would build up, that would overshadow . . . the shame or . . . the moral
restraint . . . . I guess there was the point in time where I just felt like I was out
of control, or just hopeless . . . , well, why try, so just give into it. The shame
aspect of it kind of lessened over a period of time.

Larry described a cycle in which he had no prior desire to offend but
then found that he had already committed the act. He reported his situation as being beyond his control.

R: I knew that what had happened wasn't right the first time. And it just seemed
to all of a sudden be right there and it was happening again. I mean I could
go a long time and nothing would ever happen. But yet all of a sudden it
would be like *God, no, no, no (very loudly)*. It's happened again . . . . I knew
it wasn't right and I couldn't talk to my wife because she was never there.
And I didn't know what to do so I tried to [tell myself], "Well, it'll never happen again." But yet it did. And every time it . . . happened it was like "No, I'll
make sure it'll never happen again." And it just did again.

Sidney talked about an acquired taste for offending. It was not something you like right off, because of the bad feelings afterwards, but over
time the good feelings—he said he got pleasure from dominating the
victim—became paramount. He remembered feeling that his emotions
seesawed back and forth.

R: It's a lot like . . . the first time you drink, . . . a lot of people drink and they
get a hangover, but they drink again . . . . An acquired taste seems kind of trite
to say, but . . . I think it's the same precept. I don't know anybody that liked
beer the first time they drank . . . . There [was] a period at which I was most
remorseful . . . and then that remorsefulness dropped off as the indication
that nothing had happened increased . . . . I was not seeing any outward
signs that anything I had done had really caused any harm. So I guess you
could look at it a little bit like a seesaw. And at one point in time the weight
on one side outweighed the weight on the other and it happened again.
And then it was like a cycle and I don't think it would have stopped if [she]
hadn't said something.

William stated that he too experienced the drift in and out of offending as a cycle of highs and lows. He drew a parallel to career dieters,

people who abstain from eating for a little bit, feel good about losing some weight, then binge eat.

R: For seven or eight weeks, when nothing was taking place, things seemed to feel normal and okay. I did not feel so terrible about myself. And when my daughters and I would be alone and close together, the incest would occur. After the incident would occur, I would feel so ashamed and hate myself so much that I would be strong enough to keep it from occurring for seven or eight weeks, until I would begin again to feel good, then it would reoccur. It was a cycle of . . . mood swings . . . . It is like one who begins a fad diet and thinks that he has overcome his weight problem because he didn't pig out for several weeks, only to find himself on a food binge and realize he has not overcome it at all.

Corey drew a parallel between taking a first drink or having sex for the first time. Because it feels good, it is something you want to do again, and it is very difficult to stop yourself once you have started. He related a cycle of highs and lows.

R: Just like you take that first drink, or you have that first sexual intercourse, you got to have it again . . . . Because you had the taste, you had what it tastes like, and it was good. It felt good . . . . It was a quick high and (*snaps fingers*) you were down. You were back to reality. And you went on. Then you went back up on your high (*snaps fingers*) and you were down . . . . Being drunk, . . . you feel great. Next morning you get up you have a hell of a headache. You feel bad . . . . Afterwards there was times . . . where I was starting to feel bad what I was doing. But I didn't know how to stop it.

A cycle of drift between intense feelings of guilt and pleasure wore heavily on Carl. He provided a glimpse into the emotional reality of his offending.

R: It's like an extremely bad cycle . . . . It's just one of those things where you feel so guilty you can't stand yourself, and then you kind of get over that. Then your genitals will start talking like, "But that did feel good. So perhaps we could do that again . . . ." It would be a cycle that never ended.

Ian said that offending became easier after the situation began. The initial leap was most difficult, but once he made it across the moral boundary, there was nothing really left to stop him from continuing.

R: Once it happened, it was like the door coming open. The boundaries, the constraints wore off. And even though I recognized the existence of risks and that kind of thing, . . . the desire was stronger.

Earl reported a desire to reoffend that felt like a dam bursting open, resulting in a flood that could not be contained.

R: You know it's wrong but you can't stop it. It's just like water . . . ; if you have a dam and the water just keeps on running and running and running it's going to go up and over the dam . . . . I've said it a hundred times, "I won't do that tomorrow; I won't even think about it." [But] it would come back.

The ironic reality for these men was that once they offended, there was nowhere to go for help without facing legal repercussions. Mandatory reporting laws in most states preclude offenders from seeking counseling on a voluntary basis. Because they had much to lose— their jobs, marriages, friends, freedom, and the like—they almost never went to talk to anyone about how to stop offending. Many wanted to find help, but felt trapped and afraid to do so. Consequently, they drifted further and further out of control. Both Larry and Gary, for example, became caught in their own private catch-22.

R: I should have had the guts to . . . say something . . . . If I had known the first time I molested [her] that there was someplace that I could have gone, I feel in my heart I would have went . . . . In my . . . heart I hated myself. I knew it was wrong and yet . . . I was scared to say something. I was afraid of saying something . . . ; I was afraid of losing my family . . . . I was afraid of really being persecuted all my life about it. I guess I was afraid that . . . everything would just end right then. And I didn't know that it [w]ould go on.

R: I found out in class . . . if a psychiatrist treats somebody or sees somebody and they did something illegal, . . . they have to turn them in. And that scared me even more . . . . Sure as hell, I [did] not want to go to prison . . . . I thought that's ". . . going to blow my career most likely, if I have a prison record. You can't go for help then." That pissed me off because . . . that doesn't seem fair. I mean . . . there's people that need help . . . and you can't exactly go up and talk to somebody about it. Somebody might pull out a gun and blow you away. Because a lot of people . . . , you can't really blame people for hating you.

Conclusion

The transition from one episode of sexual offending to the next, according to the men in this study, involved a panorama of emotional realities and social definitions. During sexual contact itself, offenders routinely reported strong feelings of sexual arousal and excitement. Often this was mixed with other surges of momentary pleasure such as feelings of power, acceptance, intimacy, relaxation, release of anger, and sexual safety. This was quickly replaced by an onrush of feelings of guilt toward the victim, and sometimes in relation to a spouse or partner, primarily after sexual contact had ended. Then there were attempts by offenders to cope with or numb the guilt by self-submergence in work, alcohol, television, and so forth, and/or by lecturing the victim about the immoral nature of their conduct. Between offense episodes, most men convinced themselves in various ways that what they were doing was not "really" wrong: that sexual contact was a way of helping the child, that the child would have resisted if they did not like what happened, that the victim began participating, or that the conduct the men engaged in was not really child molesting. With each new episode of offending, the men described reaching a stage at which they felt they had lost control over themselves and could not keep from offending no matter how hard they tried. Importantly, some men became locked into a cycle of offending because they feared being sent to prison and losing everything if they came forward to find help to stop what they were doing.

SEVEN

Continuing with Regular Offending

As the offenders I interviewed drifted and shifted in and out of sexual control on a subjective level, the number, frequency, and duration of the sexual violations they committed increased proportionately. How extensive was the sexual abuse in which they participated? Only four men said they molested one victim just one or two times. Conversely, 40 percent said they had engaged in sex with someone under sixteen twenty-one or more times, 57 percent eleven or more times. As a group, there were at least 1,540 estimated episodes of sexual contact.[1] The total number of offenses per offender ranged from one to over three hundred. The average number of episodes was fifty-one. Sixty percent of the men said their active involvement in offending spanned one year or longer; 40 percent said two years or longer. The overall number of victims who were molested was fifty-two; the total victims per offender ranged as high as eight (one offender, with over a hundred victims, was excluded from this total). Finally, one-third of the men admitted they molested at least two victims (see appendix C).

The question I turn to now concerns the objective dynamics of involvement in regular offending, that is, what offenders said occurred between them and their victims over time, beyond those subjective processes that were elaborated in the previous chapter. Did the level of sexual contact increase or stay the same from episode to episode? What kinds of things did offenders say or do to their victims to maintain secrecy? How did the men gain recurring access to their victims without anyone catching on to them? And why did different offenders stop at or progress to the level of sexual contact they admitted to? I focus specifically on the middle stages of the offending career, from the first episode of sexual contact onward. Rather than identifying a single consistent path that every offender followed, again, I found wide variation in offense patterns. This is similar to what has been proposed theoretically by Joel Best and David Luckenbill about deviant behavior in general: "The varied patterns of career shifts make it impossible to specify a standard deviant career path . . . . The analysis of deviant careers requires a framework which recognizes the relative lack of structure in the deviant experience."[2]

Objective Sequences of Involvement

In analyzing how regular offending unfolded, I traced what I will refer to as the basic objective offense sequences the men reported with their victims. By objective sequence, I mean a range of factors including the type or level of sexual behavior, the number of sexual violations, the total victims molested and the order by age, the length of participation by offenders, and the number of major stops and starts or breaks in sexual contact. I incorporated these factors into single coherent offending profiles, or identifiable paths of interaction with victims that offenders typically followed.[3] The objective offense sequences I documented were sometimes episodic, sometimes continuous; sometimes short-lived, sometimes long; sometimes more serious, sometimes less so; sometimes more involving of others, sometimes not at all.

One common offense sequence consisted of men who started out with less serious behavior, in particular fondling, but never increased the level of contact any further, and who limited their offending to a single victim. These offenders settled into the same scenario over and over. With this pattern, the length of involvement varied; and the frequency of contact was sometimes continuous, sometimes intermittent. Leon molested his stepdaughter for four months—sixteen episodes; Steve his stepdaughter for two years—ten episodes; Phil his biological daughter for four years—fifty to sixty episodes.

I: So how did things then progress? You described working your finger over the vaginal area . . . .

R: That was as far as they ever went as far as "steps." I did that over and over and over again . . . . Other than just running my finger along the slit, crack, or whatever you want to call it, well, that was as far as it ever got.

I: How far did things progress in terms of contact? You described touching her . . . the first time on the clitoral area.

R: Yeah, that's basically it . . . ; I mean . . . I stuck to just the stimulation. I really didn't want to touch her vaginally.

I: The first time you pulled her panties down and just looked at her . . . . How did things progress?

R: . . . I'd touch her and look with my flashlight . . . . I never inserted my finger like all the way or anything . . . . I might have just touched around the lip area. But basically touching.

A second major objective sequence was one of less serious behavior initially, and then an escalation to more serious contact over time, but with only one or mainly one victim. More men in this study fit this pattern than any other. There were a number of ways this type of progression unfolded. One variation of the model involved a stage with less serious behavior to start, then a lengthy period of abstinence from offending, routinely for a year or more, followed by a third stage involving more serious behavior when the victim was older. This type of escalation sequence was reported by Larry, who molested his stepdaughter twenty to twenty-five times over a five-year period. He described an early phase of about two years when he rubbed against the victim and fondled her breasts. Then there was a late phase, lasting about two years as well, during which he progressed to vaginal fondling, manual penetration, penis-vaginal contact, and oral sex, where things ended. In between was a period of about one year where nothing occurred because Larry had injured himself, had surgery, and was physically incapacitated.

R: It started with me just rubbing her on the outside of her clothes and then hugging her and sending her off to play. Then it got more intense where I was up under her clothes, rubbing her tits and pinching her nipples . . . . At that point I was not in her underwear yet. Then I went down to where I was playing with her vagina. I wasn't fingering her or anything. I was just rubbing the outside of it. Then it got to the place to where I . . . wasn't fingering her but I would have the lips . . . spread a little bit . . . . It really tripped me out when she got breasts . . . . There was this one time that I had not touched her in so long that the next time, I mean she had some pretty good-sized tits on her . . . . It got to the place where I was rubbing her tits after . . . she was developing. And one time I ate her out.

Conrad reported a similar career progression in his offending over an identical five-year period. There were three distinct stages. The first spanned a year, starting with genital rubbing while clothed, then undressing himself and the victim, and then rubbing his penis against the victim's vagina. The second involved an eighteen-month period of abstinence after telling his wife he had been molesting their daughter. He made this disclosure to retaliate against his wife after he learned she had a sexual affair. He claimed that he and his wife then agreed to try and put their marriage back together. The third stage spanned another year and involved sexual intercourse. All told there were over three hundred episodes of sexual contact.

R: It just started off simple. It was just like a snowball . . . ; it just got bigger and bigger and went on . . . .
I: How long did the average sexual episode with her last?
R: It lasted about, at the beginning, about ten or fifteen minutes. And then towards the end, well at the end, I'd have her with me for about an hour or an hour and a half.
I: So the time frame increased over the period?
R: Yeah, everything, I guess the picture of what happened is that it started out small and then everything about it escalated: the time, the degree of behavior. I mean it started off where we just had our clothes on and it ended up where we was having intercourse.

Eventually Conrad's offending evolved to the level of ceremonialized sexual contact with his biological daughter, which was rare in this study—it was reported in just one case. . Each offense consisted of adherence to a strict ritual—waking his daughter before dawn and escorting her to the bathroom to relieve herself, walking her to his room and undressing her, staring at her a few minutes while she stood naked, placing her on his lap with her legs around him, stroking various parts of her body, placing her on her back for intercourse, wetting her genitals with water, cleaning her up with a washcloth after, and bizarrely, on some occasions, measuring her body—neck, chest, waist, hips, thighs, sleeve, leg inseam, height—in fifteen to twenty places. The method of offending seemed to be cherished for its own sake.

Another variation in the way escalation occurred consisted of a steady progression to the most serious behavior with each new episode, then a leveling out of behavior, followed by a continuation at that final level and sometimes intermittent periods of abstinence after the leveling out occurred. When Scott first began offending, he attempted to molest his oldest stepdaughter but she rebuffed his advances. Then he quickly turned to his youngest stepdaughter. With her he reported a quick flurry of episodes that started with fondling and culminated at the level of oral sex. There was also one episode in which he attempted to insert the victim's finger in his anus, but he was unsuccessful.

R: It kind of just progressed . . . , each time I would do something a little bit different. Either I would have her . . . like rub her hand around my genital area or I would go down on her. One time I tried to put my penis in her mouth. It was just, each incident seemed to, and this was over like a probably a three-week period, it progressed. I would say there was probably ten incidents in here.

In this particular case, the victim resisted oral sex, and Scott tried a few more times to fondle the genitals of the girl, again with resistance. After about six months, he stopped for eight months, during which he moved with his wife and stepchildren to another state. Then he started again with the same stepdaughter, mainly limiting his involvement to fondling and manual penetration of the genitals, which continued steadily for two more years. In the end, Scott admitted to about a hundred episodes of sexual contact spanning a little over three years.

Sometimes there was a relatively short escalation, in terms of the seriousness of the behavior, and then everything stopped. Sidney admitted engaging in five or six episodes of sexual contact spanning a period of three months. He admitted a short progression from masturbating himself with the victim watching to being masturbated. Then there was a quick leap to penis-vaginal contact without penetration, and then the offending was stopped.

R: It progressed . . . to me having her observe me masturbate to me having her masturbate me, and it was stopped before it got much worse than that. There was one time where, in my mind I was not attempting sex with her, but in her mind I was, and that came to be a point of issue . . . , but where I actually had her . . . in the missionary position . . . . In my mind I still don't believe I attempted to penetrate her, but she thinks I did, . . . and since it's her body, I'm going to take her version of it, okay.

Other times there was a longer, more drawn out progression that just seemed to get more and more serious, escalating to the level of physical force, with no apparent stopping point. John molested two girls, his niece first and most extensively, then a half-sister twice over a two-week period. In the case of his niece, he admitted to twenty-five or more episodes of sexual contact lasting a duration of roughly two and a half years that reached the level of receiving oral sex and penis-vaginal contact with orgasm. Initially, he said, contact occurred about twice a month, then became more sporadic, with gaps depending on opportunity, and quick flurries of two or three episodes over just a few days. The situation with his half-sister was added on near the end of his involvement in offending and included the same more serious kinds of behaviors. Then he returned to his niece. The progression below was the one that involved the latter girl. He admitted reaching a stage at which he was thinking about forced rape, with one possible victim being his boss's wife.

R: For about six or eight months, whenever I wrassled with her . . . , I would manage to fondle her in some way or another . . . . After about six months there was no pretense in it at all, just go ahead and do it . . . . It progressed to the point where I would place my penis close to her vagina. Once or twice the excitement got enough so that I would ejaculate . . . . Eventually it progressed, the last two incidents, I actually placed my penis inside of her mouth . . . . Both times happened where I was actually trying to degrade her . . . . I was very close to the point of committing a major violent offense, extremely short-tempered . . . .
I: Did you ever think about, for example, rape?
R: Yeah, I think I did.

Still another main path involved switching victims, stopping more or less completely with one victim and then starting with another, then building to more serious behaviors. In the case of William, there were two victims. It began with his youngest daughter and it proceeded from hugging to having her fondle him. Then he switched to his older biological daughter and he progressed quickly to vaginal intercourse. He admitted to ten to fifteen episodes with the first victim and five or six with the second over about eighteen months. He said contact occurred about every two to three weeks. There was also an eighteen-month period of abstinence after he was arrested and then another final episode of vaginal intercourse with his oldest daughter.

R: The first was with the youngest daughter . . . ; how it had transgressed was that it started out as regular hugging and went into fondling the genital and breast areas and [then] her fondling my genital areas. There was no intercourse ever with this daughter . . . . With my oldest daughter it began much the same way but did include intercourse on maybe four or five occasions . . . . I'm not sure how it progressed into the intercourse . . . ; just one thing led to another, fondling to the intercourse.

A second such case was Ian, who molested all three of his biological daughters. He began with the oldest daughter and ended with the youngest one. His sequence involved initiating, progressing, stopping, switching, restarting, stopping, switching, and then restarting and progressing a third time. With his oldest daughter, the first victim, there were ten episodes of sexual contact across a period of approximately three months. He reported a steady and quick progression to attempted intercourse and then a leveling off during which he fondled the victim. Most of the episodes, he said, lasted only seconds.

I: What would occur? What activities? Sexual activities?

R: Just caressing and touching . . . ; mostly her breasts. But sometimes her vagina. And then it progressed to the point, after a relatively short period of time, where . . . I just continued to let . . . [it] go. I didn't put a stop to it. And I attempted to go further with it. I attempted to penetrate her once with sexual intercourse . . . .

I: How did it come about . . . that you attempted it?

R: Really it was an expansion of what we were already started the few occasions before . . . . I mean the drive is there, you might as well seek its conclusion . . . . So here I'm in this situation where obviously she's not capable of this and hey, I'm not going to force it.

When his first daughter began to resist his advances, Ian said, he stopped offending, and then roughly a year later he started up again with his middle daughter. There was only one episode of fondling and simulated intercourse while clothed. The second victim, who fell asleep on the couch lying on top of him one afternoon, woke up and reacted angrily. His oldest daughter, in reaction to the second daughter, apparently told a school counselor about being touched by her father. The welfare department investigated briefly but dropped the case. Again the offending stopped, this time for about five years. Then things began with his youngest daughter. He admitted to a hundred or more sexual episodes with her, involving manual penetration, being masturbated, oral sex, and attempted intercourse, spanning six years. During that span there were two periods of about six to eight months of abstinence from offending because his wife became ill and then died. Each time, he picked up where he left off. Eventually he reached a point at which everything became routine.

R: After a while it got to the point of her complete disrobing, and then by both of us, and masturbating her.
I: Would you penetrate her when you masturbated her?
R: . . . I might have done it twice . . . . But anyway . . . as things progressed . . . it got to the point where sometimes in the afternoons I came home first, she was alone, and we had an opportunity to have a half hour alone. Why we'd quickly get down to it . . . . I would put on a condom, . . . I would lay on my back, and she would get on top of me and rub herself off against me. And we'd both have an orgasm that way.

There were also men who reported one or two principal victims but who added on numerous other victims episodically, typically friends of their own children who were the main victims. For example, Harry said he molested seven children over a one-year period. The main victim was his stepdaughter, whom he fondled approximately eight times across roughly equal intervals of time. The other children included another younger stepdaughter, four neighborhood friends, and a stepniece, each of whom he said he fondled only once. The behavior never progressed to any more serious level beyond fondling, despite the number of victims involved.

Ken too reported this sequence of adding on victims. He had two principal victims, his biological daughter and then his stepdaughter. He began with his biological daughter, and intermittently molested three of her girlfriends when they came home to play with her. Then there was a period of no offending—primarily because his biological daughter had grown older—that spanned roughly five years. Eventually he started up again with his younger stepdaughter after he remarried, and molested three additional female friends of hers. Ken admitted to over a hundred episodes of sexual contact spanning roughly eleven years. The behaviors began with his disrobing and his being touched and fondled. Over the years things progressed, and included some kinky activities. As I reported previously, the girls he molested finger painted his genitals, shaved off his pubic hair, tied a rope to his penis and pulled him around the house, and held his penis while he urinated. He also fondled the breasts and genitals of the children, the children fondled him, and he performed and received oral sex. These latter behaviors occurred toward the end of his offending.

Keeping the Victim Quiet

Long-term engagement in child molesting, like many types of deviant behavior, hinged on the ability of offenders to control potentially discrediting information about their activities. Secrecy was especially precarious because of the unique nature of the crime: the victims knew the offenders and could identify them; the men routinely revictimized the same person over and over; and the victims had relatively immediate access to someone they could tell. Thus the men faced exposure because of victim disclosure at any point. Despite these contingencies, secrecy was something all the men sustained while they actively offended. They did so most commonly by telling their victims not to tell anyone about what had happened between them.[4] Those who admitted having said something to the victim usually insisted that they did so only once, and usually not after the first offense, but as the situation progressed. Whatever the tactic used, most offenders believed that their victims willingly agreed that keeping quiet was best.

Offenders described using two basic types of verbal requests about keeping quiet. The first type, which was less common, consisted of verbal requests without any overt or stated threat involved. Sometimes these consisted of more global requests for victims not to tell anyone in general about what had happened; occasionally there were more specific requests not to tell a particular person or category of persons, such as friends. Kevin, Tom, and Carl each recalled implementing this type of verbal control with their victims. Each said the victim seemed to agree without fanfare not to say anything. Tom especially (the second example) seemed to believe his victim understood the importance of keeping quiet to protect their relationship. The clinician who worked with Tom and his family in treatment indicated in a later interview that the stepdaughter he molested had been extremely fearful of him.

R: One time I took a shower with her. I forgot about that.
I: What happened there?
R: . . . That's when I told her, I said, "Well, this is our secret. We won't tell

nobody about this." And she said, "Okay."

I: . . . Was that the only time you said anything to her like that?

R: Uh huh [yes].

I: Where, when you said that, where did that come? Was it the first, the second, the third, or the fourth time?

R: About the third. I think . . . .

I: Did you ever threaten her in any way?

R: No.

R: I think . . . once I mentioned to her, "We really . . . shouldn't discuss this with anybody." She says, "Oh that's for sure!"

I: Was that early on? Further on?

R: . . . It was well into it. It kind of like occurred to one of us we better think about that . . . ; because we would discuss being able to hear the car come up . . . . And we'd lock the doors . . . . I don't ever recall myself really programming her, "You got to be sure." It was almost as if, "Yeah, I understand that." She once said something about "Well, I better go in and get my blouse otherwise mom might get suspicious." So she was defending it I think . . . to some extent herself.

R: The only thing I said was . . . , "If you're having sex with your little friends, you don't have to tell them about me." That's all I said . . . . There was no threats or anything like that. It was just kind of a passing statement . . . . There was nothing like "I'll kill your dog" or anything like that.

More often than not, however, when verbal requests were employed, offenders attached warnings and threats about the consequences that could result if disclosure occurred. This was the second type of verbal control strategy. The kinds of consequences mentioned to victims varied. Sidney remembered invoking the threat of "divorce" and the breakup of the family should his stepdaughter ever tell her mother. The child, he added, had already been through one divorce, and so he figured she would be highly motivated to avoid a second one.

R: The only threat I ever placed on her was that if this was ever to be found out that a divorce was going to occur from it . . . . I'd say, "For God's sake, don't tell your mom because we're going to end up in a divorce." Which I think I was using because mentally I knew it probably was one of the scariest things to her, because she'd been through it once before.

Two offenders, Gary and Mark, warned their victims that they would end up in "jail" or "prison" should the children happen to talk to anyone. Gary, in the first example, did not believe that what he said actually constituted a threat.

R: She hadn't threatened [to tell] or nothing. I mean she wasn't like that . . . . I started getting caught up with my fears and frustrations. So . . . I asked her not to tell anybody . . . .

I: What did you say to her? Do you recall?

R: . . . I said, "You know that this is wrong." And I told her, "I'd really appreciate it if you wouldn't tell anybody this!" because I just flat out told her, "I would go to prison if people find out . . . ."

I: Did you threaten her in any way if she told? That something might happen to her?

R: No. I could never do that!

R: I'd think that if I got caught I could be put in jail. I could be locked up . . . ; I could lose everything I had . . . . I remember . . . that's why I tell the child, "Do not tell nobody." . . . I said, "If you're a little uptight," I said, "Don't tell nobody that this happened because if you tell anybody I'll go to jail." And "Do you want to see me go to jail?" She said no. I said, "Well, don't tell nobody."

The most dramatic comments made by offenders to victims contained references to physical harm. In particular, George and Corey each said they told their victim or victims not to say anything to their mothers, or their mothers would "kill" both of them. George did not see his comment as a threat. When he said "kill," he claimed, he did not mean "kill" literally. But he did use force to initiate sexual contact. Corey, in contrast, acknowledged knowing that what he said was a threat. He said he repeated the same message each time he offended early on to both daughters, and later to his son, and that over time he stopped saying it because, as he put it, "finally it was going on and on and nothing was being said so they understood their dad's rule."

R: I remember telling her once . . . not to say anything to her mother. I said, "If you ever tell your mother this happened she'll kill us both . . . ."

I: When you said the word "kill," what did you mean?

R: I just meant she'd be awful upset with us. Hell, I didn't mean kill . . . .

I: Do you think she understood that?

R: I don't know. Yeah, I believe so.

R: Told them don't tell anybody because their mother would kill us . . . . Really that [was] a threat. By telling them don't tell your mother [or] she's going to kill us. It's the same thing as . . . picking you up by the collar and then saying . . . , "I'm going to knock your teeth down your throat."

A third offender, Kelly, said he told his girlfriend's daughter he molested that he would "whip" her if she told her mother. He too did not see his comments as a physical threat.

R: I remember telling her, "Don't tell mommy." I remember that.
I: Why did you tell her that?
R: I didn't want to get in trouble . . . .
I: Did you physically threaten the child?
R: No, well, no, not physically. Verbally . . . [I'd] say, "You better not tell your mom, or I'm going to have to whip your ass." I'd say that.

Finally, one other offender, Earl, silenced his common law wife's daughter with the threat that if she did tell someone about what he did, no one would believe her. He essentially tried to disarm the girl by telling her she really could not prove anything.

R: I just told her that nobody would believe her. And there's no way of really proving it ever happened because . . . you've never been penetrated. And how are you going to prove it?
I: Did she threaten to tell on you?
R: No, she never did.

In addition to using verbal strategies for ensuring silence, some men admitted letting discipline slide, being extra nice, and even offering special rewards to their victims such as candy or money with the hope that such things would keep them quiet. These offenders fit the stereotyped image of the child molester that has so often been formulated in the media and the literature. Leon and Mark both reported using this strategy of buying off, compensating, or basically bribing their victims so they would be less inclined to tell on them to protect themselves.

R: Well, I treated her probably better than I had before, . . . and that was a conscious effort, thinking that if . . . she was happy, she wouldn't be as apt to be unhappy with me because I hollered at her or something and go run and tell somebody. So I was easier on her. I let . . . a lot of the disciplinary things slide. I allowed her to do some things that she always wanted to do, like climb a tree, which I was always against, because I was afraid she was going to break a leg. I'd allow her to do those sort of things. Sometimes I'd buy her a candy bar . . . , but I didn't do that while she was sitting on my lap. Those were all things to make her happy with me, thinking that if she was happy with me, she wouldn't be as apt to tell somebody about me touching her.

R: That week . . . I tried my best to be nice to her, good to her, because of everything. Anything that she wanted she got it. When her mother was gone she could stay up until nine o'clock . . . to watch TV. I [kept] on giving her her way to keep her quiet from not telling her mother.

I: So you were nice to her to keep her quiet?

R: Yes . . . . Like I'd look on the road and . . . see the popsicle truck passing by . . . ; and I would buy the two boys a popsicle . . . ; but I would buy her two . . . . And I would hide the other one and say, "This is yours; this is yours; this is yours . . . ," trying to win back that confidence for her to stay quiet.

It has long been assumed in the empirical literature, according to research on women and children who have experienced sexual assault, that most offenders take a proactive role in trying to keep their victims silent about what has happened to them. Certainly this was the case with many of the men here, as has been documented, but not always, according to their accounts. More than a few men insisted that they never said anything to the children they molested and that they never tried to bribe them or buy them off in any way. Instead, they said they relied on the victims to keep quiet on their own. The reasons for this presumption varied, but most often offenders stated that they believed their victims were too loyal to turn on them, that their victims enjoyed what was occurring and had more to lose by telling than by not telling, that their victims would be too embarrassed to tell someone, especially if homosexual sex was involved, or that no one would really get too upset with what they were doing anyhow.

Sam seemed almost nonchalant about sex with his stepson. He recalled being discreet with his behavior, but that he never told the boy not to say anything. In part, he figured that if his wife were to find out, her reaction would be lessened by her own "immoral" sexual behavior with another man.

R: It wasn't done blatantly, but . . . there was never . . . , "Oh, I got to keep this a secret . . . ; don't tell anybody." It was . . . done on a "this is just something that we're going to do" type of thing. It was . . . private, but it wasn't a terrible secret, or I never said, "Don't tell anybody." And then I think the triad situation developed . . . as an offset there. That if I did have some concerns about the molest, that I felt by having [my wife] involved in this other three-way sex thing that she would not be nearly as upset about the molest if she found out about it.

Harry was largely oblivious to any real risk about what he was doing and figured the seven-year-old girl he molested, his principal victim, did not want anyone to know what was happening any more than he did, because telling would take away the specialness the two of them shared.

R: I don't think I was ever concerned that there was any way someone could find out because I had a lot of faith in my stepdaughter. Not because I told her not to say anything, but because she wouldn't . . . . I may have told her not to tell her mom, but I don't think so. Only if she had asked me . . . , I wouldn't have said that without her asking me . . . . I think she just knew that . . . , if everybody knew about it, we wouldn't have felt any closer because of it.

Eric never told any of the many boys he admitted molesting inside and outside his own family to remain quiet. He figured boys were naturally reluctant to talk about homosexual sex.

R: Fortunately most boys kept it to themselves. I presume because they liked me. Either that, or they were too embarrassed. They didn't want it to get out any more than I did . . . . The boys just didn't tell.

Randy was another offender who claimed he never told his victim in any way to remain silent. In part, he reasoned, it was because when he was touched sexually himself as a child, he was never told either not to say anything, and he never did.

I: Did you tell her to be quiet about what happened?
R: No . . . . At no time did I ever say a word to her about that— . . . keep this quiet or don't tell your mom or don't tell anybody.
I: . . . Were you afraid of getting caught?
R: Sure, yeah, I was afraid of getting caught . . . .
I: It just never crossed your mind to say anything?
R: No, that was never a consideration for me, to keep her quiet. I don't know if

it's the way the circumstances started . . . , with her willingness to participate . . . , why I wouldn't. I probably should have. But, granddad never told me that, be quiet.

William said he figured that his daughters naturally would not say anything because of their loyalty to him and because the act of incest was something that anyone would be reluctant to admit. He believed that his daughters wanted sex with him, that they initiated things as much as he did, and that therefore they had no reason to say anything.

I: How did you control the children?
R: There was really no control other than maybe their loyalty [or] love to me . . . .
I: How important was it to you to maintain secrecy about what you were doing with the children?
R: I never really thought about it. I never really thought about the importance of it. The nature of the act itself is not something one does in public or talks about. It carries with it its own secrecy . . . . There were no safeguards. It was just kept to ourselves . . . .
I: How come your daughters never told anyone about it?
R: . . . Probably because they realized it was wrong. And maybe because they enjoyed the experience.

Ken likewise claimed he never told the children he offended, eight of them total, not to say anything to anyone. He figured that the victims were having fun, that they were not being forced to have sex, and therefore there was no real need to worry.

R: There was no effort to maintain secrecy. I didn't at any time tell the kids to keep quiet about what we were doing. And this goes back to the fact I did not see any reason why the kids would say anything to their parents because the things we did were nothing but fun and games . . . .
I: So you never said anything [to any of them]?
R: Never said a thing. I didn't see why it would be necessary. This feeling must have had some justification because it wasn't until long after the actions had stopped that the actions were revealed.

Scott admitted being concerned about secrecy in the later stages of his offending career, but he recalled thinking that his stepdaughter was afraid to tell because of how her mother might react. He claimed he never told her not to say anything.

R: I think she was afraid to tell because she didn't want to lose everything; she didn't want to get herself in trouble; and because her mother was very hard on her. Her mother . . . was emotionally very, very hard on her . . . . And I think she was afraid that she would have been blamed for it so she might not have wanted to tell.

Scott's belief that his stepdaughter would keep quiet was confirmed to him when he was nearly caught by his wife in the bathroom one morning with his hands down the girl's pants. When confronted by an accuser, the victim remained silent. Other men also reported that the children they molested denied anything was happening to them if confronted by their mother. This undoubtedly contributed to feelings of invulnerability for some offenders and helped sustain the offending process. Scott gave the most dramatic example.

R: There was one time . . . my wife almost caught me, well did catch me really, but I kind of lied my way out of it . . . . I had my . . . hands in [my stepdaughter's] pants when she was brushing her hair in the bathroom. I heard . . . my wife coming from the bedroom so I kind of jumped back, and she came in and said, "What's going on?" I said, "I was just in here goofing around tickling [her]." My wife looked at her and said, "What's going on?" and she said, "He was just tickling me, nothing."
I: She covered for you? Literally?
R: Yeah, she literally covered for me.

Gaining Recurrent Unguarded Access

According to routine activities theory, as the amount of unguarded access to victims or targets of crime increases, the overall rate of any given crime should vary upward as well. Unguarded access, in turn, is hypothesized to vary according to people's general lifestyle patterns. Support for this theory has been demonstrated largely on the macro, or societal, level. For example, one study has shown that official burglary and theft rates increased over time with the growth of single-parent households.[5] Routine activities theory, however, is also relevant on a micro-level, at the level of individual, day-to-day behavior. Thus in this direction, a second central contingency in the cases of men who became regular offenders was the way and extent to which they secured recurrent unguarded access to their victims. Three basic patterns of regular access were reported.

One group of men were best classified as idiosyncratic offenders. They did not really plan out how to gain access to victims, but reacted spontaneously to situations, from moment to moment, if victims happened to be left unguarded. It was only when others unwittingly allowed them time alone with a particular child—for example, if they were asked to baby-sit by friends, watch a child while their spouse stepped out somewhere, or run an errand with a child—that the opportunity to offend arose. Unguarded access to victims varied with the routine activities of everyone else around them. Ian said his offending varied according to when his wife shopped. She shopped a lot, so he offended a lot. William was less specific; he noted that what he did varied depending on when his wife came and went for whatever reason. John molested his niece routinely when his mother, whom he was living with, asked him to baby-sit the girl.

R: It wasn't like it was an ongoing thing all the time. A lot of times it just happened to be circumstance; it wasn't planned ahead . . . . It was more spontaneous. The circumstances were right; home alone at the house; the mood's right . . . . Generally things were done when no one else was around the house. And that was quite often, because the oldest two loved to shop and my wife did too.

R: They were all very spontaneous, spur of the moment happenings . . . . The situations presented themselves at times my wife would not be home and I would be at home with [just] one of my daughters . . . . I think my wife must have had an idea because when she was present the daughters would still cling to me . . . , or always sit on my lap, or kiss me . . . . But she never questioned me.

R: If mom had to go somewhere she would ask me to watch [my niece]. Or [my niece] would ask to stay there with me . . . . And mom would leave and usually what would happen is I would go upstairs and call [her] up . . . . Mom had complete trust in me . . . . So whenever she wanted someone to . . . watch [my niece], . . . almost always she would leave [my niece] with me . . . . Whenever mom would leave, that would be like turning the switch . . . ; the relationship would go from emotional to physical.

There were some instances in which nonoffending parents repeatedly left a child alone with an offender, in circumstances that bordered on negligence. In these instances the offender had usually been drinking alcohol, and often in large quantities. Both George and Larry said their wives regularly left them with their stepchildren after they had been drinking. The specific offense George described below occurred after he came home from a bar. Larry reported that his wife was a heavy drinker herself.

R: Her mother asked me to come home to baby-sit . . . . I was drinking. I didn't want to come home . . . . I didn't want to leave. I was still drinking. I said, "Okay, I will anyway." So I went home to baby-sit. The younger girl was gone [too] . . . . She must have went with her mother or something.

R: My wife was staying out with her friends and drinking after work and she wouldn't come home until real late . . . . I was always drinking real bad when the molest happened too.

In the case of one idiosyncratic type of offender, the opportunity to molest varied with a complex chain of lifestyle circumstances that limited the amount of access to the victim and the overall amount of behavior. Gary started molesting his stepdaughter after he and his wife divorced. He offended on only four occasions over two years. Unguarded access depended on three factors: he had to have visitation with his biological daughter; his stepdaughter had to come along on the visit, which she did not always do; and then he had to be left alone with the girl for a while. Gary said he never planned how to gain access; he molested his stepdaughter only if the opportunity was right. The following account was from the third of four offenses.

I: It occurred in the bathroom of your girlfriend's parents' home. How did you carry that off without people finding out?
R: . . . The kids were out back playing in the yard . . . . Her parents had been gone shopping and [my girlfriend] stepped out to go to the grocery store to get some milk.
I: So . . . the adults were gone and the kids were outside playing.
R: Empty house, yeah.
I: Did you ever plan any of the episodes?
R: No . . . . It was just . . . spontaneous, just out of nowhere.

A second group of offenders fit the pattern of scheduled planners. These men organized their ongoing involvement in offending around when their spouse/partner worked outside the home. Situations in which offenders either left for work later or got home earlier, or when their spouse/partner worked a different shift created a regular window of opportunity for offending. In these cases, the men formulated what basically amounted to an offense schedule. They settled into a pattern of offending at a set time on certain days, usually weekdays and not weekends, when they knew their victims would be home alone and unguarded. If the victim was an only child, everything simply fell into place. If there were other children in the house, the schedule of the wife and the routine activities of everyone else together shaped the situation. Tom, Leon, and Conrad noted that there were regular times they were home alone with their victims, and they offended more or less according to a schedule.

I: Would you pick certain times . . . that you knew were safer?

R: Well, it was usually early afternoon, or just after she got off school. I worked nights, and my ex worked days and she would get home at about 4:30 or 5:30 or something like that. So we knew how much time, when to start, when to stop, that kind of thing.

I: Did your wife ever suspect?

R: No, I don't think so.

R: My wife started taking evening classes and was gone one evening [a week] till late. When I say late, ten o'clock . . . . Well, we'd have supper and all three kids were home most of the time. And the kids would do the dishes, then the two older ones would go to their rooms. Or the oldest one had a . . . part-time job sometimes he went to. And we were basically alone; and she, the victim, would come in . . . and we would watch television.

I: Where was your wife at the time?

R: She was at work . . . ; this was early morning . . . . She had to be at work at 4:30 in the morning so she'd leave the house about ten minutes after four. So this was even maybe 4:15, till the other kids, they got up around, some of them would start stirring at around 5:30 at the earliest. So I used that time frame of 4:15 to 5:30, or 6:00 at the latest if I knew they was going to sleep in late.

A third and final group of offenders consisted of men who were basically tactical premeditators. Rather than waiting for opportunities to be handed to them or falling into a pattern of offending when their partners were at work, these men took a more proactive and deliberate role in gaining access. They often decided days ahead of time about when and where they would offend; or they created their own opportunities to offend by setting situations up. Kevin, for example, described how he would ask his wife to do things to get her out of the house and send his son to a friend's to play, leaving him alone with his biological daughter. Corey said that planning when and where he was going to molest any of his three biological children the next time was an exciting part of the offending process. Sam mentioned planning trips and taking his step-son with him so he could have time alone with the boy.

I: Oh I set her up. I set her up big time. I did.

R: You set her up big time, what do you mean?

R: Oh . . . I would make reasons for [my ex] to leave the house, get her out of the house. Have [my son] go down and play with his friends and have [my daughter] there in the house with me . . . . There was times I planned it . . . .

I: Were you ever afraid your wife was catching onto any of this?

R: No, I never was.

R: I would . . . plan two or three days ahead of time when the next event was going to happen . . . . I'd find out . . . where the wife was going to be, who was going to be home, how long I'd have, what I could do. It was a big thrill planning it. You get anticipation, or great expectations of, tonight's the night, or today's the day . . . . I just worked it when she was never there . . . ; that was part of the planning . . . . I don't think she really knew.

R: He'd been to Philadelphia and Los Angeles with me and Yosemite sometimes alone . . . . Some I'd plan. I'd plan for that so we could be alone . . . . I'd trav-el and take him with me. Sometimes it was just short overnights, around the state, but he went with me to a number of places . . . . That would put us together for two or three days. Be able to sleep together. Which was a more satisfying relationship than just having sex standing up somewhere.

In nearly every instance, offenders engaged their victims when they were completely alone with them and no one else was around. But a few men who were tactical premeditators molested while other people— spouse, girlfriend, relatives, friends, other children—were present in the immediate setting where events transpired. In these circumstances, the men acted either when potential observers were busy and distracted with something else, particularly watching television, or in the middle of the night when everyone else was asleep. Typically the structure or layout of the house facilitated access without being seen—children who had a bedroom separated from everyone else's such as in the basement; ranch-style homes where the family or activity room was at one end, the kitchen was in the middle, and bedrooms were at the other end. Scott and Steve both offended when their spouses and other children were at home. Each admitted making up stories about what they were doing to divert attention from themselves and each took advantage of the layout of the house to molest without being seen. Both engaged their victims too by sneaking and spying on them when they were asleep.

R: God, you come up with all kinds of ideas to figure out, "How am I going to do this without her knowing about it?" . . . It was devious is what it was! "I got to go to the bathroom," or "I'm going to go down and meditate for a while . . . ." It progressed to where I would come up with ways and means to go down and touch her again . . . . My wife would be up watching TV and they [the victim and her sister] had the room downstairs. And I have an office down there . . . , "Well, I'm going to go down and do this or do that . . . ." Well of course I'd sneak in the room, the urge would come on and I'd sneak down there, lift up her underwear, and touch her.

R: My wife would be off in the living room with my older daughter; the kids [the boys] would be in their bedroom. The younger daughter [the victim] would be in her bedroom. And I'd be back listening to the radio or find some excuse to be back in the bedroom. Many times it was . . . the excuse that I was studying for . . . Bible class . . . .

I: You'd go in there while your wife was awake watching TV?

R: Yeah. Because the way the house was set up, the bedrooms were way in the back of the house; there was a long hallway that led into the kitchen and then the kitchen led into the dining room and then the . . . living room . . . . I mean there was a *long* separation between us . . . . And I could hear my wife coming and beeline out of there, which happened several times.

Drawing Sexual Boundaries

The vast majority of the men I interviewed indicated that their actions ended at a certain level of seriousness and things never went any further. Each of the following types of sexual acts were reported by offenders: 97 percent breast or genital fondling; 53 percent performing or receiving oral sex; 27 percent rubbing or stroking the penis against the vagina or anus; 13 percent manual penetration of either area; and 10 percent vaginal or anal intercourse (see appendix C).[6] The question, of course, was why things stopped where they did. Why did offenders who said their actions were limited to fondling never proceed to oral sex or intercourse? Why did offenders who ended with oral sex or penis-vaginal contact never proceed to vaginal intercourse, anal sex, or other unconventional behaviors?[7] The answers to these questions were wide ranging, but there were two general factors: first, the reaction of the victim, and second, whatever struck the offender as personally relevant at the time, especially if he perceived he had something to lose by going further than he did.

Some men said they stopped where they did in terms of the seriousness of their behavior because they believed there was a line of no return. Certain behaviors were just too serious to ever undo or explain; once certain bridges were crossed there was no getting back. Other behaviors were defined as lesser and more defensible wrongs. The line varied from offender to offender, but vaginal or anal intercourse was always mentioned as a boundary point. As Gary put it, "I knew that there was a line that we can't cross . . . . There was no vagina and no, . . . I've never probed at any woman's ass or anything like that." When behavior reached a certain level, then it became a sexual violation, but not before. There was a process of minimizing involved. Scott, who stopped at the level of oral sex, and Leon, who limited his behavior to genital fondling, elaborated about unspoken sexual boundaries of this sort.

R: It just was never something I had wanted to evolve to . . . ; how do I explain this? I think that I felt like as long as I didn't have intercourse I wasn't doing anything wrong, I wasn't sinning. Okay? I wasn't breaking the rules . . . . Somehow in my mind I felt like to have intercourse with her would be to violate her.

I: But the other [acts] weren't?

R: But the other's weren't. They weren't really violating her. They might not have been right, but they weren't really violating her.

I: Did you ever want to go beyond [further than what you did]?

R: Yes, yes I did. I wanted to insert my finger and I wanted to do a lot of things. I wanted to go down on her . . . ; I wanted her to see my penis. I wanted her to touch it. I even thought what sexual intercourse would be like, although . . . I didn't know whether she was physically able to have intercourse . . . . I wanted to do all those things, yes, but I did not.

I: And . . . why not?

R: . . . There wasn't enough time. There was normally other people in the house. And I thought those were bridges that if you crossed them you could never get back. It was almost like as if I had a defense for what I was doing [and] I would have no defense if I actually had intercourse with her, or if I had her . . . take my penis in her mouth or something.

Equally as common was the preferred or desired sexual repertoire of the offender. There were some sexual behaviors, likes and dislikes that carried over from consensual sexual relations with adults, that seemed to limit how far and in what direction offending would proceed. Men in this group, ironically, saw some sexual behaviors as abnormal, others as more normal. Decisions about the level of contact seemed to have little to do with how the victim might react or feel. Ian, Sam, and Scott mentioned sexual repertoire as defining their boundary. Again, the level of behavior varied depending on the offender.

R: As much as I like sex, I just didn't go in for anal sex, or oral sex even, or especially the real kinky stuff.
I: Was oral sex ever a part of the sexual repertoire with your daughters?
R: There was an attempt . . . but they didn't go along with it.
I: . . . Them doing it to you?
R: Yeah. I wasn't into it too much either with them. I think one or two times . . . ; I looked upon it as something unnatural. So I wasn't comfortable. And . . . I'm not into putting ice cream, and all the other, the mixed food and the whole bit. [I don't] get into all that. I just don't.

I: Why not anal intercourse or anything like that?
R: To me that was weird. That . . . just wasn't normal (*chuckles*). That's pretty [ironic], but yeah the other was more normal.

I: Why did you limit the sexual activity to the things that you did? Why didn't you go to [the level of] intercourse . . . ?
R: . . . Oral sex was more pleasureful to me than intercourse was. Intercourse was okay.
I: You thought that at the time?
R: I *know* that. I enjoyed oral sex much more than I did intercourse . . . . I mean I *enjoyed* intercourse okay, and that was great (*very loudly*). But there were times when I didn't want intercourse, I'd rather have oral sex . . . . I can see that pattern throughout my sexual activity.

While the victim's reactions to sexual contact often seemed to get ignored, redefined, or misinterpreted, a few men did take heed of physical pain and stopped what they were doing. Usually it took crying and yelling on the part of the victim to break through and touch the offender. It was the pain of the victim, then, that established the boundary about how far the offender was willing to go. The situations of Larry and Ian both illustrate this pattern.

R: It just slowly progressed to being like with her clothes off and just rubbing and then one time I did attempt to have sexual intercourse with her and she started, [my stepdaughter] started crying and said . . . that it hurt so I quit. Okay, and that was the only time, I never did successfully have intercourse with her. But I did attempt and when she cried and said that it hurt, . . . at that point I told her, I says, " . . . Don't never come into the room with me alone again." I says, "I do not like this. This is not right."

R: I was afraid I'd hurt her. And it wasn't easy; I mean there was just no way. There was no penetration at all. I didn't know exactly why. And I know there's the hymen there and all that. And I wasn't about to try to force anything even though maybe that . . . wouldn't be harmful to her. Eventually I guess . . . it does get broken . . . . But I wasn't about to try to hurt her. It was uncomfortable for her. I could tell that.

I: How so?

R: Well, because she pulled back a little bit. I mean she might've said something like "It hurts," or something to that extent. And so that to me, . . . I know some rapists or other individuals are turned on by pain, or some sexual deviants are turned on by pain. To me I'm turned off by pain and sex being associated.

Overt and explicit emotional distress on the part of the victim during sexual contact, a few men also said, was enough to stop them from trying to complete a particular behavior, at least temporarily. John noted that his victim started crying when he tried to physically force her to perform oral sex. Scott described how his stepdaughter tensed up physically when he tried to penetrate her manually. Both said they stopped with that particular behavior, though later they attempted other things.

R: [My niece] started to cry . . . and I felt angry that I'd done that, made her cry.

I: How so? Describe how you felt?

R: Just I had humiliated her to the point where she was crying.

I: When she started crying it struck you?

R: Yeah, it did, real strong . . . . I mean it was a mixture of pity and regret . . . that I'd reduced her to the point where she was crying. And [I had a] real strong desire to protect her . . . . It sounds strange, I was the one abusing her but at the same time . . . I wanted to protect her.

R: There were times when I would insert my finger in her vagina and . . . I could just physically feel her tense right up. And I knew then that . . . she didn't like that. That bothered her. That was more than what she had bargained for and I could tell that. And usually I'd quit shortly after that . . . . Just something [was] triggered . . . that said, "Hey, . . . this wasn't pleasure to her . . . " Once I noticed that, usually I would stop what I was doing and I'd go back to like maybe taking her hand and putting it in my pants.

Rather than actually seeing the victim experience pain, a few men stopped at a lower level of sexual contact because they assumed that certain behaviors would cause pain, discomfort, or injury for the child if they were to engage in them, and they felt that the child was too young. Usually this included vaginal or anal penetration of any type. Leon drew boundaries around his behavior for this reason. His offending was limited to genital fondling. John stopped at oral sex for this reason too.

I: Did you ever insert your finger into the vagina?
R: No . . . . Nothing, oh other than having your finger crooked . . . while you're rubbing back and forth, but no actual knowing penetration. I was afraid to do that because I was afraid that it would hurt and that maybe she would bleed . . . . So I wouldn't attempt that. I thought she was too young for that.

R: I assume[d] both girls were virgins at the time and I just didn't want to cause them physical pain.
I: You actually thought about that at the time?
R: Yeah . . . . Fear you know of causing them to bleed or something.

The perceived physical size of the child, the belief that the child was too small to engage in certain behaviors, constituted a stopping point for many men. Unfortunately for the victim, physical size was only a temporary barrier to more serious offending later. Conrad initially stopped offending at the level of penis-genital contact, but later his offending escalated to vaginal intercourse. Phil admitted that his involvement would have gotten much worse if he had not been caught.

I: Why didn't you penetrate her [early on]?
R: Because it would hurt . . . ; I mean I was a full-grown man and she was just a little girl.
I: So you recognized and paid attention to that and that placed a limit around your behaviors?

R: Oh yeah! Yeah, I did have boundaries on my behavior. They were just a little bit wider than what is (*laughs*) socially recognized.

I: What would keep you from going further . . . ?

R: The fact that she was too small . . . . I could see myself, if it had progressed,
as she became older, becoming sexually involved with her as far as intercourse is concerned.

I: As she had grown physically larger?

R: Yeah, as she had become larger and more mature.

I: So the only thing that restrained you is her size?

R: Right.

The possibility of causing serious physical injury to the victim struck
a chord for a couple of other men and stopped them from trying intercourse. There was a presumption that any lesser behavior was simply
not nearly as hurtful, indeed not really hurtful at all. Kelly and Gary
were two such cases. Gary noted that he had "enough sense" to stop
where he did, at the level of receiving oral sex.

R: I didn't do any intercourse . . . . That could really mess them up, I mean for
life. And you can really screw them up in there where you just can't have
kids or anything, stuff like that.

R: Luckily I had enough sense about me to know that there is no way that I
could have entered her vagina or anything because it would have tore her
up.

As much as any other variable, explicit resistance from victims, especially if it was stiff and determined, stopped some men in their tracks,
though only temporarily. Typically they would try and reinitiate later
or switch to another victim who was more compliant. These men invariably never got beyond fondling with a victim who resisted. Scott stopped
what he was doing with one stepdaughter because she told her mother
after the first incident; later he shifted to a younger sister, whom he
molested extensively. Harry and Phil, the second and third examples,
were routinely told to quit but always tried again after a few days.

R: There was one time I tried to touch my older daughter . . . and she went to her
mother and told her . . . . My wife confronted me with it and I didn't deny
it . . . . She went into a rage . . . .

I: She was *very* resistant?

R: Oh yes! Yeah. She wasn't going to put up with it anymore. Because by this time she was thirteen . . . and she was . . . very strong-minded, determined to be her own person . . . . If she didn't want it she wasn't going to let it happen.

R: She would say quit or she would roll over or something, and I wasn't trying to force her to do anything. So if she gave any kind of negative response I would just quit . . . . All she had to say was "Don't do that!" and I didn't do that.

R: There would be times . . . she'd ask me to stop and I would.

I: What would she say to you?

R: She says, "That's enough," and I would stop.

I: How quickly?

R: Very quickly. Immediately . . . . Or if she'd say I was hurting her, I'd stop immediately.

A corollary factor that shaped the direction and level of sexual contact was the perceived likes and dislikes of the victim. The boundary was what was believed to be uncomfortable, undesirable, or too much for the other person. One offender, Tom, said he asked the victim whether a behavior was okay before he did it; another offender, Ian, settled into behavior that he felt the victim would go along with. In a sense, these men forced the victim to define the limits of their behavior. They saw themselves as sensitive to the needs of the person they were victimizing. While they seemed to see the unwanted nature of a particular behavior, they could not see the larger picture that legally and morally they should not be doing anything.

I: How far did it all go? . . . Did you have intercourse . . . ?

R: No. She performed oral sex on me. I asked her to and she said okay. And I never orgasmed in her mouth. I even asked her about that. I said, "Would that bother you?" And she said, "Yeah, I think so." And I said, "Well, I won't do that."

I: And so what would you do then?

R: I would just withdraw and have her masturbate me or I'd masturbate myself and hold her close to me.

R: You find out pretty much what she likes and what she's amenable to and so you pursue it along that line and . . . , at least it was that way with me, not try to do more than what she liked. And I guess the idea of by doing what she liked that it would encourage the activity to continue. So . . . that was the focus of most of it, it was to do what she liked. And she was very much into it. There was no doubt about it.

I: What specifically did she like . . . ?

R: Being masturbated.

Sometimes it was the recognition of personal consequences for the victim or for themselves, the realization that what the offender might do would impact one or the other's lives, that seemed to sensitize certain men from proceeding to the level of intercourse. Guilt over taking away the victim's virginity or fear of getting the victim pregnant represented boundaries in this respect. Glenn and Ian stopped short of intercourse with their children for these two reasons.

R: I didn't think about penetration. I just wanted to rub it against her.

I: Was there a reason why the behaviors were limited to that?

R: [I] . . . felt that she was special and that she should be saved . . . ; she was supposed to be a virgin and she should stay a virgin. And if you ask her about that, that's how she felt. She said that several times.

R: I remember being scared to death that, now she's a developed girl, and fifteen, and she might be at risk of getting pregnant. And that just scared the hell out of me that I would ever harm my kids that way, even though you can get an abortion. That's something that would be very hard for me . . . , I mean this is hard enough, if they went through something like that, of having to be altered in some [way], surgically or whatever, it would be a very, very hard thing for me. Or to actually go ahead and deliver a baby.

Idiosyncratic situational factors also limited how far many men were willing to go. These contingencies varied from offender to offender with no consistent theme. Steve, for example, who limited his offending to fondling his stepdaughter while she was allegedly asleep, admitted to wanting to go further than he did, but the structural arrangement of the setting prohibited it. The victim slept on a bunk bed with another stepdaughter, and he was afraid of making too much noise.

R: There were times when I wanted to go further . . . ; I guess because the bunk beds kind of make a lot of noise and the chance of waking her up. That's the whole point is she was asleep.

I: What did you want to do? How far did you want to go?

R: There were times when I wanted . . . sexual intercourse. The thought of that
entered in too.

Corey stopped at fondling his victim and masturbating himself to
orgasm because that was enough for him to feel satisfied, and because he
was still being sexual with his wife and knew he would have intercourse
with her.

R: The thought was there but the mind said no . . . . Something was saying . . .
all I needed was just to touch them, have them touch me, and that was
enough satisfaction. Because I guess in my mind, back in my mind, okay,
another week or so we'd have sex, [my] wife and I would have sexual intercourse and that was where I got the other fulfillment.

Brian stopped at the level of contact he did because he got caught in
the act the first time he did anything. If he had not been caught, there is
no telling exactly how far he would have gone. He admitted that he did
not really have any boundaries. In this instance, the boundary was externally imposed.

I: How far do you think it would have gone if you weren't caught?
R: . . . As far as I could have gotten . . . ; I'd have probably had him giving me
a head job.
I: Would you have done the same?
R: Sure.

Phil limited his behavior to genital fondling because he knew that his
wife responded more to that type of stimulation and that penetration
of the vagina was not as pleasureful for her. He carried this over to his
daughter—no sense in doing something that really would not excite her.

I: How far did things progress in terms of contact? You described touching her
externally . . . .
R: Yeah, that's basically it . . . ; I stuck to just the stimulation. I really didn't
want to touch her vaginally, because . . . from my own relationship with my
wife, I discovered that vaginal contact really didn't stimulate her . . . .
I: Was there any reason why you didn't do any other behaviors?
R: . . . Probably because I hadn't really been exposed to that many different
behaviors.

Last, more than a few men stopped short of reaching ejaculation; they
chose to draw the boundary at orgasm rather than at a particular sexu-

al act per se. The reason seemed to be that this mitigated their feelings of guilt. A number of men got up and went to the bathroom to masturbate and ejaculate rather than doing this in the company of the victim. Kevin is a case in point. His victim was six in the example below.

I: How far did it go?

R: Just that, fondling. There was never any intercourse . . . . I would pull her over on top of me. I would rub her vagina against my penis . . . ; I never ejaculated on her . . . .

I: Did you ever ejaculate during any of this?

R: No.

I: . . . Did you ejaculate afterwards?

R: Uh huh [yes].

I: What would be involved in that?

R: Oh, I would just go into the bath[room]. I [got to] feeling bad or something and I'd just tell her to get up, I didn't want to play this game anymore. And I would go into the bathroom and masturbate.

There were, of course, a few men who did not really have any sexual boundaries, or who had boundaries that faded across time and victims, and who proceeded to very serious levels of sexual contact such as vaginal or anal intercourse without fanfare. The numbers were limited in this study. William said he had intercourse with his oldest biological daughter because, as he put it, "I guess I figured that's part of having sex." Asked to elaborate why he went further with one daughter than another in terms of the level of contact—intercourse versus masturbation—William indicated that it came down to the physical size of the victim. Also, unlike other men, William had no fear of getting his daughter pregnant.

R: I think the development of their bodies. The older daughter was more developed than the younger daughter.

I: How so?

R: Just more fully developed. Bigger build. Larger breasts.

I: Why did you penetrate the one child vaginally? Didn't that strike you as too much?

R: I don't think at the time I was reasoning in degrees . . . . I think when one takes pot and smokes it and then does cocaine and heroin, that is a difference in degrees, but one doesn't reason why one over the other. It was all too much.

I: Were you ever concerned about pregnancy?
R: I had a vasectomy . . . years earlier.

Conrad, who also had intercourse with his biological daughter, initially refrained from that specific behavior for about three years. For him, the victim was too small physically, but her physical development likewise sealed her unfortunate fate. Conrad took measurements of his daughter with a tape measure. When she matured he escalated his behaviors. He stated elsewhere that nothing short of the victim telling someone about what he was doing would have stopped him. He testified that no reaction on her part, no matter how emotional, would have made a difference.

I: At what point did you decide that you could penetrate her [have intercourse]? You described that early on you thought she was too small. What led you to the conclusion that you could?
R: Well, when she had grown. She was about the size of . . . her mother when I married her . . . . The measurement of her hips or butt was thirty-six inches. And . . . just by the physical size of her pelvic region, . . . well, she was big enough to take me.

Finally, in the case of Bob, the decision to engage in anal intercourse with his two victims, both boys who were eight at the start, was predicated on his own childhood experiences involving the same kind of behavior. When asked, "Did you ever think that anal intercourse with an eight-year-old boy would be painful?" he replied, "No. It wasn't with me." He had no sense that what he did might cause pain and claimed he saw no sign of any discomfort on the part of the boys involved. He also never asked the boys he sodomized whether he was hurting them. In other words, there was simply nothing to stop him. Bob defined his victims' reality for them.

Conclusion

There was no single consistent objective pathway among the men in this study in terms of how regular or sustained involvement in sexual offending unfolded. Some general patterns, however, were evident. In particular, over time, the more men offended, the more serious the sexual behavior became and the more likely there were to be additional victims. An escalation effect generally operated. When it came to maintaining secrecy, some men said they told their victims to keep quiet about things, and more often than not they attached warnings or threats about what would happen to ensure that silence was maintained. But equally as often, the men claimed they never said anything to their victims about keeping quiet, assuming that the victim had more to lose by telling. Regular offending also depended on regular access. When it came to gaining regular access to victims, some men were idiosyncratic offenders, others scheduled planners, and still others tactical premeditators. Finally, most of the men in this study claimed they drew boundaries around their behavior and stopped at a certain level of seriousness. Some men perceived a line of no return and stayed behind it, others noted limits based on their own sexual likes and dislikes, but most commonly, it was the actual or perceived reaction of the victim to a particular behavior that defined how far each offender was willing to go.

EIGHT

Exiting Offending and Public Exposure

So far this research has focused on documenting the multiple transitions and stages that explain involvement in child molesting—how the shift into the behavior unfolded and how the men who engaged in it progressed into a pattern of regular conduct. Equally as crucial, I believe, is the process of exiting from the sexual offender career,[1] the movement from the status of the "discreditable," or being a secret offender, to entry into the status of the "discredited," or becoming known to others.[2] But more, the broader concern of such an analysis is with how offenders shift out of sexual behavior with children over time and begin the process of returning to more conventional or acceptable forms of conduct. My interest is with how this shift or transition occurs on various levels. Did the men ever begin thinking about what might happen in their lives if someone discovered what they were doing? Did anyone ever stop offending on their own before the authorities intervened? How did the men ultimately get caught? What goes through the mind of an offender when he realizes that someone else knows about his secret? Are offenders more likely to deny or admit their guilt?

Exitings as social events encompass multiple and complex stages and various public versus personal dimensions.[3] For present purposes, the analysis will be limited specifically to the process of exiting from active offending. I do not investigate questions of stigma repair that undoubtedly follow legal exposure for such crimes. The respondents reported three basic stages in the transition out of active offending. First is what I call the boundary reemergence phase. Prior to being exposed as offenders, the men routinely became overwhelmed with fear and/or tried to stop themselves from offending again. This was a period of mounting regrets, self-questioning, and moral recognition of wrongdoing. Second is the detection phase of the exiting process. In the vast majority of cases, the men experienced a forced exit through confrontation by a nonoffending spouse or parent or by a victim who disclosed what had been happening. The transition was typically sudden and without forewarning. Last is the reaction and devastation phase that followed after exposure. The offenders described experiencing a wave of emotional relief and despair in the moments, hours, and early aftermath of being identified as child molesters.

Becoming Engulfed with Fear

Many of the men in this study said that early on in their offending they had little or no fear of being arrested or discovered. There were different reasons for this: they did not see what they were doing as a crime; they thought that they were smarter than everyone else and would not get caught; they believed that each time they offended they could stop themselves and would not offend again; they felt secure that the victim would not say anything to anyone else. In the later stages of their involvement, however, fear of detection seemed to become a central reality for some of the men. The more the offending progressed, the greater the anticipated threat of apprehension.[4] Over time, worry, anxiety, and feelings of paranoia began to engulf them. Commonly the men began to realize that if they got caught, they had a lot to lose—their reputation, family, friends, and job, among other things. The sexual boundary they had previously shattered with their behavior started to recrystallize in a very profound way.

Feelings of fear often arose when the victim became more independent and more difficult to control in terms of everyday childhood behavior. Faced with having to set boundaries around conduct more generally as a parent, men in these cases found their backs against the wall, believing that disclosure of what they had been doing was more likely to occur in retaliation against them. Randy had sex with his stepdaughter about a dozen times over a three-month period and then suddenly stopped offending. Three months later the situation was reported to the police.

In the interim, a period of mounting fear and paranoia set in. Randy's fears surfaced and escalated because he realized that his stepdaughter had grown incorrigible and there was nothing he could do to discipline her because she might get angry and tell on him.

R: It just started crossing my mind, . . . what if she got mad at me and told somebody? I really began to see the ramifications. Because once I stopped it she started changing towards me. She didn't want to come and talk to me . . . . She got deeper in with the kids that were running the drugs . . . . [I kept thinking] have I hurt this child? . . . Should I go see somebody? Should I tell somebody? . . . What if my employer finds out? What if friends and family find out?

I: You were really afraid of people finding out. What was that feeling [like]?

R: . . . That's a bitch! It's miserable . . . . I've always been well thought of in the community. I was a softball coach, well respected in my job. I'd sit there and think for hours on end, "Why did I do this? Why did I allow myself to get in this situation? How are you going to control her now? You can't be an authority to her now."

Other offenders—primarily those who abused one victim over a span of years—became fearful because the victim had grown older and, it might be presumed, more knowledgeable about what was happening. Sam admitted to hundreds of episodes of oral sex with his stepson from around the time the boy reached puberty. It was not until the boy was eighteen and had naturally matured and become more his own person that he began to worry about what he had to lose. Phil too became saturated with fear in part as a consequence of his biological daughter growing older.

R: I was in a position of power and control of a lot of people and a lot of money and a lot of things . . . ; I was very successful in my business; in the community [I was] highly thought of . . . . [But] I had a secret life. I had two lives. I had this pillar of society image and then this dark side . . . . And then [I] worried later; then [I] worried about being caught. It wasn't until [my stepson] really matured, until . . . he was eighteen or whatever, that I really began to worry about being caught.

R: As she became older, . . . more and more, fear became more and more involved. Fear that she may tell her mother. And then I'd be coming home from work and I'd be anticipating the police being at the house.

Fear mounted for still a couple of other men when, after having apparently sexualized the victim as a result of repetitive sexual contact, the victim began acting sexual back. Again, the offender's perception was that he had lost control over the victim and had no way to really contain the situation anymore. Larry said he experienced an unexpected spin to his offending as the situation he instigated continued over a period of five years. As he saw it, the victim, his stepdaughter, started to pursue him. He actually began to believe that the victim might tell on him if he did not agree to have sex with her when she wanted it. His entire sense of reality seemed to come unglued.

R: It had got to the place to where [my stepdaughter] was pursuing me; and at that time I was afraid if I said no that she's going to tell; that I'm going to jail and this and that and the other. And I was really, really scared! . . . I should have stopped it . . . . And I kind of . . . carried her up to a point to where she was sexually stimulated.

I: . . . What do you mean by sexually stimulated?

R: Well, . . . I think a person becomes sexually stimulated if they're left completely alone within a certain time . . . ; but [with] like touching, caressing, molesting, okay, you can bring them to a sexual peak sooner. And . . . I honestly think that that's what I had done, is just brought [my stepdaughter] slowly along to this point.

There was one episode, in particular, in which Larry's sense of what he was doing shifted and fear surfaced. He was kissing his stepdaughters good night after they had gotten into bed one evening, with no intent, he claimed, of doing anything sexual. When he got to the victim, the girl suddenly reached through his robe and started performing oral sex. His reaction was one of utter surprise. In his words, "I was really, really stunned!" It did not take Larry long to begin to realize he had created the seeds of his own destruction. The child also began acting out sexually with him, as he described, while his wife was present. The result was fear at a panic level. It started to become apparent to Larry that there was no way out.

R: It was kind of like a turn play. It got to the place there for a long time that I would stay away late and wait for them to go to bed . . . before I came home. Because I was afraid of getting caught up in a scenario I didn't want to be in . . . . I felt I was stuck between a rock and a hard spot . . . . Even with her mom sitting in the room, she would sit in my lap, and she would get herself positioned to where she was . . . sitting right on my penis. And then she would sit there and she would just constantly move her butt around . . . . And I'd get up, and I'd go to the bathroom, and when I'd come back I'd sit down, but I would sit down by [my wife] and [she] would come over and sit on my lap again. And I'd reach over and try to hold onto [my wife]. And [my wife] even got into it with me a couple of times about me not wanting the girls to sit on my lap . . . . She says, "I remember sitting in my daddy's lap all the time . . . ; I don't see what's wrong . . . ? Why don't you want them on your lap?" And I was [really] scared! I mean it had happened for so long but I was trying to figure a way out which I didn't see no end to. And I just felt trapped.

A similar account was given by Kelly, who became increasingly fearful because he came to believe, accurately or not, that his girlfriend's daughter, whom he had molested repeatedly, began to pursue and threaten him—this despite the fact that the girl was only four. Feeling that things had gotten out of his control, he began to think that there was no telling when she might blurt something out to her mother. He kept a constant watch over the victim, and took her places whenever he could, to try and limit the opportunities for a disclosure to occur.

R: She would constantly just . . . sit over on the couch . . . and watch TV and spread her legs . . . . She'd come over and say, "Touch me here. Aren't you going to touch me here?" And I was sometimes afraid if I wouldn't touch her she would tell.

I: Sounds like you had created something you couldn't [stop].

R: Yeah . . . . Until one time where she says, "If you don't touch me I'm going to tell . . . ." She did say that once and I remembered that.

I: What did you do?

R: And I went, whoa, I'm busted! . . . And I'd really have to watch over her as far as when she was with her mom. And I'd be afraid to leave sometimes because they can always get in there and throw a conversation in there real quick and I'll miss it. So I'd really watch her and take her with me wherever I was going. If she wanted a piece of candy, get a piece of candy.

Some men felt afraid because of feelings of transparency, a belief that a spouse or involved partner could see through them and recognize what they were doing.[5] Leon, for example, said that in the course of his involvement with his stepdaughter, he began to carefully monitor the frequency of sex he had with his wife. He feared that if there were any alteration in their sexual routine as a couple, she would be able to tell what he had been doing.

> R: I was getting very suspicious and paranoid. I was worried that any deviation in my normal routine or activities, she would suspect something . . . . [Sex together] . . . , if that was every three days, that's what I did. I mean I was very careful . . . to make sure that there wasn't any big change.

Phil committed his offenses in the late 1980s, when the television media began to saturate the public with movies and talk shows about incest and child sexual abuse. He remembered his wife watching those shows while he sat in front of the television with her. He began to feel that she could see through him.

> R: I was uncomfortable with seeing programs that . . . dealt with child molest. Or having my wife watch programs that dealt with child molest. Because I felt exposed.
> I: Even though your wife did not know about it?
> R: Right! . . . There was a sense of anxiety, and wondering if she'll . . . look at me as a child molester and think that I'm molesting [our] daughter.
> I: You thought she could . . . .
> R: [That] . . . she might pick up on that.

Sometimes fear seemed to engulf offenders when they suddenly realized that, because of the level of the sexual behavior involved, their female victims might get pregnant, which meant they would be found out. Glenn and John both described this fear. Neither had proceeded to the level of intercourse, but both had engaged in penis-vaginal contact. Each admitted pulling away from their victims when they realized they were going to ejaculate. Offenders who actually committed intercourse did not report the possibility of pregnancy as a source of fear because they used condoms or had other effective means of birth control such as a vasectomy, which eliminated any perceived risk.

> I: Were you fearful?
> R: Yeah. I didn't know that I was going to go to jail. I didn't know that I was going to be arrested . . . ; I wasn't fearful of that. I was fearful of if I let it go and I got my daughter pregnant. That's what I was fearful of . . . .
> I: Were you afraid of losing your marriage?
> R: Yeah, I was really afraid of that.

> R: Once or twice the excitement got enough so that I would ejaculate. Usually

I would move back away from her because, I can't explain it. One of the great fears that I had, one of the worst fears I had, was that she might become pregnant. That was the greatest fear. I mean I thought about that often. And . . . many times I said to myself, "You going to keep this up, she's going to get pregnant, and then what are you going to do? You can't do this anymore!"

Finally, in Phil's case, the source of fear was as much the perceived spiritual consequences as the legal repercussions. Being deeply religious, the more Phil offended, the more he began to fear the wrath of God. Fear of apprehension paled in comparison to the fact that he would have to face his maker and possibly be plunged into eternal damnation.

I: How afraid were you of the criminal law?
R: Well, there was fear there. But I believe God is more in control with events than the criminal justice system. So my fear was more placed with God . . . ; I mean I was terrified after the events occurred. I mean because I knew that I was in trouble . . . . The most fear I had then were of storms, when storms would be occurring, tornados. Or of an accident. Anything that may involve my dying . . . and having to stand before God and face God with what I had done . . . . Fear of the law paled much less in comparison than my fear of the eternal judgement that I would receive.

Regaining Temporary Control

Faced with mounting feelings of fear, the men I studied often—though not always—described periods in which they reassessed what they were doing and regained temporary control over their behavior.[6] They described a range of reasons that triggered attempts at abstinence, some internal, others external. Temporary stops were reported even in cases of men who had offended for years. Most who regained control spoke with great pride about having stopped offending on their own; they saw it as a major accomplishment. However, they either relapsed into offending after a period of months or years, or were caught by the legal system before they might have done so. It is difficult to tell whether this latter group of men would have resumed offending absent any formal intervention. Those who did stop but were then caught admitted or suggested that the chance that they would never have reoffended was far from certain.

Feelings of moral wrongness and guilt or the realization that maybe the victim was being harmed, for whatever reason, seemed to catch up to some men and facilitated their regaining control. In some of these cases, control seemed to surface from the inside. Kevin stopped himself from reoffending for six months because of extreme guilt, but was unsure whether or not he would have started again if he had not been arrested as a sex offender. Corey stopped himself for three months and then relapsed; Tom stopped himself cold for three years without reoffending and was then arrested.

I: Why did you stop?

R: . . . Guilt. Guilt had just gotten the best of me . . . . It got to the point where . . . about the only thing I cared about was playing with my computer and working.

I: Would you do things to keep it from happening?

R: . . . I know I avoided a lot of situations.

I: I'm just, I'm real curious how you just stopped?

R: Well, it may have started up again if things hadn't happened like they did . . . . I just know at that time I was so guilt ridden that I just didn't care much about anything.

R: At one point . . . I was going to quit. So I think I went about two or three months without doing anything during a period there.

I: Why do you think you wanted to quit?

R: Somewhere down the line something telling me . . . this was not right. I had to stop. If I stopped, everybody would forget about it.

R: I stopped it three years before it came out . . . . I had been in Presbyterian Hospital for depression. And I was comparatively drug-free . . . . Something inside of me said to myself, "You have got to stop doing this; this has got to stop. You're gambling with your daughter's sanity and psychology. You've got to quit. No matter what you may think about what you're doing, you're taking a risk. You've got no right to do that." And I got home and stopped. I told her, quote "We're not going to make love anymore because I think it makes you nervous." And she didn't say anything.

More often the guilt feelings that stopped men from offending for sustained periods did not surface from the inside, but were triggered by external events, usually things that had less to do with the victim and more to do with other people. Ian stopped himself with his youngest biological daughter on his own without legal intervention after his wife was diagnosed with a terminal illness. To him it did not seem right to have sex with his daughter while his wife was dying.

R: Everything was going quite well if you want to put it that way, as far as the relationship, immoral and everything as it might be. But then we found that . . . my wife had [this disease]. And that's what the trigger mechanism was. That's what changed things. And that put everything on hold. And I felt guilty and I'm sure she [my daughter] felt guilty.

I: You felt guilty about what?

R: . . . Well, my wife was ill, and then here we'd been involved in this relation-ship, . . . here's my wife fighting for her life, . . . and so it didn't seem right to do anything like this. So we just discontinued everything for a long, long time . . . . So I think it was, with my wife . . . in her weakened condition and dependent upon me . . . , all the more reason to be loyal to her. All the more reason to feel that I was failing her.

It did not take long, however, before Ian started up again. His wife lost her sexual drive during her fight with her illness and after about nine months Ian began to struggle over having to go without any sex. So he turned back to his daughter. Not long thereafter his wife died. She apparently never knew what he was doing. And then he continued offending even more.

R: She got into treatment and she got into remission but she lost her sexual drive . . . ; because it was uncomfortable for her and emotionally difficult for her to deal with. And so I accepted that and that wasn't a problem . . . . I felt closer to her then than any time I had in years . . . . We didn't know how long her remission was going to last. We had hoped forever. But it did-n't. So then . . . why, she went back in the hospital, and spent almost the whole summer in the hospital . . . . I tried to resume activities with the youngest one then at that point. And there was some acquiescence, there was some reluctance . . . . Well, I got to the point there where, what do I do about my sexual drive? At this point, I hadn't had intercourse with her, that's my wife now [for] six months, maybe nine months.

Corey, who had served in the military, watched a television program one night involving other men who had fought in Vietnam, as he had, and he began to realize how his life had gone astray. The external event of listening to other troubled veterans seemed to shift him out of the offending mode. This was really the end of his offending before he was reported. He had also stopped himself another time, as reported earlier, as a consequence of internal guilt, but had reoffended later.

R: I sat there one night and I listened to some other vets standing there talking about their personal lives and what happened to them and I was seeing myself in them. I was seeing myself right there on that TV set. It was them sitting there but it was me they were talking about . . . . They'd been in trouble with the law, divorce, family problems . . . ; I kept telling myself over the years that I . . . adjusted well when I come back from 'Nam. I had a family, I had a job, had three kids, nice home, what more did I want? From that point on man it just started going downhill.

Randy began to retake control over his offending when he realized that the victim, his stepdaughter, was pregnant. He knew the child was not his because he never had intercourse with her. He also paid for her to have an abortion. The scare of the pregnancy, plus the money it cost him, seemed to send a message that he was on thin ice. While he did retake control on his own, it was an external event that magnified his feelings of guilt and responsibility enough to stop.

R: I found out she was pregnant . . . . I'm just damn glad it wasn't mine . . . . I am glad that I stopped the situation and I am glad that I never went ahead and actually had sex with her. Even though I did abuse that child, and I know that I am guilty, I had enough sense. There was something within side me that said, "Hey, this is not right. You've got to stop it." And I stopped it. And I'm kind of proud of that fact. Because I knew right then that if I had any kind of a chance at all, that it was me that had to do it. It wasn't somebody else stopping me. And that cost me $325 to get rid of that baby, so I ended up paying anyway.

Randy also felt a sense of responsibility to his biological daughter; he recognized that someone else depended on him, which provided what he said was an impetus to change. As with other men, the source of his guilt had less to do with the victim per se and more to do with how others who were not directly involved might be harmed. Randy stopped himself for three months and then he was reported to the police. He never offended again.

R: Something . . . inside me . . . said, "Hey, . . . no matter what happens, you've got to get your act together. You got to get straightened up . . . . You got to carry on. You got a daughter there that's . . . really looking up to you." And I mean my own personal [biological] daughter. "You got to get your life together . . . no matter what's happened with your wife or with your stepdaughter. No matter what, . . . this other child is looking at you and you've got to be something for her." And that's the way I looked at it.

I: Is that the big reason you pulled yourself out of it? Because of the other child?

R: Yes . . . . My daughter's . . . been a big inspirational part of my life.

Some men too had decided that they needed and wanted to stop offending, but then relied on others to try to keep them from doing so. Two men in particular, ironically, believed they had put a stop to their behavior—never successfully—by giving the victim the responsibility for controlling them. Experiencing mounting feelings of guilt, William apologized to his biological daughter for molesting her and then told her to tell him no the next time.

R: I tried to stop the activities. I tried to develop a better relationship with my wife. Eventually I had a talk with my daughter and told her what we were doing was wrong and that I should never have allowed it to happen and that I was going to have to stop allowing it to happen and if I ever started to touch her again in an intimate way she was not to let me. But it continued a few times after that.

In the case of Tom, after three years of abstinence, the same feelings and desires that led him to offend initially began to resurface. The screws were starting to come loose again, and to try and maintain control, he reapproached the victim, told her what was happening, and said that he needed to hear her tell him no to quell his desires.

R: A couple of months before the suicide attempt, I told [my stepdaughter] that I was still having some of those kinds of feelings and I really needed to hear from her that *she did not want me to touch her* (*very loudly*). And she said, "No, I don't want you to touch me." And I said, "I'm glad we've got that out of the road." Because these were like little boogie men still coming up; the old stuff was starting up again and I wanted to keep it from not happening. And I knew she would say no, but I wanted to hear her say no. That helps.

Another offender, Glenn, confessed to his wife about molesting their adopted daughter out of guilt; then, rather than calling the police, she tried to monitor and control his behavior. She changed her work schedule and kept a watch over Glenn when he was at home to make sure he did not do anything else. While he initially acted out of guilt, the source of control itself was external, rather than internal, and was tenuous at best. He later reoffended.

R: We got in a big argument and I told her that I'd just stay out in the garage. I won't come back in the house . . . . We got our camper out there . . . . And she was always up and down the stairways. I think she was just checking on me to make sure. She wanted me to get help. I said no, I would leave first. I would not talk to anybody. "It was wrong what I did and I won't do it again." And it went on for about three days . . . ; and I asked her, "I don't expect you to forgive me, but please let me try to make it right." And she came around later . . . towards the end of the week and said that she wanted me to get help, but if [I] wouldn't get help, then she'll change her hours. She changed her hours! And I got upset because I felt that she was just watching over me. Everything I did, I felt everyone was watching me.

In a couple of cases, the fear of getting caught as a consequence of having experienced a very close call, a moment of near detection, led to a sustained period of nonoffending. Scott, in particular, routinely offended in the early morning hours, well before dawn, when his wife and the victim were sound asleep. One time he nearly got caught in the act—his wife saw him coming from the direction of his stepdaughters' bedroom with an erection—and he had to explain his way out of it. The close call scared him into stopping offending for eight months; then he started again.

R: I had to explain *something* to my wife because *obviously* there was something not right (*very loudly*). I came from the direction of my girls' room . . . . And my wife and I had discussed my masturbation . . . which was something that disgusted her . . . ; it really bothered her . . . . I told her that I was in the kids' bathroom masturbating. She said, "Well, what'd you go in there for?" And I said "Well, because I didn't want to bother you. I didn't want you to know." And . . . that's pretty much the line, and she accepted that . . . . And then . . . I felt like, "Pfeeww, that's over with! *That* was it." Boy, I was never going to do anything like that again. I wasn't going to go touch [my stepdaughter] no more, and for a good eight months I didn't.

Ian also experienced a near detection, which led him to stop offending for nearly six years. After the first time he molested the middle of his three biological daughters, the girl told her older sister, who told a school official her sister had been molested, and the department of welfare came to investigate at the house. The reaction of his wife was disbelief, and when the second daughter was questioned she denied she had been victimized. No one ever talked to him about this, and the crisis quickly dissipated. He remembered feeling stunned.

R: It was reported somehow through the school. My oldest girl I think said something to somebody. And . . . the next one down, she denied it . . . ; but it was still reported. And somebody came out to see my wife about it. And she just slapped it off. She didn't believe it at all. And she said something to me about it. She says, "I came home . . . and . . . somebody was here from some welfare department and said something about the school reported molesting" and this, that, and the other. And yeah, I guess I was petrified . . . ; I'd just think about my reputation and my relationship with my wife . . . . I agonized over that.

Many men reported long periods of abstinence from offending, not because of internal or external sources of guilt, but primarily because of major events in their everyday lives that diverted their interest or attention for a while. In particular, this included men who said they had moved their families long distances or men who said they had taken on a new job that made their lives busy and took up more of their idle time. In each of these cases the men returned to offending later when their lives had become more settled, because they had not experienced any fundamental shift in the meaning of offending.

Getting Caught—Audience and Self-Reports

A key aspect of the sexual abuse of children that remains largely unexplored is the dynamics by which cases come to be "officially" reported to the authorities. This is partly because of the preponderance of research on samples of adult "survivors," many of whom indicate they never told anyone about being victimized when they were young.[7] It is also partly the result of a primary emphasis on documenting how the legal and mental health system responds to childhood victims once cases do in fact get reported. The reporting process, in essence, has been lost in between.[8] At the time they were interviewed, all the men in this study either had been or were currently being processed by the criminal justice system for sexual contact with children. That is, they were all "known" offenders. The men were asked to elaborate how the transition from the world of secret offender to public "deviant" unfolded. About one-third of the cases in this study came to be reported either by third parties or by offenders themselves. It was not always the victim who came forward.

Some offenders said their cases got reported when their spouse or girlfriend, the mother of the child being molested, became suspicious and eventually put two and two together. Typically the men said they had left clues that something odd was going on between them and a specific victim, which raised suspicions. Then the mother confronted the child involved and/or confronted the offender and elicited a confession. Scott, in particular, said that his wife confronted him about whether or not he was having sex with his stepdaughter after the girl went to sleep one night and had locked the door to her bedroom. A few weeks earlier, Scott said, in the middle of the night his wife saw him walking back to bed from the direction of his stepdaughter's room nude with an erection. Another time she caught him reaching over and fondling his stepdaughter' breast after the girl had climbed into bed to sleep next to her. In both instances, he said, his wife questioned the girl, who remained silent, so she apparently interpreted the events as incidental occurrences. Eventually she caught on.

R: [My stepdaughter] had started locking her bedroom door out of fear. She went into her bedroom one night, locked the door, and fell asleep. My older daughter went to go to bed and couldn't get in. [That] made my wife think and wonder . . . ; when she started locking doors and stuff like that, my wife went upstairs and questioned her. She still denied it. She said that . . . , "No, nothing else had happened." She came downstairs and she asked me and I finally said yes. I finally confessed and told her that, "Yeah, . . . it's been going on for quite a while." And then she went back upstairs and asked my daughter and she told her that, "Your father said this is going on, now tell me what's going on!" And then my daughter finally opened up. Then she came downstairs and told me to leave. So I packed my bags and I went and slept in my office that night . . . . Now my wife was so distraught after I left that she called . . . a sheriff's office looking for a crisis line and . . . naturally the sheriff intervened.

In cases where the mother of the victim effectively pieced the situation together, it was routinely because offenders had become blatant in their sexual acting out. Steve reported that his situation quickly unraveled after he made comments to his wife about his stepdaughter, comments that had a sexual overtone, that led her to become suspicious. He basically engineered his own demise. In this case the mother of the victim then talked to her daughter and eventually confronted the offender with accusations that she had made against him. He immediately confessed his involvement. His wife then called a religious counselor, who told her she had to call the police.

R: My wife apparently had been suspicious of something going on and confronted her daughter in the bathroom one night. And it came out. And she
   confronted me.

I: Why do you think your wife got suspicious?

R: . . . I'd asked her a question about, . . . oh something to do with the development of young girls . . . . This is bizarre, she bought some underwear
   for . . . my stepdaughter . . . and I guess I made a boyish comment about
   [her] modeling it for me. Well, that triggered something right there . . . . If I
   were where I am now then, I would have been suspicious of something
   too . . . . One thing led to another. And of course then my wife confronted me.
   And I admitted to it . . . . We had a counselor that we'd been seeing for I
   don't know how many sessions . . . . She called him up. Well, he didn't know
   what the laws were. He'd never had to deal with anything like this . . . ; he
   was a Christian counselor . . . . He made some calls and found out that she
   had to report it.

There were a few men who, having decided to offend in circumstances
where others might happen upon them, simply got caught in the act.
Brian molested his girlfriend's six-year-old son, you will recall, while
parked on the side of the road in his car near a shopping center. A security guard patrolling the area approached the car and saw the boy with
his pants down. The guard began questioning Brian and did not believe
his account about what had been going on.

I: The security guard, did you see him coming or anything?

R: . . . I didn't see him at all. It's just like all of a sudden he was there I
   guess I was just lost in my own world so much and thinking about what I'd
   just done and thinking about how I felt about myself and what am I going to
   do about this now and at the same time thinking, "Well, this went well."

I: . . . What went down when this guy came up to the car?

R: When he came up to the car he knocked on the window. I rolled the window
   down. He asked me what was going on. I said, "Nothing." He shined his
   light in the car and saw the kid's clothes undone. He asked me why the kid's
   clothes were undone. I told him the kid had to go to the bathroom so I let him
   out to go to the bathroom. He couldn't button his pants [back up] and so I
   was buttoning them for him. And he didn't believe me. He asked me for my
   ID [identification].

Bob also got caught in the act of offending. He had just finished having anal intercourse with his twelve-year-old nephew, when the boy's

father, Bob's brother, opened the door to the room they were in and saw them. Thirty days later, the police called him, he turned himself in, and he was arrested. The father seemed to remain calm despite the circumstances. I interviewed Bob in prison.

R: My brother caught me and my nephew in the act . . . . He came into the room . . . ; [my nephew] was lying across the bed; his pants was down; and I was standing at the end of the bed; my penis was still erect. And he just put two and two together. He left. I'm not sure where he went. He wasn't gone very long. He'd come back and took . . . [his wife] and the kids and went home.

I: Did he leave the child in the room when he left?

R: Yes.

I: What did he say to you?

R: Nothing.

I: . . . Why do you think he didn't say anything to you when he saw what was happening?

R: Maybe he didn't know what to say.

In one case, it was not the offender who got caught in the act, but one of the victims who got caught with another child, which led directly back to the offender being arrested. Carl reported that the father of the three boys he molested overheard his youngest son, who was eight, trying to talk another boy into having sex. Apparently he had been describing what Carl had done. There was a three-month interval between when Carl committed his final offense and his subsequent discovery. It was simply by chance that he happened to get caught.

R: The youngest boy was in his bedroom trying to coax a friend to have sex with him. He was telling him about what I did to him and the father was standing outside the bedroom door and overheard . . . . He was not telling on me. He was telling the other boy how big my penis was . . . . He agonized over what to do about it. Because we were such good friends. I was just like a son to him. He sent me money all the time at school . . . . Our plan was that I would be his youth minister someday . . . . He agonized and agonized over what to do about it. He finally decided that the only way to force me to get help . . . was to have me arrested.

A couple of men claimed that they turned themselves in to the authorities to get help. This pattern was the exception rather than the rule. Both Glenn and William said they called a treatment program on their own initiative because of overwhelming feelings of guilt. Both accounts appeared plausible as presented.

R: I kept saying, "It's not going to happen again." And I said, "It did happen again." And that went on in my head for two and a half days when I called the therapy group . . . . And I told them, "I need help," that I had to talk to somebody to . . . help me leave my daughter alone.

I: Had you told your wife at that point?

R: No . . . , I had not told her. Because I came home that night and I told her . . . I was going to be arrested because I called the welfare department. And I called all three of the girls in and I said, "They're going to call me tonight and ask me to leave," and they were going to evaluate if they want me out of the house or not. And so I told them . . . , "I turned myself in . . . ." Shortly after that, the welfare department called and she says, "I want you out of that house now."

R: I contacted the county welfare department and told them what had been happening. I also had made arrangements to enter into a mental hospital for evaluation.

I: So you turned yourself in?

R: Right . . . , because I realized the importance of treatment being needed for myself and for my children . . . . It was a way of forcing myself to stop, which I had wanted to do on my own, but had not been totally successful at.

Conrad also claimed that he turned himself in to the authorities. He became agitated and upset when I asked how he got caught. As he saw it, that was not how things happened. He had been having intercourse with his biological daughter—he admitted to at least three hundred sexual episodes—and apparently decided to put a stop to things before he got her pregnant.

R: I wasn't caught by the system! I turned myself over to the system . . . ! I decided that this is not, I don't like where my life's going, and I mean I enjoyed the sexual part of having sex with my daughter, but I didn't want her to suffer the consequences of pregnancy with her father. And so I said, "Well, this ain't right," and the only way that I'm going to ensure that that doesn't happen is if I put a stop to it. And the only way I could put a stop to it was to go to the social workers and get help.

The legitimacy of his account about turning himself in became suspect later as Conrad elaborated more about how his case got reported. It seemed that his daughter wrote a note to her mother, who then confronted him about the situation. He lied to his wife about his involvement, then sought out a counselor for help, knowing that everything was about to unravel for him anyway. Conrad turned the revelation of the victim into an opportunity to confess.

R: I'd talked to her about it. I said, "This isn't right what daddy's doing with you and I need to stop." And . . . she said she wanted me to stop . . . , that she would like that . . . . I asked her, "So why haven't you said anything to anybody about it?" And . . . she didn't say why she didn't. A week or so later, she'd wrote a note to her mother saying that I had been bothering her again . . . . At the time I wasn't prepared to deal with . . . my wife. So I lied to my wife and says, "Well, I don't know what she's talking about." But at the same time I . . . went to the mental health center . . . to try to get some . . . professional help . . . to get things sorted out.

I: . . . Did you have the sense that it was all going to come out?

R: Well I knew it was going to come out. And I wasn't trying to hide it from my wife when I lied to her. I just wasn't prepared to deal with the issue with her.

Getting Caught—Victim Reports

Despite all the various routes of discovery, it was still usually disclosure by the victim, according to the men involved, that led to their detection. In this study, approximately two-thirds of the men indicated that this was what happened in their cases. When victims reported, most commonly they told their mother. They also were said to have told either a school official or a counselor, an age mate friend of the same sex, a crisis hotline, or the police. When mothers were informed first specifically by victims, unlike popular stereotypes, they usually—though not always—directly confronted the alleged offender, were described as angry and upset, and then in most instances called the police or some other professional person or agency for help.[9] Once they were confronted, nearly all the men claimed, they quickly admitted their guilt. Often they described an initial denial of guilt, but said that maintaining a front was too difficult, the pressure to tell the truth too great. When they were pressed about what happened, their stories began to break down and they confessed.

Victims disclosed things to others under various circumstances. One common pattern was that the victim was apparently cued by external information or another person who acted as a catalyst for their reporting. Kevin's biological daughter told her mother she was being touched after the family watched a movie about incest. He initially denied his involvement, then caved in.

R: I was working nights . . . and [my son], and [my daughter], and [my wife] were watching a show on molest that was on TV. I think it was on channel 20, I'm not sure.

I: A PBS special?

R: Uh huh [yes]. And when the movie was over [my wife] asked both of the kids, "If anybody ever does something like that to you, you tell me." And [my daughter] started crying and said, "mom!" So [she] told [my wife] what I had done . . . . [My wife] called me. I came home. And at first I denied it that evening; I didn't know what to say. But the next morning I went on ahead and admitted to it and started calling some people to see what we had to do.

I: Did you call the police or did your wife?

R: No. She went to see the doctor, talked to him. And when she came back she told me and so what I did was I made arrangements to turn myself in.

Mark was arrested just short of five years after he last molested his stepdaughter. At the time, he was divorced, remarried, and living with a new wife. He said his victim disclosed what he had done after a teacher provided "good-touch bad-touch" instruction at school, in which children learn what is and is not a "good" touch and what to do if they are the recipient of a "bad" touch. Despite the time frame involved, he admitted his guilt. He felt that the mother of the victim pressed the issue of his prosecution because she wanted to get back together with him after their breakup but he refused. He felt she was trying to make his life miserable as a consequence.

R: In school the teacher told her [about] good-touch bad-touch and she identified what I had done to her and she told it to her teacher. And her teacher called the social worker and the social worker reported me downtown. And they contacted my people, the National Guard. They contacted me and I went to get a lawyer and I went and surrendered.

Larry said his stepdaughter reported what he had been doing to her while she was seeing a counselor because she had been molested by another man before Larry, a temporary boarder her mother had invited into the house to live with the family. Apparently the victim felt safe enough with her counselor to disclose the rest of her abuse history. The counselor probably asked the girl whether anyone else had victimized her.

R: [My stepdaughter] was going to counseling on account of [another man] had molested her. All of my kids were going to counseling because [he] had molested them. And they'd been going for quite a while. And one day [my stepdaughter] . . . told her counselor that I had molested her . . . . I was at work . . . . [My wife] was home and I came in. And I asked [her] where the kids were. And she says, "Come in here for a minute." She said, "I need to talk to you." Okay, so I went in there and she says, "[Our daughter] . . . told a counselor that you had molested her." She says, "Is that true?" And I just kind of was awed for a minute and I thought, "Should I or shouldn't I?" And I thought, "I should . . . . It's time to end it." And I told her, "Yeah." And when I told her yes I was crying like a baby.

Frequently the men noted that there was a long chain of inference from the victim through a series of other people, starting with an age mate friend, when it came to revelations about their offending. This was what happened in the case of Leon. His victim told a girlfriend about what her stepfather was doing, and the allegation traveled from there.

R: She told our next door neighbor's daughter . . . . Now if I remember correctly, she said, "I wish my dad would stop touching me down there . . . " or something to that effect. And that girl told her mother, who told my oldest daughter, who told my wife. And I remember it all plain as day.

One night everything unraveled for Leon after he and his wife returned home from an evening out together. The sister, with the victim in company, told their mother what had been happening. Leon could not hold up under heavy questioning.

R: The two girls were sitting on the couch and when we walked in [they] got up and went into their rooms immediately. And a couple of minutes later my wife went in, I guess to check on them . . . and that's when the daughter told her . . . . I knew she was gone a long time. I didn't pay a whole lot of attention. And I remember she just came back in, had this funny look on her face, but she wasn't crying or hollering. And she made herself a drink and she sat down. And I can always tell when she's very serious because she's very quiet, very soft-spoken. And [she] told me what they had accused . . . ; and I denied it for a very brief period . . . , five minutes . . . . But I saw that I was getting nowhere so I just told her, "Yeah, I did it." I'm not a very good liar and my wife knows me well enough . . . ; I couldn't come up with the answers. I was nervous.

In the vast majority of cases, if both the victim and offender were living at home when the accusation was leveled, the authorities ordered the offender to leave the household. Sometimes the mother of the victim tossed the offender out first. In Leon's case, which was unusual, his wife wanted to have sex with him that same night after he admitted his involvement, and then threw him out of the house the next morning.

R: We had sex that night; she demanded it.
I: That strike you as odd?
R: Yes. It doesn't now. At the time she was jealous of her daughter. She admitted it. She's been through therapy too, see, so I mean we all know pretty well what went on. The next morning she said, "I think you better find a place to live." And I was just like a kid, I didn't know what to do. I mean, I was nervous and agitated. I couldn't even think. So I got in the car . . . ; I didn't say much to her. I couldn't even hardly look at her in the face.

To some men, like Leon, it was not always clear why the victim decided to tell someone about what was happening when they did. Many other men, however, seemed to have a clearer sense of the process involved. Most commonly the men said that disclosures by victims were prompted by the emergence of a crisis between the two parties. The nature of the crisis varied. John reneged on a promise he made to one of his two victims that he would not approach her for sex anymore; that seemed to precipitate her disclosure. John figured that she probably felt cornered and had no recourse but to tell.

R: I think she realized, . . . or at least thought, that I wasn't going to keep my word . . . ; I had lied to her once. And I think she saw the only [way] to stop it was to tell someone . . . . The first that I knew of it was my mom called me, telling me that [my niece] had told someone that this had happened and of course I denied it . . . . I think she'd gotten to the point . . . she'd lost that trust in me.

Other times a crisis arose and disclosures occurred, some men said, because of parenting decisions they and/or their wives made that angered the victim. Typically these involved lifestyle decisions with daughters about who they could date or how late they could stay out. Corey said he told his biological daughter she could not go out on a date with a boy she had met hanging out in a local mall. When his wife tried to talk to the girl, she revealed the molest situation. He portrayed his wife's reaction as hysterical and excessive.

R: I told [my daughter], the oldest, that she couldn't go out with somebody and she'd been furiously mad at me for two days.
I: Was it a boyfriend type thing?
R: Yeah. It was dumb; it was something I was not going to allow. She met some kid in the shopping center . . . ; he was from California . . . . She was going to go back to meet him and I told her flat no way. Well, she got real upset with me about it . . . . And [my wife] went back [to her room] to talk to [her] to see what the problem was. I was sitting there watching TV, . . . my ex-wife come out and said, "Have you been molesting the girls?" And I started to deny it and I said, "Yes I have . . . ."
I: What else did she say at that time?
R: Oh boy, . . . just a lot of yelling and screaming and carrying on.

Randy recalled that he and his wife tried to set a curfew for his step-daughter, whom he molested, but that she would not follow it. In addition, they suspected that the girl was using drugs. So his wife called the police and had her daughter arrested. The girl then told the police her stepfather had molested her. The attention, of course, immediately shift-ed to Randy. He felt that the victim told to get herself out of trouble.

R: We called the law on her, . . . or my ex-wife had called the law, . . . [because] she'd been staying out [till] midnight, 1:00 [a.m.]. [She] told her mom she hated her . . . . This was something that was ongoing even before the molest . . . . My ex-wife was going to have her, actually [took] her to jail, and so she told them that I . . . had raped her. It's the first thing that she told them. And they come in, got me out of bed, and said that there were allega-tions that had been [made] and I had to leave the house.

Yet another type of crisis that seemed to facilitate disclosure involved the case of Ian, who became angry, punitive, and forceful with his youngest biological daughter the more she refused his sexual advances. When he scaled up his approach to the victim, the victim turned to her older adult sister, whom Ian had also molested, for help. The younger girl, aged fifteen at the end, became increasingly resistant to sex as she grew older and began dating. The last time Ian tried something, he had been drinking, and he had never reacted with anger before. The girl

might have felt that her ability to thwart her father's advances was erod-
ing rapidly.

R: I came home . . . , I had a couple drinks . . . . She was . . . sitting on the
sofa . . . playing with herself again. And I reached over and put my hand on
her breast. And boy did she come up, sit up, and rebuffed me on that. And
that's the last I touched her. And I got furious . . . ; I just exploded. I didn't hit
her or hurt her. I just yelled at her . . . . Then I . . . started talking to her about,
as she left the room, "Why you haven't done this and you haven't done that."
It was like . . . I was then trying to find . . . fault with her for having [said no],
and I really was mad at her for what she didn't do!

The next day Ian's daughter did not come home after school. Instead
she went home with a girlfriend, who she then told about what he had
been doing. The girlfriend told her mother, who called the victim's older
sister. The older sister, who had also been a victim of her father, told her
husband, who was a police officer, and the two confronted the offender together. They talked for a while, then left, and the police collected evidence in the case for a few weeks. Then one day the police came to Ian's
house in force. The transition to public deviant involved a touch of the
dramatic.

I: The cops came to your house?
R: Oh yeah! In force! Three of them. Three cars. And I mean they could have
just called me and told me to meet them downtown. But I felt this was my
son-in-law's way of sticking in [the knife] and turning it . . . . And they made
a public display of things. They handcuffed me inside the house . . . ; then
paraded me outside . . . . And then the guy in full uniform, in front of all my
neighbors and everybody going by, . . . at 4:30 in the afternoon, people coming home and everybody out and about and gawking and looking at what's
going on, read me my rights. He could have done it in the car. But maybe it
was more of an impact in front of the neighborhood.

The situation for Tom also came to an end after a major crisis stage
unfolded with his victim. In this case, the discovery that his one victim,
his stepdaughter, had been involved in sex with another boy sent Tom
into a jealous rage.

R: [My stepdaughter] had told me that night that someone had gotten under
her blouse . . . . This was like a Sunday night or something. I knew something was wrong. [Her] face just looked like . . . . I said [to her], "I want to

talk to you, go downstairs." I knew something had happened . . . and I wanted to find out what it was. I wasn't sure what it was, but I wanted to find out. And she told me about that. And that, just all of a sudden, took all of those negative feelings about myself and just made them grate in. Just like, "I've lost her." And the rage, the anger, was just incredible. I wanted to destroy myself.

Tom's case also involved high drama. Later that night Tom went back down alone into the basement of his house, wielding an assault rifle and intending to commit suicide. He called his brother and said good-bye. His brother, suspecting that something was amiss, called 911. A SWAT team responded to the call, apparently because his wife and stepdaughter were in the home and it was feared he might shoot them too. The neighborhood was then sealed off until Tom eventually gave himself up. He was then hospitalized for depression and alcoholism. A few weeks later his stepdaughter learned erroneously that Tom was going to be discharged from the hospital and would be coming home. The girl called a suicide hotline and talked with someone about the incest; that person advised her to tell her mother and to call the police. Eventually his wife came to see him in the hospital and confronted him. He initially denied things but, after about five minutes, admitted his guilt, and she called the police.

A number of men insisted that, when disclosures were made by victims, they ended up being overaccused, that exaggerations were made about what really occurred. Usually the overaccusation was said to involve allegations of "rape," or penis-vaginal penetration committed with force. These same men said that the victim usually later recanted the charge of rape and then told exactly what had happened. Routinely men in this situation tried to redefine the situation to the police. Randy admitted around a dozen episodes of "fondling." The victim alleged much, much more.

I: There were allegations of rape? . . . What did you think of that?

R: Well, I was stunned, because I knew that I had never raped her. I mean, I never physically abused any of my children . . . . I didn't realize the allegations that she had made towards me when I went in and talked to the detective . . . . Nobody told me that night that that was what the allegations were. I was told later that it was rape and that she said I had sex with her thirty, forty times. And then she said finally I just fondled her. It was just over a period of time . . . she finally admitted I didn't rape her; I didn't have . . . intercourse with her.

William too stated that his oldest daughter reported he "raped" her to a friend, who then called the police. He had been arrested once before for molesting his two biological daughters and was on probation and in a treatment program. After a period of eighteen months without relapse, he reoffended, engaging in intercourse with the victim. A few minutes later, he said, he talked to the victim and told her they would have to report what happened to the welfare department. The victim, however, did not wait. She left in the middle of the night and went to a friend's house. The reoffense apparently was a major crisis for her, though he claimed she instigated it. He felt she overaccused him of wrongdoing.

R: After it was over, . . . I told my daughter that what we had done was wrong, and I could not believe we had did what we done. She agreed with me. I said come Monday morning, we were going to have to report it. I went on to bed and later around one or two . . . ; I got up to get a drink of water and my daughter was gone. My wife and I drove around looking for her. We went to a neighbor's house that was a friend of hers. There were police there. When I got out of the car, they came up to me and said I was under arrest. They took me down to the police station and said my daughter had told them I had thrown her down in the backyard, on the patio table, and raped her. Later on . . . she finally admitted her participation.

George claimed that his victim overaccused him, but he admitted to the charges anyhow. His victim reported the offense to a girlfriend, who told her to tell her mother. She did, and the mother, his wife, quickly confronted him. He immediately admitted guilt. Later, when the charges were actually filed, the victim claimed he physically forced her to have sex. He denied using force, but rather than fighting the overaccusation, as he saw it, he accepted it because he was guilty and did not think it made much difference.

R: She said in her statement that I forced her; that I threw her down and pulled her pants off. I don't remember doing that. But I didn't want to bring her into court because I was guilty and I said it don't make that much difference anyway since . . . everything I did was enough . . . . So I just let that go.

When cases did get reported by victims to either a parent, the police, or whomever, the propensity of offenders to confess their guilt cannot be understated. Another example cogently illustrates the point. Gary said that when the police came to his door he invited them in because he knew he was guilty. He saw no reason to try and lie.

R: I was taking a nap. I was in my apartment . . . . I heard a knocking at the door. So I got up and went to the door, opened it up, and there stood the police, and he read off my charges . . . . I said, "That's right! Come on in!" I mean, there was no sense in arguing. I mean, that was just going to make things worse . . . .

I: How did you feel when you opened that door and you saw two cops . . . standing there?

R: . . . In the back of my mind I was thinking, "Well, I know why they're here, but I hope they're going to ask me something else!" But I knew better than that. I said, "Yeah, come on in." I don't run from things.

Reacting to Being Discovered

Labeling theorists, who study social reactions to rule breaking, have long argued that official labels or tags that accompany the experience of arrest and criminal justice processing are pivotal to future involvement in crime or deviance.[10] Despite considerable empirical investigation of this issue, little attention has been paid to the subjective experience of people who are arrested. Few crimes carry comparable stigmatizing qualities or more moral condemnation than that of child molesting, sexual abuse, or incest. Indeed, researchers have documented the drastic social consequences of being arrested and charged with such crimes.[11] But what about the emotional impact of the label? How do men who are arrested and charged with such crimes feel inside, in the private world of the self, when they cross from the world of secret deviant to that of public villain? What is this unique sociological moment like?

The final stage in the offending process and the first stage in the career of public deviant involved the offender's reaction to being discovered. The respondents experienced three main types of reactions, which occurred in two stages. The first stage, the immediate reaction phase, was characterized by feelings of relief at having finally been discovered and/or intense panic at the prospect of losing everything. Often men said they experienced both reactions together. In the second stage, the delayed reaction phase, men hit bottom emotionally and reached what most described as the absolute lowest point they felt they could fall. It was only after they hit bottom emotionally that offenders began to take the initiative to make changes in their lives to keep themselves from reoffending.

Faced with public identification of themselves as sexual perpetrators, many of the men in this study, surprisingly, reported "breathing a sigh of relief" at having been arrested. They were glad everything was finally over and believed that with their secret out, they could finally get help for their "problems" and would never offend again. Getting caught had a cathartic impact. There was a sense among this group that a great emotional burden had finally been lifted from their shoulders. Trying to keep their deviance secret had worn most of them down to the emotional breaking point. Offenders who experienced initial feelings of relief admitted that they did not see the ramifications their exposure would eventually have on their lives. Randy, Kevin, Steve, and Phil are four examples of men who experienced relief initially.

R: When I actually admitted to the officer, it was almost like it was a load that was lifted off my shoulders. It was like finally this whole process of abuse and being an abuser was done . . . . Maybe somebody could finally help me straighten my life out . . . . I couldn't do it on my own . . . . I knew my life was screwed up. I kept thinking to myself, "Why did I do this? Why am I this way?"

I: . . . You were thinking about all this?

R: Yes, I was at the time . . . . But once this officer told me, he said, "There is help out there." And he said, "If you'll try not to abuse the system, but use the system to really look at yourself," . . . he said, "that can benefit you." And I went into it with that attitude, and I've had that attitude ever since.

I: How did you feel turning yourself in?

R: I felt good turning myself in . . . ; I felt like I was doing the right thing no matter what happened. I felt better.

I: Fearful at all?

R: Yeah, oh yeah! I was scared! But at the same time I felt good about it because one way or another it was over.

R: During this time I never thought of the repercussions. Never thought, "Well all right, it's out, now . . . ." It did feel wonderful when it came out. Like "Ahhhhh, it won't happen again." And I believed things were going to be just fine. It was like a little boy telling what he'd done wrong, and now things were okay.

R: Well, there was a great feeling of relief when the officers came, as all this was over. It was done! So I remember in my heart just saying to God, "God help me; I'm a wicked man . . . ." The relief was that it was in the open. I mean that it was exposed and that . . . it was not going to happen again . . . . That day I was thankful that it had come out . . . .

I: Any other way you can articulate what that relief feels like?

R: (*Sighs deeply.*) Oh, well basically it was just a sense of it was over and it's in the light. It can be dealt with. I don't have to hide it anymore . . . . The very thing that I feared had happened. But that was over with.

The second type of reaction many men felt when their cases became known to others was panic and desperation. Panic was a consequence of the perception by offenders that they were about to lose everything and that there was no way out of trouble. Men who panicked figured that their families would disintegrate, that arrest and public humiliation were inevitable, that they would have to do time in prison, and that life as they knew it would never be the same. Brian, Sidney, Carl, and John described this type of reaction.

R: I panicked at first . . . ; I had all these things hit me at once. I must be a weird person (*chuckles*).

I: Tell me a little bit more about that . . . ?

R: . . . It hit me that I was caught and then . . . I was worried about, well, what was going to happen. How am I going to lie this one off and get out of it and still have everything? And keep out of jail? I knew this type of offense you'd go directly to jail. Do not pass go. Do not collect $200.

R: I was working nights and my wife was working days. And one night she called me at work . . . , screaming basically almost incoherent, because [my stepdaughter] told her . . . . By the time I got home she wasn't there. She'd taken [my stepdaughter] to the hospital, which I knew meant that the doctors would report it and the police would get involved. I panicked . . . ; I was afraid I'd be arrested. I drove around town looking for a hotel . . . ; I went home shaking . . . . I was going to hide out overnight. I guess . . . I was really paranoid . . . . When I finally did go home to spend the night, I parked the car two blocks away and walked to the house. The idea of jail terrified me.

R: I was really scared. Very extremely scared. You have to realize I was Mr. Joe Everything. And there I was sitting in a jail cell with a bunch of common criminals. I certainly didn't feel like I belonged there.

R: At first I pretty much ignored it; I figured it'd just blow over . . . . But then when the detectives got into it, I got scared because then I knew I was on the verge of losing everything. Period. Everything was going to go.

Once the reactions of either relief or panic had been experienced, then came the reality of hitting bottom emotionally. At this stage, feelings of shame, guilt, remorse, and major depression became paramount. Offenders described reaching an absolute low point. There were commonly feelings of suicide and complete aloneness. Life, for these men, as they contemplated their future, was completely uncertain. Leon, William, Corey, and Bob characterized the experience of hitting the bottom of the abyss.

R: I was humiliated . . . ; I was ashamed . . . . I didn't know what to do . . . . I was like a kicked dog! I just felt terrible. And I was depressed for probably six months.

I: How depressed did you get?

R: I thought of suicide. I thought of two things. I thought of suicide and I thought of . . . leaving the state. I guess running.

I: What kept you from doing either?

R: My wife . . . ; she has supported me from the outset!

R: I went through months of depression, of hating myself, of suicidal thoughts, of detesting myself as a person. How is one supposed to feel besides how stupid could I have been. It was so stupid, very dumb. I wonder sometimes where life might have passed me by with the commonsense and ability to have said no.

I: . . . How depressed did you get?

R: I really didn't want to live. But I wasn't strong enough to kill myself either, not the ways suicide has to be done . . . . If I could have snapped my fingers into nonexistence I would have done so. I was adamant that my wife divorce me. I couldn't see how she could love me after what I did. I felt my daughters must hate me. I was very despondent.

R: Where was I at personally? About the lowest thing on earth. I couldn't look myself in the mirror. Everybody I talked to or I walked by I felt I had a sign on my back saying I was a child molester. I didn't know . . . whether I was coming or going at times. I couldn't think straight. Mainly because I didn't know what was going to happen. The unknown. What was going to become of the family? What was going to become of me? Was I going to go to jail? What was going to become of my job? How was I going to support the family? . . . I'd sit in a chair, dad had a lounge chair, and I'd sit there for hours just staring.

I: How did you feel about yourself having been caught?

R: I felt alone, as if I were the only human being left in the world. And I remembered the one question that kept going over and over and over in my mind was, "Why did I let this happen?" I thought, "What am I going to do?" That's when I decided to face whatever would happen.

Conclusion

Exiting from active offending occurred in three general stages: boundary reformulation in the form of fear engulfment and/or situational attempts to stop offending; detection and exposure of offenders, largely through confrontations by nonoffending parents or reports by victims; and subsequent reactions and emotional disorganization after the experience of being identified. Feelings of fear emerged primarily among offenders who perceived that they had lost control over the victim—because the victim was more independent, older, acting out sexually, among other reasons—and that the victim had become more capable of telling on them. Attempts to stop offending resulted from feelings of guilt or because of external factors such as the illness of a spouse, the pregnancy of the victim by someone else, hearing others tell about problems with which the offender identified, near detection experiences, or concerns about being a parent to another child. The mothers of victims, offenders admitted, played an instrumental role in their detection by confronting them and then taking action by notifying the criminal justice system. Offenders, in turn, routinely confessed their guilt rather than denying it. Often there was a long chain of communication before a case was officially reported. Finally, reactions by offenders to being discovered involved initially feelings of relief and/or panic about what was going to happen to them, followed by the experience of bottoming out emotionally and thoughts of suicide.

NINE

Answering the Question Why

The premise of this research is simple: If we want to understand why sexual abuse occurs, then we must examine the perspective of offenders about the acts in which they have been involved, on both an objective and a subjective level. Why is the study of men who molest children important? Why should we listen to the stories and accounts of the adults who engage in such behavior? The answer is obvious. Adult-child sexual contact in all its varied forms, according to the empirical research, *is an issue that dramatically affects the quality of life of millions of people* in a myriad of ways. Its occurrence is said to transcend every social grouping. Parents, in particular, are often alarmed about the possibility that their children could be abused sexually. This is an area where answers are needed, where research has the real potential to prevent future victimization and harm. The more we know about offenders, and the more familiar we become with their patterns, the more effective will be attempts to protect our children by stopping their behavior.

As I studied men who had molested children, I constantly struggled to remain value-neutral. My own feelings changed continuously throughout the research.[1] At the start, I felt excited about the prospect of studying a topic I was convinced might help people. I believed that my job as a sociologist was to give "voices" to people, to talk with and listen to those whom few others were willing to approach. I saw the research as an adventure; I felt I was moving through relatively unexplored territo-

ry. And I was convinced that a new approach to sex crimes was a theoretical necessity, especially in light of the social and scientific politics of
rape. As the research progressed, I had two daughters, and my wife, a
social worker who worked with sexual abuse victims, felt little sympathy for the offenders I often described to her. My perspective began to
change. Frequently, when I coded and wrote up the data, I felt angry
with the stories the men conveyed. I began to wonder whether what I
was analyzing was too graphic for people to read, whether the research
might arm some men with new or renewed desires for children or possibly equip them with better ways of offending.

Later, when I began to talk about my findings with colleagues, and
when I presented a paper at a professional sociology conference in a session on deviant behavior, I was alarmed and saddened by the silence of
my peers, and by their unwillingness to discuss in any detail the cases
of the men I came to know. Ironically, I found that sociologists and crim-
inologists who study and write about rules, boundaries, and public reactions seemed troubled and shocked by my research and data. In fact, at
the conference I mentioned, a speaker who made her presentation after
me, a woman who was pregnant, had to stop her own talk and regain
her composure because of what I reported. And in one job interview,
the department chair expressed concern that my research might not be
received well by the administration at that university, that hiring me
would require a hard sell. Consequently, I became worried that my colleagues saw me as an oddball with bizarre interests, and I started to
regret doing the study. Today, as I reflect on what I have finished, I feel
reluctant to continue research in this area.

Over time, I have come to recognize that child sexual abuse can probably never be studied with complete detachment. I prefer to lay my bias-
es out, up front, for the reader to consider in relation to the way the
data are reported. Still, throughout this investigation I attempted to step
back and remain open to exploring the reality of men who committed
sexual violations against children. My mission has been to present the
stories of my respondents the way they were told to me, organized in
terms of the major recurring themes. Opening myself to the data was a
constant process. I had to take breaks from the project, set it down for
a few weeks, sometimes even a few months, then reapproach it later.
My advice to other researchers studying extremely sensitive topics, especially sexual deviance, is to do the same. But most important, I suggest
that future researchers in this area anticipate and be prepared for nega-

tive and stigmatizing reactions. In the end, my attempts to remain neutral were complicated as much or more by the reactions of people who knew about my work as they were by the offenders I actually interviewed.

When I started thinking about this project in 1988, the intent was to conduct the first in-depth, qualitative, narrative-based study of men who molested their own children or the children of their friends. Over the course of the investigation, the public spotlight focused increasingly on sex crimes against children. Week after week my worries mounted that someone else would do the research conducted here. Surely, some other sociologist had to be interested in documenting the accounts of offenders. Still, seven years later, nothing yet has really been done. The only major qualitative study on sexual offenders completed since that time is research, which I have cited extensively, on a sample of men who raped adult women.[2] That book consists of a recompilation of related findings published earlier during the mid-1980s in journal articles.[3] My study, as it stands, represents one of the few works of its kind in the area. Qualitative, in-depth research on men who commit sex crimes against children is, and probably will remain, a marginal area of study in the sociology of deviant behavior. The subject matter is too unsettling and repugnant for most people to want to spend a significant portion of their lives collecting, analyzing, and writing up such data.

By focusing on the standpoint of offenders, the present research challenges some of the basic predominant images of why men molest children. In interviewing respondent after respondent, I was struck by the sexually based constructions men frequently made about their victims. Equally remarkable were the openness, explicitness, and apparent honesty of the men in conveying their stories. Unexpectedly, as I adjusted to walking in and out of a prison and to the initial challenges offenders made about my moral politics, I began to realize that most of the men were friendly, from my point of view likable, and more often than not remorseful. They seemed more like men I have known in everyday life, albeit men who had committed unspeakable acts, but without glaring pathologies. This is not to condone their actions in any way. What it does suggest is that people may engage in criminal sexual behavior more because of normal learning and interactive processes than because of something "odd" or "disturbed" about them.[4]

This study focuses on sexual contact between adults and children from an interactionist framework. Interactionist theories, in general, emphasize the situational, emergent, and changing nature of human behavior; the flow of people into, through, out of, and back into sequences of interaction; the definitions and interpretations actors construct about each other, their social activities, and especially their own self; and the continuous relationship between overt activity and internal reality. People are seen as constructing the social world, influenced by and acting in the present, orienting and reorienting themselves according to whatever contingency arises. But more than anything else, the interactionist approach emphasizes that reality varies depending on the standpoint examined.[5] Relying on victims, mental health clinicians, or criminal justice officials to tell us why offending occurs, by overstepping the ontological basis of their experience, misses a relevant view of reality and distorts what might be occurring for offenders.

Rather than using a top-down method of testing theory, I have attempted to build from data toward theory. The question addressed here, then, is what do the data reported here tell us about why men have sex with children? Why do men become involved in breaking sexual boundaries? Why do some men cross the line and engage in what to many seems unthinkable? That is, I attempt to highlight the major theoretical conclusions that can be drawn from the ground-up approach applied in this research. Throughout the analysis, the emphasis was on the stages men underwent in becoming and being offenders and the process by which involvement in active offending ended. The goal in concluding this study is to move from substantive analysis to more formal theory, and in particular, to formulate the foundation of an interactionist-based theory about why sexual offending occurs.

Boundary Contradictions

The meaning of the sexual boundary between adults and children is directly linked to current images of childhood. The concept of childhood is a relatively recent invention in Western civilization. As recently as two hundred years ago, children were viewed by parents and adults with what has been described as an attitude of indifference. Prior to that time, the historical record shows that young people were seen as marginal or almost nonexistent members of society, subject to the realities and cruelties of the adult world from early on, including sexual contact, with relatively little public or legal protection. Over the past few hundred years, children have come to be viewed differently. Childhood has evolved as a life stage increasingly separate from adulthood, a precious time to be appreciated and not wasted. Children tend to be seen as less competent and more immature than adults, requiring special attention and care to grow into healthy and happy people.[6]

Coupled with the emergence of the concept of childhood in Western culture, and in American society in particular, laws designed to ensure the sexual safekeeping of children have escalated in importance and become increasingly well defined.[7] The last fifteen years have been largely an era of "protectionism," as parents have become preoccupied with the safekeeping of their children from various perceived threats. Currently, there are few behaviors of any type, sexual or otherwise, that stir up the same fear and panic and that carry the equivalent level of potential moral condemnation as sex between adults and children.[8] Consistent with this morality, penal codes from state to state specify substantial prison sentences for sex offenders of all types, inside or outside the family (though actual sentences seem to be much less severe than what is mandated, at least according to this research).[9] If there is one boundary surrounding both sexual behavior and interaction with children that most people would seem to be aware of, it would probably be this one. Indeed, people who cross such boundaries are potentially subject to a variety of serious sanctions. As Gayle Rubin has stated:

Modern Western societies appraise sex acts according to a hierarchial system of sexual value. Marital, reproductive heterosexuals are alone at the top of the erotic pyramid . . . . The most despised sexual castes currently include . . . the lowliest of all, those whose eroticism transgresses generational boundaries . . . . As sexual behaviors . . . fall lower on the scale, the individuals who practice them are subjected to a presumption of mental illness, disreputability, criminality, restricted social and physical mobility, loss of institutional support, and economic sanctions.[10]

While moral lines have been drawn, and strict adherence to laws prohibiting sex between adults and children is expected, the experiences that underlie those boundaries are often highly variable. In the cases of the offenders in this study, there was seldom any correspondence between their own sexual histories and the erotic boundaries to which our culture has attached increasing weight. The biographies of offenders, much more often than not, were characterized by childhood sexual experiences with adults or other children that strongly contradicted the boundary. This situation of boundary contradiction dissolves the impact of sweeping attempts at boundary maintenance on people who cross over the line. The boundary means less to people who have histories that contradict it. And the expansion of the boundary in the face of such contradictions produces an even greater sense of confusion about what is right or wrong for those with such histories.

More than the mere fact of past experiences that contradict the rule of law, the content of some events as remembered by offenders seemed to render the boundary about children engaging in sex meaningless. While common feminist and mental health lore, for example, defines adult-child sexual experiences as violent and traumatic by nature,[11] some men remembered them as pleasant. And while current criminal justice policy dictates a swift response and harsh punishment when adult-child sex occurs, other men remembered no one responding with similar condemnation to those who molested them; instead, their victimization was tolerated. The same type of legal contradiction existed for offenders who described being violently assaulted by their parents as children. Not surprisingly, some men felt it extremely unjust that as adults they were being held to an entirely different set of legal and moral criteria than other adults were held to when they were children.

Coupled with these factual discrepancies between biography and boundary were broader societal contradictions that many men had come to recognize in their adult years. For example, a few offenders noted that they could not understand why our culture condoned the use of pain—hitting—in parent-child relations, but outlawed the use of something that felt good—sexual touch—to produce intimacy. Other offenders pointed out that we sexualize children in film and television, portraying and imbuing them with a sexuality,[12] but violently condemn those who become eroticized and cross the boundary into sexual activity. Still a couple of others, for example, questioned the cultural tolerance for children who have sex with each other, especially teenagers, or boys who have sex with older women, versus the panic and horror expressed when one of the partners is older or when the older person is a man. These contradictions seemed to arm offenders with rationalizations when they molested.

Boundary contradictions, as such, did not themselves cause the men who reported them to become sexual offenders. Instead, they provided a framework or resource for defining situations in a sexual direction that arose with children later and for redefining the moral boundary that surrounded their actions in a more open direction. The men often described thinking back to when they were children, during the times they became involved in sexual situations with children as adults, and attaching the same meanings to those experiences. Or they recalled invoking popular cultural images that were readily available about childhood sexuality to justify their behavior. The relevance of past biography and culture to current behavior is central to interactionist theories of social action. People develop a generalized other as children, or formulate a stock of knowledge across their lives, that they then use selectively to define situations depending on what suits their purpose at the moment to help them construct a course of conduct. To quote from Joel Charon:

The symbolic interactionist means not that what we do now is caused by the past but that the past experiences of the individual are used to help determine the kind of action to take in a situation . . . . The past is the remembered experience we use to make sense out of the present and the future . . . . We draw freely from our past. It contains our experiences, our significant others, our reference groups, our perspectives. The past is rich for us, and it provides us with the tools to define the present.[13]

Unanticipated Erotic Shifts

One of the emerging debates in the recent rape and sexual abuse literature is whether men who commit such crimes are motivated more by sexual interest or by the desire for violence, power, and aggression. There has been an increasing willingness among some scholars to explore the sexual nature of sex crimes and to focus on sexual arousal as a critical aspect of offending.[14] Others have rejected the sexual dimension and instead emphasized nonsexual needs such as anger and domination as the central motivational elements that become played out in a sexual realm.[15] Still others see sexual arousal as one contributing factor among many, such as emotional need, sexual goal blockage, social disinhibition, and the propensity of men to objectify women and children.[16] Theories of rape or sexual offending that fail to incorporate some dimension of sexual arousal simply cannot consistently explain why men choose to act in a sexual direction.

Among the men in this study, situational feelings of sexual arousal were the critical interactional event that got men to the other side of the sexual boundary with children. Feelings of sexual arousal *gave direction to their behavior*. In the cases of nearly all the men, feelings of sexual arousal surfaced as the result of an *unanticipated erotic shift*. That is,

the offending process started when the men unexpectedly found themselves in the midst of an erotic situation, experiencing feelings of sexual interest, desire, curiosity, and the like, which they experienced as spontaneous, unexpected, and unplanned. The men were able to pinpoint
exact situations in which feelings of sexual interest and desire surfaced
for them, which caught them off guard and led them to reframe their
victims in sexual terms—noticing a girl's breasts, hearing a friend's son
unexpectedly talk about penises and sex during a rest room stop, developing an erection after rubbing the back of a victim during a period of
impotence, feeling inadvertently aroused when a child spontaneously
jumps up on a lap, changing a diaper and suddenly wondering whether
the child was responsive to sexual stimulation.

Once erotic feelings surfaced, the men became unable to turn those
feelings off and return to a nonsexual state. If men were alone with the
victim when their sexual desires first emerged, and if they were in a situation in which physical contact was already occurring, they virtually
always went ahead and acted, making an *erotic leap* over the sexual
boundary. If the men were not in a situation where sexual contact could
be immediately initiated, they described fantasizing about the victim and
masturbating in private, or continually watching and looking at the victim, undergoing a buildup stage of erotic desire that quickly or eventually became uncontainable and that facilitated an *"erotic slide"* into sexual contact.[17] Each offender became immersed in a stream of experience,
an erotic stage of awareness not bounded by reflection. Whatever the
journey traveled, most men later stopped and looked back at what they
had been involved in and began to wonder where their sexual feelings
had come from and how they had gotten to where they did. Often the
experience of orgasm shocked them into awareness. Nearly all were
unable to figure out what had just happened to them. None of the men
set out to become a sex offender. They got caught by surprise and swept
along in an erotic situation only to wake up on the other side of the
moral wall.

Unanticipated erotic shifts, I contend, are not unique to men who
molest children. It may be that initial boundary crossings into other
types of sexual offending occur in similar ways. For example, some men
who rape adult women do so as an add-on sexual bonus to the commission of another crime such as burglary.[18] Such crossover crimes could
occur because of sudden erotic desires, though illicit, that surface unexpectedly in situations themselves. "Acquaintance rape" situations may

occur as a result of sexual feelings that surge at the end of dating or party situations. Men who think that "now or never is the time to make a move" may suddenly shift into an offending mode, only to realize afterwards that they got caught in a situation that they carried too far. "Marital rape" situations may likewise occur through a process of erotic combustion or explosion. It could be argued that men who rape their wives, at least the first time they do it, do not premeditate the rape. Indeed, it may be that offenders initially are as shocked by their own actions—having done something of which they never thought they were capable—as are their victims. Current images of child molesting and rape make it difficult for us to accept that initial involvements in such behavior are likely not to be premeditated.

It is not inconceivable either that such an erotic process is involved in initial forays into behaviors such as swinging or group sex, sado-masochism, bisexuality, cross-dressing, or extramarital sex. Take the latter type of situation in particular. People who work around each other may experience unanticipated erotic shifts that build into affairs. Husbands or wives who try to explain their erotic involvement with someone outside their marriage to a spouse who has discovered the situation sometimes claim that things just happened, that what occurred was not something they had planned, and that they did not set out to become attracted to the person with whom they became involved. A second illustration comes to mind as well. During the fieldwork stage of a recent study on bisexuality in which I was involved, I met a heterosexual man at a bisexual support organization who was searching for a female dominatrix as a partner. When asked why he was on such an odd quest, he said he had met a woman in a bar and had gone to her place to have sex. While he was there, she tied him to a rack and spanked and whipped him. To his surprise, he enjoyed the experience. It was something he claimed never to have thought of before. After that, his sex life was never the same. These are examples of how people discover new forms of eroticism, some consensual, some not, primarily through a process of spontaneous interaction.

Green Light Offending

We can understand sexual offending in part by drawing an analogy with driving a car. Some people, when they get behind the wheel, engage in what might be characterized as green light driving. Once they start down the road, they like to speed up to make the lights at dangerous intersections. They set their own speed limit regardless of the signs around them. If they pass a road construction site, they make no attempt to drive more carefully. Occasionally people who drive in this fashion worry about getting a ticket because they do not want to have to pay a fine, but not very often. They drive offensively, paying virtually no attention to the other drivers around them. Such drivers figure that they own the road and that the only problem to avoid is a major accident. The only rules of the road are their rules. Similar to green light driving, roughly one-third of the men in this study engaged in "green light" offending.

Men who engaged in green light offending never seemed to see much of anything wrong with what they were doing. In some cases, prior to becoming offenders, they claimed having no awareness of the concept of child sexual abuse. After they began offending, they experienced no negative emotional reaction. When asked whether they ever thought that sex with a child was something adults should not do, more often than not they admitted never having really given the question serious thought. There was little if any shame, no attempts to forget, no apologies to the victim, and they only stopped intermittently if some external constraint required them to stop, or until they got caught. Once these men got on the road and started driving, they did not see any red lights and never checked their rearview mirror. In a sense, there was no recognition of any significant moral boundary, or what boundary did exist got redefined to fit the momentary needs of the offender.

Men who offended in this fashion, to coin a phrase, became stuck in an "I" phase of self with no "Me" process attached. The "I" dimension of the self represents the "impulsive, spontaneous" component, that part of the individual that is "never fully socialized by society or controlled by the actor."[19] For these men, momentary, spontaneous, and situational sexual needs repeatedly set their conduct in motion. They crossed the boundary into offending over and over because there was nothing to stop them. This type of offending involved the most blatant examples of objectification of the victim. Bob, for example, reported frequent anal intercourse with two eight-year-old boys but claimed he never thought that it might cause them any pain. Conrad noted that his biological daughter, with whom he had intercourse hundreds of times, frequently looked off into the distance and never seemed to be emotionally present when he was having sex with her. And Sam paid his stepson thousands of dollars for oral sex and admitted he prostituted the boy.

In cases classified as green light offending, the men routinely said that they enjoyed the feeling of orgasm and the sensation of tactile physical contact that accompanied their offending above all other aspects of the experience. Reaching orgasm with the victim seemed to be the primary mission for most of the men in this category. In green light cases, the men consistently reported the most serious and frequent levels of sexual behavior with their victims. These were the respondents who in all but one case reported fifty or more episodes of sexual contact, but frequently hundreds and sometimes thousands of episodes. If vaginal or anal intercourse occurred, it was almost always with the men in this group. Bizarre and ritualistic behaviors, when they were reported, were mentioned by a couple of these respondents too. For example, Ken described being tied naked to a post in the snow in his backyard and having children throw snowballs at him. Conrad mentioned taking anthropomorphic measurements of his daughter because it fascinated him to inspect her body.

In terms of their preoffending biographies, however, there was relatively little that distinguished these men from others in the study. Some had been molested as children, some had not. Some reported early sexual contact with peers, some did not. Every type of preoffending "setup"—from feelings of entrapment to indications of sexual problems—was reported. One factor that seemed to stand out, however, was that these men frequently mentioned having either very limited or very extensive sexual biographies with other adult partners prior to their involvement in offending. Consequently, they saw their sexual biographies as incomplete, or the desire for sexual conquest became a core aspect of their everyday identity. There seemed to be no single career pattern to the ways these men organized other aspects of the offending process, for example, how they gained regular access to their victims, or what if anything they said to their victims about keeping quiet.

Red Light Offending

Red light driving is where people drive with greater awareness and caution. As they move down the road, they see signs and signals and pay more attention to them. They have a sense of understanding about the rules of the road. If they encounter a traffic jam or an accident, they take a different route. There is a greater sense that other people drive on the road too. Sometimes, however, people who drive in this fashion approach traffic lights at intersections, if they happen to be driving late at night, where no other cars are around. Most drivers in such circumstances will stop and wait for the light to turn green. Other drivers change the law based on the circumstances. They stop, check quickly for police, and then drive on through even though the light is still red. Red light drivers obey the law unless special circumstances arise.

Many men described a process of "red light" offending. These were men who prior to ever experiencing any erotic thoughts, or engaging in any sexual behavior with a child, admitted they knew full well that such behavior was wrong. They knew the boundaries and indeed often quipped that they would have been the first person to string the guy up who messed with their child. And after an episode of sexual contact occurred, bells started to ring, sirens started to sound, and the men became upset with themselves because they could not believe their own actions. The problem was that every time they got to the critical intersection where a decision had to be made at those times when they were alone on the road, despite the red signals flashing all around them, they simply decided not to stop. Two-thirds of the men in the study reported this pattern of offending.

The critical question is, why did so many men drive through the red light despite having stopped so many times before? Why did the boundary appear entirely opaque one moment and so permeable the next? What happened to the boundary and the reactions the men experienced in these cases? The answer, in part, can be found by turning to ethnomethodology and the properties of commonsense reasoning. Boundaries and rules have meanings that are "indexical" in nature. Those meanings vary for people depending on situational cues of time, place, and usage. Rules or boundaries also have an ad hoc, "et cetera" quality. We follow rules and obey them as long as no glitches occur and everything goes along smoothly. But if unanticipated circumstances arise that require the alteration of a rule or boundary, we adjust or redefine it.[20] Rules or boundaries as such do not drive or determine our behavior. Our actions determine what the rules are as much as vice versa. Warren Handel provides a straightforward definition:

"Etc." implies that additional unanticipated problems may arise that call for alteration of the routine procedure . . . . Every commonsense rule of conduct, every routine, every loose category has a list of exceptions.[21]

An offender begins with some degree of knowledge and awareness of a rule—sex with children is wrong. The rule has etcetera-like qualities. If asked for his opinion before he had engaged in sex with children, the offender would most likely agree about the unacceptableness of such behavior. Then an unanticipated and surprising erotic feeling surfaces during interaction with a child. A spontaneous foray across the boundary occurs. The man becomes an offender. An awareness shift quickly follows. The offender becomes distraught, applying the rule with which he started. He begins to adjust the meaning of the rule to fit present circumstances. He searches his past to find exceptions to the rule. He looks to the actions of the victim or to the problematic circumstances of his daily life to try and make his own behavior accountable. The offender's sense of the original rule exists, yet a new variation of the rule is being formulated. A type of *boundary slippage* occurs. Further erotic desires begin to surface. The rule has already been breached once. It no longer has the same meaning or hold that it might have had previously. The offender consequently decides to act according to his changing definition of the situation despite his knowledge of the originally existing rule. The process repeats itself.

The key difference in red light offending was that, with each new offending episode, an "awareness shift" occurred between the "I" and "Me" components of the self that did not occur with other offenders. Simply put, "the Me is the adoption of the generalized other."[22] When these men offended, they shifted into a "Me" phase of self-awareness, seeing themselves as social objects, taking the role of the victim and society to give meaning to their behavior. When they did not like what they discovered, they began redefining their conduct as an exception to the sexual boundary between adults and children. This "I" and "Me" process has been described by John Hewitt in more technical and generic terms.

The "I" and the "Me" continually alternate in ongoing conduct. At one moment, the individual acts as an "I," responding to a particular situation and to the object and people in it; at the next moment that response becomes a part of the past and so is part of the "Me"—the response now can be an object of reflection.[23]

Men who engaged in red light offending described frequent stops and restarts to their behavior. Very few in this group committed any more than twenty-five offending episodes. Most often they committed fewer than ten offenses. More serious behaviors were less common, less serious behaviors were more common. Men who never did anything more than fondling always reported this type of process of involvement. There were no systematic differences among these men in terms of their preoffense biographies. They did not seem to initially shift or drift into offending for unique reasons. What they did was respond to their activities in a markedly different manner from green light offenders. Indeed, the men who followed this pattern were the ones who most often became engulfed with fear later on and who sometimes stopped offending on their own because of feelings of guilt and wrongdoing.

Shame as a Normal Reaction

The presence or absence of an emotional reaction phase in sexual offending, as elaborated above, is far from settled in the literature. Contemporary feminist-based theories of rape, for example, more or less dismiss the possibility of an emotional career on the part of offenders. Because sex crimes are said to involve the objectification and depersonalization of the victim, the presumption is that there is little in the way of any emotional feeling or regret following such behavior. This idea is elaborated by Diana Scully in her research on male rapists of women.

> The majority do not experience guilt or shame as a result of raping, nor do they report feeling any emotions for their victims during or following the rape. Instead of experiencing feelings that might constrain their sexually violent behavior, these men indicate that rape causes them to feel nothing or to feel good . . . . Men are able to rape because their victims have no real or symbolic meaning or value outside of the role rapists force them to perform.[24]

Contrary to feminist-based theories that emphasize the absence of emotion, the sexual addiction model of sexual deviance posits that feelings of intense shame about sex and self in general drive rape or sexual abuse. The key to this theory is that feelings of shame represent an underlying core pathology in some people, originating from abusive sexual experiences in childhood or the experience of being raised in a dysfunctional family system with overly rigid sexual boundaries. Shame-based people, according to Patrick Carnes, get caught in a never ending cycle from which they are unable to escape.

> Following the climax experience, the addict plummets into shame and despair more deeply with each repetition of the cycle. Despair becomes the connecting

link in all addictive cycles, creating the need to begin the cycle again. Whether the focus is food, drugs, alcohol, gambling, or sex, the addict relieves the low or withdrawal by getting high again. That is, to take away the pain of despair, he or she reenters the obsessive preoccupation, thus completing the cycle . . . . The purpose of the cycle in the addict's life is to keep pain at bay.[25]

Most men reacted with emotion, some men did not. It may be that emotional after-reactions are more common when the victims of sexual offending are children rather than adults. Precisely why some men experience emotional reactions while others do not is not completely clear. Contrary to the sexual addiction model of offending, however, feelings of shame and guilt that did follow for offenders seemed primarily situational rather than a consequence of some fundamental personality flaw. Along this line, as argued earlier, feelings of erotic shame are characteristic of all forms of sexual relating that diverge from reproductive, monogamous, heterosexual, conventional ideals. Modern Western culture imbues most forms of sexual activity with guilt and shame. The more distant the behavior from the conventional boundary, the more intense the level of shame attached.[26] The question, then, is not why some men who offend experience guilt and shame, but why certain men do not.

Sexual Momentum

Momentum refers to the tendency of an object to keep moving against resistance once it has started. Erotic constructions that people make about others sometimes gain what I refer to as *sexual momentum*. Once people attach sexual meaning to others, it becomes difficult for them to deconstruct that meaning and return to a nonsexual frame of understanding. Erotic frames tend to maintain themselves and to escalate unless they are met by a force that shatters them or they burn out as a consequence of boredom. This seemed to be the case with men who molested children. Once feelings of erotic desire were attached to a child, a sexual momentum process unfolded. The men reported being unable to stop their sexual feelings, which tended to take on a life of their own, occurring over and over, often building in strength, surging and resurging, reaching a stage at which many men perceived they were out of sexual control. Sexual momentum is why most men became repetitive offenders.

Once erotic desire became turned on, there were more factors that facilitated a process of sexual momentum than obstacles to stop it. Such factors consisted of a range of *erotic pushes and pulls*. One contingency was the perceived vulnerability of the child who became the object of attention. Many men noted that they had picked a particular child they believed to be an easy or willing mark. Another contingency was the relative ease with which most offenders were able to choose appropriate approach strategies to overcome whatever resistance victims offered. Offenders enjoyed physical and intellectual advantages as well as strategical experience in the realm of sex. Also providing pushes and pulls were the various erotic and emotional surges of pleasure, the quick high the men reported experiencing, each time sexual contact occurred. The unique and banned nature of the offending situation, in particular, provided added intensity to the erotic context. Still more, adding to the momentum process was the regular unguarded access men had to their victims. Time alone with a victim was directly related to the frequency and number of sexual episodes.

The one erotic contingency that more than all others facilitated sexual momentum—the continual buildup and resurgence of erotic desire that provided the impetus to further offending—was the context of isolation and secrecy in which offenders became embedded. The men I interviewed nearly always felt cut off sexually and emotionally from their spouses and other meaningful relationships from the start to finish of the offenses they committed. Many had reached a point at which whatever sexual desires they might be experiencing, there was nowhere left to channel them. As sexual frustration, boredom, inactivity, and problems built in one realm, there was a spillover effect in an illicit direction. The men in a sense became unglued or unanchored from the realm of traditional sex. And as illicit desires began to take hold, the men were often so disconnected emotionally that they routinely felt they had no one they could turn to and talk with to try and stop what was happening. Once offending unfolded, the secrecy offenders began to sustain to keep from getting caught marginalized them even more. And as the offending situation continued, there were no external observers to impact and halt the abuse.

Erotic desires ebb and flow according to the socially available channels that close and open around people.[27] As closure occurred in the conventional realm, the doors began to open elsewhere. A type of self-fulfilling prophecy started to take hold. Offenders became encapsulated completely alone with their erotic desires and feelings. They typically struggled to find an explanation for what they had been doing but were nearly always unsuccessful. Having no one else to talk to and no linguistic framework or vocabulary to make sense of their illicit desires, they began to interpret and experience those desires and feelings as sexual compulsions.[28] To them, a mysterious force took hold of their lives and controlled them more than they were able to control it. A process of sexual momentum unfolded. Ironically, the societal reaction attached to sexual offending against children, one characterized by intense hatred and condemnation expressed on a public level, would seem to foster the very conditions that facilitate the buildup of sexual momentum for offenders. The more our culture encourages conditions of isolation and secrecy because of such reactions, the more extreme the forms of offending that could develop.

Power played a part in the momentum process as well. Erotic desire seemed to flourish for men when they were in control of their victims. It appeared to dissipate when they were not. *Power seemed to act as an erotic catalyst.* Some men seemed to eroticize power. Most explanations of sexual offending presume that offenders always have all the power and are always in control. This is why they are able to offend and, it is often said, why they desire to do so as well. According to the men in this study, power was more dynamic. Most of the time offenders admitted they were in control, but sometimes they also felt it was the victim who was in control of them. *Power switches* for offenders seemed to occur as the victims they molested got older. Some victims became wiser with age and appeared to figure things out. The men felt that the victims began to use sex and their knowledge of what had been occurring to gain leverage, to enhance their freedom and economic situation. Other men admitted that they lost power when the victim started to initiate sex back. There was a revealing irony to this experience as the men themselves became victims of their own actions. In these instances, erotic interest dissipated, sexual momentum essentially stopped, and offenders began to search for ways out of the situation.

Sexual momentum should not be confused with sexual compulsion or sexual addiction. They are not the same things. Sexual momentum is a routine aspect of sexual desire in general. It can occur with all types of sexual activities. Husbands and wives sometimes experience sexual momentum, for example, if they develop a relentless desire for regular daily sex, which they cannot wait to get home to at night. Sexual addiction is a pathological construct or label that gets attached to people who engage in sexual behavior that has an illicit quality to it—high-volume masturbation, extramarital sex, use of pornography, and so forth. Sexual momentum is facilitated by external situational contingencies and pleasures that act as catalysts for sexual feelings. Sexual addiction is theorized to be driven by pathological shame that can be traced to a person's family of origin. Importantly, sexual momentum gets defined as sexual addiction or compulsion when people cross the line into illicit behavior. A man who has sex with his wife once or twice a day and who cannot stop desiring her is perceived as sexually healthy. But if the same erotic feelings and behavior occur in an extramarital liaison, or if the actor prefers dirty films over his wife, it tends to get defined as sexual addiction. The first is an actor-relevant concept, the second is an observer-based interpretation.

Depersonalization and Repersonalization

A person's ability to take the role of the other is a core symbolic process that shapes the emergence of self and the direction of interaction with other people. Taking the role of the other consists of trying to gauge how others see and experience the world of which the actor is a part, looking at social life through the eyes of the other person. Indeed, it is this ability that makes people distinctly human. It is what makes us able to act nonviolently and consensually in relation to each other. It is a crucial component of mutual, cooperative sexual interaction. Again, I quote from Joel Charon:

> We imagine the other's perspective, we communicate that perspective to self on the basis of what we see and hear the other do . . . . Individuals tell themselves how others see things and how other people's perspectives operate . . . . That is the essence of taking the role of the other.[29]

When the men in this study molested their victims, rather than actively taking the role of the other, they suspended doing so. Instead, they shifted into an interactive mode that consisted of a pattern of "depersonalization" and "unresponsiveness" with their victims.[30] However the younger person might have reacted to what was happening, the men either ignored or redefined the reality of the other party during the immediate context of offending. Victims were almost always seen as enjoying the experience, as willing participants, as old enough to make up their own minds about sex regardless of their age, as having not offered enough resistance. At the same time, offenders admitted that they virtually never asked their victims whether they wanted to have sex, that their victims were often silent or outright resistive, and that signs of distress were continually visible around them.

What occurred while the men offended was a process of selective filtering of reality consistent with Mead's philosophy of pragmatism. Again to quote Joel Charon, "People see what they want to see and remember what they want to remember . . . . Objects we encounter are defined according to their use for us."[31] That is to say, the reality of offenders was organized around a "closed awareness context."[32] This closing off of the self to the reactions of others, of seeing things as one wants to see them, basically involves a pattern of overt objectification. John Stoltenberg explains the term as such:

When a man sexually objectifies someone—that is, when he regards another person's body as a thing, not another self, for the purpose of his own subjective sexual stimulation—he is not terribly likely to be perceptive of what is happening to anyone other than himself. Actually, the man is likely to be completely oblivious to what is happening to the person he is objectifying, because once he objectifies that person—once he reduces the person in his mind to the object he desires—then the person, to him, is by definition not a real subject like himself . . . . This person is not worth any real empathy at all because this person simply does not exist as someone who could have a valid experience apart from, much less contrary to, his own.[33]

To the same degree that involvement in offending was facilitated through a process of depersonalization, the overall seriousness of sexual contact was likewise mitigated as a result of intermittent episodes of repersonalization by offenders in relation to their victims. Repersonalization occurred when men began taking the role of the other, recognizing how their actions were affecting or might affect the younger person while they were actually offending. Routinely it took a major reaction from the victim for the men to begin drawing sexual boundaries around the overall level of their behavior, to shock them aware, so to speak: if the victim expressed feelings of physical pain, offered firm resistance, or displayed emotional distress either verbally or by crying. Some men, in addition, stopped at a lower level of contact because they anticipated that penetration or intercourse would probably cause physical pain or injury due to the size of the victim.

While occasional role taking was evident among offenders as they offended, there probably is no systematic way for children to stop adults from molesting them or to stop them from proceeding to more serious levels of contact once an episode of sexual contact begins.[34] Different men attended to different factors and drew sexual boundaries in different places. And some men admitted during the interviews that there was nothing the child could have done to stop them. While resistance and signs of pain clearly stopped some from offending or from escalating the situation, others used coercion or force to initiate contact or to carry sex to the next level. Still, referring to what A. Nicholas Groth has written about men who have committed predatory rape against adult women, it was when the victim "said or did something that registered with the offender and communicated to him that she was a real person and not just an object" that offending was most likely to stop at the level it did.[35] The best advice is for victims to tell someone about what happened to them afterwards as quickly as possible to stop the situation from recurring.

Situational Definitions and Offending

Causal theories about men who commit sex crimes or who molest children almost always are based on a static model of motive. Motive is nearly always seen as something that is preset prior to actual behavior. Usually an offender is said to be driven by a single core motive emanating from earlier life experiences or from some essential feature of the individual's personality. For example, in one study, four subtypes of child molesters were delineated based on an identification of core motive: physiological sexual arousal, cognitive distortion about the victim, a negative affective state such as depression, or personality problems or disorders.[36] Other typologies based on core motive have also been formulated. Distinctions between "fixated" versus "regressed" offenders and between "power," "anger," and "sadistic" offenders are widely cited.[37] And most recently is a classification of five essential types of offenders: "sexually preoccupied," "adolescent regressives," "instrumental self-gratifiers," "emotionally dependent" offenders, and "angry retaliators."[38]

Interactionist theorists, in contrast, view reasons for conduct as emergent, ongoing, multiple, and changing depending on the definition of the situation constructed by actors as interaction unfolds. Actors continually redefine experiences and situations as they occur, acting often in ways unintended and unplanned at first, but becoming more clearly refined across the course of involvement. Definitions rather than a priori motives thus shape social action. Joel Charon provides the following distinction:

> Action is to be explained not by deep-seated stable motives but by shifting goals and definitions of the situation . . . . If we imagine human action as being the result of individual motives, there is a tendency to see action determined by an internal state . . . . Motives are conceptualized as . . . preceding situations and action, and motives are thought to stay relatively stable in situations guiding the actor, despite the interaction that takes place there . . . . To emphasize motive . . . is to divert attention away from action as a stream of action with a history, directed by actors defining goals and objects as the action unfolds over time.[39]

Attempts to typecast offenders as acting based on a single, unchanging, predetermined motive miss the dynamic, unfolding, and complex mix of realities that shape the boundary-crossing process. Definitions that emerged and were formulated in the context of interaction with victims and before and after offending occurred all played a part in what the men did. Most men reported a web of definitions that told their own unique stories about how they became involved as offenders. While erotic definitions seemed to focus the choices of men in a sexual direction, other definitions that revolved around power, escape, anger, victim participation, risk of detection, intimacy, thrill, victim vulnerability, use of force or coercion, childhood experiences, relations with spouses, lifestyle problems, opportunity, and victim consequences all tended to get blurred, built up, layered, and mixed together. Indeed, it was not uncommon for men who started out offending for what they identified as one reason, to recount that they offended for quite different reasons in the middle, and then again for yet other reasons at the end. People in the business of social control who rely on unidimensional types might be locking themselves into a misleading picture about men who become offenders.

The Myth of Abnormality

One of the predominant views about men who become sex offenders is that they are fundamentally different in some way from men who do not offend. Essentialist-based models about offenders dominate the sex crimes literature.[40] The data supplied by the men in this study suggest otherwise, that male offenders as a group are not particularly different from men in general. The accounts that respondents provided showed typical aspects of male sexual reality, and some routine aspects of social life more generally. The one exception is the data on the early childhood histories of the men, in particular their reports of a greater incidence of childhood sexual contact with adults than is commonly found in the general population. We can see the mundane aspects of the men's actions most clearly if we deconstruct their offending accounts, strip out any reference to children or adolescents, and remove the one factor that makes these reported interactions seem "deviant" or "bizarre." The result is an extraordinary glimpse at what would appear to be relatively ordinary gender-stereotyped behavior.

The men became interested in sex with children for the same reasons they do with any other adult—they were curious, they began noticing, they responded to what they perceived as a sexual cue, they experienced an erection from nonsexual touching, they chose someone they perceived as accessible to them. They experienced sex in the same ways men generally experience sex—they enjoyed the touch and the feeling of ejaculating, it was exciting because it was something new, they felt young again, it helped them forget all the stress in their lives, it was a thrill, they felt closer and more intimate. They approached and engaged the other party in ways men routinely initiate sex—by trying to seduce the person, trying to talk the person into it, being a little forceful, grabbing at the person, attempting to introduce sex in stages, taking over if they thought the other person started things. They reacted afterwards often with feelings of shame, or sometimes no guilt at all, just like the range of reactions others elicit if they are involved in behavior of any type that society frowns heavily on. And they adjusted and coped with these feelings in ways that are commonplace as well—by apologizing to the injured party, by burying themselves in work or alcohol, by denying that what they did was really all that bad or harmful.

This is the critical point about the data here. There is nothing about how the men acted on a generic level that, in and of itself, is abnormal or "odd" for men per se. Offenders and their behavior are frequently seen as abnormal because defining them as such absolves nonoffending men of all responsibility. Importantly, this does not make what offenders do acceptable or tolerable in any way. It is not to give license to men in general to do as they please to others. Indeed, it is to implicate male culture generally as problematic. It raises the question about whether men are willing to reassess their status and worldview as men. And it leads to the obvious question, not about why men offend, but as has also been suggested by Scully and Marolla in regard to men who rape adult women, why some men do not.[41] Ultimately the men appeared to treat the children they victimized as sexual objects, felt eroticized doing so, sometimes felt a bit guilty or sometimes did not, and then did it again and again, much as they might with any adult partner. There does not seem to be much that differentiates these men from men who are not offenders except that they crossed what appears to be a thin boundary between ordinary sexual relations and what is defined culturally as extreme sexual deviation.

Over the last couple of years, I have heard heated argument from numerous male students and male sociology colleagues about this point. They adamantly insist that their view of sex is quite different from that of the men I studied. Frequently they personalize their view to illustrate how they are different, stating that they have never had a sexual thought about a child in their lives. Even more, many add they have never, even in the remote recesses of their minds, entertained thoughts of raping a woman.[42] Interestingly, nearly all the men I interviewed said the same things before they became offenders. It is difficult for men to accept that they might be participants in a culture of rape or sexual abuse. I frequently ask men who reject my argument to answer specific questions about themselves before reaching any final conclusions: Have you ever asked or tried to talk a girlfriend or your wife into having sex when she did not want to? Have you ever looked at a child and thought or commented strongly about his or her looks? Have you ever looked at a group of young females and noticed that some were attractive even though you did not know their ages? What is the difference between you and someone who rapes or engages in child molesting? What are the similarities? Obviously not all men are going to commit sexual violations. But many could have a facilitating framework for doing so.

Confronting the Problem of Sexual Abuse

Having analyzed the involvement of men in child sexual abuse, we must still consider what all of this tells us about stopping the behavior. What do we need to do as parents and as a community to solve the problem? How can we keep some men from becoming reoffenders? How can we prevent other men who might become offenders from crossing over into the unspeakable? Today, the rhetoric and approach to social control that many of us endorse involves what has been referred to as a "war model" strategy.[43] In our culture, when we want to solve crime problems, we go to war. We engage in combat. We attempt to wipe out the enemy. We frame crime control in a war context. The war on drugs. The war on violent crime. The war on gangs. The war on organized crime. The war on child sexual abuse. And if we capture the enemy, we encourage tossing the prisoners of these wars into institutions where they can attack each other instead of us. We also react with suspicion toward social programs that might offer some hope. Imagine working as a clinician with molestation offenders in the context of this control framework and trying to repair what has gone wrong.

The concern I raise is whether or not we can really prevent or stop sexual violations against children from occurring in this general way. Can we really teach people to respect other people's boundaries by going to war? Does treatment itself administered in a war context become a form of coercion, which we are supposed to be teaching offenders not to do? Let me state up front that I am not a mental health clinician. I do not claim the expertise of a counselor in the trenches who has some sense of what does and does not specifically work with offenders. But I do want to suggest on a broader level, drawing on what my research has shown, something about where some of our control priorities ought to lie, especially in situations of family-based sexual abuse like the cases I analyzed here. My concern is not with going easy on offenders. I am just as outraged by sexual abuse as the next person. But I do endorse on a general level what is known as the "peacemaking" model in criminal justice.[44] This approach posits treating interpersonal violations such as unwanted sex more as violations of respect and trust rather than as criminal acts. Thus the goal of effective control is to try and rebuild respect and trust between people where it has broken down, to negotiate and settle the conflicts that separate them, to teach people to be more responsive with each other, and to bring those who do terrible things back into the community in a more positive way.

With this in mind, what exactly do I recommend? First, we need to carefully reassess the implications that the registration of sex offenders and mass announcements about their release back into the community will have on the commission of sexual abuse in the long run, especially family-based sexual abuse. Is the best solution to brand all offenders as public deviants? Think about this. If child sexual abuse results, in part, from factors such as too much stress, the erosion of social connections, emotional disorganization, feelings of anger or powerlessness, and the need to escape, what are we doing when we react as a community in this fashion? Are we not creating the very conditions that facilitated the behavior we want to stop? Talk about creating stress, frustration, and powerlessness, this is certainly one good way to do it. Are we really protecting ourselves? As a matter of policy, I believe it is imperative that we clearly distinguish with preset criteria which offenders we want to deal with in this fashion. Should all child sex offenders be grouped together and made the focus of public awareness? Is this something you would advocate if the offender was your brother, or father, or uncle, or husband? Should family-based offenders be included in this policy? Or should we reserve such designations strictly for people who are evaluated as dangerously violent predators who have molested children previously unknown to them? And if so, what criteria do we use to determine dangerousness?

Second, community treatment should be the first line of defense in stopping family-based sexual abuse, and incarceration should be the last line. It is widely presumed in our society that men who commit sexual crimes are highly likely to recidivate and that when they do, the crimes they commit later on are much more heinous and violent than the first time around. Much of our perception in this regard is colored by the tragic extreme cases of sexual abuse and murder we see reported in the mass media. Such cases are the exception and not the rule. Some sexual offenders do repeat their crimes. Others, with effective intervention, do not. I interviewed one offender who had completed a year of treatment while released in the community on bond. There were letters in his case file from counselors describing the substantial progress the offender had made and urging more treatment because he was a low-risk case. Then he came up for sentencing. He received eight years and was placed in a high-security institution where no one had any training in sex offender therapy. I asked him after three years whether he thought it likely he would ever reoffend. He said he did not know. Meanwhile, he lost a high-paying job, spent all his money on lawyers, could no longer assist his wife and three children paying the bills, and had nothing left to help the eight children he molested (two of whom were his own children) pay for counseling. Why did we handle this case this way? Most sex offenders we sentence to prison are going to get out sometime. We made this man more dangerous.

Critics will argue that sexual abuse offenders can receive treatment while they are in prison or after they get out. This is true, and they should. But penal institutions are invariably problematic places for offering treatment of any kind, let alone working with incest or family-based offenders. The presence of other inmates who have committed other nonsexual crimes who harass inmates incarcerated for child sexual abuse discourages many such men from seeking help. Also, in cases of family-based sexual abuse, treatment is much more likely to be effective when entire families are involved and when they work together where willing. Prisons, however, are not particularly conducive places for wives and children. But even if they were, many offenders are sent to prisons that are far away from their families. While prisons protect the community from offenders during the period they are incarcerated, they place us even more at risk when those same violators, who could have been better helped elsewhere, are released. This is why we should give a priority to treatment where possible.

Third, if it is agreed that public priority lies with treatment, communities need to enact mechanisms by which offenders can come forward and voluntarily seek help to stop what they are doing, rather than waiting for victims or someone else to report what is happening. On the surface this would seem to be a far-fetched idea. But it did not seem unusual at all to some of the men I interviewed. I found that many offenders, though certainly not all, tried to put the brakes on their behavior at various times. Those who did then faced a huge disincentive to seek more official qualified help because coming forward and talking to a counselor meant they would be charged and prosecuted as criminals. So they tried to solve their problems themselves, which they were unable to do successfully. One offender recommended the declaration of a period of amnesty, during which men involved in child sexual abuse who had not inflicted major physical injury or abducted anyone, who came forward and turned themselves in, and who actively participated in treatment would in exchange not be prosecuted or incarcerated. Those men who decided to keep offending instead of seeking help, or who reoffended after treatment, as he saw it, ought then to be prosecuted more severely. The idea is an interesting possibility, especially with family-based offenders. I think we need to put more priority on figuring out how to stop the behavior as early as we can as opposed to waiting until later and then instituting harsh punishment. Every new offense means more damage to victims.

Closely related to this third point is a fourth idea. If we hope to stop future abuse, we need to encourage ways to open a full dialogue with known offenders who are evaluated as amenable to treatment. Successful treatment requires that we know the full range of fantasies and violations offenders have been involved in with victims so that a more effective attempt can be made to reorganize their sexuality. Full disclosure also breaks down the wall of secrecy that surrounds sexual abuse situations. Every separate sexual act in which an offender has engaged is a prosecutable offense. If an offender is charged with one level of conduct, but actually did something more severe, disclosure of previously unknown acts very well could mean additional criminal prosecution. Sex offenders are often seen as people who lie about and minimize their behavior. It seems surprising that anyone would expect any sex offender to be willing to talk about his behavior with full disclosure, given the potential legal ramifications. It is thus essential to provide mechanisms for offenders to report every aspect of their involvement. For example, maybe physically nonviolent offenders like the men I interviewed here who admit a fuller spectrum of activity than their charges or convictions indicate should be exempt from further prosecution. Maybe we should prosecute and sentence on a general level only—nonviolent sexual abuse, or violent sexual abuse—rather than for each individual behavior. My experience was that when I promised offenders their stories would not be used to prosecute them, they opened up and shared substantial detail about their cases.

Fifth, whatever the form of treatment offenders receive, one of the core components should consist of instilling empathy toward victims. Indeed, many treatment programs already emphasize this important goal. For example, treatment should include core lectures and discussions about the impact of sexual abuse on victims. These should be supplemented with some of the documentary films about victims now available that involve personal accounts of the devastating impact of sexual abuse. There should also be extensive efforts in treatment to break down rationalizations offenders assemble around their behavior. But more, creating empathy should include, in the cases of willing victims, sessions at which offenders hear their victims talk about their experience and present their emotional reality. In turn, structured "apology" sessions should be incorporated as a component of all treatment programs.[45] In structured apology sessions, offenders take responsibility for their behavior in front of victims in a mutually supportive environment. And finally, an offender should be required to pay for part or all of the victim's mental health treatment, depending on what he earns.

Sixth, sex offender treatment programs should also include the formulation and implementation of explicit external rules for offenders—and families where applicable—to follow to prevent any future reoffending. In the treatment settings where I sampled offenders, these rules were referred to as a "protection plan." Each offender constructed his own protection plan, with the guidance of his therapist, and in consideration of the needs of his spouse and victims where possible. Protection plans were basic: a rank item list of who offenders should call or talk to if erotic thoughts returned; specific dress code rules for family members to minimize voyeurism; use of locks on bathroom and bedroom doors to prevent unwanted entries; names and phone numbers of people spouses and children should call in the case of renewed victimization; pledges that offenders and spouses would work together on family problems instead of fighting over power. The protection plan was written as a contract and signed by the offender. While such plans obviously convey an image of families and victims under constant threat and siege, they also provide structural mechanisms to stop sexual abuse situations before they reoccur, versus relying strictly on internal changes in offenders for such protection.

Reframing our approach toward offenders is not enough by itself to stop the problem of child sexual abuse. Realistically, this is akin to treating the symptom and not the cause, of patching things up after the fact. Thus, it is also crucial that we focus on social reform in a broader sense.[46] Indeed, this is an idea that feminist scholars have long advocated. Men who engaged in sexual abuse, like many men in general, tended to rank sex as an extremely high priority in life. They tended to focus on looks and body structure. They tended to get angry and vindictive if their female partners defied them in any way. These are patterns of relating that men in general need to take some responsibility for changing. Men as a group need to learn to focus less on bodily attributes and more on the whole person. They need to learn to share power and privilege more than exerting power and control over others. And they need to become more aware of the ways others signal them to stop their sexual advances when such advances are unwanted.

There are a few additional possibilities for social control that might help protect children from sexual harm. We need to give high priority to working with boys who have been sexually abused to reestablish the importance of the moral boundary surrounding such behavior. We need to do the same thing with boys who commit sexual violations as children to prevent any carryover later in adult life. Education too is necessary. High school and college courses that focus on the family, sex education, or public health should contain discussion about behaviors that constitute child sexual abuse. In addition, there should be active public and community involvement in perpetrator treatment programs to reaffirm the moral outrage people feel when children are victimized. For example, every treatment group could contain a panel of citizens who confront offenders. Finally, every parent should take the time to read at least one book on sexual victimization so that they will be more aware of possible situations involving their children and what they can do. And most critical of all, the government should provide research funds for the study of child sexual abuse offenders and rapists. We need to keep asking offenders how they view sexual boundaries and why they acted as they did. This study of thirty cases is not nearly enough to provide any definitive answers. Just because we abhor the act does not mean we should ignore research in this direction.

Looking Ahead

While the present study has provided a rich and detailed portrait of the social reality of child molesting from the standpoint of the men involved, additional avenues of research remain to be pursued. In particular, similar interactionist- and reality-based research on more diverse groups of offenders would certainly yield more generalizable results. The number of cases discussed here was relatively small and consisted entirely of adult men, all of whom were either biological fathers, stepfathers, or close family friends of their victims, who molested primarily females, tended to use only minimal levels of physical violence if any, and claimed to prefer adults as sexual partners. In what ways would the stages of involvement documented among respondents here vary for other groups of offenders? For example, would the same processes hold for adolescent offenders? For female offenders? For adult men who molest children in stranger-based circumstances? For offenders who admit a strong erotic preference for children? For men who commit more ritualistic, violent, or sadistic offenses? For homosexual or bisexual offenders, who represented only a fraction of the offenders in these data?

Other unexplored dimensions of the lives of men who have molested children remain to be studied as well. The current research concluded at the point at which men were exposed as offenders. Another fruitful avenue of inquiry would be to investigate what happens from that point on. What kinds of reactions and labeling by others are experienced by men who have been publicly identified as sex offenders? How are they treated afterwards by their nonoffending spouse, family friends, parents—some of whom molested them too—other relatives, any other children of theirs who were not victims, inmates if incarcerated, employers, or even police, prison guards, therapists, or prosecutors? Also, how do offenders adjust to being sexually stigmatized on both a social and personal level? Do they attempt to deny responsibility or engage in a process of deviance disavowal? Do they ever acknowledge wrongdoing and reorganize how they view their victims later? Is there a process of adjustment that unfolds in stages too? And, depending on the eventual legal outcome of their cases, do offenders think they received justice, given the hostility that surrounds the issue of child molesting? Last, do offenders themselves believe they are likely to reoffend, and what kinds of things do they think might best keep this from happening?

Beyond the study of offenders, further interactionist- and standpoint-based research needs to be conducted with other parties involved in sexual abuse situations in order to fill out a more complete picture of the dynamics of sexual offending. This would include, for instance, more rigorous unbiased research with both female and male children involved in adult-child sexual contact, studies that move beyond trauma symptom checklists or presumptions of violence, injury, force, and harm,[47] and that instead focus on interactional processes.[48] This would also include research with victims that moves beyond loose clinical evidence or otherwise potentially useful qualitative research that groups together men who rape adult women and men who molest children.[49] A more complete interactionist model of sexual offending against children requires an examination of all the relevant standpoints in any offending situation. When offending occurs in the family environment, this would include data on nonoffending spouses and other nonvictimized children who live in the same household.[50] One interactionist-based research design that might yield more valid results in cases of family-based offending would be to conduct depth interviews with entire families as a sampling unit. The goal would be to piece together a more dynamic and interactive portrait of how offending in family-based contexts occurs.

As more interactionist-based studies on both offenders and victims in particular are completed, some attempt needs to be made to compare the accounts that both parties provide about reported offenses. Do offenders and victims construct similar portraits about what occurs in offending situations? If not, where exactly do their accounts differ? Returning briefly to the data in this research, some men claimed that the children they molested misreported what actually happened—accusing them of more serious sexual contact when they claimed they had not gone that far, grossly overestimating the number of offending episodes that transpired, stating that force was used or that threats of injury or harm were made when offenders said they were not, and denying that they participated in or instigated the sexual situation when offenders believed they had. Comparisons between the accounts of offenders and sporadic data in the official record for roughly two-thirds of the men confirmed, as offenders had reported, that these were common areas of discrepancy.

While these findings are at best speculative in this research and require further investigation, they do of course raise the provocative question about who is more accurate in their reconstruction of events. Today, ideology dictates that victims invariably tell the truth and that offenders are more likely than not to be dishonest. For researchers to question otherwise places them at serious risk of scholarly attack from members of the clinical and scientific community who deal with these issues. But an interactionist-based theory provides a modest solution to this dilemma. It may be that both sides are telling what is real to them, and that neither party is deliberately fabricating what occurred. To quote Joel Charon one final time, "It is difficult for us to accept that all of us may be telling the truth. We might see things differently if we imagine that each . . . sees a different reality."[51] Victims who feel traumatized are not going to define the situation the same way as offenders who become sexually aroused toward and engage in sex with someone who should be off limits. Resolution of this issue is critical for the treatment of offenders who are routinely required to accept the victims' version of events in order to receive a favorable and cooperative evaluation from their clinicians.

What type of prospects loom for children in terms of the sexual risks they face? Will rates of victimization go up or down in the future? Three factors in particular could contribute to an increased rate of family-based sexual abuse in the years ahead. The first factor is the increase in the number of wives/mothers working outside the home. As fathers in general spend more time with their children, especially time alone with their children because their spouses work, the rate of sexual victimization could possibly increase. In this study, offenders often commented that they began offending after periods of extensive involvement with their children when their spouses were not around and that the frequency of sexual contact varied with their spouses' schedule. The second factor is the continued proliferation of the stepparent family. There were more stepfathers in this study than any other category of offender. Stepfathers are less familiar with their stepchildren and thus, it could be argued, more prone to develop erotic feelings toward them.[52] One warning signal might be stepfathers who spend more time with their wives' children than with their wives. The third factor is the culture of hate and condemnation that surrounds the phenomenon of sexual offending at present. Sexual offending is an unsettling reality. But until we find a way to encourage offenders to come forward with their stories rather than hide and continue with what they are doing, the situation is only bound to get worse.

Some Final Thoughts about Offending

Understanding why people commit child sexual abuse, I argue, requires answers to two interrelated but different questions. First, where does the desire or interest in having sex with a child start? What triggers the idea? What factors facilitate such a reality and what kinds of things prevent it? This in many ways, I think, is the easier of the two questions to answer. Many circumstances can trigger erotic thoughts in unexpected directions, especially if you happen to be a man who often thinks about sex. Second, if such an interest or desire in the unspeakable does surface, why are offenders not able to construct a boundary that is strong enough to stop themselves? What happens to the moral boundary that should contain the actor in these situations? How do offenders get across it? Do they even construct a boundary? In contrast, how are people who do attach erotic meanings to children but who also stop or keep themselves from acting able to do so? How does their image of the sexual abuse boundary differ?

When we stand back and look at child sexual abuse situations from a distance—for instance, we see a television program or hear about a child who was molested at school by a teacher—the boundary between right and wrong is unquestionably opaque for many of us. We wonder how somebody could do such a thing; we feel both amazed and horrified. We reaffirm to each other that there are some really weird characters out there in the world who live by a different moral code than we do. But what if any one of us, you or the next person, happened to notice, for whatever reason, something erotic about a child? And what if, like the men here, you found that you spent a lot of time alone in the company of that child? What would you do? Would the boundary disappear? Are you sure that you would be able to construct a boundary to erase your thoughts or to stop yourself? Is there anything any of us could do to ensure that this is how we would react? Where could we go in such circumstances if we needed help?

I would like to think that many of us would build a concrete wall and do it immediately, that if nothing else the threat of punishment or social shame would stop us. Yet after talking to the men here, I wonder. The moral code we articulate for others may be quite different from what we institute for ourselves at the critical moments we need to in life. If you think about it, who really ever stopped to teach us why doing something sexual with a child is wrong? How strong can the boundary be for each of us in this culture if such lessons in morality are rare? What is a boundary anyway, besides a definition we can change if we decide to do so? Is a boundary a brick wall that blocks our way? More like a fence with lots of openings that we can squeeze through? Or is it like a wall of water we can walk right on through if we choose? The question is important, the image we settle on crucial, when we discuss how to protect our children.

Table 1

Recent Studies Measuring Incidence of "Sexual Abuse" during Childhood and Adolescence

Author (Year)	Sample	Method	Type of Sexual Behavior	Relation of Victim to Offender	Age of Victim	Victimization Criteria	Percentage Ever Abused	
							Female	Male
Doll et al. (1992)	1,001 self-identified or actively homosexual men aged 18 or older from STD clinics	standard interview	kissed or hugged sexually, received invitation, exhibitionism, or any type of genital contact	any	18 or under	subject said the other person was older or more powerful		37
Finkelhor (1979)	796 college students from six New England schools in social science courses	classroom questionnaire	kissed or hugged sexually, received overture, exhibitionism, or any type of genital contact	any	16 or under	subject said the other person was at least 5 years older if aged 12 or younger, 10 years older if aged 13 to 16	19.2	8.6
Finkelhor (1984)	521 Boston parents with children aged 6 to 14	depth interview	any type of attempted or completed sexual things	any	under 16	subject said the other person was at least 5 years older and defined the situation as sexual abuse	15	6

Table 1 (*continued*)
Recent Studies Measuring Incidence of "Sexual Abuse" during Childhood and Adolescence

Author (Year)	Sample	Method	Type of Sexual Behavior	Relation of Victim to Offender	Age of Victim	Victimization Criteria	Percentage Ever Abused Female	Percentage Ever Abused Male
Finkelhor et al. (1990)	2,626 citizens aged 18 or older from all 50 states	telephone survey	kissed or touched sexually, photographed or shown a sex act, exhibitionism, or any type of genital contact	any	18 or under	subject defined the situation as sexual abuse	27	16
Fritz, Stoll, and Wagner (1981)	952 undergrad students at Univ. of Washington	classroom questionnaire	physical contact of any overtly sexual nature	any	before puberty	subject said the other person was post-adolescent	7.7	4.8
Kercher and McShane (1984)	1,056 licensed Texas drivers aged 17 or older	mail questionnaire	any type of interaction where child was used for stimulation, or was photographed or prostituted	any	child	subject indicated having been sexually abused	11	3
Russell (1986)	930 adult females from San Francisco	depth interview	any type of attempted or completed physical breast or genital contact	relative . . . . . nonrelative . . . . . any	under 18 . . . . . under 18 . . . . . under 18	subject said the other person was at least 5 years older or coders classified the situation as unwanted	16 . . . 31 . . . 38	. . . . . .

Table 1 (*continued*)
Recent Studies Measuring Incidence of "Sexual Abuse" during Childhood and Adolescence

Author (Year)	Sample	Method	Type of Sexual Behavior	Relation of Victim to Offender	Age of Victim	Victimization Criteria	Percentage Ever Abused Female	Male
Simari & Baskin (1982)	29 lesbians and 54 gay males aged 22 to 65 from New York City	handout questionnaire	sexual event of any nature	relative	any	not specified	38	46
Wellman (1993)	824 college students in psychology courses from one school in New England	classroom questionnaire	not specified	any	child or teenager	subject indicated having been sexually abused	13	6
Wyatt (1985)	248 Black and White females from Los Angeles county aged 18 to 30	standard interview	received solicitation, exhibitionism, or any type of genital contact	any	under 18	subject said the other person was at least 5 years older *or* defined the situation as unwanted	62	

Note: Complete citations for these studies are listed in notes 2 and 3 of chapter 1.

Appendix A
Topical Interview Guide

Personal Information
    Age, race, sex, education, income
    Married, number of times
    Number of children, type (biological/step), ages
    Religion, religiosity
    Military experience, Vietnam combat
    Employment, length, wage/salary, supervise at work

Criminal Record
    Number of times arrested, convicted
    Date, charge, offense class for each
    Bond amount, conviction, plea/trial for each
    Sentence, date, days served and where for each

Family Background
    What family life was like over the years
        Structure, stability
        Quality of relations
    Adequacy of food, clothing, shelter
    Parents' education, job, income
    Hit or harmed as child
        Number of times, by whom, what was it like

Any family member problems with law
Open or closed family socially
Other significant positive or negative events
Overall happiness of family life
Feelings about, effects of family experiences
Relation of anything to molest

Sexual Development

How sexuality unfolded over the years
Sex as child with anyone older
    Number of times, with whom, what was it like
Childhood, adolescent sex play
Early dating patterns
First sex, first intercourse
Relationships, later dating
Sexual difficulties
Any sex education
Gender preference, age preference
Other significant positive or negative events
Overall happiness about sexuality
Feelings about, effects of sexual events
Relation of anything to molest

Life Leading up to Offending

Quality of marriage
Was spouse a molest victim
Was spouse nonmonogamous
Sex life, frequency, difficulties, complaints
Family environment
Use of alcohol, drugs
Social interactions, network
Economic situation, job
Other significant positive or negative events
Sense of self, overall happiness with life
Feelings about, effects of life events
Relation of anything to molest

Being Sexual with Children under Sixteen

Number of children with whom sexual contact was made

Ages of children when it began, when it ended
Your age when it began, when it ended
Victims' race, gender, your relationship to them
What was each child like as a person
Describe events, starting with first thoughts and actions
    What brought on interest
Any dreams, fantasies, masturbation
Number of episodes, average length
Behaviors over time, how sustained, how progressed
Plan first, subsequent episodes, where others were
Command, threaten child in any manner
Any resistance, how controlled

Meaning of Sexual Contact

What was it like to have sex with child
Thoughts, feelings as you did it
What you think child felt about what was happening
Any evidence of interest or distress
Why stop with certain acts, why not, why penetrate
Was sex painful for child in any way
    Your response to pain
What you did after first episode, between episodes
Why continued contact over time
Anything arousing about child to you
    Physical attributes, personality, mannerisms
Strength of attraction to child
    Did attraction arise before or after first act
Was affection, love, romance a component
    Did these arise before or after first act
Why not have sexual affair with adult
Any difference being natural father, stepfather, etc.
Why you think you did it
    Distinguish reasons then and now
    Break through scripts
Ever believe behavior to be wrong
    Distinguish view then and now
Aware of criminal penalties
How dealt with morality
Feelings about behavior across episodes

Feelings about self across episodes
Should adults be allowed to have sex with children
    Distinguish thinking then and now
Opinion about adults who have sex with children
    Distinguish position then and now
Ever think you might be harming child
    Distinguish view then and now
What you got out of experience
    Benefits and drawbacks
    Likes and dislikes

Secrecy and Discovery

Anyone ever suspect what you were doing
How you kept things secret
Ever say anything to child
How important was secrecy
Ever fear getting caught
Effects of secrecy on you, on child
How case got reported to officials, by whom
Feelings about self when caught
Feelings about behavior when caught
What you did when you realized you had been caught
    Admit or deny

Societal Reaction and Effects

Movement through justice system
Attitudes, comments of various authorities
    Your responses, feelings, the effects
Who knows about your crimes
    Spouse, family, friends, work mates, neighbors
    Type of reactions, comments
    Status of various relationships
    Your responses, feelings, the effects
Ever try to hide situation
Offense get any media publicity
    What followed as consequence
    Your responses, feelings, the effects
What is it like in prison/treatment
    How treated by DOC staff/therapist

Inmates'/other offenders' reactions, comments
Your responses, feelings, the effects
Why you think you got prison/treatment
Know any other molest offenders
What you think of them, what they think of you
Type of relationship with them
Talked to child involved since apprehension
What would you say if you could
Perceived impact on child
Why so little negative reaction
What you suppose public thinks about people who do this
Was overall treatment fair, just
Legally, socially, publicly
Feelings about what you did at this point
Other feelings about self given reactions
What would you do if someone molested your child
Believe you will ever reoffend
Has being labeled had an effect
How will you prevent it
How do you feel being around children now
How do you deal with the legal stigma
What do you think of the label "child molester"
What do you think your life will be like in future
Ever try to make amends

Personal Character

Greatest, worst attribute as person
Are women equals, should women do what men ask
See yourself as powerful, controlling
Like, dislike children in general
Biggest goal in life
What would you like to tell public

Interview Notes

Appendix B
Research Consent Forms

Human Subjects Statement

This research takes an in-depth look at men who have been convicted of sexual activity with persons under the age of sixteen. The main goal is to develop an understanding of the experiences and feelings of such men before, during, and after their involvement in the criminal justice system. In order to accomplish this, I would like to conduct a face-to-face interview with you. This is a chance for you to report your view of events to an impartial observer.

If you agree to participate, there are a number of steps that will be taken to protect your identity: (1) your name will not be recorded in the data; (2) only I and a university research committee will examine the data; (3) the data will be stored in a secure location under lock and key; (4) your location (agency, facility) will be kept secret; and (5) you will not be cited as the sole example in any formal write-up. Care will be taken to keep your involvement in this study confidential.

There are a few other points I must convey to you as well. About myself; I am a sociologist from [name of university]. I am not affiliated with any legal organization. Thus your participation is not a condition of your treatment or release from prison. I will be using the data you provide only to complete a Ph.D. dissertation and to write essays for publication and presentation.

Also, you can discontinue your involvement in this research at any point. If you would rather not answer a question I ask or prefer to keep a statement off the record, that is okay. Finally, during the interview, I will either be writing the information you provide on paper or I will tape-record our conversation, depending on your preference. In a minute, I will read you a statement about the benefits and risks of tape-recording to help you decide which of these methods you prefer. If you want to review the data from any portion of the interview, I will be glad to do so with you after we are finished.

At this time, if you have any questions or concerns, I will be happy to talk with you in more detail, and to provide answers as best I can. If not, I need you to initial your case number and date a consent waiver form to show you freely agree to participate. Thank you.

Respondent Agreement to Participate

I hereby consent, freely and by my own choosing, to participate in a social science research project (the nature of which is not stated here, for my own protection). I acknowledge that I have been informed about the purpose of the research as well as my rights as a human subject in a statement that was read to me or that I read. I acknowledge that I was given the opportunity to ask any questions I had about the research before participating and that these were answered to my satisfaction. I also understand that I am not obligated to participate in this study for any reason and that I can terminate my involvement at any point. Finally, I realize that my participation is not a requirement or condition of my treatment or release from prison.

sign here: _____

CASE NUMBER   DATE

Request to Tape-Record

I would like to ask your permission to tape-record our interview together. *THIS PROCEDURE IS OPTIONAL.* Tape-recording has certain benefits over recording data by hand: it shortens the time involved in doing an interview and increases the accuracy of the data. However, tape-recording also has certain drawbacks: it may make you feel uncomfortable and more vulnerable to identification. Therefore, *YOU SHOULD NOT AGREE TO THIS PROCEDURE IF YOU FEEL ANY RESERVATIONS ABOUT DOING SO.* Tape-recorded data will be managed as follows: (1) a transcript will be produced and stored in a personal computer locked in a university office; (2) all names or places that might identify the respondent will be left out of the transcript; (3) audio tapes will be stored in a locked file cabinet in a locked building at all times; (4) all tapes will be erased when the transcript is typed. All other protections previously outlined will still apply. Also, if you prefer to keep a statement off tape, the tape recorder will be stopped at your request. If you consent to this additional procedure, then please sign your case number and today's date below.

sign here: _____
CASE NUMBER   DATE

Release of Information Request

I, [case number], hereby grant permission for information maintained on me by [name of agency/sample site] to be used in the research project for which I have been interviewed. I understand that all the procedures in regard to confidentiality that were discussed in the safeguard statements presented to me prior to my interview will still apply. I acknowledge I have been fully informed about the purpose of the additional data I am agreeing to provide, which will aid as a supplement to the interview data. Further, I have received sufficient answers to any questions I asked about the procedure. The case file materials that might potentially be examined include but are not limited to psychological workups, presentence reports, prison classifications, autobiographical sketches, and personal correspondence. I will note any materials below that I do not want reviewed. Finally, I realize that by initialing my case number and the current date I am giving [name of agency/sample site] permission to release the information described.

sign here: _____
CASE NUMBER   DATE

Respondent Comments:

Appendix C
Statistical Data on Cases

Social Characteristics of the Men

Education at onset ($N = 30$): 13 percent less than high school; 33 percent completed high school or G.E.D.; 47 percent some college; 7 percent completed college. One Ph.D.

Average age at onset ($N = 29$): 32.9 years; range: 20–52 years.

Average age at end ($N = 30$): 35.7 years; range: 20–52 years.

Average age at interview ($N = 30$): 38.5 years; range: 20–58 years.

Married at onset ($N = 30$): 70 percent yes; at interview ($N = 30$): 50 percent yes.

Religion at onset ($N = 29$): 52 percent Protestant; 34 percent no affiliation; 14 percent other—Catholic, Jehovah's Witness.

Employed at onset ($N = 29$): 93 percent yes; at interview ($N = 30$): 73 percent yes.

Occupation at onset ($N = 28$): carpet layer, sign painter, farmhand, basket weaver, kitchen assistant, construction worker, night security guard, assembly line factory worker, forklift operator, machinist ($n = 2$), truck driver (*n* = 2), butcher, automobile repair mechanic (*n* = 2), race car driver, manager of donation store, National Guard staff (*n* = 2), college student, jet aircraft mechanic, photocopy machine servicer, news writer, computer operator/programmer (*n* = 4), gospel singer, insurance salesperson, aircraft electrical engineer, agricultural scientist, national political lobbyist. (Note: Some men worked more than one job.)

Highest personal income for any year between onset and interview (*N* = 29): 28 percent less than $14,999; 52 percent $15,000 to $34,999; 21 percent $35,000 or more. Highest yearly income in sample: $100,000.

Prior criminal arrest (*N* = 30): 43 percent yes.

Ever in military (*N* = 30): 57 percent yes.

Description of the offenses and the victims

Total minimum episodes of sexual contact for all men (*N* = 30): 1,540.

Average minimum episodes of sexual contact per offender (*N* = 30): 51; range: 1 to over 300.

Overall episodes of sexual contact per offender (*N* = 30): 13 percent one or two episodes; 30 percent three to ten episodes; 17 percent eleven to twenty episodes; 40 percent twenty-one or more episodes.

Total number of victims (*N* = 29): 52. (One offender, who had more than 100 male victims, was not included in total.)

Number of victims per offender (*N* = 30): 67 percent one victim only; 33 percent two or more victims; range: 1 to 8. (One offender again had more than 100 victims.)

Sex of victims (*N* = 52): 83 percent female; 17 percent male.

Offender gender preference with victims (*N* = 30): 77 percent girls only; 20 percent boys only; 3 percent both sexes.

Average age of victim at onset (*N* = 52): 9.4 years; range: 2–14 years.

Average age of victim at end (*N* = 52): 11.0 years; range: 6–20 years.

Duration of involvement of offenders (*N* = 30): 40 percent less than one year; 20 percent one to two years; 40 percent more than two years.

Offender relationship to victim (*N* = 52): 23 percent biological father; 38 percent stepfather/adopted father/mother's boyfriend; 12 percent other relative; 27 percent acquaintance.

Admitted behavior with any victim (*N* = 30): 97 percent breast or genital fondling; 53 percent performing or receiving oral sex; 27 percent penis-vaginal or penis-anal touching; 13 percent manual penetration of vagina or anus; 10 percent vaginal or anal intercourse.

Legal Dimensions of the Cases

Bail status at charging (*N* = 29): 45 percent released on bail set at $10,000 or less and less than $1,000 posted; 14 percent released on bail set at over $10,000 and more than $1,000 posted; 21 percent released on own recognizance; 21 percent could not make bail. Highest bail: $125,000.

Conviction status at interview (*N* = 30): 63 percent pled guilty to felony child molesting; 20 percent pled guilty to lesser misdemeanor—usually battery; 10 percent case still pending; 7 percent never charged due to statute of limitations or no state jurisdiction.

Length of sentence (*N* = 30): 33 percent none or less than one week; 37 percent one week to six months; 30 percent one to ten years. Longest effective sentence: five years.

Length of probation (*N* = 27): 33 percent none or one year or less; 19 percent two years; 37 percent three to five years; 11 percent six years or more. Longest probation period: ten years.

Duration of counseling at interview (*N* = 30): 20 percent none or less than one year; 47 percent one to two years; 33 percent over two years. Longest involvement in counseling: five years and two months.

Appendix D
The Retrospective Interpretation Problem

One of my major methodological concerns throughout the course of this research was the potential validity problem of retrospective interpretation by the men in the interviews. Retrospective interpretation refers to the fact that a person's views and interpretations change over time; past behavior is reinterpreted in light of new information and experiences. This is especially likely when people are forced to undergo mental health treatment or spend time in jail or prison. In such circumstances, the accounts people formulate about their lives are likely to be shaped by the institutional context in which they are embedded. The longer the time between the offense and the interview, the worse the potential overall contamination as well.

The men in this study were asked to provide a detailed reconstruction of their offenses, sometimes events that occurred years earlier. The period between the onset of sexual contact with a child and the date of the interview was on average six years. In addition, the men were asked to remember details even further in their past, such as their sexual development. In conjunction with this, all the men had been exposed to sex offender treatment, prison, jail, or all three. The question then is whether or not their version of events is still valid, given their experiences and the passage of time. Admittedly the best research design would have been to interview respondents before, during, and after their involvement in offending, or to track childhood victims of sexual, physical, and emotional abuse to see whether, when, and how they become offenders. Unfortunately, neither of these research designs was a practical or legally sound option.

The problem of retrospective interpretation is endemic in most depth interview research. Whenever people are asked to tell about events in their lives, their responses are always retrospective. The question then becomes one of degree—how can the effect be reduced. In this respect, three strategies were used to minimize the problem of retrospective interpretation: (1) respondents were asked about many aspects of their past, in time order, starting from early childhood, to bring them forward through their lives the way they had lived; (2) respondents were asked repeatedly whether what they said reflected how they felt in the past or in the present, and to offer distinctions where necessary; and (3) respondents were continually pressed and probed for minute detail in different ways to try and fill in past situations. Still, the accounts the men have provided about their involvement in sexual offending probably vary from what actually occurred and what they were thinking at the exact moment they acted.

Notes

Chapter 1 *Studying Offenders and Their Behavior*

1. One study, in particular, documented the emotional reactions of 521 parents to the actual or hypothetical "sexual abuse" of their children. Ninety percent of the parents in the sample with children who had been victims said they remembered feeling "anger," 88 percent felt "upset," and 81 percent felt "frightened" when they learned about what had occurred. The proportion of parents with children who had not been sexually abused who said they would react in the same ways if their children were to be victimized was even higher. See David Finkelhor, *Child Sexual Abuse: New Theory and Research*, New York: Free Press, 1984, pp. 75–84. Two other studies that address the societal reaction to child sexual abuse include Cheryl Regehr, "Parental responses to extrafamilial child sexual assault," *Child Abuse and Neglect*, 14, 1990, pp. 113–20; Ann H. Tyler and Marla R. Brassard, "Abuse in the investigation and treatment of intrafamilial child sexual abuse," *Child Abuse and Neglect*, 8, 1984, pp. 47–53.

2. David Finkelhor, Gerald Hotaling, I. A. Lewis, and Christine Smith, "Sexual abuse in a national survey of adult men and women: Prevalence, characteristics, and risk factors," *Child Abuse and Neglect*, 14, 1990, pp. 19–28; David Finkelhor, *Child Sexual Abuse*, 1984, pp. 69–74; David Finkelhor, *Sexually Victimized Children*, New York: Free Press, 1979, pp. 34–57; Gregory S. Fritz, Kim Stoll, and Nathaniel N. Wagner, "A comparison of males and females who were sexually molested as children," *Journal of Sex and Marital Therapy*, 7, 1981, pp. 54–59; Glen A. Kercher and Marilyn McShane, "The prevalence of child sexual abuse victimization in an adult sample of Texas residents," *Child Abuse and Neglect*, 8, 1984, pp. 495–501; Diana E. H. Russell, *The Secret Trauma: Incest in the Lives of Girls and Women*, New York: Basic Books, 1986, pp. 60–74; Mary Wellman, "Child sexual abuse and gender differences: Attitudes and prevalence," *Child Abuse and Neglect*, 17, 1993, pp. 539–47; and Gail E. Wyatt, "The sexual abuse of Afro-American and white American women in childhood," *Child Abuse and Neglect*, 9, 1985, pp. 507–19.

3. Lynda S. Doll, Dan Joy, Brad N. Bartholow, Janet S. Harrison, Gail Bolan, John M. Douglas, Linda E. Saltzman, Patricia M. Moss, and Wanda Delgado, "Self-reported

childhood and adolescent sexual abuse among adult homosexual and bisexual men," *Child Abuse and Neglect*, 16, 1992, pp. 855–64; and C. Georgia Simari and David Baskin, "Incestuous experiences within homosexual populations: A preliminary study," *Archives of Sexual Behavior*, 11, 1982, pp. 329–44.

4. David Finkelhor, "Epidemiological factors in the clinical identification of child sexual abuse," *Child Abuse and Neglect*, 17, 1993, p. 67.

5. There are scores of empirical studies and clinical books that examine the trauma and personal devastation linked to child sexual abuse victimization. The citations I provide are by no means an exhaustive list but rather a general sampling of what is available. Joseph H. Beitchman, Kenneth J. Zucker, Jane E. Hood, Granville A. DaCosta, and Donna Akman, "A review of the short-term effects of child sexual abuse," *Child Abuse and Neglect*, 15, 1991, pp. 537–56; Joseph H. Beitchman, Kenneth J. Zucker, Jane E. Hood, Granville A. DaCosta, Donna Akman, and Erika Cassavia, "A review of the long-term effects of child sexual abuse," *Child Abuse and Neglect*, 16, 1992, pp. 101–18; John N. Briere, *Child Abuse Trauma: Theory and Treatment of the Lasting Effects*, Newbury Park, CA: Sage, 1992; John Briere, *Therapy for Adults Molested as Children: Beyond Survival*, New York: Springer, 1989; Alan A. Cavaiola and Matthew Schiff, "Behavioral sequelae of physical and/or sexual abuse in adolescents," *Child Abuse and Neglect*, 12, 1988, pp. 181–88; Dianne Cleveland, *Incest: The Story of Three Women*, Lexington, MA: Lexington Books, 1986; Jon R. Conte and John R. Schuerman, "Factors associated with an increased impact of child sexual abuse," *Child Abuse and Neglect*, 11, 1987, pp. 201–11; Jean Goodwin, "Suicide attempts in sexual abuse victims and their mothers," *Child Abuse and Neglect*, 5, 1981, pp. 217–21; Evan Greenwald and Harold Leitenberg, "Long-term effects of sexual experiences with siblings and nonsiblings during childhood," *Archives of Sexual Behavior*, 18, 1989, pp. 389–99; Kenneth J. Gruber and Robert J. Jones, "Does sexual abuse lead to delinquent behavior? A critical look at the evidence," *Victimology*, 6, 1981, pp. 85–91; Carol R. Hartman and Ann W. Burgess, "Child sexual abuse: Generic roots of the victim experience," in Terry S. Trepper and Mary J. Barrett (eds.), *Treating Incest: A Multimodal Systems Perspective*, New York: Haworth, 1986, pp. 83–92; Roberta A. Hibbard and Georgia L. Hartman, "Behavioral problems in alleged sexual abuse victims," *Child Abuse and Neglect*, 16, 1992, pp. 755–62; Joan L. Jackson, Karen S. Calhoun, Angelynne E. Amick, Heather M. Maddever, and Valerie L. Habif, "Young adult women who report childhood intrafamilial sexual abuse: Subsequent adjustment," *Archives of Sexual Behavior*, 19, 1990, pp. 211–17; Johannes Kinzl and Wilfried Biebl, "Long-term effects of incest: Life events triggering mental disorders in female patients with sexual abuse in childhood," *Child Abuse and Neglect*, 16, 1992, pp. 567–73; Frederick H. Lindberg and Lois J. Distad, "Post-traumatic stress disorders in women who experienced childhood incest," *Child Abuse and Neglect*, 9, 1985, pp. 329–34; Jon McClellan, Julie Adams, Donna Douglas, Chris McCurry, and Mick Storck, "Clinical characteristics related to severity of sexual abuse: A study of seriously mentally ill youth," *Child Abuse and Neglect*, 19, 1995, 1245–54; Debra A. F. Miller, Kathleen McCluskey-Fawcett, and Lori M. Irving, "The relationship between childhood sexual abuse and subsequent onset of bulimia nervosa," *Child Abuse and Neglect*, 17, 1993, pp. 305–14; Michael F. Myers, "Men sexually assaulted as adults and sexually abused as boys," *Archives of Sexual Behavior*, 18, 1989, pp. 203–15; Peter E. Olson, "The sexual abuse of boys: A study of the long-term psychological effects," in Mic Hunter (ed.), *The Sexually Abused Male*, New York: Lexington Books, 1990, pp. 137–52; Anderson B. Rowan, David W. Foy, Ned Rodriguez, and Susan Ryan, "Post-traumatic stress disorder in a clinical sample of adults sexually abused as children," *Child Abuse and Neglect*, 18,

1994, pp. 51–61; Diana E. H. Russell, *The Secret Trauma*, 1986; Mimi H. Silbert and Ayala M. Pines, "Sexual abuse as an antecedent to prostitution," *Child Abuse and Neglect*, 5, 1981, pp. 407–11; Brandt F. Steele and Helen Alexander, "Long-term effects of sexual abuse in childhood," in Patricia B. Mrazek and C. Henry Kempe (eds.), *Sexually Abused Children and Their Families*, Oxford: Pergamon, 1981, pp. 223–33; Arlene R. Stiffman, "Physical and sexual abuse in runaway youths," *Child Abuse and Neglect*, 13, 1989, pp. 417–26; Liz Tong, Kim Oates, and Michael McDowell, "Personality development following sexual abuse," *Child Abuse and Neglect*, 11, 1987, pp. 371–83; Anthony J. Urquiza and Maria Capra, "The impact of sexual abuse: Initial and long-term effects," in Mic Hunter (ed.), *The Sexually Abused Male*, New York: Lexington Books, 1990, pp. 105–36; Brenda J. Vander Mey, "The sexual victimization of male children: A review of previous research," *Child Abuse and Neglect*, 12, 1988, pp. 61–71; Theresa Wozencraft, William Wagner, and Alicia Pellegrin, "Depression and suicidal ideation in sexually abused children," *Child Abuse and Neglect*, 15, 1991, pp. 505–11; Gail E. Wyatt, "The aftermath of child sexual abuse of African-American and White American women: The victim's experience," *Journal of Family Violence*, 5, 1990, pp. 61–81; Rodney E. Young, Thomas A. Bergandi, and Thomas G. Titus, "Comparison of the effects of sexual abuse on male and female latency-aged children," *Journal of Interpersonal Violence*, 9, 1994, pp. 291–306.

6. Roxane L. Silver, Cheryl Boon, and Mary H. Stones, "Searching for meaning in misfortune: Making sense of incest," *Journal of Social Issues*, 39, 1983, pp. 81–102.

7. I refer here specifically to five cases in the 1980s and 1990s that were dramatically reported in the national media: the story of Elizabeth Morgan, who spent roughly two years in jail for contempt of court after sending her daughter, who was allegedly molested by her ex-husband, into hiding through the Underground Railroad; the McMartin preschool trial that involved allegations of ritual and satanic sexual abuse from dozens of children but resulted in no criminal convictions against the accused; the child custody battle between Woody Allen and Mia Farrow after their separation, which eroded into allegations that he had committed sexual abuse against one of their adopted children; the sexual accusations leveled by one boy against Michael Jackson, which were settled quietly between attorneys; and finally, probably the most dramatic case, the situation of Ellie Nessler, who shot and killed a man during his preliminary hearing in court; the man had been accused of molesting her son. This claim of unprecedented media attention on the crime of child sexual abuse is also advanced in a recent article: Erna Olafson, David L. Corwin, and Roland C. Summit, "Modern history of child sexual abuse awareness: Cycles of discovery and suppression," *Child Abuse and Neglect*, 17, 1993, p. 16.

8. A recent example was the release of Joseph Gallardo in the state of Washington after he had served eighteen months for what was described in one news article as the rape of a ten-year-old girl. He was convicted for a crime involving oral sex with his victim. Local law enforcement officials notified the citizens of the town where the offender had lived, and where he was planning to return after his release, that he was "an extremely dangerous untreated sex offender," and that he "still fantasizes about torture, sexual assault, human sacrifice, bondage and the murder of young children." His house was subsequently burned to the ground. Robert Davis and Deeann Glamser, "Sex offender notification: Help or harassment?" *USA Today*, July 16, 1993, p. 2A. Gallardo then relocated with a brother who was a minister in New Mexico, and both men soon left town after local officials again released fliers to citizens cautioning them about the potential danger that lurked in the community. Gary Fields, "Convicted rapist forced to move again," *USA Today*, July 19, 1993, p. 3A.

9. For example, one widely watched television show was the 1993 special on incest

produced by Oprah Winfrey called "Breaking the Silence." Another show, which aired earlier in 1990, was a segment of *48 Hours* entitled "Don't Touch My Child." Recent movies that have portrayed themes about child molestation include *Nuts, Istanbul, The Prince of Tides, Something about Amelia, I Know My First Name Is Steven,* and *Little Girl Lost,* to name a few. In 1993 as well, there was a four-hour documentary written by Ofra Bikel entitled *Innocence Lost: The Verdict,* about alleged sexual abuse at a preschool in Edenton, North Carolina. The documentary portrayed the convictions of the adults who ran the school as most likely false. The topic of sexual abuse has also received coverage on *60 Minutes, Sally Jesse Raphael, Donahue,* and *Geraldo,* and in the Ann Landers advice column, among other places.

10. SLAM is a national reform organization founded in 1980 in California by a woman whose two-and-a-half-year-old grandaughter was molested and murdered by a man with a long prior criminal record of sex crimes against children. The mission of SLAM is to ensure long sentences for convicted child molesters. Chapters of SLAM have started up in different states. I picked up a *SLAM of Indiana* brochure in a local store one day while I was conducting this research. The pamphlet, stenciled on white paper, was undated, and on the cover was stated the following: "How you can help wipe out the crime of child molestation . . . ." There was also an address: P.O. Box 1013, Greenwood, IN 46142. ARCH, or Alliance for the Rights of Children, is a national tax-deductible lobby organization that works to ensure that children who have been abused are adequately protected by the justice system. Their newsletter, *ARCH Advocate,* is available to members. The address of ARCH is P.O. Box 3826, Merrifield, VA 22116. The Underground Railroad has been described as a covert network of safe houses and volunteers who offer sanctuary to victims of incest and their mothers. Some mothers decide to live on the run with their children when local courts dismiss allegations of sexual abuse involving fathers. The Underground Railroad, thus, is the last resort for mothers who do not feel they received "justice" from the courts. I read two stories about the Underground Railroad published in my local paper in the early stages of this research. Susan Baer, "America's hidden children," *Indianapolis Star,* March 5, 1989, pp. F1, F7; Susan Baer, "Scared families on the run alter names, looks," *Indianapolis Star,* March 5, 1989, p. F7.

11. Suzanne M. Sgroi, "Sexual molestation of children: The last frontier in child abuse," *Children Today,* 4, 1975, pp. 18–21, 44.

12. The data I cite throughout this paragraph are all from one source. Kathleen Maguire and Ann L. Pastore (eds.), *Sourcebook of Criminal Justice Statistics—1993,* Washington, DC, U.S. Department of Justice, Bureau of Justice Statistics, 1994, pp. 427, 623, 638–40. The approximate 12.6 percent figure I report was arrived at by adding the number of incarcerated sex offenders listed in the *Sourcebook* table on pages 638–40 and dividing by the total state prison population for the same year, which is also listed in the table.

13. R. A. Keller, L. F. Cicchinelli, and D. M. Gardner, "Characteristics of child sexual abuse treatment programs," *Child Abuse and Neglect,* 13, 1989, pp. 361–68.

14. Kathleen Maguire and Ann L. Pastore (eds.), *Sourcebook of Criminal Justice Statistics—1993,* 1994, pp. 638–40.

15. The address for the American Professional Society on the Abuse of Children (APSAC) is 332 South Michigan Avenue, Suite 1600, Chicago, IL 60604, phone: (312) 554-0166. The main resource publication of this organization is *The Advisor.* Two other professional organizations that may be of interest to readers are the Association for the Treatment of Sexual Abusers (ATSA), P.O. Box 866, Lake Oswego, OR 97034-0140; and

the Family Violence and Sexual Assault Institute, 1310 Clinic Drive, Tyler, TX 75701. They also publish a periodical information booklet entitled *Family Violence and Sexual Assault Bulletin.*

16. The best-known book of this genre is Ellen Bass and Laura Davis, *The Courage to Heal: A Guide for Women Survivors of Child Sexual Abuse,* New York: Harper and Row, 1988. Along with the main text is a supplemental workbook for suvivors of sexual abuse: Laura Davis, *The Courage to Heal Workbook: For Women and Men Survivors of Child Sexual Abuse,* New York: Harper and Row, 1990. There is also a third text in the series for people with partners who were molested as children: Laura Davis, *Allies in Healing: When the Person You Love Was Sexually Abused as a Child,* New York: HarperCollins, 1991. See also Euan Bear and Peter Dimock, *Adults Molested as Children: A Survivor's Manual for Women and Men,* Orwell, VT: Safer Society Press, 1988; E. Sue Blume, *Secret Survivors: Uncovering Incest and Its Aftereffects in Women,* New York: Ballantine Books, 1990; Eliana Gil, *Outgrowing the Pain: A Book for and about Adults Abused as Children,* New York: Dell, 1983; Katheryn Hagans and Joyce Case, *When Your Child Has Been Molested: A Parent's Guide to Healing and Recovery,* Lexington, MA: Lexington Books, 1988; Wendy Maltz, *The Sexual Healing Journey: A Guide for Survivors of Sexual Abuse,* New York: Harper Perennial, 1992; Wendy Maltz and Beverly Holman, *Incest and Sexuality: A Guide to Understanding and Healing,* Lexington, MA: Lexington Books, 1987; Carol Poston and Karen Lison, *Reclaiming Our Lives: Hope for Adult Survivors of Incest,* Boston: Little, Brown, 1989.

17. WTHR 13 News with Tom Cochran, pamphlet *What Everyone Should Know about the Sexual Abuse of Children,* South Deerfield, MA: Channing L. Bete, 1985. When I started this research, I was very interested in the moral boundary about sexual abuse that was being constructed in the community where I lived. Two related public information materials that were widely circulated in the late 1980s around my home area and that helped to "alarm" the public included Indianapolis Police Department, *PARENTS BEWARE: Child Sexual Abuse Awareness and Prevention,* undated. The booklet warns, "It affects boys and girls of all ages . . . . It is not as uncommon as we would like to believe . . . . It . . . may occur over and over again before it is detected . . . . In most cases the offender is someone known and trusted . . . . Offenders come from all walks of life." Sam Stall, "Suffer the children," *Indianapolis Monthly,* March 1988, pp. 84–91. The writer of this article reported, "A tidal wave of child abuse is breaking over Indianapolis." Later, a social worker is cited: "It's an epidemic that's spreading," and a police investigator is quoted: "We assume we're getting one report for every 10 incidents . . . . But I'm not sure that's accurate. We could be getting one out of 20, or one out of 50." These types of widespread horrific claims, assuming they are read by some people, would seem to crystallize the sexual abuse boundary.

18. Bill Roberts, "Castration bill defeated by large margin in house," *Indianapolis News,* March 3, 1989, p. A14.

19. I cite three researchers across a period spanning ten years as evidence of this point. C. Henry Kempe, "Incest and other forms of sexual abuse," in C. Henry Kempe and Ray E. Helfer (eds.), *The Battered Child,* 3d ed., Chicago: University of Chicago Press, 1980, p. 198:

Sexual abuse is defined as the involvement of dependent, . . . immature children and adolescents in sexual activities they do not fully comprehend, to which they are unable to give informed consent . . . . Indeed, these children are exploited, because sexual abuse robs . . .[them] . . . of their . . . control over their own bodies.

Suzanne M. Sgroi, Linda C. Blick, and Frances S. Porter, "A conceptual framework for child sexual abuse," in Suzanne M. Sgroi (ed.), *Handbook of Clinical Intervention in Child Sexual Abuse*, Lexington, MA: Lexington Books, 1982, p. 9:

Child sexual abuse is a sexual act imposed on a child who lacks emotional, maturational, and cognitive development. The ability to lure a child into a sexual relationship is based upon the all-powerful and dominant position of the adult . . . which is in sharp contrast to the child's age, dependency, and subordinate position.

Jim Struve, "Dancing with patriarchy: The politics of sexual abuse," in Mic Hunter (ed.), *The Sexually Abused Male*, New York: Lexington Books, 1990, p. 9:

An essential ingredient in sexually abusive behavior is a general lack of empathy by the adult for the child's stage of development and abilities. Additionally, the adult places the satisfaction of his or her own needs above those of the child. In so doing, the essence of child sexual abuse becomes clear: the exploitation of a child for the purpose of satisfying an adult.

20. Brenda J. Vander Mey and Ronald L. Neff, *Incest as Child Abuse: Research and Applications*, New York: Praeger, 1986, pp. 1, 3, 38.

21. I cite many sources in relation to research on victims in notes 2, 3, 5, and 6 that revolve around these three themes. In addition are a range of other studies that provide descriptions of victims in various respects: Diane H. Browning and Bonny Boatman, "Incest: Children at risk," *American Journal of Psychiatry*, 134, 1977, pp. 69–72; Ann W. Burgess, *Child Pornography and Sex Rings*, Lexington, MA: Lexington Books, 1982; J. Michael Cupoli and Pamela M. Sewell, "One thousand fifty-nine children with a chief complaint of sexual abuse," *Child Abuse and Neglect*, 12, 1988, pp. 151–62; Mary De Young, *The Sexual Victimization of Children*, Jefferson, NC: McFarland, 1982; Robert Dube and Martin Hebert, "Sexual abuse of children under 12 years of age: A review of 511 cases," *Child Abuse and Neglect*, 12, 1988, pp. 321–30; David Finkelhor, "The sexual abuse of boys," *Victimology*, 6, 1981, pp. 76–84; John H. Gagnon, "Female child victims of sex offenses," *Social Problems*, 13, 1965, pp. 176–92; Michael Gordon, "The family environment of sexual abuse: A comparison of natal and stepfather abuse," *Child Abuse and Neglect*, 13, 1989, pp. 121–30; Judith L. Herman, *Father-Daughter Incest*, Cambridge: Harvard University Press, 1981; Judith Herman and Lisa Hirschman, "Father-daughter incest," *Signs: Journal of Women in Culture and Society*, 2, 1977, pp. 735–56; Kathleen A. Kendall-Tackett and Arthur F. Simon, "Molestation and the onset of puberty: Data from 365 adults molested as children," *Child Abuse and Neglect*, 12, 1988, pp. 73–81; Leslie Margolin, "Sexual abuse by grandparents," *Child Abuse and Neglect*, 16, 1992, pp. 735–41; Arlene McCormack, Mark-David Janus, and Ann W. Burgess, "Runaway youths and sexual victimization: Gender differences in an adolescent runaway population," *Child Abuse and Neglect*, 10, 1986, pp. 387–95; Paul Okami, "Self-reports of positive childhood and adolescent sexual contacts with older persons: An exploratory study," *Archives of Sexual Behavior*, 20, 1991, pp. 437–57; Patricia Phelan, "The process of incest: Biologic father and stepfather families," *Child Abuse and Neglect*, 10, 1986, pp. 531–39; Robert L. Pierce and Lois H. Pierce, "The sexually abused child: A comparison of male and female victims," *Child Abuse and Neglect*, 9, 1985, pp. 191–99; Robert L. Pierce and Lois H. Pierce, "Race as a factor in the sexual abuse of children," *Social Work Research and Abstracts*, 20, 1984, pp. 9–14; Michael A. Reinhart, "Sexually abused boys," *Child Abuse and Neglect*, 11, 1987, pp. 229–35; J. Weiss, E. Rogers, M. R. Darwin, and C. E. Dutton, "A study of girl sex victims," *Psychiatric Quarterly*, 29, 1955, pp. 1–27.

22. To illustrate my point, the following studies, while both groundbreaking and informative, frame images of offenders that are filtered through victim, clinician, or official

realities, without firsthand data from offenders themselves. Lucy Berliner and Jon R. Conte, "The process of victimization: The victims' perspective," *Child Abuse and Neglect*, 14, 1989, pp. 29–40; Judith L. Herman, *Father-Daughter Incest*, 1981, pp. 67–95, 109–24; Lynda L. Holmstrom and Ann W. Burgess, "Rapists' talk: Linguistic strategies to control the victim," *Deviant Behavior*, 1, 1979, pp. 101–25; Marisa Laviola, "Effects of older brother-younger sister incest: A study of the dynamics of 17 cases," *Child Abuse and Neglect*, 16, 1992, pp. 409–21; Leslie Margolin, "Sexual abuse by grandparents," 1992, pp. 735–41; Patricia Phelan, "The process of incest: Biologic father and stepfather families," 1986, pp. 531–39; Diana E. H. Russell, *The Secret Trauma*, 1986, pp. 93–101, 124–36, 216–385; Suzanne M. Sgroi et al., "A conceptual framework for child sexual abuse," 1982, pp. 9–38; Laurie Taylor, "The significance and interpretation of replies to motivational questions: The case of sex offenders," *Sociology*, 6, 1972, pp. 23–39. In *The Secret Trauma*, for example, Russell asked the incest victims she studied why they thought their offenders violated them sexually. This approach to studying men who sexually abuse children is speculative at best. To provide two less emotional examples, this type of ontology is like trying to understand people who commit armed robbery by interviewing the store clerks from whom they steal, or trying to understand the perspective of minority gang members by talking to white urban police officers. Such data, presented alone, without other corroborating testimony, are insufficient for drawing conclusions about offenders. Other examples of research on offenders or victims that provide partial looks at offense situations and/or that touch on the internal reality of offenders specifically about their crimes and victims to a limited degree are Gene G. Abel, Judith V. Becker, Mary Mittleman, Jerry Cunningham-Rathner et al., "Self-reported sex crimes of nonincarcerated paraphiliacs," *Journal of Interpersonal Violence*, 2, 1987, pp. 3–25; Ann W. Burgess and Lynda L. Holmstrom, "Accessory to sex: Pressure, sex, and secrecy," in Ann W. Burgess, A. Nicholas Groth, Lynda L. Holmstrom, and Suzanne M. Sgroi (eds.), *Sexual Assault of Children and Adolescents*, Lexington, MA: Lexington Books, 1978, pp. 85–98; W. D. Erickson, N. H. Walbek, and R. K. Seely, "Behavior patterns of child molesters," *Archives of Sexual Behavior*, 17, 1988, pp. 77–86; Louise V. Frisbie, *Another Look at Sex Offenders in California*, California Department of Mental Hygiene, Research Monograph 12, 1969; Paul H. Gebhard, John H. Gagnon, Wardell B. Pomeroy, and Cornelia V. Christenson, *Sex Offenders: An Analysis of Types*, New York: Harper and Row, 1965; A. Nicholas Groth and H. Jean Birnbaum, "Adult sexual orientation and attraction to underage persons," *Archives of Sexual Behavior*, 7, 1978, pp. 175–81; A. Nicholas Groth and Ann W. Burgess, "Motivational intent in the sexual assault of children," *Criminal Justice and Behavior*, 4, 1977, pp. 253–65; Lynda L. Holmstrom and Ann W. Burgess, "Sexual behavior of assailants during reported rapes," *Archives of Sexual Behavior*, 9, 1980, pp. 427–39; Blair Justice and Rita Justice, *The Broken Taboo: Sex in the Family*, New York: Human Sciences Press, 1979; Leslie Margolin, "Child sexual abuse by uncles: A risk assessment," *Child Abuse and Neglect*, 18, 1994, pp. 215–24; J. W. Mohr, R. E. Turner, and M. B. Jerry, *Pedophilia and Exhibitionism*, Toronto: University of Toronto Press, 1964; K. Nedoma, J. Mellan, and J. Pondelickova, "Sexual behavior and its development in pedophilic men," *Archives of Sexual Behavior*, 1, 1971, pp. 267–71; Asher R. Pacht and James E. Cowden, "An exploratory study of 500 sex offenders," *Criminal Justice and Behavior*, 1, 1974, pp. 13–20; Richard T. Rada, "Alcoholism and the child molester," *Annals of the New York Academy of Science*, 273, 1976, pp. 492–96; Mark I. Singer, David Hussey, and Kimberly J. Strom, "Grooming the victim: An analysis of a perpetrator's seduction letter," *Child Abuse and Neglect*, 16, 1992, pp. 877–86; Lana Stermac, Kathryn Hall, and Marianne Henskens, "Violence among child molesters," *Journal of*

Sex Research, 26, 1989, pp. 450–59; Roland Summit and JoAnn Kryso, "Sexual abuse of children: A clinical spectrum," *American Journal of Orthopsychiatry*, 48, 1978, pp. 237–51; David W. Swanson, "Adult sexual abuse of children: The man and the circumstances," *Diseases of the Nervous System*, 29, 1968, pp. 677–83. Probably the most in-depth investigations that explore the reality of men who have engaged in sex with children include Lee E. Budin and Charles F. Johnson, "Sex abuse prevention programs: Offenders' attitudes about their efficacy," *Child Abuse and Neglect*, 13, 1989, pp. 77–87; Jon R. Conte, Steven Wolf, and Tim Smith, "What sexual offenders tell us about prevention strategies," *Child Abuse and Neglect*, 13, 1989, pp. 293–301; A. Nicholas Groth, *Men Who Rape*, New York: Plenum, 1979, pp. 141–64; Charles H. McCaghy, "Child molesters: A study of their careers as deviants," in Marshall B. Clinard and Richard Quinney (eds.), *Criminal Behavior Systems: A Typology*, New York: Holt, Rinehart and Winston, 1967, pp. 75–88; Charles H. McCaghy, "Drinking and deviance disavowal: The case of child molesters," *Social Problems*, 16, 1968, pp. 43–49; Parker Rossman, *Sexual Experience between Men and Boys: Exploring the Pederast Underground*, New York: Association Press, 1976. My study varies from Rossman's in that he studied men who for the most part indicated a sexual preference for children. The respondents I sampled, as I discuss later, did not.

23. For example, see Gene G. Abel, Judith V. Becker, William D. Murphy, and Barry Flanagan, "Identifying dangerous child molesters," in Richard B. Stuart (ed.), *Violent Behavior: Social Learning Approaches to Prediction, Management and Treatment*, New York: Brumer/Mazel, 1981, pp. 116–37; H. E. Barbaree and W. L. Marshall, "Erectile responses among heterosexual child molesters, father-daughter incest offenders, and matched offenders: Five distinct age-preference profiles," *Canadian Journal of Behavioural Science*, 21, 1989, pp. 70–82; R. R. Frenzl and R. A. Lang, "Identifying sexual preferences in intrafamilial and extrafamilial child sexual abusers," *Annals of Sex Research*, 2, 1989, pp. 255–75; Kurt Freund, "Diagnosing homo- or heterosexuality and erotic age preference by means of a psychophysiological test," *Behavior Research and Therapy*, 5, 1967, pp. 209–28; Kurt Freund and Ray Blanchard, "Phallometric diagnosis of pedophilia," *Journal of Consulting and Clinical Psychology*, 57, 1989, pp. 100–105; Kurt Freund and Ron Langevin, "Bisexuality in homosexual pedophilia," *Archives of Sexual Behavior*, 5, 1976, pp. 415–23; Kurt Freund and Robin Watson, "Assessment of the sensitivity and specificity of a phallometric test: An update of phallometric diagnosis of pedophilia," *Psychological Assessment: A Journal of Consulting and Clinical Psychology*, 3, 1991, pp. 254–60; Kurt Freund, Robin Watson, and Robert Dickey, "Sex offenses against female children perpetrated by men who are not pedophiles," *Journal of Sex Research*, 28, 1991, pp. 402–23; R. A. Lang, E. L. Black, R. R. Frenzl, and K. L. Checkley, "Aggression and erotic attraction toward children in incestuous and pedophilic men," *Annals of Sex Research*, 1, 1988, 417–41; Ron Langevin, Stephen J. Hucker, Mark H. Ben-Aron, John E. Purins, and Helen J. Hook, "Why are pedophiles attracted to children? Further studies of erotic preference in heterosexual pedophilia," in Ron Langevin (ed.), *Erotic Preference, Gender Identity, and Aggression in Men*, Hillsdale, NJ: Lawrence Erlbaum Associates, 1985, pp. 181–207; P. Bruce Malcolm, D. A. Andrews, and Vernon L. Quinsey, "Discriminant and predictive validity of phallometrically measured sexual age and gender preference," *Journal of Interpersonal Violence*, 8, 1993, pp. 486–501; W. L. Marshall, H. E. Barbaree, and Jennifer Butt, "Sexual offenders against children: Sexual preference for gender, age of victim and type of behavior," *Behavior Research and Therapy*, 26, 1988, 383–91; Vernon L. Quinsey and Terry C. Chaplin, "Penile responses of child molesters and normals to descriptions of encounters with children involving sex

and violence," *Journal of Interpersonal Violence*, 3, 1988, 259–74.

24. For example, see Mark Dadds, Michelle Smith, Yvonne Webber, and Anthony Robinson, "An exploration of family and individual profiles following father-daughter incest," *Child Abuse and Neglect*, 15, 1991, pp. 575–86; G. Fisher, "Psychological needs of heterosexual pedophiles," *Diseases of the Nervous System*, 30, 1969, pp. 419–21; G. Fisher and L. M. Howell, "Psychological needs of homosexual pedophiles," *Diseases of the Nervous System*, 31, 1970, pp. 623–25; Gordon C. Nagayama Hall, Roland D. Maiuro, Peter P. Vitaliano, and William C. Proctor, "The utility of the MMPI with men who have sexually assaulted children," *Journal of Consulting and Clinical Psychology*, 54, 1986, pp. 493–96; Diane S. Hayashino, Sandy K. Wurtele, and Kelli J. Klebe, "Child molesters: An examination of cognitive factors," *Journal of Interpersonal Violence*, 10, 1995, pp. 106–16; Seth C. Kalichman, "Psychopathology and personality characteristics of criminal sexual offenders as a function of victim age," *Archives of Sexual Behavior*, 20, 1991, pp. 187–97; Seth C. Kalichman and Margit C. Henderson, "MMPI profile subtypes of nonincarcerated child molesters: A cross validation study," *Criminal Justice and Behavior*, 18, 1991, pp. 379–96; Seth C. Kalichman, Margit C. Henderson, Lucinda S. Shealy, and Margretta Dwyer, "Psychometric properties of the multiphasic sex inventory in assessing sex offenders," *Criminal Justice and Behavior*, 19, 1992, pp. 384–96; Ron Langevin, Stephen J. Hucker, Lorraine Handy, John E. Purins, Anne E. Russon, and Helen J. Hook, "Erotic preference and aggression in pedophilia: A comparison of heterosexual, homosexual, and bisexual types," in Ron Langevin (ed.), *Erotic Preference, Gender Identity, and Aggression in Men*, Hillsdale, NJ: Lawrence Erlbaum Associates, 1985, pp. 137–60; Ron Langevin, Lorraine Handy, Anne E. Russon, and David Day, "Are incestuous fathers pedophilic, aggressive, and alcoholic?" in Ron Langevin (ed.), *Erotic Preference, Gender Identity, and Aggression in Men*, Hillsdale, NJ: Lawrence Erlbaum Associates, 1985, pp. 161–79; Saul M. Levin and Lawrence Stava, "Personality characteristics of sex offenders: A review," *Archives of Sexual Behavior*, 16, 1987, pp. 57–79; William D. Murphy and James M. Peters, "Profiling child sexual abusers: Psychological considerations," *Criminal Justice and Behavior*, 19, 1992, pp. 24–37; Paul Okami and Amy Goldberg, "Personality correlates of pedophilia: Are they reliable indicators?" *Journal of Sex Research*, 29, 1992, pp. 297–328; James H. Panton, "MMPI profile configurations associated with incestuous and non-incestuous child molesting," *Psychological Reports*, 45, 1979, pp. 335–38; Joseph J. Peters, "Children who are victims of sexual assault and the psychology of offenders," *American Journal of Psychotherapy*, 30, 1976, pp. 398–421; Ronald L. Scott and David A. Stone, "MMPI profile constellations in incest families," *Journal of Consulting and Clinical Psychology*, 54, 1986, pp. 364–68.

25. For example, see Gene G. Abel, Mary Mittleman, Judith V. Becker, Jerry Cuningham-Rathner, and J. L. Rouleau, "Predicting child molesters' response to treatment," *Annals of the New York Academy of Science*, 1988, pp. 223–35; Judith V. Becker and John A. Hunter, "Evaluation of treatment outcome for adult perpetrators of child sexual abuse," *Criminal Justice and Behavior*, 19, 1992, pp. 74–92; Judith V. Becker and Vernon L. Quinsey, "Assessing suspected child molesters," *Child Abuse and Neglect*, 17, 1993, pp. 169–74; Mark Chaffin, "Factors associated with treatment completion and progress among intrafamilial sexual abusers," *Child Abuse and Neglect*, 16, 1992, pp. 251–64; Jon R. Conte and Lucy Berliner, "Prosecution of the offender in cases of sexual assault against children," *Victimology*, 6, 1981, pp. 102–9; David A. Crawford, "Treatment approaches with pedophiles," in Mark Cook and Kevin Howells (eds.), *Adult Sexual Interest in Children*, London: Academic Press, 1981, pp. 181–217; David A. Crawford and Judith V. Allen, "A social skills training programme with sex offenders," in Mark

Cook and Glenn Wilson (eds.), *International Conference on Love and Attraction*, Oxford: Pergamon, 1977, pp. 527–36; Robert E. Freeman-Longo and Ronald V. Wall, "Changing a lifetime of sexual crime," *Psychology Today*, March 1986, pp. 58–64; Henry Giarretto, "A comprehensive child sexual abuse treatment program," in Patricia B. Mrazek and C. Henry Kempe (eds.), *Sexually Abused Children and Their Families*, Oxford: Pergamon, 1981, pp. 179–97; Anne L. Horton, Barry L. Johnson, Lynn M. Roundy, and Doran Williams, *The Incest Perpetrator: A Family Member No One Wants to Treat*, Newbury Park, CA: Sage, 1990; Robert A. Keller et al., "Characteristics of child sexual abuse treatment programs," 1989, pp. 361–68; W. Marshall and H. Barbaree, "The long-term evaluation of a behavioral treatment for child molesters," *Behavior Research and Therapy*, 26, 1988, pp. 499–511; William O'Donohue and Elizabeth Letourneau, "A brief group treatment for the modification of denial in child sexual abusers: Outcome and follow-up," *Child Abuse and Neglect*, 17, 1993, pp. 299–304; Ronnie Priest and Annalee Smith, "Counseling adult sex offenders: Unique challenges and treatment paradigms," *Journal of Counseling and Development*, 71, 1992, pp. 27–32; Marnie E. Rice, Vernon L. Quinsey, and Grant T. Harris, "Sexual recidivism among child molesters released from a maximum security psychiatric institution," *Journal of Consulting and Clinical Psychology*, 59, 1991, pp. 381–86; Inger J. Sagatun, "The effects of court ordered therapy on incest offenders," *Journal of Offender Counseling, Services, and Rehabilitation*, 5, 1981, pp. 99–103; Anna C. Salter, *Treating Child Sex Offenders and Victims: A Practical Guide*, Newbury Park, CA: Sage, 1988; D. J. West, "Adult sexual interest in children: Implications for social control," in Mark Cook and Kevin Howells (eds.), *Adult Sexual Interest in Children*, London: Academic Press, 1981, pp. 251–70.

26. Citations are provided for each listed category of offender in the order presented in the text. Fixated versus regressed: A. Nicholas Groth, "Patterns of sexual assault against children and adolescents," in Ann W. Burgess, A. Nicholas Groth, Lynda L. Holmstrom, and Suzanne M. Sgroi (eds.), *Sexual Assault of Children and Adolescents*, Lexington, MA: Lexington Books, 1978, pp. 6–10; A. Nicholas Groth, "The incest offender," in Suzanne M. Sgroi (ed.), *Handbook of Clinical Intervention in Child Sexual Abuse*, Lexington, MA: Lexington Books, 1982, pp. 216–17; A. Nicholas Groth and H. Jean Birnbaum, "Adult sexual orientation and attraction to underage persons," 1978, pp. 175–81. This distinction generally refers to men who prefer children as sexual partners compared to those who turn to children for sex when the stress in their lives becomes unmanageable. Alcoholic: Blair Justice and Rita Justice, *The Broken Taboo*, 1979, pp. 80–82; Ron Langevin et al., "Are incestuous fathers pedophilic, aggressive, and alcoholic?" 1985, pp. 164, 176–77. Psychopathic: J. H. Fitch, "Men convicted of sexual offenses against children," *British Journal of Criminology*, 3, 1962, pp. 18–37; Blair Justice and Rita Justice, *The Broken Taboo*, 1979, pp. 83–89; Ralph C. Serin, P. Bruce Malcolm, Arunima Khanna, and Howard E. Barbaree, "Psychopathy and deviant sexual arousal in incarcerated sexual offenders," *Journal of Interpersonal Violence*, 9, 1994, pp. 3–11; David W. Swanson, "Adult sexual abuse of children: The man and the circumstances," 1968, p. 680. Sexually addicted: Patrick Carnes, *Contrary to Love: Helping the Sexual Addict*, Minneapolis: CompCare Publishers, 1989; Steven C. Wolf, "A multi-factor model of deviant sexuality," paper presented at the Third International Conference on Victimology, Lisbon, Portugal, 1984, pp. 2–10. Senile or senescent: Charles H. McCaghy, "Child molesters: A study of their careers as deviants," 1967, p. 87; J. W. Mohr et al., *Pedophilia and Exhibitionism*, 1964, p. 95. Narcissistic: Morris Fraser, *The Death of Narcissus*, London: Secker and Warburg, 1976; A. Nicholas Groth, William F. Hobson, and Thomas S. Gary, "The child molester: Clinical observations," *Journal of Social Work and Human*

Sexuality, 1, 1982, pp. 129–44; William Kraemer, *The Forbidden Love: The Normal and the Abnormal Love of Children*, London: Sheldon Press, 1976; Robert A. Prentky, Raymond A. Knight, Ruth Rosenberg, and Austin Lee, "A path analytic approach to the validation of a taxonomic system for child molesters," *Journal of Quantitative Criminology*, 5, 1989, 231–57. Sadistic: A. Nicholas Groth, *Men Who Rape*, 1979, pp. 160–63; A. Nicholas Groth and Ann W. Burgess, "Motivational intent in the sexual assault of children," 1977, p. 261. Perverse: Kevin Howells, "Adult sexual interest in children: Considerations relevant to theories of aetiology," in Mark Cook and Kevin Howells (eds.), *Adult Sexual Interest in Children*, London: Academic Press, 1981, pp. 58–59; Roland Summit and JoAnn Kryso, "Sexual abuse of children: A clinical spectrum," 1978, p. 247. Psychotic: Blair Justice and Rita Justice, *The Broken Taboo*, 1979, p. 91; Ron Langevin et al., "Erotic preference and aggression in pedophilia: A comparison of heterosexual, homosexual, and bisexual types," 1985, pp. 148–50, 155; Roland Summit and JoAnn Kryso, "Sexual abuse of children: A clinical spectrum," 1978, p. 242. Passive-dependent: A. Nicholas Groth, "The incest offender," 1982, pp. 218–22; Kevin Howells, "Some meanings of children for pedophiles," in Mark Cook and Glenn Wilson (eds.), *International Conference on Love and Attraction*, New York: Pergamon, 1977, pp. 519–26; Roger C. Katz, "Psychosocial adjustment in adolescent child molesters," *Child Abuse and Neglect*, 14, 1990, pp. 567–75; Joseph J. Peters, "Children who are victims of sexual assault and the psychology of offenders," 1976, pp. 410–11. Two recent articles provide a thorough review of the research literature on the personality attributes of pedophiles and incarcerated molesters. See Saul M. Levin and Lawrence Stava, "Personality characteristics of sex offenders: A review," 1987, pp. 57–79; Paul Okami and Amy Goldberg, "Personality correlates of pedophilia: Are they reliable indicators?" 1992, pp. 297–328.

27. I drew from a handful of well-known sources in putting together this brief list of social-based theories about why men commit child sexual abuse. Constance Avery-Clark, Joyce A. O'Neil, and D. R. Laws, "A comparison of intrafamilial sexual and physical child abuse," in Mark Cook and Kevin Howells (eds.), *Adult Sexual Interest in Children*, London: Academic Press, 1981, pp. 3–39; David Finkelhor, *Child Sexual Abuse*, 1984, pp. 23–68; David Finkelhor and Sharon Araji, "Explanations of pedophilia: A four factor model," *Journal of Sex Research*, 22, 1986, pp. 145–61; R. K. Hanson and S. Slater, "Sexual victimization in the history of sexual abusers: A review," *Annals of Sex Research*, 1, 1988, pp. 485–99; Judith L. Herman, *Father-Daughter Incest*, 1981, pp. 36–63; Judith Herman and Lisa Hirschman, "Father-daughter incest," 1977, pp. 735–56; Kevin Howells, "Adult sexual interest in children: Considerations relevant to theories of aetiology," 1981, pp. 55–94; Noel R. Larson and James W. Maddock, "Structural and functional variables in incest family systems: Implications for assessment and treatment," in Terry S. Trepper and Mary J. Barrett (eds.), *Treating Incest: A Multimodal Systems Perspective*, New York: Haworth, 1986, pp. 27–44; Kevin McIntyre, "Role of mothers in father-daughter incest: A feminist analysis," *Social Work*, 26, 1981, pp. 462–66; Patricia B. Mrazek, "The nature of incest: A review of contributing factors," in Patricia B. Mrazek and C. Henry Kempe (eds.), *Sexually Abused Children and Their Families*, Oxford: Pergamon, 1981, pp. 97–107; Parker Rossman, *Sexual Experience between Men and Boys*, 1976; Florence Rush, *The Best Kept Secret*, New York: McGraw-Hill, 1980; Diana E. H. Russell, *The Secret Trauma*, 1986, pp. 5–16, 103–14, 384–94; Kathleen J. Tierney and David L. Corwin, "Exploring intrafamilial child sexual abuse," in David Finkelhor, Richard J. Gelles, Gerald T. Hotaling, and Murray A. Strauss (eds.), *The Dark Side of Families: Current Family Violence Research*, Beverly Hills, CA: Sage, 1983, pp. 102–16.

28. A. Nicholas Groth, "Sexual trauma in the life histories of rapists and child molesters," *Victimology*, 4, 1979, p. 10.

29. I elaborate on the dimensions of this debate in my closing chapter. One view is that rape, incest, and other related sex crimes are crimes of violence motivated by non-sexual needs such as anger, power, or sadism. Susan Brownmiller, *Against Our Will: Men, Women, and Rape*, New York: Simon and Schuster, 1975; A. Nicholas Groth, *Men Who Rape*, 1979, pp. 2–7; Lynda L. Holmstrom and Ann W. Burgess, "Sexual behavior of assailants during reported rapes," 1980, pp. 427–39. The opposite view, one being raised by some male scholars in particular, is that sexual arousal, albeit misdirected, underlies sexual offending. Neil Frude, "The sexual nature of sexual abuse: A review of the literature," *Child Abuse and Neglect*, 6, 1982, pp. 211–23; Kevin Howells, "Adult sexual interest in children: Considerations relevant to theories of aetiology," 1981, pp. 65–70; Craig T. Palmer, "Twelve reasons why rape is not sexually motivated: A skeptical examination," *Journal of Sex Research*, 25, 1982, pp. 512–30. The middle-range view is that both types of motivations may be relevant. Lee Ellis, *Theories of Rape: Inquires into the Cause of Sexual Aggression*, New York: Hemisphere, 1989, pp. 57–80; Richard B. Felson and Marvin Krohn, "Motives for rape," *Journal of Research in Crime and Delinquency*, 27, 1990, pp. 222–42; David Finkelhor, *Child Sexual Abuse*, 1984, pp. 33–43; Diana Scully, *Understanding Sexual Violence: A Study of Convicted Rapists*, London: Harper Collins, 1990, pp. 142–49. For many years, the climate of political correctness surrounding the study of sex crimes has largely driven interpretations and theories about offenders away from the sexual and toward the violent and the pathological.

30. In formulating this argument about the implicit problem of the activation of background factors in the commission of child sexual abuse, I borrow heavily here and other places from Jack Katz, *Seductions of Crime: Moral and Sensual Attractions of Doing Evil*, New York: Basic Books, 1988, pp. 3–10, 310–24 esp.

31. This is an issue I explore in great detail in chapter 2. My purpose here is to simply point out that one of the most widely accepted arguments about offenders is far from fully explained, understood, or confirmed in the research literature.

32. While males of nearly every age have been documented as sexual offenders against children, most commonly the age of onset is between the late twenties and the mid-fifties; the mean age is usually thirties or early forties, regardless of the gender of the victim. See, among others Jon R. Conte et al., "What sexual offenders tell us about prevention strategies," 1989, p. 295; Robert Dube and Martin Hebert, "Sexual abuse of children under 12 years of age: A review of 511 cases," 1988, p. 325; A. Nicholas Groth, "Patterns of sexual assault against children and adolescents," 1978, p. 4; A. Nicholas Groth and H. Jean Birnbaum, "Adult sexual orientation and attraction to underage persons," 1978, pp. 178–79; Charles H. McCaghy, "Child molesters: A study of their careers as deviants," 1967, p. 79; Diana E. H. Russell, *The Secret Trauma*, 1986, p. 222; Lawrence Simkins, "Characteristics of sexually repressed child molesters," *Journal of Interpersonal Violence*, 8, 1993, p. 7; Lana Stermac et al., "Violence among child molesters," 1989, p. 454.

33. Central to my theoretical approach is the search for what has been referred to as generic, general, or basic social processes, that is, stages of social experience that are common to many or all people. I am interested in the recurrent stages offenders report in crossing highly restricted sexual boundaries. It may be that such stages are characteristic of all types of interpersonal boundary violations. A generic or basic social process would by definition extend beyond a particular type of substantive event. Carl J. Couch, "Symbolic interaction and generic sociological principles," *Symbolic Interaction*, 7, 1984, pp. 1–13; Barney G. Glaser, *Theoretical Sensitivity: Advances in the Methodology of Ground-*

ed Theory, Mill Valley, CA: Sociology Press, 1978, pp. 93–115; Robert Prus, "Generic social processes: Maximizing conceptual development in ethnographic research," *Journal of Contemporary Ethnography*, 16, 1987, pp. 250–93.

34. The concept of "career" refers to the entire sequence of movements of individuals into, through, and out of a particular social status or experience. While the term "career" traditionally refers to occupations, it has also been applied to the study of deviant behavior. The term is basically synonymous with the concept of social process, though there may be many social processes that constitute an overall career. See Howard S. Becker, *Outsiders: Studies in the Sociology of Deviance*, Glencoe, IL: Free Press, 1963, p. 24.

35. There are a handful of core studies that analyze the internal and/or external dynamics of involvement in various deviant careers, from which I build in my research. Patricia Adler, *Wheeling and Dealing*, New York: Columbia University Press, 1985; Joel Best and David F. Luckenbill, *Organizing Deviance*, 2d ed., Englewood Cliffs, NJ: Prentice-Hall, 1994; Mary O. Cameron, *The Booster and the Snitch*, Glencoe, IL: Free Press, 1964, esp. pp. 159–66; Nanette J. Davis, "Prostitutes," in Earl Rubington and Martin S. Weinberg (eds.), *Deviance: The Interactionist Perspective*, 4th ed., New York: Macmillan, 1981, pp. 305–13; Kathleen J. Ferraro and John M. Johnson, "How women experience battering: The process of victimization," *Social Problems*, 30, 1983, pp. 325–35; Erving Goffman, *Asylums*, Englewood Cliffs, NJ: Doubleday, 1961, esp. pp. 125–70; John Lofland, *Deviance and Identity*, Englewood Cliffs, NJ: Prentice-Hall, 1969; Edwin M. Lemert, *Human Deviance, Social Problems, and Social Control*, Englewood Cliffs, NJ: Prentice-Hall, 1967, pp. 40–64, 99–134; David F. Luckenbill, "Deviant career mobility: The case of male prostitutes," *Social Problems*, 33, 1986, pp. 283–96; David F. Luckenbill, "Entering male prostitution," *Urban Life*, 14, 1985, pp. 131–53; David Matza, *Becoming Deviant*, Englewood Cliffs, NJ: Prentice-Hall, 1969; Erdwin H. Pfuhl, *The Deviance Process*, 2d ed., Belmont, CA: Wadsworth, 1986; Prue Rains, "Deviant careers," in M. Michael Rosenberg, Robert A. Stebbins, and Allan Turowitz (eds.), *The Sociology of Deviance*, New York: St. Martin's, 1982, pp. 21–41; Neal Shover, "The later stages of ordinary property offender careers," *Social Problems*, 31, 1984, pp. 208–18.

36. For a general discussion of this and related methodological issues, see James Reed, "Injustice in the academy: A look at scholarship and child sexual offenders," paper presented at the Annual Meetings of the Society for the Study of Social Problems, Cincinnati, OH, 1991, pp. 5–6.

37. Nearly all studies on sexual offenders, either rapists or child molesters, have been based on samples drawn from official populations. The likely biased and thus unrepresentative nature of such samples is a common criticism of this research. One exception is a study that looked at over six hundred pedophiles sampled from around the world, many of whom were still actively involved in sex with boys and who remained outside the purview of the law. That research, curiously, is seldom cited by mainstream scholars studying sex crimes. See Parker Rossman, *Sexual Experience between Men and Boys*, 1976. To attack the integrity of a sample is a convenient criticism, yet the alternative, the study of active offenders, is not really a practical option, given the legal and moral risks. Legal and scholarly attempts to censure areas of sensitive research, especially on topics involving sexual deviance or sexual situations involving children, and to seize data and even file criminal charges have been documented. See Raymond M. Lee, *Doing Research on Sensitive Topics*, Newbury Park, CA: Sage, 1993, pp. 164–70; David Sonenschein, "On having one's research seized," *Journal of Sex Research*, 23, 1987, pp. 408–14.

38. Raymond M. Lee, *Doing Research on Sensitive Topics*, 1993, pp. 65–69.

39. I borrow words here from two authors to convey the marginal, disreputable, and

disposable status child sexual offenders have within institutions of social control, and to emphasize the courtesy stigma that can rub off on people who specialize in these kinds of cases. John Irwin, *Jail: Managing the Underclass in American Society*, Berkeley: University of California Press, 1985, p. 2; Steven Spitzer, "Toward a Marxian theory of deviance," in Stuart H. Traub and Craig B. Little (eds.), *Theories of Deviance*, 4th ed., Itasca, IL: F. E. Peacock, 1994, p. 404. In the prison I frequented, men who had committed sexual abuse against children were referred to as "baby raper" by most other inmates, rather than being called by their actual names. For more on the social status of sex offenders in the prison context, see Malin Akerstrom, "Outcasts in prison: the cases of informers and sex offenders," *Deviant Behavior*, 7, 1986, pp. 1–12.

40. This field strategy of conducting preliminary background research about a setting, and gathering insider information from gatekeepers within a setting, to figure out what you need to know to gain access to others who are embedded in that setting has been discussed elsewhere. John M. Johnson, *Doing Field Research*, New York: Free Press, 1975, pp. 60–63; Raymond M. Lee, *Doing Research on Sensitive Topics*, 1993, pp. 121–24.

41. For example, when I asked the gatekeepers I was working with, who were mental health practitioners, why they thought some men turned to children for sex, the most common reply was "because they wanted to," or some related variation of this theme. This script, of course, is about the locus of responsibility for behavior. In fact, one clinician elaborated on this theme, saying that many men are for a long time simply unable to figure out why they become involved in offending, that they dwell on their childhoods or their marriages, instead of admitting the real reason. That is, he steered his clients away from social-based theories of behavior. Later, when I actually asked the men I interviewed why they thought they did what they did, when I probed for their explanation of events, I frequently was told, "because I wanted to." The account, as such, was largely scripted for them by their clinicians. When I asked the men whether this was a conclusion they had reached in treatment, the reply was yes. Consequently, I asked these men to step back, to try to remember what they were thinking and feeling when they began offending and what was going on in their lives at the time. It was at this point that the accounts tended to become very rich. This process of eliciting or demanding acquiescence is a well-known dynamic of institutional settings. Erving Goffman, *Asylums*, 1961, pp. 146–69; Thomas J. Scheff, *Being Mentally Ill: A Sociological Theory*, New York: Aldine, 1984, pp. 65–66, 127–42.

42. Usually sponsor-based access is gained by befriending someone in the life, so to speak, in relation to the people the researcher wants to study. Patricia Adler, *Wheeling and Dealing*, 1985; John Hagedorn, *People and Folks: Gangs, Crime, and the Underclass in a Rustbelt City*, Chicago: Lake View Press, 1988; William F. Whyte, *Street Corner Society*, 2d ed., Chicago: University of Chicago Press, 1955; Raymond M. Lee, *Doing Research on Sensitive Topics*, 1993, pp. 121–24. The clinicians I worked with were generally respected by the offenders, primarily because of their perceived willingness to help them, while most other outsiders were seen as a source of potential or actual shame or condemnation.

43. Barney G. Glaser and Anselm L. Strauss, *The Discovery of Grounded Theory: Strategies for Qualitative Research*, New York: Aldine, 1967, p. 48, and pp. 45–77 generally. See also Barney G. Glaser, *Theoretical Sensitivity*, 1978, pp. 36–54.

44. I adopt a broader, nuclear family definition of incest, as opposed to a narrow, genetic definition. Ray H. Bixler, "The multiple meanings of incest," *Journal of Sex Research*, 19, 1983, pp. 197–200.

45. David Finkelhor, *Child Sexual Abuse*, 1984, pp. 36–37, 53, 62; Diana E. H. Russell, *The Secret Trauma*, 1986, p. 390.

46. Penis transducer research, which examines changes in penis size following exposure to audio depictions of sex or nude pictures involving children, has shown in general that men who have molested two or more children or children of the same sex, and nonincest offenders rather than incest offenders, display higher levels of sexual arousal toward children and thus stronger pedophilic desires. See the extensive citations listed in note 23. On a related note, it has been estimated that 90 percent of incest offenders may be regressed or situational offenders. A. Nicholas Groth, "The incest offender," 1982, p. 218. In one recent study of 580 offenders, on average, intrafamilial offenders who molested girls or boys reported fewer than 2 victims, but extrafamilial offenders who molested girls reported nearly 20 victims, and extrafamilial offenders who molested boys just over 150 victims. Gene G. Abel et al., "Self-reported sex crimes of nonincarcerated paraphiliacs," 1987, pp. 3–25. Research has likewise revealed that girls are more likely to be molested by a relative than are boys. See David Finkelhor, "The sexual abuse of boys," 1981, p. 78; David Finkelhor et al., "Sexual abuse in a national survey of adult men and women: Prevalence, characteristics, and risk factors," 1990, p. 21; Mary Wellman, "Child sexual abuse and gender differences: Attitudes and prevalence," 1993, p. 543. Finally, stepfathers and biological fathers appear to commit more offenses per victim over a longer period than any other group. See Patricia Phelan, "The process of incest: Biologic father and stepfather families," 1986, pp. 535–37; Diana E. H. Russell, *The Secret Trauma*, 1986, pp. 224, 234.

47. For descriptions of these other types of sexual offenders, see Ann W. Burgess, *Child Pornography and Sex Rings*, 1982; John M. MacDonald, "Sexual deviance: The adult offender," in Patricia B. Mrazek and C. Henry Kempe (eds.), *Sexually Abused Children and Their Families*, Oxford: Pergamon, 1981, pp. 89–95; J. W. Mohr et al., *Pedophilia and Exhibitionism*, 1964; Magnus J. Seng, "Sexual behavior between adults and children: Some issues of definition," *Journal of Offender Counseling, Services, and Rehabilitation*, 11, 1986, pp. 47–61.

48. Adolescent perpetrators may not be as uncommon as first thoughts suggest. For example, in one study of hospital cases of sexual abuse against children under twelve, 26 percent of the alleged perpetrators were fifteen or younger. Robert Dube and Martin Hebert, "Sexual abuse of children under 12 years of age: A review of 511 cases," 1988, pp. 324–25. In fact, research on adolescent offenders appears to be the most recent vogue topic in the literature on child sexual abuse. Other examples of adolescent perpetrators can be found in the following: Naomi A. Adler and Joseph Schutz, "Sibling incest offenders," *Child Abuse and Neglect*, 19, 1995, pp. 811–19; Judith V. Becker, Cathi D. Harris, and Bruce D. Sales, "Juveniles who commit sexual offenses: A critical review of research," in Gordon C. Nagayama Hall, Richard Hirschman, John R. Graham, and Maira S. Zaragoza, *Sexual Aggression: Issues in Etiology, Assessment, and Treatment*, Washington, DC: Taylor and Francis, 1993, pp. 215–28; Karen E. Gerdes, M. Michelle Gourley, and Monette C. Nash, "Assessing juvenile sex offenders to determine adequate levels of supervision," *Child Abuse and Neglect*, 19, 1995, pp. 953–61; Toni C. Johnson, "Female child perpetrators: Children who molest other children," *Child Abuse and Neglect*, 13, 1989, 571–85; Carlos M. Loredo, "Sibling incest," in Suzanne M. Sgroi (ed.), *Handbook of Clinical Intervention in Child Sexual Abuse*, Lexington, MA: Lexington Books, 1982, pp. 177–89, J. W. Mohr et al., *Pedophilia and Exhibitionism*, 1964, pp. 41, 94. Numerous studies report on female perpetrators as well, more often with boys as victims, though not always. Still, the vast majority of offenders are known to be male. Following are a

few sources that mention female offenders. David Finkelhor et al., "Sexual abuse in a national survey of adult men and women: Prevalence, characteristics, and risk factors," 1990, pp. 21–22; Charlotte D. Kasl, "Female perpetrators of sexual abuse: A feminist view," in Mic Hunter (ed.), *The Sexually Abused Male*, New York: Lexington Books, 1990, pp. 259–74; Christine Lawson, "Mother-son sexual abuse: Rare or underreported? A critique of the research," *Child Abuse and Neglect*, 17, 1993, pp. 261–69; Margaret M. Rudin, Christine Zalewski, and Jeffrey Bodmer-Turner, "Characteristics of child sexual abuse victims according to perpetrator gender," *Child Abuse and Neglect*, 19, 1995, pp. 963–73; Philip M. Sarrel and William H. Masters, "Sexual molestation of men by women," *Archives of Sexual Behavior*, 11, 1982, pp. 117–31; Ruth Mathews, Jane Matthews, and Kate Speltz, "Female sexual offenders," in Mic Hunter (ed.), *The Sexually Abused Male*, New York: Lexington Books, 1990, pp. 275–94. Evidence of the female accomplice/male perpetrator instigator hypothesis is documented in at least three studies. See Kathleen C. Faller, "Polyincestuous families: An exploratory study," *Journal of Interpersonal Violence*, 6, 1991, p. 312; David Finkelhor and Gerald T. Hotaling, "Sexual abuse in the national incidence study of child abuse and neglect: An appraisal," *Child Abuse and Neglect*, 8, 1984, p. 27; Keith L. Kaufman, Anne M. Wallace, Charles F. Johnson, and Mark L. Reeder, "Comparing female and male perpetrators' modus operandi: Victims' reports of sexual abuse," *Journal of Interpersonal Violence*, 10, 1995, pp. 322–33.

49. Gender preference toward victims among male child sexual perpetrators is usually measured by official statistics. Thus in five studies, 4 percent to 20 percent of known offenders were arrested or convicted for molesting children of both sexes. W. D. Erickson et al., "Behavior patterns of child molesters," 1988, p. 82; A. Nicholas Groth and H. Jean Birnbaum, "Adult sexual orientation and attraction to underage persons," 1978, p. 179; K. Nedoma et al., "Sexual behavior and its development in pedophilic men," 1971, p. 267; Lana Stermac et al., "Violence among child molesters," 1989, p. 456; Brenda J. Vander Mey and Ronald L. Neff, *Incest as Child Abuse*, 1986, p. 96.

50. I drew heavily on two resources for information about conducting face-to-face intensive interviews. Raymond Gorden, *Basic Interviewing Skills*, Itasca, IL: F. E. Peacock, 1992; Grant McCracken, *The Long Interview*, Newbury Park, CA: Sage, 1988.

51. The use of this type of personal investment exchange strategy for building trust and encouraging participation in research has been implemented in different and more involved forms by others. Patricia Adler, *Wheeling and Dealing*, 1985, pp. 16–18; Rosalie H. Wax, "Reciprocity as a field technique," *Human Organization*, 11, 1952, pp. 34–37.

52. John M. Johnson, *Doing Field Research*, 1975, p. 109.

53. Raymond M. Lee, *Doing Research on Sensitive Topics*, 1993, p. 139.

54. Raymond M. Lee, *Doing Research on Sensitive Topics*, 1993, p. 120.

55. The salience of this problem in the case of sex offenders is argued in one recent book on male rapists of adult women. Diana Scully, *Understanding Sexual Violence*, 1990, pp. 26–28.

56. David F. Luckenbill, "Criminal homicide as a situated transaction," *Social Problems*, 25, 1977, pp. 176–86; Diana Scully, *Understanding Sexual Violence*, 1990, pp. 26–28.

57. Harold Garfinkel, *Studies in Ethnomethodology*, Englewood Cliffs, NJ: Prentice-Hall, 1967, pp. 186–207. I refer in particular to his discussion about how organizational records get put together. People who assemble case folders tend to include only that information that makes them accountable within the context of the organization they are working in. Missing information is a consistent problem in official records.

Chapter 2: *Blurring of Boundaries in Childhood*

1. Research on the possible relationship between being the victim of sexual abuse or early sex perpetrated by an adult during childhood and subsequent involvement in child molesting, pedophilic behavior, or even rape years later is far from conclusive. Some studies have shown that there is either only a small increased probability or no difference between various groups of sexual offenders versus nonoffender controls on this background factor. See Kurt Freund, Robin Watson, and Robert Dickey, "Does sexual abuse in childhood cause pedophilia: An exploratory study," *Archives of Sexual Behavior*, 19, 1990, pp. 557–68; R. K. Hanson and S. Slater, "Sexual victimization in the history of sexual abusers: A review," 1988, pp. 485–99; Diana Scully, *Understanding Sexual Violence*, 1990, pp. 68–70. Other studies, however, have reported that early sexual contact as such is a strong factor in the offending careers of men. See Kathleen C. Faller, "Why sexual abuse: An exploration of the intergenerational hypothesis," *Child Abuse and Neglect*, 13, 1989, pp. 543–48; Heidi Vanderbilt, "Incest: A chilling report," in John J. Sullivan and Joseph L. Victor (eds.), *Criminal Justice: Annual Editions—93/94*, Guilford, CT: Dushkin Publishing, 1993, pp. 82–83. Vanderbilt cites current unpublished research by David Finkelhor and Linda M. Williams on 118 incestuous fathers. Paul N. Gerber, "Victims becoming offenders: A study of ambiguities," in Mic Hunter (ed.), *The Sexually Abused Male*, New York: Lexington Books, 1990, pp. 153–76; A. Nicholas Groth, "Sexual trauma in the life histories of rapists and child molesters," 1979, pp. 10–16; T. Seghorn, R. Boucher, and R. Prentky, "Childhood sexual abuse in the lives of sexually aggressive offenders," *Journal of the American Academy of Child and Adolescent Psychiatry*, 26, 1987, pp. 262–67. Across this literature, the reported incidence of childhood sexual contact with someone older reported by offenders has ranged from a low of 9 percent to a high of 70 percent.

2. The relationship between child physical abuse and adult sexual offending against children or even against other adults has only rarely been examined. Child physical abuse has been correlated with delinquent and adult criminal behavior in general. See Beverly Rivera and Cathy S. Widom, "Childhood victimization and violent offending," *Violence and Victims*, 5, 1990, pp. 19–35; Cathy S. Widom, "Child abuse, neglect, and violent criminal behavior," *Criminology*, 27, 1989, pp. 251–71. It has also been linked with physically abusive behavior against children later. See Constance Avery-Clark et al., "A comparison of intrafamilial sexual and physical child abuse," 1981, pp. 3–39; Ruth S. Kempe and C. Henry Kempe, *Child Abuse*, Cambridge: Harvard University Press, 1978, pp. 12–14. One study did examine the relationship between serious physical violence experienced in childhood and involvement in rape against women as an adult. Rapists were not any more likely than other felons who did not commit sex crimes to report such a history, 34 versus 32 percent. These data are used to dismiss any connection between physical child abuse and later rape. Another possibility, of course, is that violence during childhood may be related to involvement in both sexual and nonsexual crimes down the road. After all, one-third of offenders in both groups did experience major violence. A more appropriate control group would be men with no criminal history. Diana Scully, *Understanding Sexual Violence*, 1990, pp. 68–69. Overall, however, child physical abuse and child sexual abuse have almost always been studied as independent phenomena leading to separate outcomes for people in their adult lives. This trend is surprising, given the long accepted premise that sexual offending of any nature is an act of violence and not an act of sex, and also given descriptions of sexual offenses that include elements of physical force, power, anger, and even sadism. Susan Brownmiller, *Against Our Will*, 1975; A. Nicholas Groth, *Men Who Rape*, 1979.

3. Researchers are equally uncertain about the possible consequences of peer and/or sibling sexual contact during childhood. A large contingent of researchers argue that sexual activity between children is not uncommon and in fact is quite "normal." They do not see such experiences as harmful, but rather a regular phase of sexual development. See Robert Crooks and Karla Baur, *Our Sexuality*, 2d ed., Menlo Park, CA: Benjamin/Cummings, 1983, pp. 411–16; William N. Friedrich, Patricia Grambsch, Daniel Broughton, James Kuiper, and Robert L. Beilke, "Normative sexual behavior in children," *Pediatrics*, 88, 1991, pp. 456–64; John H. Gagnon and William Simon, *Sexual Conduct: The Social Sources of Human Sexuality*, Chicago: Aldine, 1973; Evan Greenwald and Harold Leitenberg, "Long-term effects of sexual experiences with siblings and nonsiblings during childhood," 1989, pp. 389–99; Alfred C. Kinsey, Wardell B. Pomeroy, and Clyde E. Martin, *Sexual Behavior in the Human Male*, Philadelphia: W. B. Saunders, 1948; Sharon Lamb and Mary Coakley, "Normal childhood sexual play and games: Differentiating play from abuse," *Child Abuse and Neglect*, 17, 1993, pp. 515–26; Harold Lietenberg, Evan Greenwald, and Matthew J. Tarran, "The relation between sexual activity among children during preadolescence and/or early adolescence and sexual behavior and sexual adjustment in young adulthood," *Archives of Sexual Behavior*, 18, 1989, pp. 299–313; Floyd M. Martinson, "Eroticism in infancy and childhood," *Journal of Sex Research*, 12, 1976, pp. 251–62. Others have suggested, however, that certain forms of sexual behavior between children, if left unchecked, may represent activating experiences and function as a prelude to subsequent adolescent or adult sexual offending. See Alan P. Bell and Calvin S. Hall, "The personality of a child molester," in Martin S. Weinberg (ed.), *Sex Research: Studies from the Kinsey Institute*, 1976, pp. 184–201; Allan R. DeJong, "Sexual interactions among siblings and cousins: Experimentation or exploitation?" *Child Abuse and Neglect*, 13, 1989, pp. 271–79; David Finkelhor, "Sex among siblings: A survey on prevalence, variety, and effects," *Archives of Sexual Behavior*, 9, 1980, pp. 171–94; Robert E. Freeman-Longo and A. Nicholas Groth, "Juvenile sexual offenses in the histories of adult rapists and child molesters," *International Journal of Offender Therapy and Comparative Criminology*, 27, 1983, pp. 150–55; W. L. Marshall, H. E. Barbaree, and A. Eckles, "Early onset and deviant sexuality in child molesters," *Journal of Interpersonal Violence*, 6, 1993, pp. 323–36; Alayne Yates, "Children eroticized by incest," *American Journal of Psychiatry*, 139, 1982, pp. 482–85. The nature and extent of early genital sex with peers in the cases of family-based molestation offenders and the interpretations and meanings attached to those experiences have yet to really be explored. For a history of the research and theoretical views on the impact of early peer or early sex with adults on children, see Dean D. Knudsen, "Sex in childhood: Abuse, aversion, or right," paper presented at the Annual Meeting of the Society for the Study of Social Problems, Washington, DC, 1985.

4. Considerable data show that the vast majority of adult sexual offenders against children are male. Eighty-three percent or more of offenders who have molested either girls or boys identified in different studies have been men. See David Finkelhor et al., "Sexual abuse in a national survey of adult men and women: Prevalence, characteristics, and risk factors," 1990, p. 21; David Finkelhor and Gerald T. Hotaling, "Sexual abuse in the national incidence study of child abuse and neglect: An appraisal," 1984, p. 27. This is a conservative estimate, because most reported figures are between 93 percent and 98 percent. See J. Michael Cupoli and Pamela M. Sewell, "One thousand fifty-nine children with a chief complaint of sexual abuse," 1988, p. 154; Lynda S. Doll et al., "Self-reported childhood and adolescent sexual abuse among adult homosexual and bisexual men," 1992, p. 858; Robert Dube and Martin Hebert, "Sexual abuse of children under 12 years

of age: A review of 511 cases," 1988, p. 324; Leslie Margolin, "Sexual abuse by grandparents," 1992, p. 737; Robert L. Pierce and Lois H. Pierce, "The sexually abused child: A comparison of male and female victims," 1985, p. 194; Robert L. Pierce and Lois H. Pierce, "Race as a factor in the sexual abuse of children," 1984, p. 11; Diana E. H. Russell, *The Secret Trauma*, 1986, p. 216; Roxane L. Silver et al., "Searching for meaning in misfortune: Making sense of incest," 1983, p. 85; Brenda J. Vander Mey and Ronald L. Neff, *Incest as Child Abuse*, 1986, p. 96; Gail E. Wyatt, "The sexual abuse of Afro-American and white American women in childhood," 1985, p. 516. The pattern holds whether the victims are boys or girls, though in two studies male victims were more likely to mention being molested by female offenders than were female victims: 17 percent versus 2 percent and 37 percent versus 12 percent. David Finkelhor et al., "Sexual abuse in a national survey of adult men and women: Prevalence, characteristics, and risk factors," 1990, p. 21; Paul Okami, "Self-reports of positive childhood and adolescent sexual contacts with older persons: An exploratory study," 1991, p. 443, respectively. Drawing on these data, we may say that the ratio of male to female offenders is roughly thirty to one.

5. I am not the first person to make this argument. The other researcher who formulated this line of thinking carried it out is a study on adult male rapists. Diana Scully, *Understanding Sexual Violence*, 1990, pp. 69–70. In her research, she found that male rapists were not any more likely to have been sexually abused as children than a comparison group of other felons who were not sex offenders, 9 percent versus 7 percent. Since women are raped much more than men, Scully suggests that one would intuitively expect more women than men to be rapists. Further, since rapists who are sexually abused as children are usually victimized by a male, one would expect them to rape other males, not females. One problem with her research is that the proportion of perpetrators who report child sexual abuse experiences in their backgrounds is extremely low compared to other studies. In fact, in note 1, I cited a range of studies that examine this question. If we exclude her findings, the remaining research shows that between 20 percent and 70 percent of offenders have histories of sexual abuse as children. The reason for the difference is most likely selection bias, since all these studies are based on availability rather than probability samples of offenders. But more, it is important to recognize that men and women do have different physical abilities. Men in general certainly have a greater physical capacity to overpower women than vice versa. Thus it is misleading to expect that women would rape more than men despite a higher incidence of a specific background event that might explain such behavior. In addition, gender differences especially in relation to issues of power and emotional affect may impact strongly on the long-term consequences of child sexual abuse victimization. There is some evidence of different outcome effects. For example, women who are sexually abused as children may be more likely than their male counterparts to become involved in prostitution. Nanette J. Davis, "Prostitutes," 1981, pp. 305–6; Diana Gray, "Teenage prostitution," in Leonard D. Savitz and Norman Johnston (eds.), *Crime and Society*, New York: John Wiley, 1978, pp. 791–92; Mimi H. Silbert and Ayala M. Pines, "Sexual abuse as an antecedent to prostitution," 1981, pp. 407–11. Finally, it may be that being the victim of child sexual abuse is more strongly related to subsequent involvement in sex crimes against children later as an adult rather than to the commission of sex crimes against other adults.

6. Ellen Bass and Laura Davis, *The Courage to Heal*, 1988, pp. 20–39; Diana E. H. Russell, *The Secret Trauma*, 1986, pp. 138–57. Additional extensive citations can be found in note 5 of chapter 1.

7. Martin S. Weinberg, Colin J. Williams, and Douglas W. Pryor, *Dual Attraction: Understanding Bisexuality*, New York: Oxford University Press, 1994, p. 140.

8. Nanette J. Davis, "Prostitutes," 1981, p. 305; Diana Gray, "Teenage prostitution," 1978, p. 791.

9. Harold E. Pepinsky, *The Geometry of Violence and Democracy*, Bloomington: Indiana University Press, 1991, pp. 8–33.

Chapter 3: *Escalating Problems in Adulthood*

1. Life sequences of unresolvable problems, escalating unhappiness, and turning points have been identified as a major stage in theoretical models of deviance situations other than child molesting. For example, attempted suicide among adolescents has been documented as the result of five progressive factors: long-standing and escalating life problems, an ongoing failure to cope, increasing social isolation, the final loss of a major social relationship, and the onset of feelings of hopelessness. Jerry Jacobs, *Adolescent Suicide*, New York: Irvington, 1980, pp. 27–28. Likewise, it has been reported that religious conversion and religious cult membership are more common among people who have experienced long-standing acute life dissatisfaction, coupled with the inability to solve those problems through conventional psychiatric or political means. John Lofland, "Conversion to the doomsday cult," in Earl Rubington and Martin S. Weinberg (eds.), *Deviance: The Interactionist Perspective*, 5th ed., New York: Macmillan, 1987, pp. 232–34. Also, the process of becoming involved in embezzlement or prostitution, according to two classic studies, follows from the emergence of nonshareable problems or marginalization from conventional social circles. Donald R. Cressey, *Other People's Money: The Social Psychology of Embezzlement*, Belmont, CA: Wadsworth, 1971, pp. 34–36; Nanette J. Davis, "Prostitutes," 1981, p. 307. In the cases of men who molested children, the process was similar, though the dimensions of the problems that were experienced were substantively different. This situational reality of mounting problems, drift, and emotional and social disconnection is, of course, the flip side of control theory. See Travis Hirschi, *Causes of Delinquency*, Berkeley: University of California Press, 1969. I prefer the term "decontrol" or "disintegration" theory to conceptualize what happened with the men I studied.

2. A turning point has been defined as "an event that mobilizes and focuses awareness that old lines of action are complete, have failed, have been disrupted, or are no longer personally satisfying." Helen R. F. Ebaugh, *Becoming an EX: The Process of Role Exit*, Chicago: University of Chicago Press, 1988, p. 123. See also John Lofland, "Conversion to the doomsday cult," 1987, p. 234.

3. Neil Frude, "The sexual nature of sexual abuse: A review of the literature," 1982, pp. 213–15. For other discussions of this explanation of rape, see Lee Ellis, *Theories of Rape*, 1989, p. 9; Blair Justice and Rita Justice, *The Broken Taboo*, 1979, pp. 118–19.

4. This sexual theory was not found to be supported in one detailed study of 114 adult male rapists of women. In particular, compared to a sample of seventy-five convicted felons who had not committed sex crimes, rapists reported similar levels of consensual sexual behavior prior to being incarcerated. Roughly 90 percent of the men in both groups reported having sex twice a week or more, about 40 percent every day. Unfortunately, there is no time frame for this variable, so it is unclear whether the measured level of sexual outlet refers to the last week, month, year, or when exactly. In addition, just 16 percent described their relationships or marriages as unsatisfactory in some way, while the majority talked about their partners in positive terms. Diana Scully, *Understanding Sexual Violence*, 1990, pp. 70–74. One possible explanation for the different finding in my research is that the rapists in the other study may have been exaggerating, fabricating, and putting a positive spin on their sexual histories, especially to a female interviewer. In

support of this point is the fact that the overall sexual outlet reported by the men in prison in the rape study is considerably higher than that reported by men in general in a national study of sexual behavior, in which only 34 percent stated they had sex two or more times a week. Robert T. Michael, John H. Gagnon, Edward O. Laumann, and Gina Kolata, *Sex in America: A Definitive Survey*, Boston: Little, Brown, 1994, pp. 115–16. In addition, it may be that feelings of sexual frustration are more salient in the situations of men who molest their own children within the immediate context of the family. For example, when incest victims were asked why they felt the person who molested them had done so, they sometimes mentioned that the offender had talked about sexual problems or a lack of sexual outlet with a spouse. Diana E. H Russell, *The Secret Trauma*, 1986, p. 135. Such feelings may be less central in the etiology of predatory stranger rape of adult women, which is the focus of much of the study on adult rapists.

5. The frequency of this offender's reported sexual outlet is not a misprint.

6. More often the opposite power dynamic is reported, that men who commit sexual abuse are absolute authoritarians who dominate and exact obedience over everyone in their families. Susan Brownmiller, *Against Our Will*, 1975, p. 281; Judith L. Herman, *Father-Daughter Incest*, 1981, pp. 71–80; Blair Justice and Rita Justice, *The Broken Taboo*, 1979, pp. 77–80; Diana E. H. Russell, *The Secret Trauma*, 1986, pp. 374–84; Suzanne M. Sgroi et al., "A conceptual framework for child sexual abuse," 1982, pp. 27, 32–33; Roland Summit and JoAnn Kryso, "Sexual abuse of children: A clinical spectrum," 1978, pp. 245–46; Brenda J. Vander Mey and Ronald L. Neff, *Incest as Child Abuse*, 1986, pp. 80–88. The portrait of offenders as powerless and passive in relation to their spouses is not as widely discussed. A. Nicholas Groth, "The incest offender," 1982, p. 218; Joseph J. Peters, "Children who are victims of sexual assault and the psychology of offenders," 1976, p. 411; Kathleen J. Tierney and David L. Corwin, "Exploring intrafamilial child sexual abuse," 1983, p. 108.

7. Patrick Carnes, *Contrary to Love*, 1989, pp. 43–102.

8. For a description of the frequency of different types of sexual problems among homosexual, bisexual, and heterosexual men, see Martin S. Weinberg, Colin J. Williams, and Douglas W. Pryor, *Dual Attraction*, 1994, pp. 171–73.

9. This relationship between sexual problems that block adult sexual outlet and sexual offending against children has been proposed theoretically and discussed elsewhere. David Finkelhor, *Child Sexual Abuse*, 1984, pp. 43–44; David Finkelhor and Sharon Araji, "Explanations of pedophilia: A four factor model," 1986, pp. 153–54. One recent study along this line found that incest and nonincestuous offenders do not differ from each other in terms of types of sexual problems, but both have more sexual dysfunctions than men in the general population. Anne E. Pawlak, John R. Boulet, and John M. W. Bradford, "Discriminant analysis of a sexual-functioning inventory with intrafamilial and extrafamilial child molesters," *Archives of Sexual Behavior*, 20, 1991, pp. 27–34.

Chapter 4: *Shifting into an Offending Mode*

1. As noted earlier, this categorization of offenders is generally associated with one particular clinical psychologist: A. Nicholas Groth, "Patterns of sexual assault against children and adolescents," 1978, pp. 6–10; A. Nicholas Groth, "The incest offender," 1982, pp. 216–17; A. Nicholas Groth and H. Jean Birnbaum, "Adult sexual orientation and attraction to underage persons," 1978, pp. 175–81. See also Kevin Howells, "Adult sexual interest in children: Considerations relevant to theories of aetiology," 1981, pp. 76–79; Blair Justice and Rita Justice, *The Broken Taboo*, 1979, pp. 89–91, 112–17.

2. Jack Katz, *Seductions of Crime*, 1988, pp. 3–4. My theoretical framing of this

chapter extends directly from the phenomenological approach to explaining crime recently formulated by Jack Katz. His argument is that it is critical to look at the immediate "foreground" of events, the realities people experience and the meanings they construct in the context of social interaction, in order to understand why they do what they do. Definitions and interpretations, more than antecedent biography, is what provides the push and pull needed to organize and shape the actions of people in a given situation. To quote:

> The study of crime has been preoccupied with a search for background forces, usually defects in the offenders' psychological backgrounds or social environments, to the neglect of the positive, often wonderful attractions within the lived experience of criminality . . . . Only rarely have sociologists taken up the challenge of explaining the qualities of deviant experience . . . . Whatever the relevance of antecedent events. . . , something causally essential happens in the very moments in which a crime is committed. The assailant must sense, then and there, a distinctive constraint or seductive appeal that he did not sense a little while before . . . . Although his economic status, . . . Oedipal conflicts, genetic makeup, internalized machismo, history of child abuse, and the like remain the same, he must suddenly become propelled to commit the crime. (pp. 3–4)

3. The importance of the physical appearance of a particular child as an activating factor in the onset of sexual abuse has been discussed in other research. However, there is very little actual data to support this possibility, especially in relation to how offenders viewed their actual victims versus, for example, how they react to seeing children in pictures in controlled laboratory conditions. In particular, I extend beyond this limited literature by showing the dynamics by which the sexual noticing of victims occurred. See Lee E. Budin and Charles F. Johnson, "Sex abuse prevention programs: Offenders' attitudes about their efficacy," 1989, p. 79; Jon R. Conte et al., "What sexual offenders tell us about prevention strategies," 1989, p. 296; Neil Frude, "The sexual nature of sexual abuse: A review of the literature," 1982, p. 215; Kevin Howells, "Some meanings of children for pedophiles," 1977, p. 524.

4. My intent here is not to reawaken the sexual seduction hypothesis, that young daughters in particular tease their fathers into sexual activity. Instead, I focus on how offenders framed their victims, or attached sexual meaning to situations, irrespective of whatever reality may have been operating for the other party. In fact, I have only one side of the story, that of offenders, and imply no claims about the reality of victims. But more, if children do express a sexuality at times in the midst of older adults, it is the adult who must be responsible and channel that behavior in socially acceptable directions.

5. I paraphrase William I. Thomas, who stated more precisely, "If men define situations as real, they are real in their consequences." As cited in George Ritzer, *Sociological Theory*, 3d ed., New York: McGraw-Hill, 1992, p. 197.

6. Kevin Howells, "Adult sexual interest in children: Considerations relevant to theories of aetiology," 1981, p. 68.

7. See Richard B. Felson and Marvin Krohn, "Motives for rape," 1990, pp. 227–29, 237–39; A. Nicholas Groth, *Men Who Rape*, 1979, pp. 13–24; Diana Scully, *Understanding Sexual Violence*, 1990, pp. 137–40; Diana Scully and Joseph Marolla, "Riding the bull at Gilley's: Convicted rapists describe the rewards of rape," *Social Problems*, 32, 1985, pp. 255–57.

8. It has been reported elsewhere that many offenders deliberately select children they perceive as vulnerable targets based on various criteria, including physical accessibility (for example, children who live with one parent), and emotional vulnerability (for example, children who are more passive, unhappy, or needy). Jon R. Conte et al., "What sexual offenders tell us about prevention strategies," 1989, p. 299; David Finkelhor, *Child Sexual Abuse*, 1984, pp. 60–61.

9. This latter moralistic inhibition against extramarital sex is briefly mentioned in at least one theory about sexual abuse. See David Finkelhor, *Child Sexual Abuse*, 1984, pp. 43–44; David Finkelhor and Sharon Araji, "Explanations of pedophilia: A four factor model," 1986, pp. 153–54.

Chapter 5: *Approaching and Engaging the Victim*

1. This is by no means a complete list of the various methods by which sexual offenses against children are perpetrated, but they do seem to be the most common access methods mentioned in the literature. There also seems to be more interest in documenting what occurred to victims than in analyzing how it occurred. For more on this topic, see Lucy Berliner and Jon R. Conte, "The process of victimization: The victims' perspective," 1989, pp. 33–35; Lee E. Budin and Charles F. Johnson, "Sex abuse prevention programs: Offenders' attitudes about their efficacy," 1989, pp. 80–82; Ann W. Burgess and Lynda L. Holmstrom, "Accessory to sex: Pressure, sex, and secrecy," 1978, pp. 85–88; Suzanne M. Sgroi et al., "A conceptual framework for child sexual abuse," 1982, p. 13; Jon R. Conte et al., "What sexual offenders tell us about prevention strategies," 1989, pp. 296–98; Robert Dube and Martin Hebert, "Sexual abuse of children under 12 years of age: A review of 511 cases," 1988, p. 324; David Finkelhor, *Child Sexual Abuse*, 1984, pp. 60–61; Neil Frude, "The sexual nature of sexual abuse: A review of the literature," 1982, p. 215; A. Nicholas Groth, *Men Who Rape*, 1979, pp. 142–44; A. Nicholas Groth and Ann W. Burgess, "Motivational intent in the sexual assault of children," 1977, pp. 257–62; Lynda L. Holmstrom and Ann W. Burgess, "Rapists' talk: Linguistic strategies to control the victim," 1979, pp. 105–9; Leslie Margolin, "Sexual abuse by grandparents," 1992, p. 738; Joseph J. Peters, "Children who are victims of sexual assault and the psychology of offenders," 1976, pp. 412–16; Diana E. H. Russell, *The Secret Trauma*, 1986, pp. 229–30; Gail E. Wyatt, "The sexual abuse of Afro-American and white American women in childhood," 1985, p. 517.

2. My distinction in this analysis between surreptitious and overt coercion-based exploitive transactions in relation to sexual abuse is based on a theoretical formulation proposed by other researchers in the sociology of deviance. Joel Best and David F. Luckenbill, *Organizing Deviance*, 1994, pp. 141–64. They distinguish between two types of exploitive deviant transactions depending on whether the target or victim is aware or unaware of what is happening. The range of transactions sexual abuse offenders employed clearly illustrates both dimensions of their dichotomy. Thus even in a single type of deviant behavior, the nature of the transactions can vary widely. It may be misleading to classify any one form of deviant behavior as involving a single type of deviant transaction.

3. This pattern is consistent with what has been reported in other research on child sexual abuse. The majority of offenders are not known to use overt physical force to complete a molestation. In at least thirteen studies, anywhere from half to 90 percent of the reported cases or episodes of sexual contact were identified as nonforceful. John Briere and Marsha Runtz, "Symptomatology associated with childhood sexual victimization in a nonclinical adult sample," *Child Abuse and Neglect*, 12, 1988, p. 53; Lynda S. Doll et al., "Self-reported childhood and adolescent sexual abuse among adult homosexual and bisexual men," 1992, p. 859; Robert Dube and Martin Hebert, "Sexual abuse of children under 12 years of age: A review of 511 cases," 1988, p. 324; David Finkelhor et al., "Sexual abuse in a national survey of adult men and women: Prevalence, characteristics, and risk factors," 1990, p. 21; John H. Gagnon, "Female child victims of sex offenses," 1965, p. 181; Gordon C. Nagayama Hall et al., "The utility of the MMPI with men who have sexually assaulted children," 1986, p. 494; Judith Herman and Lisa Hirschman,

"Father-daughter incest," 1977, p. 743; Leslie Margolin, "Sexual abuse by grandparents," 1992, p. 738; W. L. Marshall and M. M. Christie, "Pedophilia and aggression," *Criminal Justice and Behavior*, 8, 1981, pp. 145–58; Charles H. McCaghy, "Child molesters: A study of their careers as deviants," 1967, p. 80; Joseph J. Peters, "Children who are victims of sexual assault and the psychology of offenders," 1976, p. 416; Diana E. H. Russell, *The Secret Trauma*, 1986, p. 96; Gail E. Wyatt, "The sexual abuse of Afro-American and white American women in childhood," 1985, p. 517. One exception is a study in which 100 percent of the incest cases and 78.4 percent of the nonincest cases examined were rated by coders as violent. Lana Stermac et al., "Violence among child molesters," 1989, p. 456. When force is used, it is usually of low severity, consisting of grabbing, pinning, or pushing. The incidence of less severe force used against victims ranged from 17 percent to 50 percent in four studies. Charles H. McCaghy, "Child molesters: A study of their careers as deviants," 1967, p. 79; Diana E. H. Russell, *The Secret Trauma*, 1986, p. 96; Roxane L. Silver et al., "Searching for meaning in misfortune: Making sense of incest," 1983, p. 85; Gail E. Wyatt, "The sexual abuse of Afro-American and white American women in childhood," 1985, p. 517. In one study, force was found to be more likely with male than female victims, 45 percent versus 30 percent. Robert L. Pierce and Lois H. Pierce, "The sexually abused child: A comparison of male and female victims," 1985, p. 195. According to the same research above and other research, severe violence is uncommon in the commission of offenses, and use of a weapon or killing is very rare. See W. D. Erickson et al., "Behavior patterns of child molesters," 1988, p. 85; J. W. Mohr et al., *Pedophilia and Exhibitionism*, 1964, pp. 77–78; D. J. West, "Adult sexual interest in children: Implications for social control," 1981, pp. 259–61.

Chapter 6: *Snowballing from One Act to Many*

1. Repetitive involvement in sex crimes against children is a well- supported research finding. For example, in incest cases, especially situations involving stepfathers or biological fathers, when the perpetrator lives around the victim, the duration of sexual behavior can span years. In one study of forty victims molested by their fathers, 75 percent said they were victimized more than once; 43 percent said the incest spanned three years or longer. Judith L. Herman, *Father-Daughter Incest*, 1981, p. 84. In a second survey of four therapists who provided data on thirty-one cases, 80 percent of the biological fathers and 64 percent of the stepfathers were said to have molested their victims for a period of at least one year. Patricia Phelan, "The process of incest: Biologic father and stepfather families," 1986, p. 535. Three other studies that report data on the duration of sexual abuse but that extend beyond cases involving biological fathers or stepfathers reveal a similar trend. Thus, in a third study of fifty-seven male and female adults who answered a research advertisement asking whether they had been child victims of unwanted sex, one-third of the females in the sample indicated that they had been abused for a span of over five years, and over half said their abuse had occurred weekly. Sharon Lamb and Susan Edgar-Smith, "Aspects of disclosure: Mediators of outcome of childhood sexual abuse," *Journal of Interpersonal Violence*, 9, 1994, pp. 314–15. In a fourth study of 365 adults molested as children, 85 percent indicated that they had been ongoingly molested over a period of one year or more. Kathleen A. Kendall-Tackett and Arthur F. Simon, "Molestation and the onset of puberty: Data from 365 adults molested as children," 1988, pp. 78–79. In a fifth study of 930 women, 187 of whom were incest victims, 57 percent indicated being molested two or more times, 27 percent six or more times. Diana E. H. Russell, *The Secret Trauma*, 1986, p. 93. Many offenders also report molesting more than one victim. In one study of twenty sexual offenders against children who were sampled

from a treatment program, seventeen indicated having two or more victims; the number of victims went as high as forty. Jon R. Conte et al., "What sexual offenders tell us about prevention strategies," 1989, p. 295. In yet another study of 580 molestation offenders, which I cited earlier, intrafamilial offenders against girls reported an average of 1.8 victims, intrafamilial offenders against boys 1.7 victims, extrafamilial offenders against girls 19.8 victims, and extrafamilial offenders who molested boys 150.2 victims. Gene G. Abel et al., "Self-reported sex crimes of nonincarcerated paraphiliacs," 1987, pp. 3–25. Finally, in a study of 72 men incarcerated for child sexual abuse, the median number of female victims reported in the sample was 2; the median number of male victims was 3.5. Lee E. Budin and Charles F. Johnson, "Sex abuse prevention programs: Offenders' attitudes about their efficacy," 1989, p. 79.

2. Erving Goffman, *Asylums*, 1961, p. 128.

3. Howard S. Becker, *Outsiders*, 1963, p. 42.

4. David Matza, *Becoming Deviant*, 1969, p. 177. For a more recent discussion of this concept, see Erdwin H. Pfuhl, *The Deviance Process*, 1986, pp. 33–35.

5. Diana Scully, *Understanding Sexual Violence*, 1990, p. 158, and also pp. 137–57. The offenders she interviewed who raped adult women described "feeling good" about what they had done. Typically there was an absence of any negative emotion and there were various perceived rewards that were attached to the act of rape. The rewards offenders mentioned included revenge and justice, a pleasureful bonus to another crime, sexual access to someone that could not be accomplished through consensual routes, increased feelings of power and sexual confidence, and a sense of excitement and adventure. In comparison, what I refer to as "feeling good at first" is a more specific stage in the overall sexual offender career, a stage followed by a sequence of other stages as well. I report a range of physical and emotional reactions offenders remembered experiencing at the time they were actively molesting their victims. I focus more on the phenomenology of the offense itself, whereas the rapists in the first study seem to step back and assess what they generally got out of the situation, or how they benefited from raping. Still, it is useful to make comparisons between what rapists of adult women state about their behavior and what child molesters report. The men in my study reported a few of the same, but also numerous other, positive feelings.

6. For an excellent discussion of the genesis and various arguments underlying the nonsexual view of sex crimes, see Craig T. Palmer, "Twelve reasons why rape is not sexually motivated: A skeptical examination," 1982, pp. 512–30.

7. Jack Katz, *Seductions of Crime*, 1988, pp. 52–79.

8. This phrase of course refers to the theme of the show *Star Trek*, which one offender I interviewed made reference to a few times in describing why he was interested in having sex with his biological daughter.

9. A. Nicholas Groth and Ann W. Burgess, "Motivational intent in the sexual assault of children," 1977, p. 255. For the broader application of this argument to rape in general, see A. Nicholas Groth, *Men Who Rape*, 1979, pp. 2–7.

10. The power domination theme is reported in other research on men who rape adult women or who commit child sexual abuse. A. Nicholas Groth and Ann W. Burgess, "Motivational intent in the sexual assault of children," 1977, pp. 257–62; A. Nicholas Groth, *Men Who Rape*, 1979, pp. 155–60; Judith L. Herman, *Father-Daughter Incest*, 1981, p. 87; Diana Scully, *Understanding Sexual Violence*, 1990, esp. pp. 149–50, 156.

11. For a brief discussion of this idea, see A. Nicholas Groth, *Men Who Rape*, 1979, p. 152.

12. Mordechai Rotenberg, "Self-labeling: A missing link in the social reaction theory

of deviance," *Sociological Review*, 22, 1974, pp. 335–54. While shame has been identified as an important dimension of involvement in deviant behavior, especially in relation to the process of secondary deviance, there are opposite views on the centrality of feelings of shame in the commission of sex crimes. One view is that shame is pervasive among some men who engage in illicit sex. Patrick Carnes, *Contrary to Love*, 1989, pp. 67–69. The other view is that most men who commit sex crimes, rape in particular, feel no shame, and that is why they do what they do. Diana Scully, *Understanding Sexual Violence*, 1990, p. 165. I take up this debate in more detail in my closing chapter.

13. See, among many other textbook discussions, Allen E. Liska, *Perspectives on Deviance*, 2d ed., Englewood Cliffs, NJ: Prentice-Hall, 1987, pp. 93–113.

14. My definition and use of this concept are directly adapted from the work of Stanley Cohen and Laurie Taylor, *Escape Attempts*, London: Allen Lane, 1976.

15. Stanley Cohen and Laurie Taylor, *Escape Attempts*, 1976, pp. 97–113.

16. Stanley Cohen and Laurie Taylor, *Escape Attempts*, 1976, pp. 129–37.

17. Carol A. B. Warren, "Destigmatization of identity: From deviant to charismatic," *Qualitative Sociology*, 3, 1980, pp. 59–72.

18. Gresham M. Sykes and David Matza, "Techniques of neutralization: A theory of delinquency," *American Sociological Review*, 22, 1957, pp. 664–70.

19. Marvin B. Scott and Stanford M. Lyman, "Accounts," *American Sociological Review*, 33, 1968, pp. 46–62.

20. Most relevant to this research is a recent typology of male rapists based on the types of neutralizations they formulated to account for their behavior: "deniers" versus "admitters." Diana Scully, *Understanding Sexual Violence*, 1990, pp. 97–135, 163–65; Diana Scully and Joseph Marolla, "Convicted rapists' vocabulary of motive: Excuses and justifications," *Social Problems*, 31, 1984, pp. 530–44. Like the respondents here, deniers justified their actions on grounds that the victim was willing or got what she deserved. Accounts by perpetrators that their victims seduced them or had a reputation for sleeping around are examples. Deniers did not believe they had really committed rape and were said to be "unaware of their victims' feelings." Admitters, in contrast, acknowledged they committed rape but excused their actions by denying responsibility. Blaming of behavior on alcohol or personal problems are examples. The same distinction, between deniers and admitters, did not seem to hold true in my data. There were no essential types in this respect. Rather, each method of neutralization seemed to be a phase in the process of offending that every offender passed through. Denial came first, while offending. Admitting and excusing came later, after the men had gotten caught.

21. Similar illustrations of this teacher and protector type account of sexual abuse can be found in Judith L. Herman, *Father-Daughter Incest*, 1981, p. 85; Blair Justice and Rita Justice, *The Broken Taboo*, 1979, pp. 70–74.

22. John P. Hewitt and Randall Stokes, "Disclaimers," *American Sociological Review*, 40, 1975, pp. 1–11.

23. This is a parallel account to the justifications documented among male rapists that their victims were seductive or that they really enjoyed what happened. Diana Scully, *Understanding Sexual Violence*, 1990, pp. 102–3, 105–7.

24. This is an extension of the idea that "nice girls don't get raped," which has been documented among male rapists of women. Diana Scully, *Understanding Sexual Violence*, 1990, pp. 107–10.

25. Once more, this is a variation of the belief among some male rapists that their behavior was really a minor transgression. Diana Scully, *Understanding Sexual Violence*, 1990, pp. 110–11.

26. As defined in Erdwin H. Pfuhl, *The Deviance Process*, 1986, pp. 162–63.

27. This type of neutralization, attacking condemnors, has been documented in other research on lifestyle pedophiles. Parker Rossman, *Sexual Experience between Men and Boys*, 1976, pp. 187–91; Mary De Young, "The indignant page: Techniques of neutralization in the publications of pedophile organizations," *Child Abuse and Neglect*, 12, 1988, pp. 588–89.

Chapter 7: *Continuing with Regular Offending*

1. I asked the offenders I interviewed to estimate the total number of episodes of sexual contact they remembered engaging in with each child they admitted having molested. Some men could not give a precise answer because there were simply too many episodes to recall. In these instances they provided a range, for example, three hundred to four hundred times. I selected the conservative or low number in the range to figure this overall group estimate.

2. Joel Best and David F. Luckenbill, *Organizing Deviance*, 1994, pp. 231–32.

3. Other descriptions about the sexual victimization of children generally report three basic objective career patterns among offenders. First, there is usually a gradual escalation in the level of sexual contact. See, for example, W. D. Erickson et al., "Behavior patterns of child molesters," 1988, p. 83; Neil Frude, "The sexual nature of sexual abuse: A review of the literature," 1982, p. 221; Judith L. Herman, *Father-Daughter Incest*, 1981, p. 83; Suzanne M. Sgroi et al., "A conceptual framework for child sexual abuse," 1982, p. 15. Second and third, as I cited in note 1, offenders frequently molest more than one victim and often continue molesting over a long period of time. I found that the picture was more complex, that escalation was the most common pattern, but not the only one, and it did not always occur in a simple linear progression. I attempt to portray the varied patterns of long-term involvement in offending in a more complete fashion than is found elsewhere in the literature.

4. Offenders' widespread use of threats, pleas, apologies, and material rewards to maintain secrecy is well documented in the research literature on victims. Lucy Berliner and Jon R. Conte, "The process of victimization: The victim's perspective," 1989, pp. 34–35; Ann W. Burgess and Lynda L. Holmstrom, "Accessory to sex: Pressure, sex, and secrecy," 1978, pp. 88–90; Judith L. Herman, *Father-Daughter Incest*, 1981, p. 88; Lynda L. Holmstrom and Ann W. Burgess, "Rapists' talk: Linguistic strategies to control the victim," 1979; pp. 120–22; Diana E. H. Russell, *The Secret Trauma*, 1986, p. 132; Suzanne M. Sgroi et al., "A conceptual framework for child sexual abuse," 1982, pp. 15–17. In comparison, I examine the other side of the coin, what offenders said they did.

5. Lawrence E. Cohen and Marcus Felson, "Social change and crime rate trends: A routine activity approach," *American Sociological Review*, 44, 1979, pp. 588–608.

6. The behaviors the men reported are generally consistent with other research that measures types of sexual contact. The same order of descending frequency is widely documented. Boys, according to some studies, are more likely to be the victims of oral sex. Girls are more likely to be the victims of intercourse as they get older and if the offender is a biological father or stepfather. See, for example, Robert Dube and Martin Hebert, "Sexual abuse of children under 12 years of age: A review of 511 cases," 1988, pp. 323–24; W. D. Erickson et al., "Behavior patterns of child molesters," 1988, pp. 82–83; John H. Gagnon, "Female child victims of sex offenses," 1965, pp. 182–83; A. Nicholas Groth, *Men Who Rape*, 1979, p. 151; Leslie Margolin, "Sexual abuse by grandparents," 1992, pp. 737–38; J. W. Mohr et al., *Pedophilia and Exhibitionism*, 1964, p. 32; Patricia Phelan, "The process of incest: Biologic father and stepfather families," 1986, p. 535;

Robert L. Pierce and Lois H. Pierce, "The sexually abused child: A comparison of male and female victims," 1985, p. 194; Diana E. H. Russell, *The Secret Trauma*, 1986, pp. 98–99, 226.

7. The flip side of this question is the types of resistance strategies victims report they employ to try and stop sexual attacks from occurring. Common documented forms of resistance include fighting back, fleeing, screaming, vigorously protesting, pleading, seeking help from a third party, crying or showing emotional distress, and avoiding coming home or running away. See Diana E. H. Russell, *The Secret Trauma*, 1986, pp. 126–27, 205. It is interesting to compare what victims say they did to what offenders indicated they attended to in drawing boundaries around their behavior.

Chapter 8: *Exiting Offending and Public Exposure*

1. It was Becker who emphasized the importance of analyzing both ends of involvement in deviant behavior: "We should not confine our interest to those who follow a career that leads them into ever-increasing deviance . . . . We should also consider those . . . whose careers lead them away from it into conventional ways of life." Howard S. Becker, *Outsiders*, 1963, pp. 24–25.

2. Erving Goffman, *Stigma: Notes on the Management of Spoiled Identity*, Englewood Cliffs, NJ: Prentice-Hall, 1963, pp. 41–42.

3. The ways exitings occur are one of the least-examined and least-understood aspects of deviant behavior in general. According to the small group of studies that have been done in this direction, exitings differ according to the objective nature of the transition: forced (at the hands of others) or voluntary (self-initiated). They likewise differ according to the time frame of the transition: abrupt (sudden), or long-term (sometimes spanning years); as well as whether the exit is intermittent or final. There are also distinct phases of the exiting process: endings of active involvements in behaviors versus attempts to shed labels and redefine identity as nondeviant or normal. Exitings, depending on the behavior involved, sometimes occur in a group context (e.g., Alcoholics Anonymous or Synanon), or they may be experienced individually. Finally, the factors that facilitate exits may consist of objective contingencies—witnesses, job opportunities, marrying or having children, policing priorities, and so forth; they may also include subjective criteria—self-doubts, searching out alternatives, burnout or aging experiences, heightened feelings of risk, loss of interest, and the like. The core studies on exitings include Patricia Adler, *Wheeling and Dealing*, 1985, pp. 130–42; Joel Best and David F. Luckenbill, *Organizing Deviance*, 1994, pp. 239–44, Helen R. F. Ebaugh, *Becoming an EX*, 1988; Barbara Laslett and Carol A. B. Warren, "Losing weight: The organizational promotion of behavior change," *Social Problems*, 23, 1975, pp. 69–80; John Lofland, *Deviance and Identity*, 1969, pp. 209–95; Thomas N. Meisenhelder, "Becoming normal: Certification as a stage in exiting crime," *Deviant Behavior*, 3, 1982, pp. 137–53; Thomas N. Meisenhelder, "An exploratory study of exiting from criminal careers," *Criminology*, 15, 1977, pp. 319–34; Marsh Ray, "Abstinence cycles and heroin addicts," *Social Problems*, 9, 1961, pp. 132–40; Neal Shover, "The later stages of ordinary property offender careers," 1984, pp. 208–18; Harrison M. Trice and Paul M. Roman, "Delabeling, relabeling and Alcoholics Anonymous," *Social Problems*, 17, 1970, pp. 536–48.

4. This career contingency is similar to what has been reported about the exiting processes of drug dealers, check forgers, and property offenders. See Patricia Adler, *Wheeling and Dealing*, 1985, pp. 131–32; Edwin M. Lemert, "The check forger and his identity," in Earl Rubington and Martin S. Weinberg (eds.), *Deviance: The Interactionist Per-*

spective, 4th ed., New York: Macmillan, 1981, pp. 453–59; Neal Shover, "The later stages of ordinary property offender careers," 1984, pp. 214–15.

5. David Matza, *Becoming Deviant*, 1969, pp. 150–55. See also Erdwin H. Pfuhl, *The Deviance Process*, 1986, pp. 138–40.

6. Again, "phaseout" and "reentry" patterns have been documented for drug dealers and drug users, among others. See Patricia Adler, *Wheeling and Dealing*, 1985, pp. 137–39; Marsh Ray, "Abstinence cycles and heroin addicts," 1961, pp. 132–40.

7. For example, in one study, 58 percent of the forty incest survivors who were surveyed never told anyone about being sexually abused while they lived in the home where their victimization was occurring. Judith L. Herman, *Father-Daughter Incest*, 1981, p. 88. In a second study, only 5 percent of the cases of documented sexual abuse prior to age eighteen were reported to the police. Diana E. H. Russell, *The Secret Trauma*, 1986, pp. 85–86. In a third national survey of the general population, 42 percent of the men who admitted being sexually abused as children, and 33 percent of the women, never reported the situation to anyone. Another 14 percent of the men and 24 percent of the women said they did report but it took them at least one year to do so. David Finkelhor et al., "Sexual abuse in a national survey of adult men and women: Prevalence, characteristics, and risk factors," 1990, p. 22. Finally, in one other study, 64 percent of a sample of fifty-seven adult women and men who were child sexual abuse victims said they did not disclose what happened to them until adulthood. Sharon Lamb and Susan Edgar-Smith, "Aspects of disclosure: Mediators of outcome of childhood sexual abuse," 1994, p. 316.

8. The few studies that describe disclosures typically have found that most often disclosures occur because the victim decides to tell someone, that usually this happens when the victim becomes older, and that sometimes the victim is not believed or is pressured by family or the offender to recant. Such studies also include cursory lists of other ways disclosure results, for example, someone else told, the victim was physically injured, and the like. Lucy Berliner and Jon R. Conte, "The process of victimization: The victims' perspective," 1989, p. 36; Suzanne M. Sgroi et al., "A conceptual framework for child sexual abuse," 1982, pp. 17–21. I have seen only one study that looks at the disclosure process in close detail, but from the angle of nonoffending mothers. My research presents an interesting source of comparison. Actually there is remarkable consistency between this other study and my own. My study is the only one I know of that provides an account from the offender's standpoint. Janis T. Johnson, *Mothers of Incest Survivors*, Bloomington: Indiana University Press, 1992, pp. 18–28.

9. In Johnson's study of mothers of children who were incest victims, the mothers described what happened to their children as disgusting. If action was needed to intervene and stop the offenders, the study indicated, they took it. This is in sharp contrast to the more passive and helpless stereotype of mothers who simply allow sexual abuse to continue. Janis T. Johnson, *Mothers of Incest Survivors*, 1992, pp. 50–75.

10. Among the many discussions, see Barry Glassner, "Labeling theory," in M. Michael Rosenberg, Robert A. Stebbins, and Allan Turowetz (eds.), *The Sociology of Deviance*, New York: St. Martin's, 1982, pp. 71–90; John Lofland, *Deviance and Identity*, 1969, pp. 209–95; Edwin M. Lemert, *Social Pathology*, New York: McGraw-Hill, 1951, pp. 75–78; Erdwin H. Pfuhl, *The Deviance Process*, 1986, pp. 125–56; Edwin H. Schur, *Labeling Deviant Behavior*, New York: Harper and Row, 1971.

11. Malin Akerstrom, "Outcasts in prison: The cases of informers and sex offenders," 1986, pp. 1–12; Cheryl Regehr, "Parental responses to extrafamilial child sexual assault," 1990, pp. 113–20; Ann H. Tyler and Marla R. Brassard, "Abuse in the investigation and treatment of intrafamilial child sexual abuse," 1984, pp. 47–53.

Chapter 9: *Answering the Question Why*

1. For a broader discussion of the salience of emotions in qualitative research, see Sheryl Kleinman and Martha A. Copp, *Emotions and Fieldwork*, Newbury Park, CA: Sage, 1993.

2. Diana Scully, *Understanding Sexual Violence*, 1990.

3. Diana Scully and Joseph Marolla, "Convicted rapists' vocabulary of motive: Excuses and justifications," 1984, pp. 530–44; Diana Scully and Joseph Marolla, "Riding the bull at Gilley's: Convicted rapists describe the rewards of rape," 1985, pp. 251–63.

4. For the origin of this idea, see Edwin H. Sutherland and Donald R. Cressey, "The theory of differential association," in Stuart H. Traub and Craig B. Little (eds.), *Theories of Deviance*, 4th ed., Itasca, IL: F. E. Peacock, 1994, pp. 188–94.

5. I draw heavily from three sources in outlining the basic elements of the interactionist approach in sociology: Joel M. Charon, *Symbolic Interactionism: An Introduction, an Interpretation, an Integration*, 2d ed., Englewood Cliffs, NJ: Prentice-Hall, 1985; John P. Hewitt, *Self and Society: A Symbolic Interactionist Social Psychology*, 2d ed., Boston: Allyn and Bacon, 1979; Erdwin H. Pfuhl, *The Deviance Process*, 1986, pp. 1–42.

6. Lamar T. Empey, *American Delinquency: Its Meaning and Construction*, Homewood, IL: Dorsey Press, 1982, pp. 17–74. See also Carl N. Degler, *At Odds: Women and the Family in America from the Revolution to the Present*, New York: Oxford University Press, 1980, pp. 66–85.

7. For a general review of the evolution of these laws, see Erna Olafson et al., "Modern history of child sexual abuse awareness: Cycles of discovery and suppression," 1993, pp. 7–24; Edwin H. Sutherland, "The diffusion of sexual psychopath laws," *American Journal of Sociology*, 56, 1950, pp. 142–48.

8. In support of this point, parents in one study ranked sexual abuse as the most serious trauma or most harmful experience that could happen to their child. Parental divorce or a friend dying were ranked as less serious. David Finkelhor, *Child Sexual Abuse*, 1984, p. 89.

9. The Indiana penal code of 1990 illustrates this point. Consider the maximum possible penalties for each of the following crimes with aggravating circumstances present: sexual intercourse or deviate sexual conduct with a child under sixteen involving the use of a weapon—up to fifty years; the same act against a child under twelve without a weapon—up to twenty years; the same act with a child aged twelve to fifteen, again without a weapon—up to eight years; fondling or touching a child under twelve—up to eight years; fondling or touching a child aged twelve to fifteen—up to three years. The penalties the offenders in this study received were considerably less in comparison (see appendix C).

10. Gayle Rubin, "Thinking sex: Notes for a radical theory of the politics of sexuality," in Carol S. Vance (ed.), *Pleasure and Danger: Exploring Female Sexuality*, Boston: Routledge and Kegan Paul, 1984, p. 279.

11. See, for example, Diana E. H. Russell, *The Secret Trauma*, 1986, pp. 138–57; Ellen Bass and Laura Davis, *The Courage to Heal*, 1988, p. 20.

12. Evidence of this cultural reality is documented in at least two places: James W. Trivelpiece, "Adjusting the frame: Cinematic treatment of sexual abuse and rape of men and boys," in Mic Hunter (ed.), *The Sexually Abused Male*, New York: Lexington Books, 1990, pp. 47–72; Florence Rush, *The Best Kept Secret*, 1980, pp. 116–33.

13. Joel M. Charon, *Symbolic Interactionism*, 1985, p. 126.

14. I return here to the debate I mentioned in chapter 1. See Neil Frude, "The sexual nature of sexual abuse," 1982, pp. 211–23; Kevin Howells, "Adult sexual interest in chil-

dren: Considerations relevant to theories of aetiology," 1981, pp. 65–70; Craig T. Palmer, "Twelve reasons why rape is not sexually motivated: A skeptical examination," 1982, pp. 512–30.

15. Susan Brownmiller, *Against Our Will*, 1975; A. Nicholas Groth, *Men Who Rape*, 1979, pp. 2–7; Kate Millett, *Sexual Politics*, New York: Ballantine Books, 1970, pp. 3–81.

16. Lee Ellis, *Theories of Rape*, 1989, pp. 57–80; Richard B. Felson and Marvin Krohn, "Motives for rape," 1990, pp. 222–42; David Finkelhor, *Child Sexual Abuse*, 1984, pp. 33–43; Diana Scully, *Understanding Sexual Violence*, 1990, pp. 142–49.

17. The concept of "erotic slide" is adapted from the work of Murray S. Davis, *Smut: Erotic Reality/Obscene Ideology*, Chicago: University of Chicago Press, 1983, pp. 45–85. The author refers to "the sensual slide into erotic reality."

18. Diana Scully, *Understanding Sexual Violence*, 1990, pp. 141–42.

19. Joel M. Charon, *Symbolic Interactionism*, 1985, p. 126.

20. Harold Garfinkel, *Studies in Ethnomethodology*, 1967, pp. 4–22, 73–74.

21. Warren Handel, *Ethnomethodology: How People Make-Sense*, Englewood Cliffs, NJ: Prentice-Hall, 1982, p. 89.

22. George Ritzer, *Sociological Theory*, 1992, p. 346.

23. John P. Hewitt, *Self and Society*, 1979, p. 71.

24. Diana Scully, *Understanding Sexual Violence*, 1990, p. 165.

25. Patrick Carnes, *Contrary to Love*, 1989, p. 67.

26. Gayle Rubin, "Thinking sex: Notes for a radical theory of the politics of sexuality," 1984, pp. 278–83.

27. The importance of sexual opportunity in shaping sexual desire and outlet is a central theme in another co-authored book of mine: Martin S. Weinberg, Colin J. Williams, and Douglas W. Pryor, *Dual Attraction*, 1994, pp. 292–97.

28. This process of defining deviant behavior as a compulsion is outlined elsewhere. See Donald R. Cressey, "Role theory, differential association, and compulsive crimes," in Donald R. Cressey and David A. Ward (eds.), *Delinquency, Crime, and Social Process*, New York: Harper and Row, 1969, pp. 1114–30.

29. Joel M. Charon, *Symbolic Interactionism*, 1985, p. 100.

30. Harold E. Pepinsky, *The Geometry of Violence and Democracy*, 1991, pp. 18–19.

31. Joel M. Charon, *Symbolic Interactionism*, 1985, p. 28.

32. Barney G. Glaser and Anselm L. Strauss, "Awareness contexts and social interaction," in Jerome G. Manis and Bernard N. Meltzer (eds.), *Symbolic Interaction: A Reader in Social Psychology*, 2d ed., Boston: Allyn and Bacon, 1972, p. 449.

33. John Stoltenberg, *Refusing to Be a Man: Essays on Sex and Justice*, Portland, OR: Breitenbush Books, 1989, p. 48.

34. I concur in my view of this with A. Nicholas Groth, *Men Who Rape*, 1979, p. 59.

35. A. Nicholas Groth, *Men Who Rape*, 1979, p. 59.

36. Gordon C. Nagayama Hall and Richard Hirschman, "Sexual aggression against children: A conceptual perspective of etiology," *Criminal Justice and Behavior*, 19, 1992, pp. 17–20.

37. A. Nicholas Groth, *Men Who Rape*, 1979, pp. 151–63; A. Nicholas Groth and H. Jean Birnbaum, "Adult sexual orientation and attraction to underage persons," 1978, pp. 175–81; A. Nicholas Groth, "The incest offender," 1982, pp. 215–18.

38. Heidi Vanderbilt, "Incest: A chilling report," 1993, pp. 82–83. Vanderbilt describes this essentialist-based typology from current unpublished research by David Finkelhor and Linda M. Williams on 118 incestuous fathers.

39. Joel M. Charon, *Symbolic Interactionism*, 1985, pp. 127–28.

40. Essentialist models portray offenders as deviant, weird, or sick people, as having something wrong that explains their disturbed behavior.

41. Diana Scully and Joseph Marolla, "Riding the bull at Gilley's: Convicted rapists describe the rewards of rape," 1985, p. 262. This is the basic premise of control theory applied to the question of child molesting.

42. These claims, of course, run counter to research on rape proclivity among males. In one review of the literature on this topic, it was estimated that 35 percent of the male students (mainly college students) who have been surveyed in different studies reported at least some likelihood they would consider raping a woman if they thought they could get away with it. In addition, male students who admitted they might rape have been found to share a range of rape myths similar to those of convicted rapists. The author of this review article also cite another study of male high school students in which over 50 percent said they thought it was acceptable to use physical force to hold a girl down and have intercourse with her in certain circumstances, for example, if the respondent thought the female involved had done something to get him excited or if she had initially said yes but changed her mind. The point is that thoughts about rape may not be all that uncommon among men in general. Neil M. Malamuth, "Rape proclivity among males," *Journal of Social Issues*, 37, 1981, pp. 138–57. Also, in one early phallometric study of male college students and male immigrants who were described as nondeviant in terms of their sexual histories, both groups of subjects were found to respond erotically to pictures of body parts displaying the pubic region and buttocks of female children as young as six. Kurt Freund, C. K. McKnight, R. Langevin, and S. Cibiri, "The female child as a surrogate object," *Archives of Sexual Behavior*, 2, 1972, pp. 119–33. The fine line between attitudes conducive to rape and normal male behavior is also presented in a book in which men speak personally on the issue of rape. Timothy Beneke, *Men on Rape: What They Have to Say about Sexual Violence*, New York: St. Martin's, 1982, pp. 36–70. Finally, in one other study germane to this point based on a small sample of 193 male undergraduate students, 21 percent admitted previously having felt sexually attracted to a child, 9 percent having had fantasies about children, and 7 percent that they might consider having sex with a child if they knew they would not get caught. John Briere and Marsha Runtz, "University males' sexual interest in children: Predicting potential indices of pedophilia in a nonforensic sample," *Child Abuse and Neglect*, 13, 1989, pp. 65–75.

43. Fay H. Knopp, "Community solutions to sexual violence: Feminist/abolitionist perspectives," in Harold E. Pepinsky and Richard Quinney (eds.), *Criminology as Peacemaking*, Bloomington: Indiana University Press, 1991, pp. 182–83. She provides an excellent discussion of the war model that dominates criminal justice thinking.

44. My interest in the concept of peacemaking has surfaced through personal communications with Hal Pepinsky. I also draw heavily on two of his recent books: Harold E. Pepinsky, *The Geometry of Violence and Democracy*, 1991; Harold E. Pepinsky and Richard Quinney (eds.), *Criminology as Peacemaking*, Bloomington: Indiana University Press, 1991.

45. For an excellent working example of how to structure and run an apology session with fathers who have molested one or more of their children, see Terry S. Trepper, "The apology session," in Terry S. Trepper and Mary J. Barrett (eds.), *Treating Incest: A Multimodal Systems Perspective*, New York: Haworth, 1986, pp. 93–101. Two other sources about the use of mediation and dispute resolution between crime victims and offenders and some of the problems with this approach are also worth reading: Joseph A. Scimecca, "Conflict resolution and a critique of alternative dispute resolution," in Harold E. Pepinsky and Richard Quinney (eds.), *Criminology as Peacemaking*, Bloomington:

Indiana University Press, 1991, pp. 263–79; Maria R. Volpe, "Mediation in the criminal justice system: Process, promises, problems," in Harold E. Pepinsky and Richard Quinney (eds.), *Criminology as Peacemaking*, Bloomington: Indiana University Press, 1991, pp. 194–206.

46. For a general discussion of the issue of social reform in relation to sexual offending, see Susan Caringella-MacDonald and Drew Humphries, "Sexual assault, women, and the community: Organizing to prevent sexual violence," in Harold E. Pepinsky and Richard Quinney (eds.), *Criminology as Peacemaking*, Bloomington: Indiana University Press, 1991, pp. 98–113; M. Kay Harris, "Moving into the new millennium: Toward a feminist vision of justice," in Harold E. Pepinsky and Richard Quinney (eds.), *Criminology as Peacemaking*, Bloomington: Indiana University Press, 1991, pp. 83–97.

47. Three examples among many of this kind of research include Diana M. Elliot and John Briere, "Sexual abuse trauma among professional women: Validating the trauma symptom checklist-40," *Child Abuse and Neglect*, 16, 1992, pp. 391–98; Diana E. H. Russell, *The Secret Trauma*, 1986, pp. 137–211; Lana Stermac et al., "Violence among child molesters," 1989, pp. 450–59.

48. Two articles that make a beginning attempt in this direction are Lucy Berliner and Jon R. Conte, "The process of victimization: The victims' perspective," 1989, pp. 29–40; Jon R. Conte et al., "What sexual offenders tell us about prevention strategies," 1989, pp. 293–301.

49. One study in particular in which this separation in cases would have been extremely helpful is Lynda L. Holmstrom and Ann W. Burgess, "Rapists' talk: Linguistic strategies to control the victim," 1979, pp. 101–25.

50. As I cited previously, some research on mothers of victims has recently been done. Janis T. Johnson, *Mothers of Incest Survivors*, 1992. In this study, however, only six mothers were included in the sample. Studies on more nonoffending mothers are thus highly needed. One other early study on nonoffending mothers is Thomas B. Garrett and Richard Wright, "Wives of rapists and incest offenders," *Journal of Sex Research*, 11, 1975, pp. 149–57.

51. Joel M. Charon, *Symbolic Interactionism*, 1985, pp. 2–3.

52. The opposite has been argued about biological fathers. Edward Westermarck, *The History of Human Marriage*, London: Clay and Sons, 1894. See also Lewellyn Hendrix, "A problem in the biosocial account of incest: Why do parents avoid sex with their offspring?" paper presented at the Annual Meetings of the Society for Cross-Cultural Research, Santa Fe, NM, 1994.

Suggested Reading

Bass, Ellen, and Laura Davis. *The Courage to Heal: A Guide for Women Survivors of Child Sexual Abuse*. New York: Harper and Row, 1988.

> Probably the most widely read self-help manual for women who were molested as children. The authors maintain that a person who has experienced childhood sexual abuse is better thought of as a "survivor" rather than a victim; they argue that such experiences are life altering in nature. They show the multiple stages survivors go through in attempting to repair their lives and suggest that anger is a critical stage in overcoming abuse experiences.

Beitchman, Joseph H., Kenneth J. Zucker, Jane E. Hood, Granville A. DaCosta, and Donna Akman. "A review of the short-term effects of child sexual abuse." *Child Abuse and Neglect*, 15, 1991, pp. 537–56. Beitchman, Joseph H., Kenneth J. Zucker, Jane E. Hood, Granville A. DaCosta, Donna Akman, and Erika Cassavia. "A review of the long-term effects of child sexual abuse." *Child Abuse and Neglect*, 16, 1992, pp. 101–18.

> Both articles provide relatively recent overviews of the massive literature on the short- and long-term effects of sexual abuse in the lives of female and male childhood victims. An excellent source for quick knowledge of the literature in this area. Contains references to most of the critical studies.

Beneke, Timothy. *Men on Rape: What They Have to Say about Sexual Violence*. New York: St. Martin's, 1982.

A book that explores the voices and thoughts of men in everyday life and their views about women and rape. Reveals that some men hold attitudes of tolerance toward rape. Also explores the men's reactions, from various standpoints as involved partners, friends, doctors, lawyers, and police, to women they learned had been raped.

Berliner, Lucy, and Jon R. Conte. "The process of victimization: The victims' perspective." *Child Abuse and Neglect*, 14, 1989, pp. 29–40. Conte, Jon R., Steven Wolf, and Tim Smith. "What sexual offenders tell us about prevention strategies." *Child Abuse and Neglect*, 13, 1989, pp. 293–301.

These articles, both coauthored by Jon R. Conte, take an initial, brief, qualitative look from the perspectives of victims and offenders at how child sexual abuse situations get started. The analysis in both articles is somewhat disorganized, and offenders are depicted as excessively predatory, but there is little other available qualitative research of any sort on child sexual abuse situations. A good starting point.

Briere, John N. *Child Abuse Trauma: Theory and Treatment of the Lasting Effects*. Newbury Park, CA: Sage, 1992. Idem. *Therapy for Adults Molested as Children: Beyond Survival*. New York: Springer, 1989.

From one of the most widely known treatment researchers in the field, and one of the first to develop the idea of symptom checklists for the diagnosis of child sexual abuse, these two books focus on psychotherapeutic methods for child abuse victims of all types, but especially sexual abuse victims. In particular, in the first book listed, the author advocates the view that most people are maltreated in some way as children and that people often overlook how such experiences shape their lives.

Carnes, Patrick. *Contrary to Love: Helping the Sexual Addict*. Minneapolis: CompCare Publishers, 1989.

This book, by one of the inventors of the concept of sexual addiction, describes the process by which some people lose control over their sexual desires and behaviors to the point where their lives begin to crumble, and some of the things that can be done to regain control. People who like sex multiple times a day and have a history of violating the sexual boundaries of others, including children, might fit within the framework of this book.

Cleveland, Dianne. *Incest: The Story of Three Women*. Lexington, MA: Lexington Books, 1986.

An oral-history, microscopic view of the adult lives of three women who were the victims of extensive incest as children. The three cases illustrate the varying ways that family sexual abuse experiences can become integrated in later life, from destructive to more functional adaptations. Reveals how victims can make different things out of their lives depending on the circumstances.

Finkelhor, David. *Child Sexual Abuse: New Theory and Research*. New York: Free Press, 1984.

In a field starved for compelling explanations of child sexual abuse, this book presents probably the most widely cited theory about why child sexual abuse occurs. The author presents a four-factor theory of child sexual abuse, focusing on possible motivations to offend, the breakdown of internal and external inhibitions, and conditions that put children at risk. There is also widely cited research on the incidence of childhood victimization as well as on public knowledge and views about child sexual abuse.

Frude, Neal. "The sexual nature of sexual abuse: A review of the literature." *Child Abuse and Neglect*, 6, 1982, pp. 211–23.

One of two main articles in the research literature that attempt to reframe child sexual abuse as motivated by sexual needs, however unwarranted, as much or more so than by desires to commit violence or to dominate someone more helpless.

Groth, A. Nicholas. *Men Who Rape*. New York: Plenum, 1979.

The original clinically based qualitative study of male rapists that defines rape as a nonsexual crime. Distinguishes between three types of rape: power, anger, and sadistic rape. The author also provides a short description of child sexual abuse and addresses some of the early myths surrounding offenders, for example, that they are dirty old men, usually strangers, are crazy, and the like. A graphic read, not for the faint of heart.

Hall, Gordon C. Nagayama, Richard Hirschman, John R. Graham, and Maira S. Zaragoza, eds. *Sexual Aggression: Issues in Etiology, Assessment, and Treatment*. Washington, DC: Taylor and Francis, 1993.

Strictly for the academic reader, this edited volume, heavily technical in style, focuses on both the biological and cognitive approaches in research on rape. A good book for sociologists who want to juxtapose their research against other disciplines. One chapter on adolescent sex offenders contains a detailed review of the literature in this area. Otherwise, the focus of the book is on rapists of adult women.

Herman, Judith L. *Father-Daughter Incest*. Cambridge: Harvard University Press, 1981.

> A groundbreaking feminist analysis of one specific type of incest and the role of patriarchy in facilitating such situations. Attacks and breaks down conceptions that incest is harmless and that mothers and daughters are responsible for its occurrence. Presents data on forty victims and their stories about incest with their fathers.

Hunter, Mic, ed. *The Sexually Abused Male: Prevalence, Impact, and Treatment*. New York: Lexington Books, 1990.

> One of the few available edited volumes to explore the issue of males who experience unwanted sex during childhood. There are chapters on prevalence, impact, intervention, and female perpetrators, though most of the chapters present little original empirical data on the situation of male victimization.

Johnson, Janis Tyler. *Mothers of Incest Survivors: Another Side of the Story*. Bloomington: Indiana University Press, 1992.

> A relatively unknown but compelling portrait of the lives of six mothers who discovered that their husbands had molested their daughters. Shatters some of the taken for granted myths about mothers of incest victims as collusive and powerless, and presents a more protective side of women in such situations. Explores the changes in families that result after the revelation of incest.

Justice, Blair, and Rita Justice. *The Broken Taboo: Sex in the Family*. New York: Human Sciences Press, 1979.

> This research is based on group therapy with 20 parents and a survey of 112 families in which incest was reported, though it is never clear who exactly constituted the sample—mothers, victims, or offenders. The authors present various types of incest offenders, including introverts, rationalizers, tyrants, alcoholics, and psychopaths. In addition, they discuss how marital erosion is often a turning point in incest, provide a list of cues that incest might be occurring, explore the effects of incest on the family, and offer various suggestions for stopping incest.

Kercher, Glen A., and Marilyn McShane. "The prevalence of child sexual abuse victimization in an adult sample of Texas residents." *Child Abuse and Neglect*, 8, 1984, pp. 495–501.

> A large sample of 1,056 adult men and women, a reasonable definition of child sexual abuse as sexual contact or interaction between a child and an adult in which the child is being used for sexual stimulation, and a credible measure of incidence, 11 percent of females and 3 percent of males.

Maltz, Wendy. *The Sexual Healing Journey: A Guide for Survivors of Sexual Abuse*. New York: Harper Perennial, 1992.

> A no-nonsense, readable, practical, and encouraging guide for child sexual abuse victims who are experiencing sexual difficulties; the book's aim is to help them put their problems in perspective, try to move beyond these problems, and establish more happy sexual lives. Contains an important chapter on how to deconstruct negative views of sex and replace them with a more positive framework or approach.

McCaghy, Charles H. "Child molesters: A study of their careers as deviants." In *Criminal Behavior Systems: A Typology*, edited by Marshall B. Clinard and Richard Quinney, pp. 75–88. New York: Holt, Rinehart and Winston, 1967. Idem. "Drinking and deviance disavowal: The case of child molesters." *Social Problems*, 16, 1968, pp. 43–49.

> McCaghy's research provides some early distinctions between types of child molesters—minimal, limited, and high interaction with children—and how the offenders' conception of their own behavior changes after arrest: denying guilt, wanting to forget, blaming the victim, or invoking their own abuse as an excuse. He also illustrates the role of alcohol in mitigating feelings of wrongdoing. An important source for people conducting qualitative research on child sexual abuse.

Olafson, Erna, David L. Corwin, and Roland C. Summit. "Modern history of child sexual abuse awareness: Cycles of discovery and suppression." *Child Abuse and Neglect*, 17, 1993, pp. 7–24.

> This article, which traces back over a hundred years, is the best available historical analysis of how societal and legal views of child sexual abuse have fluctuated and become increasingly crystallized in recent times in the United States.

Palmer, Craig T. "Twelve reasons why rape is not sexually motivated: A skeptical examination." *Journal of Sex Research*, 25, 1982, pp. 512–30.

This article is at the heart of the recent paradigm shift in research on rape and child sexual abuse that has now begun to focus on sexual motives and desires as critical to sexual violence. Attacks the specter of political correctness that hangs over research in the field.

Rossman, Parker. *Sexual Experience between Men and Boys: Exploring the Pederast Underground*. New York: Association Press, 1976.

A book ahead of its time on the issue of adult-child sex. Rossman conducts the definitive study on men with sexual preferences toward boys and the international subculture in which they live and look for sex. The analysis is based on a sample of active and undetected boy lovers. One chapter in particular focuses on the stages men go through as they become pederasts.

Rush, Florence. *The Best Kept Secret: Sexual Abuse of Children*. New York: McGraw-Hill, 1980.

Another book in the genre of early feminist work on the sexual exploitation of children. A polemical historical analysis of how different male-dominated cultures past and present have ignored, tolerated, and promoted sexual abuse in a myriad of ways. The author maintains that many laws are inadequate for protecting children.

Russell, Diana E. H. *The Secret Trauma: Incest in the Lives of Girls and Women*. New York: Basic Books, 1986.

Based on a sample of 930 women, this widely cited study focuses on the incidence rate of sexual abuse among girls and the short- and long-term impact of becoming a victim. It provides profiles based on victim accounts of offense situations and the offenders who molested them. A rich source of data for the new researcher.

Salter, Anna C. *Treating Child Sex Offenders and Victims: A Practical Guide*. Newbury Park, CA: Sage, 1988.

The main contribution of this book is the section on evaluation and treatment of offenders and forms of denial among offenders in the treatment process. Contains examples of treatment program initiatives. A good place to start for communities and therapists attempting to put together a sex offender treatment approach.

Scully, Diana. *Understanding Sexual Violence: A Study of Convicted Rapists*. London: Harper Collins, 1990.

An in-depth interview study of 114 convicted rapists and a comparison group of 75 other felons in prison. Constructs a chilling portrait of the situational rewards offenders said they received from raping and the rationalizations about their victims and behavior they constructed. Attempts to dismiss notions that rape results in part from child sexual abuse, child physical abuse, being raised by a single mother, an unhappy marriage, or from adult sexual deprivation.

Sgroi, Suzanne M., ed. *Handbook of Clinical Intervention in Child Sexual Abuse*. Lexington, MA: Lexington Books, 1982.

An older, but still useful and informative, edited volume of papers on different aspects of child sexual abuse experiences and intervention. Contains chapters on victims, offenders, and sibling incest. There are also various discussions on individual, group, family, and art therapy, as well as papers on the role of law enforcement and team and case management approaches in responding to reports of victimization.

Silver, Roxane L., Cheryl Boon, and Mary H. Stones. "Searching for meaning in misfortune: Making sense of incest." *Journal of Social Issues*, 39, 1983, pp. 81–102.

Study of a sample of 77 women, 80 percent of whom reported that even after 20 years, they were still searching off and on for a way to resolve their incest experiences and still thought at times about what had happened to them as children.

Trepper, Terry S., and Mary Jo Barrett, eds. *Treating Incest: A Multimodal Systems Perspective*. New York: Haworth, 1986.

An edited volume of papers that lay out the family systems and systemic model for explaining and treating sexual abuse within the family. There is an interesting chapter on the use of the apology session between victims and offenders as part of the treatment and family reunification process.

Index

Unanticipated erotic shift (*Cont.*)
unconventional sexual behavior, 259.
See also Crossing sexual boundary;
Shift into offending
Underground Railroad, 3, 305 n. 7,
306 n. 10
Unguarded access, 204–9, 220, 261,
266, 271; idiosyncratic offenders,
205–6, 220; routine activities theory,
204; scheduled planners, 206–7, 220;
tactical premeditators, 130–31, 142,
207–9, 220. *See also* Opportunity
with victim
Unreported sexual abuse, 331 n. 7

Verbal control of victims, 197–201;
without threat, 197–98; with threat of
divorce, 198; with threat of jail for
offender, 199; with threat mother

would kill, 199–200; with threat of
not being believed, 200; with threat
of whipping, 200
Victim disclosure, 238–46; after
bad–touch lecture, 239; after crisis
with offender, 241–43; after seeing
movie, 239; by telling friend, 240;
while seeing counselor, 239
Victims, molested: descriptive profile of,
1, 23, 298–99; relationship to offender, 23, 299
Violence, physical, during childhood,
31–32, 49, 54–60, 110, 319 n. 2, 342
Violent nonsexual view of sex crimes, 7,
158, 160, 257, 280, 314 n. 29, 319 n.
2, 327 n. 10, 338

War model of control, 274, 334 n. 43